P9-EDN-264

By Bennett Cerf

LAUGH DAY

RIDDLE-DE-DEE

OUT ON A LIMERICK

THE LAUGH'S ON ME

READING FOR PLEASURE

THE LIFE OF THE PARTY

AN ENCYCLOPEDIA OF MODERN AMERICAN HUMOR

GOOD FOR A LAUGH

LAUGHTER, INCORPORATED

SHAKE WELL BEFORE USING

ANYTHING FOR A LAUGH

LAUGHING STOCK

TRY AND STOP ME

Edited by Leonora Hornblow and Bennett Cerf

BENNETT CERF'S TAKE ALONG TREASURY

LAUGH DAY

LAUGH DAY

LAUGH DAY

*A New Treasury of Over 1000
Humorous Stories and
Anecdotes*

BENNETT CERF

With Illustrations by Michael K. Frith

DOUBLEDAY & COMPANY, INC., GARDEN CITY, NEW YORK

Copyright © 1965 by Bennett Cerf
Illustrations Copyright © 1965 by Michael K. Frith
All rights reserved. Printed in the United States of America

Contents

Introduction

Two of my favorite girls in all the world are my diffident wife, Phyllis, and my sometime collaborator, Leonora (Zsa Zsa) Hornblow. Both of them are superb housekeepers, able to open a can of beans with the best of them, preside with assurance over the most difficult dinner party, almost balance a check book, and dress to the Queen's taste on not a cent more than a hundred thousand dollars a year. They have but one serious failing: a sadly deficient sense of humor. This failing manifests itself most clearly—and predictably—when my own sparkling sallies are unveiled before them—only to wither in the icy silence and exchange of "How-much-longer-can-we-endure-this?" looks that ensue.

Even I, with the patience of Job, have been known on rare occasions to protest mildly at this ludicrous lack of appreciation. The end result was not precisely what I had bargained for. The two ladies—sometimes known as "The Twitter Girls" because, when together, they communicate in a series of weird and continuous chirps that only they and a very few highly inbred, supersensitive dogs can decipher, came up with a semi-annual ceremony of which I do not entirely approve. The ceremony has been designated by them as "Laugh Day," when—Zsa Zsa installed as a guest—from the moment I sally forth for a day's labors at my usual hour of 7:00 A.M., the pair of them roll on the floor laughing hysterically at every remark that passes my lips. A "Good morning, girls" brings shrieks of girlish merriment. A "Who the hell has been messing up my copy of the morning *Times?*" sends them into obscene convulsions. By about 7:08 A.M. my justly acclaimed patience has been exhausted, and I am ready to murder them both in cold blood.

That my two sons have seen fit to join in this outrageous

Laugh Day conspiracy is a development that pains me even more deeply, but they are sturdy, fun-loving lads, and I cling to the hope that their appreciation of true wit, despite their stints on the editorial board of the Harvard *Lampoon*, will ripen and mature as they shake off the influences of the Beatles, James Bond, and the New York Rangers hockey team.

Meanwhile, there remained the problem of what name to affix to this compendium of tales and anecdotes—the ninth of my lifetime and my first in five long years. The imminence of 1965's first Laugh Day—duly heralded and savored by everybody concerned but myself—suddenly gave me an inspiration. *Laugh Day* would be the name of the book. And, in my dreams at any rate, it would go marching to glory, hoisting the originators of Laugh Day on their own diabolical petards.

I don't think Americans are laughing enough these days. We're worrying too much about our "image," and whether other people love us enough. The strongest country in the world needs respect from others more than love. And it needs the saving grace—and courage—to be able to laugh a little bit at *itself*. The country that can no longer chuckle sometimes at its own foibles is in trouble. We've become too thin-skinned—and, yes, too pompous.

Laughter is the greatest humanizer and medicine God has given us. It can relieve tension and hysteria faster than all of the newest pills rolled into one. There is no more beautiful, soul-satisfying sound in all the world than a solid, reverberating "belly laugh."

May *Laugh Day* provoke a few from you!

Cordially,

Bennett Cerf

Mount Kisco, New York
Summer, 1965

LAUGH DAY

1. A Look at the Record

SOME OF THIS, GENTLEMEN, WAS HISTORY!

To begin at the beginning, rumor has it that Father Adam got bored with life in the Garden of Eden in general, and his wife Eve in particular, and went on a bender one fine Saturday evening. When he returned home he fell into a deep, deep slumber. When he awoke Eve was bending solicitously over him—counting his ribs.

* * *

The most incontrovertible statement of the year 1965 was made by a fifteen-year-old on an essay submitted to a students' prize contest on the subject of "Prehistoric Times." "In pre-historic times," stated the fifteen-year-old boldly, "books were very scarce."

* * *

One of those researchers who doesn't care how he spends his time came up with a dubious bit of history concerning Alexander the Great. According to this researcher, Alexander whipped up a crude timepiece for his soldiers, consisting of a chemically treated cloth worn on the left forearm. Under the heat of the sun, the cloth changed colors every hour, pro-viding the Macedonian warriors with the world's first wrist watch. Among historians, adds the researcher, the device is known as "Alexander's Rag Timeband."

* * *

Burt Shafer pictures the boy Nero practicing his violin les-son with obvious reluctance while his mother in the background confides to a neighbor, "I'm afraid my son will never set the world on fire."

* * *

After his conquest of Turkey, the legendary Tamerlane, it is told, found out that the local keeper of the exchequer had falsified his books and was getting rich on loot. Tamerlane ordered him to appear with his records, tore them into pieces, and made his terrified subordinate eat them on the spot.

The successor to this unfortunate grafter was a great deal wiser. When Tamerlane demanded that he appear with *his* financial reports, it turned out that they had all been neatly inscribed on a platterful of griddle cakes!

* * *

Mike Connolly relays a story about an Indian brave who glumly watched Christopher Columbus land and grumbled, "Well, there goes the neighborhood!"

* * *

Fellow who claims he was there quotes Christopher Columbus at a banquet honoring him for discovering the New World. Columbus, claiming he had not expected to be called on for a speech, smiled at Queen Isabella and began, "A funny thing happened to me on my way to India . . ."

* * *

Charles V of France was determined that everybody in his realm was going to subscribe to his own religious beliefs, and killed thousands who refused to conform. Finally, realizing he had failed, he abdicated and retired to a monastery, where he amused himself by trying to make a dozen clocks run absolutely together.

When he failed in this endeavor, he exclaimed, "How foolish I was to think that I could make all men think alike about religion when I cannot even make two clocks run together!"

* * *

"The principle of spending money to be paid by posterity, under the name of funding, is but swindling posterity on a large scale."

An anti-Administration blast by a conservative banker made

in Washington the other day? Not at all. It was said by Thomas Jefferson, almost two hundred years ago!

❋ ❋ ❋

At the height of the French Revolution, Robespierre, mainly responsible for the Reign of Terror, had his heart set on capturing a bold and elusive count who was the head of an effective resistance movement near Versailles. Finally the count was captured, but all efforts to persuade him to reveal the names of his lieutenants failed. He was led to the guillotine. At the very last moment, his nerve failed and he cried, "I'll talk! I'll tell all!" Alas! The blade had already been released, and it severed the count's head clean as a whistle.

Robespierre was outraged by the news, and gave the executioner a terrific dressing down. "How often have I cautioned you," he thundered, "NOT TO HATCHET YOUR COUNTS BEFORE THEY CHICKEN??"

❋ ❋ ❋

What was everyday life like in Paris during the French Revolution—"The Days of the Terror?" Reveals André Castelot in his engrossing book, *Paris 1783–1871*, "Chateaubriand's concierge enthused, 'Ah, those were the days! Every morning there went past my window little duchesses whose necks were white as snow when they were guillotined! Now it's all over. The people's pleasures have been taken from them!'"

❋ ❋ ❋

Judge Carl Friebolin insists that this note was found among the possessions of the Empress Josephine after her death: "Dear Josie: I seem to have misplaced one of my gloves, and since it's mighty cold here near Moscow, I wish you'd look in my top bureau drawer to see if I left it there. If you find it, please rush it to me by special courier, since I now have to keep one hand in my waistcoat—and the troops seem to find this amusing. Your devoted husband, Nappy."

❋ ❋ ❋

A familiar American legend—as rewritten by a Detroit wag:

A Chinese father summoned his four sons and addressed them thus: "Honorable sons, which one of you sullied the honor of our family by pushing outhouse in creek?" Number two son bowed ceremoniously, and admitted, "Honorable Father, I cannot tell a lie. I pushed outhouse in creek." Number two son thereupon received beating of his life.

At conclusion of whomping, bruised Number two son said, "Honorable Father, must point out that great President George Washington never beat son for telling truth. Is not so?"

"Is indeed so," agreed Honorable Father, "but big difference should be noted: great President George Washington not sitting in cherry tree."

* * *

Indefatigable researcher Norman Cousins has found out how electricity really was discovered. Benjamin Franklin tried to date a hoity-toity Colonial damsel—and she told him to "go fly a kite."

* * *

Little Olde New York (Statistics assembled by Sam Himmell): Broad Street in 1637 was called the "Heere Graft" and Wall Street was known as the "Cingle." . . . Peter Kock, who appears to have been the first houseowner—at No. 1 Broadway in 1633—also is credited with concocting the first Martini cocktail ever served in America. . . . In 1664, at the present Peck Slip and Pearl, intrepid voyagers wishing to be ferried across the East River to Brooklyn would blow a blast on a long metal horn suspended from a tree growing close to the water's edge. Upon hearing the blast, Commodore Rudo Kaplan, an imbiber, would saunter out of the beerstube, don his uniform, find his paddle, and propel them over to "Breukelen." . . . Gas was introduced into the city in 1825, and cabs were first launched on New York streets in 1840, with three in service in front of the old Astor House. . . . In July 1842, New York celebrated the opening of Croton Aqueduct, providing the city with an adequate water supply for the first time. . . . In 1845 the New York Knickerbockers, the first regular baseball club, was organized in New York City. . . . The first practicable passenger elevator was installed by the Otis Elevator Company in Haughwout's Store on Broadway in 1857; and the Tower Building, thirteen stories high at 50 Broadway, was the first steel-structure building in New York, erected in 1888. . . . In May 1883, the Brooklyn Bridge was finished by John A. Roebling & Sons. . . . In 1869–70, the first "El" was constructed in New York City. It ran on Greenwich Street from Battery Place to Thirtieth Street. . . . In June 1885, the French vessel S/S *Isère* arrived at Bedloe's Island with twenty-two tons of the Statue of Liberty in 210 wooden cases. A great celebration greeted her arrival.

❆ ❆ ❆

Shortly before the outbreak of the Civil War, President Lincoln had a mild attack of smallpox (the doctors called it varioloid) to add to his troubles. Informed of the nature of his illness, Lincoln didn't lose his precious sense of humor. "It is too bad," he noted dryly, "that this one time while I have something to give everybody—no one comes near me!"

❆ ❆ ❆

Another Abraham Lincoln anecdote: Lincoln had in his Cabinet one maverick who was against every move proposed, and automatically disputed every statement the President made. Lincoln, however, was adamant when advisers begged him to get rid of the dissenter. In explanation, Lincoln told about a farmer he once encountered who was trying to plow with a decrepit horse. Lincoln noticed a big horsefly on the flank of the animal and was about to brush it off when the farmer cried, "Don't you bother that fly, Abe! If it wasn't for that fly this danged old hoss wouldn't move an inch!"

❆ ❆ ❆

One of those sick comedians swears that an earnest do-gooder was heard asking, "Wouldn't you like to contribute to Indian relief, Mrs. Custer?"

* * *

Only yesterday, it seems, schoolboys were learning that "the sun never sets on the British Empire." History is made so rapidly today, the day-to-day changes are so radical, that it's almost impossible to keep abreast of events. A member of the U. S. Foreign Service was saying the other evening that it was in what now seems like another era—shortly before the outbreak of World War II—that an English delegation visited then President Franklin D. Roosevelt to discuss a tiny uninhabited island which Britain, among other nations, was claiming as its own. "What is the basis for your claim?" asked F.D.R. The head of the English delegation thought for a moment, then explained frankly, "It's always been colored red in the Encyclopædia Britannica!"

* * *

They say that just three days before the final fall of Nazi Germany, Hitler summoned the heads of his disintegrating Air Force, Navy, and Army to the Berlin bunker in which he was holed up and demanded, "How are we doing?"

The Air Force head announced, "We have one plane left: a 1914 model." The top admiral reported, "Our only boat afloat is a flat-bottom rowboat in the park." And the ranking general mourned, "Our remaining troops are undisciplined, unequipped, and in panic."

Hitler brooded momentarily, then brought his hand down sharply on his desk. "That settles it, gentlemen," he cried. "NO MORE NICE GUY!"

* * *

Are there ghosts in the White House? If so, none seem to have manifested themselves to the Johnsons—as yet, at any rate. But former President Truman, Mrs. Coolidge, and Mrs. Theodore Roosevelt all reported apparitions of Abraham Lincoln, and other strange occurrences—never under oath, however. It is a matter of record that when Queen Wilhelmina of the Netherlands was a guest at the White House, she swore that she saw Mrs. Lincoln march straight into her drawing room—and fainted dead away. Mrs. Woodrow Wilson was convinced that the ghost of Dolly Madison dropped in one evening to pay her respects. Even Winston Churchill reported strange noises and visitations while he stayed at the White House during World War II (for top-secret conferences with F.D.R. and Harry Hopkins).

Maybe these are the very ghosts who are writing those so-called "inside stories" of doings in top Washington echelons?

* * *

Had the equivalent of modern-day draft boards been in existence in times gone by, many of the world's most famous military figures, pointed out Dr. Logan Clendenning, would have been turned down cold for the following reasons: George Washington had false teeth, U. S. Grant was a confirmed alcoholic, Bismarck was grossly overweight, the Duke of Wellington was underweight, Nelson had only one eye, Kaiser Wilhelm had a withered arm, Napoleon had ulcers of the stomach, and Julius Caesar was an epileptic!

* * *

An insensitive lady at a dinner party demanded of fellow guest Herbert Hoover, "What do retired U. S. Presidents do to pass the time?" The late President answered graciously, "Madam, we spend our time taking pills and dedicating libraries."

* * *

Bill Nichols has a few encouraging statistics for self-doubters who fear they may not be getting ahead quickly enough:

1. In 1882, a German couple worried that their three-year-old son had not yet learned to speak a word. At twenty, the son was a grubby little office worker—with a side interest in obscure mathematics. The side interest eventually paid off. The son's name was Albert Einstein.

2. A happy-go-lucky drifter was turned down by West Point, and got successive jobs as a soda-jerk and clerk in a haberdashery. The drifter's name: Harry S. Truman.

3. A French lad, born in 1841, got into so much trouble in Paris that his father exiled him to America where he taught French in a girls' finishing school until he paid too much attention to his pupils after hours. Back home in France, he finally settled down to serious business. His name: Georges Clemenceau.

The late starters often cross the finish line first!

* * *

In light of the fact that the United States will soon be celebrating the two hundredth anniversary of the signing of the Declaration of Independence, an anonymous statistician points out that the average of former great civilizations was just about two hundred years—and that each of them passed through the following evolutions:

1. From bondage to spiritual faith.
2. From spiritual faith to great courage.
3. From courage to liberty.
4. From liberty to abundance.
5. From abundance to selfishness.
6. From selfishness to complacency.
7. From complacency to apathy.
8. From apathy to dependency.
9. From dependency right back to the bondage where it all started.

How far along this cycle will *we* have moved by 1976? And can we profit by the lessons of history?

POLITICS

A stanch Republican commuter had this complaint to register: "The Democrats have made it tough for me to get out of New York these days. I have to go out the Franklin D. Roosevelt Drive, past four Johnson restaurants, to Kennedy Airport, and pay my toll with a Kennedy half-dollar."

His companion, Jerry Beatty, advised him, "Why not save up enough Lincoln pennies, buy a ticket to Hoover Dam—and jump off!"

* * *

Fellow running for office in November against a popular incumbent was asked by a voter, "I'd like to know your views on what the main issues of this campaign are." "Main issues?" echoed the candidate. "There's just one, the way I see it. That so-and-so has the job—and I want it."

* * *

"Remember," the late Mayor Curley of Boston always advised his young political protégés, "that every time you do a favor for a constituent, you make nine enemies and one ingrate."

* * *

Somebody once remarked bitterly to Benjamin Franklin that the Constitution of the U.S. was a booby trap. "Where is all the happiness it is supposed to guarantee for us?" jeered the cynic. "Look at the bickering, the injustice, the poverty."

Franklin smiled tolerantly and replied, "All that the Constitution of the United States guarantees, my friend, is the *pursuit* of happiness. You have to catch up with it yourself."

* * *

Wonderful are the ways of Washington bureaucracy! Here's a story about a Californian who applied through regular channels for a job in Washington he knew he was qualified to fill. While cooling his heels awaiting a reply, he happened to meet in person in San Francisco, the head of the very agency to which he had applied, and was given the position on the spot.

The scene now shifts to Washington. Our Californian had been doing a fine job there for three months when a letter was forwarded to him from his old address telling him that, unfortunately, his application for the job he was now holding down had been denied because he lacked the necessary qualifications.

And here's the kicker. The letter had been signed by himself.

* * *

A candidate for Congress in Wisconsin was out drumming up support among his constituents when he spotted one of them milking a cow. Never the one to miss an opportunity, the candidate seized a pail and set out to help.

"That dumb opponent of mine," he began cheerfully. "Has he been around to talk to you yet?"

"He sure has," nodded the constituent. "Matter of fact, he's working the other side of this cow right now."

* * *

At New York's Dutch Treat Club, the late Frank Crowninshield was once obliged to introduce a politician who had just been clobbered unmercifully in a bid for re-election to Congress. "Gentlemen," began Crowninshield in silky tones, "our next speaker bears a strong resemblance to the earth. You will recall that the earth is not a perfect spheroid, because it is flattened at the poles. That's precisely what happened to our next speaker."

* * *

Charlie Rice, no great admirer of committees, recalls the definition somebody once coined for a camel: "a horse designed by a committee"; also William Sumner's warning, "If you live in a town that is run by a committee, you had better be on it yourself." Rice sums up:

> Committees of twenty deliberate plenty,
> Committees of ten act now and then,
> But most jobs are done by committees of one.

* * *

"City Hall," said the phone operator, answering a call. There wasn't a sound at the other end of the wire. "City Hall," the operator repeated. "With whom do you wish to speak, please?" Finally the caller admitted sheepishly, "Nobody, I guess. I just found this number in my husband's pocket."

* * *

Rex Stout was week-ending recently in a Southern town where two prominent Democrats were seeking the nomination for mayor. The town was split about fifty-fifty and feelings were running high. "Who are you going to declare for?" Stout asked the editor. "I haven't decided yet," admitted the editor, "but when I do—I'm going to be mighty bitter!"

* * *

New Hampshire conservatives couldn't get over the fact that the state legislature had approved a sweepstakes lottery. "To think," marveled one, "that it wasn't until 1947 that they legalized hand-holding up here!"

* * *

Overheard at the New York World's Fair:
Lady Number One: "What do you think of Cabot Lodge?"
Lady Number Two: "I prefer Grossinger's."

* * *

Don Maclean heard a congressman tell one of his secretaries, "You've been here two months now and I'm glad to note your typing has improved miraculously. However, it's not so good that you can stop wearing those tight sweaters yet!"

* * *

A town in South Dakota was in the process of electing a new mayor and board of advisers, and Mrs. Hubbard thought it would be educational to take her seven-year-old daughter with her to the polling booth. On the way home the daughter asked, "Mom, do you always vote for the men you love most?"

"Whatever put an idea like that in your mind?" wondered Mrs. Hubbard.

"Well," said the daughter, "I saw you put kisses next to their names."

* * *

Senator Borah of Idaho mailed out more letters to constituents than any of his colleagues—and the bulk of them went to his bitterest political enemies. "No point in sending copies of my speeches to friends who already agree with me," Borah explained. "My enemies, however, read every word I say— looking for mistakes."

* * *

A candidate for a high state office in Arkansas was accused by his opponent of merely posing as a "son of very poor parents." "As a matter of fact," thundered the opponent, "my adversary comes from the richest family in his county." The candidate answered calmly, "It's quite true I wasn't born in a log cabin. *But we moved to one as soon as we could afford it.*"

* * *

Eugene Field once told how a large group of Illinois legislators were vacation-bound on a train that was held up by bandits. "After relieving the bandits of their cash and watches," concluded Field, "the legislators proceeded on their journey with increased enthusiasm and *joie de vivre.*"

* * *

A windy, unreconstructed Southern senator put in an unexpected appearance at a big country picnic one late summer afternoon and announced that if a platform could be provided, he happened to have a few words to say to his constituents.

Reluctantly, somebody pulled up a farm wagon which the senator mounted. He then whipped a long speech out of his pocket and began to read it, while some two hundred picnickers, slices of watermelon or ears of corn in their hands, gathered lackadaisically to hear.

When he reached the bottom of page twelve, the senator looked up for the first time. His audience had simply melted away—with the exception of one bedraggled, pop-eyed farmer who stood motionless before him. The outraged senator bellowed, "I thank you, my good friend, for being the one voter in this county who is sufficiently interested in world affairs to stay and listen to my comments. I am grateful to you, sir."

The farmer shook his head vehemently. "I don't care a hoot for your comments on international affairs," he admitted, "but you're standing on my wagon!"

* * *

Philip Stern's controversial book, *The Great Treasury Raid,* points out the vast difference between illegal income tax *evasion* and entirely legal tax *avoidance.* Judge Learned Hand once observed, "There is nothing sinister in arranging one's affairs so as to keep taxes as low as possible. Nobody owes any public duty to pay more than the law demands. To ask for more in the name of morals is mere cant." Senator Pat Harrison summed it up with, "There's nothing that says a man has to take a toll bridge across a river when there's a free bridge nearby."

*　*　*

How much did Adlai Stevenson enjoy living in New York? Well, in 1964, he told a story in Washington—and with great relish, too—about a family about to move to Manhattan. The young daughter was saying her very last prayer in her old home. It went as follows: "Bless my daddy, bless my mommy, bless my brother Freddy. And now, dear Lord, I'll have to say goodbye to You. We are moving to New York. Amen."

*　*　*

John Straley tells about a lovely German fraulein in Washington who was suspected of some hanky-panky with government officials. So an investigator asked her if she'd ever been away on trips with senators. Indignantly, she replied, "Nein" —so she was deported.

*　*　*

Martin Levin predicts this airwave bulletin one hundred years from today: WASHINGTON: The President checked into the Walter Reed Army Hospital early this morning. Doctors say it may be twins. . . . NEW YORK: Traffic Commissioner Bargle has warned motorists that the city will crack down on litterbugs who fail to deposit their disposable automobiles in trash receptacles. . . . UN HEADQUARTERS: A visiting Dodger spokesman has denied a rumor that the team will move to Tangier. "We'll never leave Kuwait," he declared. . . . DETROIT: The Ford Foundation has granted $750,000 to an educational experiment which will investigate the use of books as possible visual aids. . . .

*　*　*

Leon Harris in *The Fine Art of Political Wit* has collected these telling observations by the late Adlai Stevenson:

1. An editor is one who separates the wheat from the chaff and prints the chaff.

2. Eggheads of the world, arise. You have nothing to lose but your yolks.

3. Someone must fill the gap between platitudes and bayonets.

4. Much of our foreign policy in the fifties was based on the power of positive brinking.

5. As scarce as truth is, the supply seems greater than the demand.

6. I understand that Mrs. Karl Marx, at the end of a long and bleak life, remarked, "How good it would have been if Karl had made some capital instead of writing so much about it."

❀　❀　❀

Pierre Salinger recalls a day when George Reedy, then the two-hundred-pound Press Secretary at the White House, was ordered to a hospital to go on a strict diet and lose some weight. When his office staff sent him a big basket of flowers, Reedy acknowledged the gift with this wire: "Thank you for the flowers. They were delicious."

❀　❀　❀

From an Indian on a New Mexico reservation came this bit of advice to Vice President Hubert Humphrey: "Dear V.P.: Be careful in revising those immigration laws of yours. We got careless with ours. (Signed) A Native American."

Our Vice President admits he's thoroughly fed up by this time with the story of the male camel with one hump who married a female camel with two humps. They had a baby with no humps, and named it, naturally, Humphrey.

LATTER-DAY PRESIDENTS

William Beebe, in *The Book of Naturalists*, tells about a little game he and President Teddy Roosevelt used to play in the latter's summer home at Sagamore Hill. After an evening of conversation, they would go out on the lawn and search the skies until they found a faint spot of light mist beyond the lower left-hand corner of the great square of Pegasus. Then T.R. would intone gravely, "There is the spiral galaxy of Andromeda. It is as large as our Milky Way. It is one of the hundred million galaxies. It consists of one hundred million suns, each larger than our own sun."

T.R. invariably would pause at this point, grin, and conclude, "Well, Will, I guess we realize again how small we are. Let's go to bed!"

* * *

President William Howard Taft was holding a reception one day when his tailor arrived to try on his new Prince Albert. The tailor was hustled into the reception line by zealous guards. When he reached the President, Taft remarked, "You look very familiar to me." "Naturally, Mr. President," chuckled the tailor. "I made your pants."

"Ah, yes," nodded the President. "How do you do, Major Pants."

* * *

Somebody once asked Woodrow Wilson how long it took him to prepare a ten-minute speech. "About two weeks," he estimated. "And a one-hour speech?" "That would take me a week," he said. "And a two-hour speech?" "Oh," laughed the President, "if you'll let me ramble on for two hours, I'm ready now."

* * *

When Woodrow Wilson was President, he often complimented author Oliver Herford, and, in fact, liked to repeat Herford's better quips in his political speeches. This didn't please Herford at all, because he considered Wilson a political accident and a piece of bad luck visited on a helpless populace. So the dedication in Herford's next book, *This Giddy Globe*, ran, "To President Wilson: with all his faults he quotes me still."

✿   ✿   ✿

Woodrow Wilson's valiant fight for the League of Nations ruined his health to a point where rumors hinted that his mind had been affected. Senator Albert Fall, a bitter Republican foe of Wilson, called to see what truth there might be in these rumors. "Well, Mr. President," was Fall's greeting, "we all have been praying for you." Wilson answered, "Which way, Senator?"

✿   ✿   ✿

When Calvin Coolidge occupied the White House, he ducked reporters so consistently that one day they formed a conspiracy against him. Before a conference to which he reluctantly agreed, each one wrote out precisely the same question: "Are you going to run again in 1928?" Coolidge read each slip carefully, without comment or change of expression, then threw them all in the trash basket.

"Gentlemen," he said, "the only question in this lot I care to answer today concerns public schools in Puerto Rico." He then delivered a fifteen-minute talk on the subject, full of statistics. The reporters never tried *that* trick on him again.

✿   ✿   ✿

A story President Hoover loved to tell about his predecessor, Calvin Coolidge, concerned the day the Coolidges entertained a missionary at their Northampton home before the visitor delivered a scheduled address at the Congregational Church. Grace Coolidge cooked a special dinner, but the missionary wouldn't eat a bite of it—explaining that a meal would spoil his delivery.

Mrs. C. was so annoyed she stayed home, so Mr. Coolidge escorted the missionary alone to the church. When he came home, Mrs. Coolidge asked, "How did it go?" Cal's laconic reply was, "He might as well have et!"

✿   ✿   ✿

A frequent caller at the White House during F.D.R.'s tenure of office was the self-satisfied Alexander Woollcott, who liked to tell the President just what books to read. At one dinner, he inquired testily whether or not F.D.R. had gotten around to a new detective story he had recommended. "I have not," said the President.

Later, F.D.R. told attorney Morris Ernst, "I did read it—and enjoyed it, too—but I was darned if I'd give Woollcott the satisfaction of telling him so."

* * *

Rear Admiral William Mott, who once worked in the White House Map Room, tells about the day President Franklin D. Roosevelt came in to inspect the map collection. "Somehow," recalls Admiral Mott, "I managed to get his wheelchair stuck between the map of North Africa and a filing cabinet. The more I tried to pull him loose, the more we seemed to get tangled up with the cabinet. Finally the President looked up and said with the hint of a smile, "Young man, are you trying to file me?"

* * *

"President Harry Truman," recalls H. Allen Smith, "always gloried in being a country boy, scornful of the pretensions of the stuck-up sassiety folks in the East. Back home, whenever someone got gussied up in a boiled shirt, Harry had a standard taunt: 'You look like a jackass peerin' over a whitewashed fence.'

"Once when he was being given an honorary degree, President Truman tripped over his academic gown. 'Whoops,' he muttered. 'I forgot to pull up my dress!'"

*   *   *

Truman likes to tell of the day, a year or so after he left the White House, that he went calling on a friend on Park Avenue and rang the wrong doorbell. The man who answered accepted his apology, then did a double take, and exclaimed:

"Say, did anybody ever tell you you're the spitting image of that old ———, Harry Truman?"

*   *   *

Former President Harry Truman revealed to Marianne Means for her book, *The Woman in the White House,* that he once discovered his good wife Bess on her knees in their Independence, Missouri residence, burning papers in the fireplace. He asked her what she was doing. "I'm burning your letters to me," she said, shoveling in the remainder. "Bess, you oughtn't do that," he reprimanded her. "Think of history!" "I have," said Mrs. Truman.

*   *   *

Robert Keith Gray tells in his book, *Eighteen Acres Under Glass,* about the time a little girl in the Midwest invited President and Mrs. Eisenhower to a surprise party she was cooking up for her mother. In a postscript she added, "I am also inviting the Queen of England and Lassie."

* * *

If you can believe Allen and Rossi, a country club attendant stepped up to former President Eisenhower in the locker room and asked, "Do you notice anything different since you left the White House?" "Yes," was the rueful answer. "A lot more golfers are beating me."

* * *

A young reporter in Wichita rode in an open car down the main street with Jack Kennedy during his 1960 campaign tour. While the onlookers cheered lustily, the reporter begged, "Won't you tell the driver he's going too fast?" "It's all right," the soon-to-be President assured him. "They all know who I am."

"I know," grinned the reporter, "but I'd like to give them a chance to see who's riding with you."

* * *

The difficulty of making good on expensive campaign promises was something John F. Kennedy understood thoroughly long before he even dreamed of being President of the United States. In his book *Profiles in Courage,* the late President quoted this letter, sent by a California congressman to one of his more persistent constituents:

"Sir: One of the countless drawbacks of being in Congress is that I am compelled to receive impertinent letters from a jackass like you in which you say I promised to have the Sierra Madre mountains reforested and I have been in Congress two months and haven't done it. Will you please take two running jumps and go to hell. (Signed) John Steven McGroarty."

* * *

Merriman Smith tells of one of the most unusual phone calls ever received at the White House. It came in via a pay telephone just off the lobby. A voice with a distinct Southern drawl announced, "I'd like mighty well to talk to Miss Mary, please." The Secret Service man who had answered chuckled, "There's no Miss Mary here. This is the White House!"

There was a moment of silence. Then the awed caller whispered, "Pardon me, Mr. President. I sure didn't mean to bother you!"

* * *

A certain governor who had the presidential bee buzzing furiously and conspicuously in his bonnet in 1964 was observed rushing out of his private office in a swivet one morning, shouting to his secretary, "Quick! Where's that list of people I call by their first names?"

* * *

An understandable reaction from G. Barker:

The more I examine the world's sorry mess,
The more I would like to be President less!

* * *

An enterprising New York youngster, with infinite faith in the Lord, wrote Him this note recently: "I would like to give my mother, who takes such good care of me and my four sisters, a nice birthday present but I have no money at all, so won't You please send me $100 right away." He addressed the envelope simply, "For God."

Somebody in the New York Post Office was intrigued by the note and impulsively readdressed it to the White House, where it duly reached the attention of President Johnson. The President promptly sent the youngster a check for five dollars with a cheery greeting clipped thereto.

Three days later the youngster wrote another note addressed to God. "It was wonderful of You," ran this one, "to send me the hundred dollars I asked for. But why did you send it through Washington? As usual those birds down there deducted 95 per cent of it!"

* * *

Some of the problems Harry Truman encountered as President of the United States are reflected in a comment he made just before turning over the reins to Dwight Eisenhower. "He'll sit there at the White House," predicted Truman, "and he'll say, 'Do this! Do that!'—and then absolutely nothing will happen!"

* * *

Some examples of the trigger-quick wit of the late President Kennedy:

1. Upon receiving an honorary degree at Yale in June 1962: "It might be said that I now have the best of both worlds: a Harvard education and a Yale degree."

2. An inscription on a copy of a photograph of the President, snapped by Senator Goldwater: "For Barry Goldwater, whom I urge to follow the career for which he has shown such outstanding talent—photography. From his friend, John Kennedy."

3. On appointing his brother, Bobby Kennedy, as Attorney General in 1961: "I see nothing wrong with giving Robert some legal experience as Attorney General before he goes out to practice law."

4. To a Los Angeles crowd, while campaigning in 1960, he began, "I appreciate your welcome. As the cow said to the Maine farmer, 'Thank you for a warm hand on a cold morning.'"

5. At SHAPE Headquarters in Paris, in June 1961: "I do not think it altogether inappropriate to introduce myself to this audience. I am the man who accompanied Jacqueline Kennedy to Paris—and I have enjoyed it."

6. Asked by a small boy at Cape Cod, "Mr. President, how did you become a war hero?" he replied, "It was absolutely involuntary. They sank my boat."

7. To a White House dinner for Nobel Prize winners, he

commented, "I think this is the most extraordinary collection of talent and human knowledge that has ever been gathered together at the White House—with the possible exception of when Thomas Jefferson dined alone."

* * *

Dwight Eisenhower joins the growing list of people demanding shorter presidential campaigns. "By golly," he recalls, "I sure got tired of all that clackety-clack!"

When Calvin Coolidge was campaigning, somebody asked him why he didn't play up more to famous novelists and poets. Answered Coolidge, "I knew a poet once, when I was in Amherst. Class poet, name of Smith. Never heard of him since."

* * *

The United States continues to subject incoming Presidents to attacks of pneumonia and worse by insisting that they take the oath of office outdoors in often foul midwinter weather in Washington. Ed Newman, however, points out gradual evolutions in the inauguration ceremonies.

It was James Madison, for instance, who first resolved to wear only American-made clothes at his inauguration. Martin Van Buren introduced the ceremonial ride the length of Pennsylvania Avenue. William Henry Harrison spoke the longest —a solid hour and forty minutes in sub-zero cold. It's a wonder the crowd didn't demand his impeachment then and there!

McKinley's Inaugural Address, incidentally, was the first covered by motion picture cameras; Coolidge's the first broadcast on radio, and Truman's in 1949 the first flashed on a TV network.

* * *

President Lyndon Johnson received a letter at the White House recently whose envelope was marked "Personal." The letter began, "I'm sure you'll remember me. I sent you a get-well card in 1953. . . ."

* * *

Loquacious V.P. Hubert Humphrey won the hearts of all the ladies at a Women's National Press dinner when, on the eve of Inauguration Day, he told them, tongue-in-cheek, "President Johnson has given me only two instructions for the next four years. Number one is that I must keep my eyes open. As for number two—well, I don't think I have to mention that!"

2. *Always in Good Humor*

A PAUSE WITH THE PROS

A hypocritical business pirate once told Mark Twain, "Before I die I mean to make a pilgrimage to the Holy Land. I will climb to the top of Mount Sinai and read the Ten Commandments aloud." "I have a better idea," said Twain. "Why don't you stay right at home in Boston and keep them?"

A reporter visiting Mark Twain's boyhood haunts in Hannibal, Missouri, some years back found one old gaffer who discounted the glory and fame of his erstwhile school chum. "Shucks," he said. "I knew as many stories as Sam Clemens. He just writ them down."

* * *

From a letter written by Mark Twain in the twilight of his career: "Twenty-four years ago, madam, I was incredibly handsome. The remains of it are still visible through the rifts of time. I was so handsome that women became spellbound when I came in view. In San Francisco, in rainy season, I was frequently mistaken for a cloudless day. . . ."

* * *

From the notebooks of the immortal Will Rogers:

"In the early days of the Indian Territory, there were no such things as birth certificates. You being there was certificate enough."

"I had just enough white man's blood in me to make my honesty questionable."

"Once you are a showman you are plum ruined for manual labor again."

"Being a front-page hero is about the shortest-lived profession on earth."

(Referring to Calvin Coolidge): "He was the first President to discover that what the American people want most is to be left alone."

(When he was named Honorary Mayor of Beverly Hills): "I've never seen a Mayor who wasn't funny—and when he puts on a silk hat, he's even funnier. What this country needs is more ex-mayors."

* * *

The late George S. Kaufman once explained to the Dutch Treat Club why it took him over a year to write *Dinner at Eight* in collaboration with Edna Ferber. "Edna," he remarked with some bitterness, "worked from 8:00 A.M. until 3:10 P.M. I worked from 3:00 P.M. until 8:00 P.M. That gave us exactly ten minutes a day together."

* * *

A group of Montreal nature lovers once invited the great Canadian humorist, Stephen Leacock, to accompany them on a pre-dawn bird-watching expedition. "Ladies," Mr. Leacock told them candidly, "I freely admit that I am the kind of man who would have absolutely no interest in an oriole building a nest unless it built it in my hat in the check room at my club."

* * *

Other memorable lines attributed to Stephen Leacock:

1. There is only one beautiful child in the world, and every mother has it.

2. Many a man in love with a dimple makes the mistake of marrying the whole girl.

3. A friend is a man who has the same enemies you have.

4. Many college graduates need that sheepskin they get to cover their intellectual nakedness.

* * *

A neglected humorous classic, says Frank Sullivan, is Stephen Leacock's *Gertrude the Governess*. Sullivan, a famous humorist himself, particularly likes Leacock's opening paragraph: "It was a wild and stormy night on the west coast of Scotland. This, however, is immaterial to the present story, as the scene is not laid in the west of Scotland. As a matter of fact, the weather was just as bad on the east coast of Ireland. But the scene of this narrative is laid in the south of England."

Later on in *Gertrude the Governess*, one will encounter the oft-quoted "Lord Ronald said nothing: he flung himself from the room, flung himself upon his horse, and rode madly off in all directions."

* * *

Moments of high comedy on the stage that are lovingly recalled by Frank Sullivan:

1. When Ed Wynn, telling another character in a musical about something frightening that had happened to a friend, said, "Why, he turned as white as your shirt." With this, Wynn took a closer look at the shirt, and added, "Whiter!"

MKF
AFTER THE GREAT
GW

2. When Bob Benchley reminisced in a monologue, "While rummaging through a bureau drawer in my youth, I came across some old snow."

3. When Bobby Clark, sampling a bowl of soup in a beanery, was asked by a solicitous waiter, "How's the soup, sir?" and answered pensively, "To tell you the truth, I'm kinda sorry I stirred it."

❖ ❖ ❖

Many of the late Jim Thurber's finest humorous pieces were devoted to affectionate chronicles of the oddballs in his own family. Of his own mother, he wrote, "For some reason or other, during storms, she always took the telephone receiver off the hook and let it hang. And she lived the latter years of her life in the horrible suspicion that electricity was dripping invisibly all over the house. It leaked, she contended, out of empty sockets."

Thurber's great-uncle, maintained Jim, met with a unique fate: "He caught," noted Mr. Thurber, "the same disease that was killing off a lot of chestnut trees one year and passed away.

It was the only case in history where a tree doctor had to be called in to spray a person."

❋ ❋ ❋

James Thurber once encountered a lady at a cocktail party who assured him that his books were even funnier in French. "Ah, yes," mused Mr. Thurber, "I lose something in the original."

❋ ❋ ❋

In the last piece that James Thurber wrote, the greatest humorist America has produced in the past thirty years took a dim view of modern trends in his chosen field. "Comedy," he noted, "didn't die; it just went crazy. It has identified itself with the very tension and terror it once did so much to alleviate. The roost is ruled today by what has been called the comedy of menace: horror jokes, magazines known as Horror Comics, and sick comedians. . . . Life at the moment is a tale told in an idiom, full of unsoundness and fury, signifying nonism."

❋ ❋ ❋

Meanwhile—back at the high schools—what are a few of the "sick jokes" our teenagers are now circulating?

1. "I guess I've lost another pupil," sighed the professor as his glass eye slid down the drain.

2. James McNeill Whistler came home one evening to find his mother sprawled out on the living room floor. "How come, ma?" he chided her. "You off your rocker?"

3. "Better hurry over here, Mom. Junior just ate the raisins off that sticky brown paper."

4. "But, Oswald, that isn't our baby." "Quiet, you fool; it's a better carriage."

THE PERENNIAL EAVESDROPPER

1. Driving instructor to confused student: "Lady, those steel objects you complain are keeping you from concentrating are the accelerator, the brake, and the clutch."

2. Door-to-door salesman to housewife: "Let me show you a little item your neighbors said you couldn't afford. . . ."

3. One rat in a laboratory cage to another: "I've finally got Dr. Skinner conditioned. Now every time I press the bar and stand on my head he gives me a piece of cheese."

4. In a golf course shelter during a thunderstorm: "When I met my wife, I got a lump in my throat. She was a judo expert."

5. At a hamburger stand: "Who was that cute little blonde I saw you outwit Tuesday night?"

6. Mother, tucking youngster into bed: "Honey child, if you want anything at all during the night, just call Mommy—and she'll send Daddy in."

7. Tulane senior to his girl: "I'll phone you tonight or dial in the attempt."

8. In a crowded department store elevator: "Take your hands off me, you cad! No, not you! YOU!"

9. Little boy leaving a movie: "I like television better. It's not so far to the bathroom."

10. Fight manager to his new heavyweight: "Don't be so terrified. Remember: if he was any good, he wouldn't be fighting you."

11. At Baylor University in Waco: "In my calculus exam this morning I was mighty close to the right answers. They were only two seats away."

12. In the garment district: "I'm truly sorry, Max, but if I let you take off two hours for lunch today, I'd have to do the same thing for every other cutter in the place whose wife gave birth to quintuplets!"

13. At a big cocktail party: "Every time I turned around, he was kissing my wife. So I stopped turning around."

14. In a barber shop: "Just give me a shave. I haven't got time to listen to a haircut."

15. Young lady in phone booth to impatient man waiting to replace her: "This won't take much longer. I just want to hang up on him."

16. Eight-year-old reporting to his favorite teacher: "Pop

came in very late last night and crashed into the garage doors. It's a lucky thing he didn't have the car!"

17. Visitor from outer space getting his first glimpse of a skating rink: "Well, well! People on the rocks!"

18. Darling old lady at an airline ticket counter: "How long a hangover will I have in St. Louis?"

19. Chiropractor giving patient a massage: "It's going to rain. I can feel it in your bones!"

20. Long-winded Rotarian at the microphone: "I will have to conclude this discourse because of my throat. Several members have threatened to cut it."

21. In a locker room: "There's only one way I can let the kids know when I'm home from the office. I walk in front of the television set."

22. At Aqueduct Race Track: "I haven't got a cent to bet today. My wife just blew our entire bankroll on the rent."

23. Dignified Harvardite resisting the advances of an ardent Radcliffe-Hanger: "Please, Miss Arbuthnot: you're steaming my glasses."

24. Golfer, yelling from the woods: "Never mind about my ball, caddy. Come find *me!*"

25. Newlywed to his bride: "Save the recipe for that tapioca pudding, darling. I have to mend a patch in the driveway."

26. Father to son asking for money: "Junior, have you ever considered being a professional fund-raiser?"

27. At Danny's Hideaway: "No wonder she's gushing. The fellow she's dining with owns two hundred oil wells."

28. Complaint by a member of a trio specializing in folk songs: "My son loosened one of the strings on my gee-tar and he won't tell me which one!"

29. On a Fifth Avenue bus: "Grandma can never find her glasses any more—so now she drinks from the can."

30. In an Eskimo igloo: "My wife is driving me nuts. She keeps asking me to buy her a *cloth* coat!"

31. At Schrafft's: "My fiancé likes the same thing I do—only he likes to save it and I like to spend it."

32. Near M.I.T.: "My wife doesn't understand me. I'm a nuclear physicist."

33. Off Broadway: "That man tosses money around like a boomerang."

34. At a party honoring a film star just back from a safari in Africa: "He's the first man the head shrinkers ever failed with."

35. In a big office: "A fresh goof tried to pick me up in his big convertible last night. Boy, what an apartment he's got!"

36. From a customer in a branch post office: "This package contains a very fragile vase—so please throw it underhand."

37. In St. Petersburg, Florida: "When I was a kid, ten cents was a lot of money. How dimes have changed!"

38. Mr. Meek to his domineering wife: "I will NOT take you to '21' this evening—and that's semi-final!"

39. At a commencement dance at a seaboard university: "I'll give you exactly forty-five minutes to get your hand off my knee."

40. At a shopping center: "You don't sell used cars? What kind of a drugstore is this?"

41. Man with a terrible hangover hollering at his cat: "Confound it! Stop stamping your bloody feet!"

42. At a bridge party: "My son's new girl friend is so hefty she could play fullback for Ohio State. You know what she wears on her charm bracelet? *Old license plates!*"

43. At Toots Shor's: "I come from a long line of boxers—except for an uncle who was a Doberman pinscher."

44. At a downtown lunch counter: "My boss is so incompetent this restaurant refused to serve him the businessman's lunch."

45. Disgusted drill sergeant, after marching a new lot of draftees around the parade ground: "I've seen better drilling by cans of beer on my TV screen!"

46. In a girls' dormitory on the University of Wisconsin campus: "The important thing in saying good night is to keep your feet on the ground."

47. Broadway star in Dr. Pullman's Dental Parlor: "It's the one in the first row, right, in the balcony."

48. A lady at a bank teller's window: "I want to make this withdrawal from my husband's half of our joint account."

49. Leader of a flock of geese to the birds following: "Stop that infernal honking! If you want to pass, pass!"

50. At a cannibal conclave: "Don't tell me you hate your mother-in-law's guts. Just push them to one side and eat the vegetables!"

QUICKIES

Brevity is a virtue appreciated today by practically everybody but political orators, burlesque show censors, perpetrators of TV deodorant commercials, and authors of current novels.

And whatever else you may say about the thirty-seven "short shorts" in this section, you'll have to admit they're brief. It won't take more than a few seconds to read—or retell—any one of them!

1. Two angels were enjoying an idle conversation aboard a cloud. Finally one asked the other, "Do you believe in the heretofore?"

2. A wife suggested to her husband, "Let's buy Junior a bicycle." "Do you think it might improve his behavior?" asked

the ever-hopeful husband. "I do not," admitted the wife, "but at least it will spread it over the neighborhood."

3. A bargain hunter went to a gigantic fire sale last week—and bought a gigantic fire.

4. Have you heard about the absent-minded Siamese twin? Everything went into one ear and out of his brother's.

5. A pert miss at a soda counter sighed wistfully, "What I really crave is one of those darling foreign sports cars—with the foreign sport still in it."

6. "Phew," sighed a relieved surgeon as he joined his colleague in the hospital's executive dining room. "I just got under the wire with that last emergency operation! Another hour and the patient would have recovered without it."

7. A movie star saw a fellow thespian enter a restaurant with a beautiful girl on his arm. "That's his wife," he was told. "His wife!" echoed the star. "What a publicity stunt!"

8. Eve Backer has discovered a snazzy new restaurant just off Park Avenue where the prices are so outrageous that when you find a pearl in your oyster you break even.

9. A sporting goods store in Duluth advertised a mammoth removal sale and had spectacular results within four hours. Burglars who read the papers removed the entire stock of the store that very evening.

10. There's at least one understanding wife in Las Cruces who lets her husband go out one night every week with the boys. He's a scoutmaster.

11. There's also a bridegroom there, however, who knew he was going to be henpecked right from the start. As he carried her over the threshold she warned him, "Wipe your shoes."

12. A grouchy boss kept rattling his box of pens and penpoints. "I wonder," whispered his secretary to the phone operator, "what's the matter with his nibs."

13. Two prominent figures in a nudist camp became involved in a bitter argument. The more temperate of the two finally laid a restraining hand on the other's shoulder and counseled, "Hector, Hector! Keep your shirt off!"

14. One thing you'll have to concede to a wolf: he whistles while he works.

15. A brokerage clerk admitted to his folks, "Since I'm married, I've really learned how to meet expenses. My wife introduces them to me."

16. In the Bronx Park Zoo a tipsy gentleman regarded a huge hippopotamus reproachfully and beseeched, "Don't look at me that way, my love! I can explain everything."

17. In a boardwalk auction parlor, a triumphant auctioneer clamped down the cover on a box of garish chinaware and declared, "Sold—to the stout lady with her husband's hand over her mouth."

18. A sailor went peacefully to sleep on a Riverside Drive bench, with this sign hung over his shoes: "Please do not disturb. The fleet's all in."

19. An octopus fell into a cement mixer. Just a crazy, mixed-up squid.

20. Larry Wolters knows a conservative teen-ager who drives a warm-rod.

21. A worker in a violin repair shop claims he restrings an average of fourteen instruments a day. "And that, gentlemen," he adds, "takes guts!"

22. Steve Allen has sent his wife Jayne to U.C.L.A. to improve her cooking. The name of the course she's signed up for is "advanced defrosting."

23. Sign in a Washington merchant's window: "You can fool some of the people some of the time, and generally speaking, that's enough to allow for a profit."

24. There are four things, insists Herb Caen, that every bona fide Hollywood star simply *must* have: a Japanese gardener, a Filipino houseboy, a French maid—and a Mexican divorce.

25. Ralph Henderson maintains that his golf game is looking up: he played a full round of eighteen holes the other day without falling off his golf cart once.

26. A harassed office manager was asked, "Who are you working for these days?" His answer: "Same old outfit: my wife and six kids."

27. A Vassar senior told a plastic surgeon she yearned for a "turned up" nose. The doctor turned it up a trifle too far. Now every time the poor girl sneezes she blows her hat off.

28. A Texas debutante returned her boy friend's friendship ring. She found out his definition of friendship.

29. A gangster's son spent four years learning how to be a successful safe-cracker. He was determined to follow in his father's fingerprints.

30. Two Indian fakirs discovered a tub of nails outside their tent. So they had a pillow fight.

31. There exists one bride who treats her husband like a Greek god. At every meal she places a burnt offering before him.

32. Bob Campbell reports the sad case of the nitwit who fell into a lens-grinding machine—and made a spectacle of himself.

33. Overheard in the Lonesome Pine country:
Door-to-door salesman: Madam, I represent the Stretchit Woolen Mills. Could I interest you in some coarse yarns?
Mrs. Hatfield McCoy: Sure. Tell me a couple.

34. Comic Joey Bishop spotted a midget friend exiting from a health spa steam room and told him, "I warned you, Sam! You can take only so much of that stuff and no more!"

35. A character parading about Fort Lauderdale, Florida,

insists that his name is Seven-and-One-Eighth Flannery. Explains that his parents picked his name out of a hat.

36. A tenderhearted big league baseball manager sought out his third baseman in the locker room. "Joe," he said, putting his arm around the player's shoulder, "it's okay for you to forget all those batting tips I gave you. We just traded you to Kansas City."

37. Robert Q. Lewis, TV philosopher, was in a butcher shop when a lady customer complained bitterly, "That chicken I bought here yesterday had no wishbone." The butcher answered earnestly: "Madam, the chickens we sell here are so happy, they have nothing to wish for."

SHAGGY DOGGEREL

To the surprise of everybody at a recent stupendous, all-star benefit performance, the hit of the evening was scored by a miniature talking poodle who brought down the house with a series of superb imitations and snappy new jokes. While the applause of the audience was at its height, however, a large dog shot out of the wings, grabbed the triumphant poodle by the scruff of the neck, and pulled him offstage.

"Sorry, folks," yelled the poodle as he disappeared into the wings. "It's my mother. She always wanted me to be a doctor."

❋   ❋   ❋

Two "at liberty" vaudevillians met at a bar one afternoon, and one demanded, "Say, whatever became of that talking dog of yours?" "I gave him away," admitted the other. "An actor has to have *some* pride." "But that dog was one in a million," said the first. "Yeah," nodded the other, "but he got too smart for me. First, he took more curtain calls than I did, then he demanded top billing. But the climax came when he started making out his own income tax returns—and tried to list me as a dependent!"

❋   ❋   ❋

Two flies met on top of a huckleberry cake. "How's the world treating you, Mrs. Buzz?" asked one. "Not so good," was the weary reply. "Junior's been in such a pet I've had to walk the ceiling with him all week."

* * *

A man selling two-dollar tickets at the Aqueduct horse racing track registered considerable surprise when a horse stepped up to the window and asked to bet on himself. "What's the matter," snorted the horse. "Are you astonished that I can talk?" "Not at all," said the man. "I'm astonished that you think you can win."

* * *

Dolores Duck was the most seductive fowl that ever had paraded on Lake Lookout, but proud, sullen Darwin Drake remained impervious to her charms.

Dolores had just decided he wasn't worth any more of her time when she spotted a hunter in the reeds drawing a bead on the two. "Look out, Darwin," she quacked as she dove to safety.

When she resurfaced the hunter was gone—but where the handsome Drake had been there floated nothing but a bunch of splinters.

"Ah, ha," nodded Dolores in a flash of understanding. "Wooden duck, eh?"

* * *

A missionary and a very un-Elsa-like lion met head-on in an impenetrable jungle. Flight was out of the question; the missionary sank to his knees and prayed. To his astonishment, the lion did likewise.

"How miraculous," babbled the missionary, "to join you in prayer when just a moment ago I gave myself up for lost!"

"Quiet," ordered the lion severely. "I'm saying grace."

* * *

In a well-stocked clothes closet, a moth and his mate came upon a pair of all-woolen spats and had a feast for themselves. Later the moth flew about a bit to digest his dinner and bumped into a pal who caroled, "Hi boy! How ya doin'?" "Not so hot," admitted the moth, "I just had a spat with my wife."

* * *

Jerome Beatty tells about a doctor whose doorbell began ringing frantically in the middle of the night. He rushed to answer it and found on his doorstep a man on whose head a pelican was roosting.

"Say, Doc," begged the pelican, "can you get this thing off my feet?"

* * *

A family of bears, rummaging in a Yellowstone National Park garbage dump, looked up when a car crammed with eight tourists pulled up at the side of the road. "It's cruel," commented Papa Bear to his brood, "to keep them caged up like that!"

* * *

Hugh Downs submits the story of the leopard who visited his optometrist to complain, "Every time I look at my wife, I see spots before my eyes." "What do you expect?" scoffed the optometrist. "You're a leopard, aren't you?" "Of course I am," conceded the leopard, "but my wife is a zebra."

* * *

Gertrude Bayne avers that she heard two sharks talking off Sandy Hook Light recently. "Take my tip and stay clear of Coney Island," one shark was advising the other. "Irving was swimming down there last weekend and he got mugged."

*   *   *

A theatrical agent would have no part of an applicant who claimed he could do any kind of bird imitation.

"At least listen to my act," begged the applicant.

"Haven't got time," snapped the agent. "Bird imitators died with vaudeville."

"Okay, if that's the way you feel about it," concluded the offended artist—and flew out of the window.

*   *   *

According to Dick Rodgers, there was once a vacationing bartender who encountered a grasshopper in a field. "Do you know," inquired the bartender respectfully, "that a very popular new drink has been named after you?" "Golly," nodded the grasshopper, obviously impressed. "Who could have dreamed there'd be a drink named Leonard!"

*   *   *

According to the always-reliable Jack Lemmon, a lobster strolled into a restaurant and sat down at a table by the window. "What would you like, sir?" asked a waiter, and the lobster answered, "A little mayonnaise."

*   *   *

En route to the seashore for a weekend engagement, a trainer and his talking dog were speeding along in a new sports car when a motorcycle cop started closing in on them. The dog advised the trembling trainer, "Better pull up at that parking area, and remember—when he gets here, *let me do the talking.*"

3. *All the World's a Stage*

ACTRESSES AND ACTORS

Two grizzled acrobats who had been the opening act in countless dilapidated vaudeville houses throughout the country wound up one night in Boston lodged in jail, charged with assault and battery in the first degree. They summoned a local lawyer, who asked, "What happened?"

"Well, Bertie here and me," explained the elder acrobat, "had a night before our new show opened so we decided to spend it improving our minds. We hadn't been to a concert in twenty years and I said, 'Bertie, this Boston Symphony is supposed to be the cat's whiskers. So that's where we'll go.' We buy seats in Row A, and watch the conductor come out in white tie and tails. We're impressed. Then he raises his baton and what do you think that orchestra does? PLAYS OUR ENTIRE OPENING NUMBER!"

* * *

Another acrobatic duo finally got a chance to play a top Broadway showcase after long, weary years in the sticks. "If you make good in this house," their agent promised, "I'll get you a fifty-week contract playing the whole circuit. But keep your eyes on an owl the manager keeps on the balcony railing. The manager takes great stock in that owl. If he keeps his eyes open during the act, you're in like Sinatra. But if it blinks— good night, Charlie!"

The opening night arrived and the acrobats advanced to the footlights, their wives watching nervously from the wings. Suddenly one acrobat whispered to the other, "Do you see what I see, Joe? That ventriloquist has your wife in his arms and is kissing her madly."

"Never mind my wife," hissed the other. "Keep your eyes on that owl!"

* * *

No admirer of child actors was acidulous drama critic George Jean Nathan. When a more indulgent colleague declared, "In my opinion, 90 per cent of all children are natural actors," Nathan's sharp rejoinder was, "What a pity the other 10 per cent go on the stage!"

* * *

The late Sir Cedric Hardwicke, accomplished British actor, liked best of all his press notices on accolades bestowed upon him by George Bernard Shaw. "Hardwicke," wrote Shaw, "is my fifth favorite actor, the first four being the Marx Brothers."

* * *

King George had a little trouble the day he knighted Sir Cedric. As Hardwicke knelt before him, the Lord Chamberlain read his name. The King said sharply, "Who?" He didn't get it the second time, either, then demanded, "Spell it." "For an actor's name to be spelled out," confessed Hardwicke, "is his greatest humiliation."

It turns out that spelling didn't help King George a bit. He finally whacked Sir Cedric on the back with his jeweled sword, and dubbed him, rather testily, "Sir Samuel Pickwick."

*   *   *

Very early in their fabulous career, the Four Marx Brothers were booked for a vaudeville tour through the Middle West, and their father took a train from New York to Chicago to arrange the details of their itinerary. It was by far the longest train journey any Marx had undertaken to that date, and the entire family trooped over to the 125th Street station to see him off. There were speeches, cheers, and even a few tears as Papa Marx hopped aboard the train. Fifteen minutes later he hopped off again—at Grand Central Station. He had boarded an incoming train instead of an outgoing one.

*   *   *

During World War I, the immortal Will Rogers was delivering his monologue in the Ziegfeld Follies one evening when a hatchet-faced woman in the ninth row called out, "Why aren't you in the Army?" Rogers gave everybody in the audience time to turn around and look at his heckler, then drawled, "For the same reason, Madam, that you aren't in the Follies: *physical disabilities.*"

*   *   *

Peter Lind Hayes delights in reminiscing about his erratic old friend, stuttering Joe Frisco. Joe was in constant terror of being robbed, says Hayes. One night he checked into a fleabag in Altoona, and searched every corner of the room before retiring to make sure no robber was lying in wait for him.

Then he double-locked the door and dove into bed. He took one more precaution even then. In the darkness he called out, "Oh, Lord, here I am in Altoona again—dead broke!"

✿ ✿ ✿

"There," said a diner at Sardi's, "is an actor who's going places." "Have they given him featured billing?" asked a companion. "No, no," answered the diner impatiently. "I mean his wife is out of town."

✿ ✿ ✿

Several years after she had married Charlie MacArthur, great star Helen Hayes announced to him and their young son James that she had secretly been taking cooking lessons, and proposed to cook dinner for them that very evening. "If I spoil it," she ordered, "I don't want to hear a word from either of you. We'll just get up from the table, *without* comment, and go to a restaurant for dinner."

A short time later, she entered the dining room, bearing aloft the first steak she ever had cooked. Mr. MacArthur and Son Jamie were sitting in silence at the table—with their hats and coats on.

✿ ✿ ✿

Radie Harris tells of a time Rosalind Russell was doing a series of one-night stands. She was resting for a performance after a 250-mile journey from her last engagement, and hung a "Do Not Disturb" sign very carefully outside her dressing room.

A half hour later she was awakened from a delicious doze by a persistent knock on the door. She jumped up to open the door and found a little girl with the "Do Not Disturb" sign in her hand. She thrust it at Miss Russell and said, "Please autograph this for me."

* * *

Gypsy Rose Lee would have you believe that this is how she embarked upon her career as a stripper: "I was trying out for a singing role in a musical comedy. I sang my heart out, in fact. When I had finished, a brute of a director said, "Well, don't just stand there, young lady. Un-do something!"

* * *

A ventriloquist told veteran showman Bill Kennedy he had developed the sock novelty act of the year. "I throw my mother-in-law's voice," he beamed. "What's so unusual about that?" scoffed Kennedy. "You don't dig this yet," the ventriloquist explained earnestly. "I throw her voice while it's still in her."

* * *

In the Players' Club, the death mask of Richard Sheridan invariably intrigues visiting celebrities. A hard-to-impress author once grumbled to a member, "Hmph! He looks mighty dour for a celebrated humorist." The member patiently pointed out, "You must remember he was not at his best when this mask was made."

* * *

Barbra Streisand, the new toast of Broadway and shining star of *Funny Girl*, was christened Barbara at birth, but later took an "a" out of it just to confuse everybody. Now she says, "I don't care what you write about me—so long as you spell my name wrong." Once she considered changing her name entirely—to Angella Scarangella for no particular reason—but desisted in the nick of time.

She told her first interviewer that she was born in Madagascar and grew up in Rangoon. Investigation proved, however, that she never left Brooklyn until she was fifteen and was an "A" student at Erasmus High there. Nothing ever has stopped her since and, obviously, nothing will. Miss Streisand is a law unto herself.

* * *

George Abbott advised a group studying acting for the experimental theater, "Always be extremely careful of the scenery. There's no telling who had it in his mouth just before you."

*　*　*

Billy Rose tells the story of a well-known ham actor who gave up Broadway and became a surgeon. He removed an appendix so skillfully one morning that several doctors watching him started to applaud. Whereupon he bowed gratefully and cut out the patient's gall bladder for an encore.

*　*　*

"My wallet," boasted an old Shakespearian ham, "is bursting with big bills." Then he added sadly, "If only some of them were paid!"

*　*　*

Oscar-award-winner Peter Ustinov submits to a great deal of kidding about his beard, but refuses to give it up. "People can hear me better," he explains, "when I speak above a whisker. Besides it gives babies something to hold on to when they're climbing into my lap."

Ustinov admits his beard got him into some difficulty when he was riding in a New York elevator. The operator gave it a playful yank (pulling out several hairs in the process) and exclaimed, "I know you! You're that crooked wrestler on TV!"

*　*　*

Off Broadway, they tell of a performer who tried to impress an agent with a brand new act. "I catch razor-sharp butcher knives with my teeth," he boasted, then, noting an incredulous look in the agent's eye, added, "I suppose you think I'm smiling!"

*　*　*

Carol Burnett is a great big star these days, but still likes to tell stories in which she figures as the patsy. One of her favorites concerns the out-of-towner who grabbed her arm in the

Waldorf lobby one morning and called loudly to his wife, "Hey, Mae, here's What's-her-name! And you know what? She ain't such a dog after all!"

* * *

Pat O'Brien tells of an old ham actor who was happy to secure a bit part in a new Broadway play, laid in an East Side saloon. He was to portray a customer in Act 1, and again in Act 3.

On the opening night, the director grabbed him when he made his exit in the first act and roared, "You dummy! You left your hat on the bar and the whole audience noticed it." The contrite actor made sure to retrieve the hat when he appeared in Act 3. When he placed it on his head, the audience surprised him by bursting into laughter and applause. "What did I do now?" asked the actor when he escaped to the wings. "Idiot!" bellowed the director. "This last scene is supposed to be fifteen years later!"

* * *

Deems Taylor tells a story to demonstrate that even the greatest stars suffer twinges of jealousy. He attended an audition of budding talent with Alfred Lunt and Lynn Fontanne. The participants—mostly female—groped their way through the sleepwalking scene in *Macbeth*.

Afterward, Miss Fontanne whispered to Deems Taylor, "Absolutely no talent in the whole group"—and added, "Thank God!"

CIRCUSES AND FAIRS

A beautiful and adventurous girl ran away from home and joined the circus. "I don't want to make the usual beginner's mistakes," she told the ringmaster. "Can you give me a few helpful hints?" "Well, for one thing," mused the ringmaster, "don't ever undress around the bearded lady."

* * *

At a convention in Chicago, a magician whispered to the toastmaster, "Boss, I've got a great act for you. Out of the air I pick two hundred lighted cigars, puff on them, and then swallow them." "You mean to say you swallow two hundred lighted cigars?" challenged the toastmaster. "Nothing to it," shrugged the magician. "I buy 'em wholesale."

* * *

George Kirgo, making a survey of new circus acts in Europe, came across one troupe that features a man diving two hundred feet into a sofa pillow. "Of course," amplifies Kirgo, "they use a different man every night."

* * *

For generations, one of the standard products offered for sale by circus hawkers has been "pink lemonade." The origin of this peculiar potation, according to John Ringling North, goes back to the day when one Peter Conklin was handling the refreshment concession for Mabie's Mighty Circus in the South.

One afternoon was such a scorcher that lemonade sales reached unprecedented heights, and Pete Conklin ran out of his principal ingredient: water. He rushed into the dressing room of Fannie Jamieson, the Fat Lady, and heedless of her protests, seized a tub of water in which she had been soaking her bespangled red dress. "Analine dye never hurt nobody," pronounced Pete.

To the reddened water he added a spot of tartaric acid and sugar, and promptly began shouting, "This way for the only lemonade in the world guaranteed PINK." The customers were enchanted, and when nobody came down with even a mild convulsion, pink lemonade became standard equipment in the refreshment tent.

* * *

When Billy Rose's Aquacade was turning them away at the 1939 World's Fair, the diminutive showman was enraged to hear that an unknown had opened a pet shop just outside the Fair grounds with a big sign outside proclaiming "BILLY

ROSE'S PET SHOP." Billy rushed over to tell the unknown, "If you haven't got that sign down by tomorrow morning, I'm going to get out an injunction to close you up permanently." The proprietor replied calmly, "I have a birth certificate handy to prove that Billy Rose is my real name. What's yours?" Showman Rose knew when he was licked. He bought a canary.

✿ ✿ ✿

The star tightrope walker of the Ringling Brothers and Barnum & Bailey Circus one winter discovered that she was going to have a baby, but managed to conceal her condition from the management and fellow artists by adroit use of costume and parasol.

At the end of her seventh month, however, the artiste sought out a leading doctor in Boston and asked how much longer she could safely continue doing her act in the circus.

"The circus!" exclaimed the astonished doctor. "What do you do in the circus?"

"I walk the tightrope," she told him proudly.

"Holy smoke!" said the doctor. "You do your act tonight, because I have tickets. But *tomorrow morning*, you *quit!*"

✿ ✿ ✿

A circus owner caught his trainer administering a merciless beating to the most valuable elephant in the troupe. "Stop!"

roared the owner. "What's the idea of beating that poor animal?"

The trainer explained grimly, "He tripped in the middle of his act this evening." The owner cried, "Do you mean to say you're beating him just because he tripped?" "Just because he tripped, my left eyebrow," said the trainer—or words to that effect. "He tore the tails out of all your eleven other elephants."

THE FLICKS

Lives there a writer with pockets so lined with gold he never once has succumbed to the siren songs of the movie and TV magnates in Hollywood? I doubt it.

Even James Thurber, one of America's greatest and most uncompromising humorists, hankered after some of that California gold on one occasion, and set out to do a screen version of his own story, "The Catbird Seat." He was assigned a secretary and started to dictate some dialogue. "I'm sorry," interrupted the secretary, "but I don't take dialogue. I only take letters."

Thurber proved equal to the occasion. He began the dictation of every scene with the salutation, "Dear Sam," and he and the secretary got along perfectly.

*　*　*

George Bernard Shaw was no lover of motion pictures. "Films bore me," he explained, "because they show interminably people getting in and out of limousines, trains, and buses. I am not interested in how people get to different places, but what they do when they get there."

*　*　*

That great comedian W. C. Fields was definitely anti-author, particularly after he hit Hollywood. After one full day's shooting on a new script, Fields returned to his dressing room in an unusually jovial mood. "This was a day to remember," he explained happily. "I didn't say one word the so-and-so wrote for me!"

* * *

Gene Fowler once caught the irascible Fields violently kicking a rose bush in his garden. "Bloom, damn you," Fields was muttering.

* * *

When Dorothy Parker was writing screenplays in Hollywood, the bejeweled wife of an important producer named Pizitz bore down upon her in her cubicle in the executives' building and pinned her down for a dinner party eight weeks in advance. Thinking the wife had gone, Miss Parker instructed her secretary, "Remind me to write those illiterate, phony boors that I can't attend their confounded party because . . ."

At this point, Miss Parker looked up and saw to her dismay that the lady was listening, frozen, in the doorway. "Because," Miss Parker improvised hastily, "I am dining that evening with the Pizitzes!"

* * *

A world-famous director tried in vain to cajole a star into throwing himself down a mobile staircase. Finally he exploded, "You coward! I'll show you myself how easy it is."

After his demonstration, while still lying at the foot of the staircase, he sneered at the star, "Well, do you think you can do it now?" "I guess so," said the star reluctantly.

"Okay," said the director. "Go ahead. And while you're at it, tell somebody to call for an ambulance. I've broken a leg."

* * *

Jayne Mansfield recalls that when she was a sweet young co-ed at the University of Texas she once walked into a dress shop and inquired of the manager, "May I try on that bathing suit in the window?" The manager eyed her appreciatively and urged, "Go ahead. It might help business."

* * *

A Hollywood bit player who fancies himself as an irresistible Lothario was boasting about his conquests on location in the San Joaquin Valley. "My very first night there," he revealed, "I had dates with Sally, Irene, and Fido."

"Fido!" echoed a friend. "That sounds like a dog to me."

"If you think Fido was a dog," admitted the bit player reluctantly, "you should have seen Sally and Irene."

* * *

Anita Loos recalls a summer day in Hollywood when Aldous Huxley, Bertrand Russell, one of the top professors at U.C.L.A., Charlie Chaplin, and Greta Garbo joined her for a picnic. The dazzling group parked in a shady glen, and not one of them noticed the "No Trespassing" sign tacked to a sheltering tree. Just as they were unpacking the caviar and champagne, an angry sheriff hove into view and demanded, "Don't anybody in this gang know how to read?"

* * *

Kirk Douglas, dressed as a Roman soldier of Caesar's legions for a big historical picture, took advantage of a break in the day's shooting schedule to repair to a nearby bistro for a drink. He took with him two lesser actors in similar garb.

The bartender wasn't used to serving movie actors in costume, and his eyes popped when Douglas and his friends walked in. Douglas, noting his astonishment, asked casually, "What's the matter, pop? Don't you cater to servicemen here?"

* * *

Filming outdoor shots for a Western film, Director John Rich had to reshoot one scene seven times because of such extraneous noises as yelping canines and jets flying overhead. A passing lady motorist stopped to watch, and finally interrupted the director to ask, "Why do you persist in shooting the same scene so many times?" Rich answered patiently, "Madam, have you stopped to consider how many theaters there are in this country?"

The lady drove on—satisfied.

* * *

One of those new movie stars with extraordinary measurements is so candid and unpredictable that her studio has assigned two press agents to do her talking for her. An enterprising reporter, however, cornered her when the press agents were out to lunch and came back with an interview that was a sizzler. The star confessed, for instance, that she liked to "wear dresses so tight that the men can't breathe." She also suggested a sure-fire way to keep children from biting their fingernails. "Other mothers should just do what I did," she proposed cheerfully. "I knocked my little boy's teeth out!"

Asked why she was seen so frequently with a wealthy and publicity-mad octogenarian, she explained, "He possesses that rarest of masculine virtues—about fifteen million dollars."

* * *

A pretentious movie producer, always boasting about his rare books, became such a bore that his associates decided to cut him down a peg. They hired an actor from the East and introduced him as a country doctor from Ioway. Quickly, the conversation was brought around to rare books.

"Personally," asserted the good doctor, "I loathe very old books. They're moldy and I can't stand their smell. Only a couple of days ago I threw out an old German Bible that had been in the family, I reckon, for generations."

"Old German Bible?" repeated the producer hastily. "You don't happen to remember who printed it?"

"I think it was Guten-something or other," yawned the doctor.

"Not GUTENBERG!" shrieked the producer. "You fool, you have thrown away a great fortune. We must fly back to Iowa at once and try to retrieve that Bible before it is destroyed!"

"Hold your horses," counseled the doctor with elaborate unconcern. "This particular Bible couldn't be worth anything, no matter who printed it. Some character named Martin Luther had scribbled his name all over it!"

HOLLYWOOD SHORTS.

— Life in Hollywood is like this: a big bad man-about-town was having difficulty persuading a sweet thing to go home and hear his hi-fi set. "Look," he implored, "how long have I known you?" "About three-quarters of an hour," she estimated coyly. "All right then," he stormed, "have I ever lied to you?"

— Will Jones avers that the evening he visited a movie theater in the Middle East, he saw the man next to him tap the lady in front of him and ask her, "Would you mind removing your jug?"

— Envious whisper to a movie star who had had four husbands by a virtual novice who had had only two: "You're two chumps ahead of me!"

— Driving on one of California's jammed-up freeways, observes Matt Weinstock, you can watch a drive-in movie, follow a revolving searchlight in the sky, and wave at a blonde in a sports car—all in the same accident.

— A studio head summoned his assistant, embraced him warmly, and told him, "Mac, old boy, this new project of ours calls for ingenuity, imagination, clear thinking, and hard work. That's why I called you in on it! I want you to resign."

— Mike Connolly cites a Hollywood star who knew instinctively how to behave when invited to the Flower Show. He got potted. Mike has also discovered the one way to keep a couple of jumps ahead of his wife. He plays checkers with her.

— "Husbands," warns Zsa Zsa Gabor, "are like fires. They go out when unattended."

— An indignant chorus girl pointed to a friend, "Remember that fellow I told you about who got me by saying he makes Westerns? The phony cuts up the ham, onions, and green peppers for omelets at the Automat!"

— One of Hollywood's most famous word assassins was invited to a party recently. "I can't make it," he announced regretfully, "but I hope you'll give me a raincoat."

— "I looked too thin in my last rushes," complained a petulant film star to her cameraman. "Can't you do something to make me look round?" The cameraman did something and the star slapped him in the face.

— A reigning Hollywood movie queen told an interviewer earnestly, "I believe very firmly in early marriages. I always get married before noon."

— A movie starlet determined to have her nose fixed, but was appalled to discover that the surgeon demanded five hundred dollars for the operation. "Surely," she persisted, "there must be a less expensive way of doing it." "There is," agreed the surgeon (a mean one, as you shall see). "Why don't you try walking into a brick wall?"

— Two ladies in Atlantic City were watching the emoting of a current blonde favorite in a movie theatre on the Boardwalk.

"I wonder who made her dress," mused one.

"I imagine," replied the other, "it was the police."

* * *

Walter Slezak visited Hollywood for a brief chore and while there, called an old, old friend to ask, "How's it going with you?"

"I was in a bad auto crash recently," reported the friend, "but I can't kick."

"Tough break," sympathized Slezak. "And your wife?"

"She ran away with my agent last week, but I can't kick."

"I'm sorry to hear that, but at least you still have that soft job at Paramount."

"What job? They fired me three months ago—but I can't kick."

"With all that bad luck," marveled Slezak, "why do you keep telling me you can't kick?"

"Because," moaned the friend, "I'm in a cast from the waist down!"

* * *

Into a Hollywood restaurant walked an ill-matched couple who had already caught the attention of the gossip columnists: a middle-aged widow whose husband had left her millions and a handsome, but not too fastidious young leading man. The gifts the widow was showering on him proved more than the leading man's longtime sweetheart could counterbalance.

Said sweetheart saw him enter the restaurant this particular evening. So did her companion who said, "What on earth can those two find to talk about?" The sweetheart bared her fangs and explained, "It's very simple. She's giving him a complete course in *nouveau riche!*"

* * *

The late head of a big film studio in Hollywood was an ardent do-gooder who thought every picture should emphasize the rewards to be won by clean living and the American way. Unfortunately, most of his productions lacked box-office appeal and the fortunes of his studio declined sharply. "Poor Hugo," sighed one of his big stockholders. "He's selling out our company for a pot of message!"

* * *

A hopeful Manhattan bachelor read that Kim Novak was looking for a de luxe New York penthouse. "You can have mine for nothing," he wired her posthaste, "if you will put up with a few things. Me, for instance."

* * *

Here are just a few of the honest-to-goodness names of current movie heroes and heroines:

Kirk Douglas is really Issur Danielovitch; Rock Hudson: Roy Fitzgerald; Tab Hunter: Arthur Gelien; Red Buttons: Aaron Chwatt; Bill Holden: William Beedle. On the distaff side, Shelley Winters is really Shirley Schrift; Cyd Charisse: Tula Finklea; Doris Day: Doris Kappelhoff!

✿ ✿ ✿

Doris Day was dining in Chicago's famous Pump Room one evening when a waiter hustled by with a serving of shish kebob (lamb held aloft on a flaming sword—a specialty of the house). "What the heck is *that?*" inquired Miss Day. Jimmy Durante, sitting next to her, explained, "A customer who left only a ten-dollar tip."

✿ ✿ ✿

A heartwarming scene was enacted at the poolside of a Beverly Hills hotel the other day. A grandmother was explaining to two impatient youngsters that they simply could not go in the water until the lifeguard returned from lunch. A famous starlet arose from her deck chair and announced that she would be happy to take the kiddies in wading. "How thoughtful! How unselfish of this supposedly spoiled and beautiful girl," thought the grateful grandmother—until the starlet explained candidly when she returned the youngsters, "I had to have some excuse for staying at the shallow end. I can't swim."

✿ ✿ ✿

Herb Stein tells of a Hollywood merchant whose wife fell so madly in love with Cary Grant (whom she never had met, of course) that she could talk of virtually nothing else. The merchant finally went to his barber, and pleaded for a haircut that would make him look as much like Cary Grant as possible.

"Leave it to me," said the barber confidently, and went to work with a will. Soon big clumps of hair were falling in all directions. Increasingly concerned, the merchant finally asked, "Are you quite sure you know what Cary Grant looks like?" "Of course I'm sure," asserted the barber. "I saw him four times in *The King and I.*"

NIGHT CLUBS

Before each of them became famous singly on Broadway, Judy Holliday, Betty Comden, and Adolph Green had a night club act that sent audiences into gales of laughter. They repeated their triumph when invited to perform for the Dutch Treat Club—but one famous gentleman at a table directly in front of them never smiled once. It was the late President Herbert Hoover, and Judy Holliday in particular was determined to break down his resistance.

"If this number doesn't get him," she whispered to me, "I give up." Alas, Mr. Hoover again watched impassively and his rather solemn expression never changed.

Directly after the meeting was adjourned, however, Mr. Hoover came up to the three young performers and told them warmly, "You kids have the jolliest, most original act I've seen in years. I don't remember when I've had a better time. You're going to go very far!" "But Mr. President," interrupted the delighted Judy Holliday, "we were watching you particularly, and you never smiled once!" "I know," nodded Mr. Hoover. "I never have learned to smile on the outside. But inside, I was smiling all over!"

*   *   *

Eyeing the scantily clad chorus girls at a popular night club recently, comedian Joe E. Lewis sighed, "They don't make them like they used to." Even more wistfully, he added, "At least I don't!"

*   *   *

A new girl in the check room of a popular night club whispered to a veteran employee, "What does it mean when a college student slips you a dollar tip?" "It means," answered the knowing veteran, "that you have given him the wrong coat."

*   *   *

Milton Berle once broke in a new routine in Sioux City. Late that night he wired his agent, "I won't say I died out here, but when I picked up my suitcase to check out, it had eight handles on it."

*   *   *

Herb Stein, in Las Vegas to cover the opening of Mitzi Gaynor's new night club act, overheard a fellow guest at the Sands Hotel complaining, "I'll never share a room again with the fellow I came down here with from San Francisco. At three this morning the desk clerk called to say, 'You'll have to get your friend to stop snoring. They're trying to have a party next door!'"

*   *   *

One of the best remembered of the wild parties staged during Prohibition days was the one hosted by producer Earl Carroll, in which he offered a chorus girl fifty dollars to take a bath for the entertainment and enlightenment of his fastidious guests. The gendarmes broke up the party, and Carroll never got around to paying the girl her fifty dollars. Several mothers of other girls in the same chorus line expressed deep concern —not at the bathtub routine, but at the non-payment. As one of them put it, "WHERE was her mother?"

*   *   *

George Burns acknowledges a debt of gratitude to one loyal fan named Feldman who came to see his night club act thirty-seven times in succession. Every evening at eight, Feldman's five sons deposited him in a seat in the orchestra, and every night at eleven one of the sons returned to take him home.
"You may ask," continues Burns, "why it took five sons to bring the old gentleman to the theatre and only one son to take him home. The answer is that Feldman fought like a steer."

*   *   *

Frank Gilchrist, top executive of a Southwestern oil combine, has a framed picture in his office that depicts a lightly clad night club dancer showing a snapshot to her sidekick. "This is my new fiancé," she is boasting. "He's a clumsy, funny-looking lout, I'll admit. That thing behind his house in the background is an oil well."

* * *

The proprietor of a small night club in Los Angeles has been featuring a singer who, he claims, has a soothing effect on the customers. She calls herself Tranquil Liza.

* * *

Overheard backstage at the Copacabana: "I go with him because he has a will of his own—and it's made out in my favor!"

* * *

Before he won fame and fortune as a night club entertainer and TV standby, Sam Levenson eked out a modest living as a teacher in a Brooklyn elementary school. In the corridor of this school one day, a brash pupil yelled, "Hey, Levenson!" Sam, enraged, grabbed the fresh student by the collar, shook him violently, then admonished him, "In the first place, boy, hay is for horses. In the second place, you owe your teacher a minimum of courtesy and consideration."

A look of utter mystification on the boy's face stopped Levenson short. "What's the matter," he asked in a much gentler tone. "Don't you know what the words 'a minimum of courtesy and consideration' mean?"

"Teacher," faltered the boy, "I didn't even know hay was for horses."

* * *

Alan King complains that his wife is such a compulsive shopper, every department store in town that is planning a sale phones her first to make sure she's available. King also confides that the town he hails from is so small the barbershop quartet consists of three people.

King says that his wife, incidentally, was working in the same office he did when they met. "I took to whispering sweet nothings in her ear," he recalls, "and she whispered back sweet nothing-doings."

* * *

Mrs. Housewife persuaded her overworked husband to take her to a night club—the first one he had tried, he proclaimed, since he had been a junior at Princeton. The doorman at the club, however, greeted him as an old and valued customer and the scantily clad cigarette girl cooed, "Back again, eh, cutie pie?" Mrs. Housewife, without batting an eye, extended a hand and murmured, "I don't believe we've met. I'm Mrs. Pie."

* * *

That talented crooner, Tony Bennett, is worried lest the telephone company's craving for code area numbers seeps over into the field of popular songs. Even now Tony can envisage the day when he will be requested to render a chorus or two of "Moon Over 305," "312, 312, That Wonderful Town," "Shuffle Off to 716," "Way Down Yonder in 504," or "I Left My Heart in 415."

Phone buffs will know that 305 is the code area number for Miami, 312 for Chicago, 716 for Buffalo, 504 for New Orleans, and 415 for San Francisco.

* * *

Vaughn Meader, who became famous for his uncanny impersonation of the late President Kennedy, had, of course, to revamp not only his entire act, but his personality as well, when the President was assassinated. That the new act was off to a big start immediately was a tribute to his skill and versatility. Now he conducts a seminar for pet owners in which he portrays the pipe-puffing Dr. Bow-Wow. To the typical question, "What can I do if my dog has ticks?" he answers imperturbably, "Don't wind him."

Reminiscing about his home town, Waterville, Maine, Meader observes that "It's so small, the local Howard Johnson branch has only one flavor."

TV AND RADIO

The late Fred Allen, one of the canniest and best-loved personalities in all show business, spotted the drift in television early in the game. "The only performers who will last in this medium," he predicted accurately, "will be the 'pointers.' Pointers never do anything themselves. They merely stand in the center of the stage, point to another performer, and announce, 'See that fellow? He's going to do the darndest trick you ever saw!' Then the other fellow comes out and does the trick. A week later, the pointer is back gesturing at somebody else, but the fellow who did the great trick has already given his all and is out in the cold. TV can eliminate pointers if times get tough enough. They can teach dogs to do the same routine simply by smearing meat on the actors!"

◊　◊　◊

Almost every important official in television circles has a very definite opinion on the supreme value—or worthlessness —of ratings. The trouble is that practically none of the opinions coincide. Columnist George Frazier once wrote caustically that he knew of one show that actually registered a *minus* rating in the Greater Boston area. "Not only does nobody watch it," reported Frazier, "but there's one fellow in Swampscott who calls up every day to knock it."

* * *

Jack Paar, entertaining a glittering assemblage of television nabobs, assured them, "You fellows have made astonishing progress. I can remember the days when commercials were no louder than the rest of the show!"

* * *

James Reston, of the New York *Times,* is one man who has no fear that television ever will replace the newspapers. "One of the great things about a newspaper," Reston points out, "is that, especially on Sunday, you can split the thing up and let everybody in the family settle into a quiet trance with the section he likes best. TV makes you listen to all the news you don't want to hear in order to get around to the news you do want to hear. You can't split up Chet Huntley or throw away part of Dave Brinkley."

* * *

There's a motel on Route 1 in Maryland that reserves one of its units for newly marrieds. A little sign over the door says, "Welcome to Honeymoon Inn." A long-married visitor noticed the unit as he was checking out one morning, and said, "Your 'Honeymoon Inn' doesn't look a bit different to me than any of the other units." "It isn't," agreed the proprietor. "But the TV set inside it is busted. So far not one guest has noticed it!"

* * *

At a rehearsal of one of his big Sunday night shows, Ed Sullivan asked a visiting TV star if he knew whose face adorned a ten-thousand-dollar bill. "I'll give you three clues," volunteered Sullivan. (The face is that of Salmon P. Chase.) "His first name is a fish, his middle initial is a soup, and his last name is what college boys do after girls."

The TV star pondered momentarily, then reached for his wallet. "Mind if I take a peek?" he asked.

* * *

Professional comedians rarely appreciate each other's talents, but George Burns and Jack Benny are notable exceptions to the rule. Not only have they been fast friends for thirty-odd years, but Burns can break Benny up by merely sticking his tongue out at him. Benny calls Burns up from all corners of the globe just to gab with him, and keeps yakking so long that Burns usually ends up by hanging up on him.

Benny, in fact, now counts on this so that one day in Hollywood he told an agent named Rubin, "I'm calling George Burns in Chicago in ten minutes and I'll bet you twenty-five dollars he hangs up on me." Rubin accepted the bet. When Benny got George Burns on the wire, their usual kidding, desultory conversation ensued. Finally Benny, sounding puzzled, said, "Well, George, aren't you going to hang up on me in your usual insulting fashion?"

"I certainly am not," declared Burns, then added, "and by the way, Rubin called me and gave me half his bet."

* * *

A radio quiz show moderator told the contestants, "I'm going to ask you to name some famous episodes in history associated with animals. First, what animal do we associate with Lady Godiva?" An eager young lady contestant blurted out, "Bear."

* * *

There's a fellow at Random House whose face is full of cuts and slashes every morning. He insists on trying to shave himself as fast as they do it on television.

* * *

Abel Green saw the pilot of a new Western TV show, updated to appeal to 1965 audiences. In it, the outlaws beat the stagecoach holdup rap—but are convicted for income tax evasion.

* * *

The wife of the stingiest man in a Western TV station gave birth to twin boys, and the father, in a rare burst of generosity, announced, "If anybody has a cigar, I'll be happy to light it for him."

* * *

During the height of a blizzard in Philadelphia last winter, a local radio station went on the air with a list of events that faced cancellation unless the snowfall ceased. Caskie Stinnett swears he heard this announcement: "The Back-to-Nature Club still plans to hold its scheduled hike tomorrow—provided the Market Street subway is operating."

Televisionaries . . .

—Zsa Zsa Gabor once found time in her busy life to moderate a TV show devoted to husband-and-wife problems. The first guest on the show confessed, "I'm breaking my engagement to a very wealthy man who has already given me a beautiful home, a sable coat, diamonds, a stove, and a Rolls-Royce. Miss Gabor, what should I do?" Zsa Zsa counseled, "Give back the stove."

—Jack Leonard, the stylish stout comedian, squeezed himself laboriously into one of those horrible new miniature taxicabs and instructed the driver, "Take me to a larger cab."

— "TV cameras," frets Kitty Carlisle, "seem to add ten pounds to me. So I make it a policy never to eat TV cameras."

— "Sunday was always the noisiest day of the week in my family," confided Buddy Hackett. "Everybody sang at the top of his lungs in the bathtub." "You all must have been full of animal spirits," commented a friend. "What do you mean, animal spirits?" countered Hackett. "Our bathroom door had no lock."

— Tennessee Ernie Ford before the first broadcast of a new TV series: "I'm as nervous as a tomcat in a roomful of rocking chairs."

— One of Groucho Marx's most famous rejoinders was made when a friend stopped short on Sunset Boulevard and exclaimed, "I must find a Western Union office. I've got to wire my father." "What's the matter?" demanded Groucho. "Can't he stand up by himself?"

— Among Woody Allen's so-called autobiographical notes: "When I was born, my family was so poor my mother couldn't afford to use talcum powder on me. So she used to douse me with kitchen baking soda. The result was most unfortunate. About once every month I'd break out in a severe case of cookies." . . . "I had a terrible education. I attended a school for

emotionally disturbed teachers." . . . "The Boy Scouts kicked
me out because I tried to rub one stick together to make a fire.
This is very Zen—but definitely not Boy Scout." . . . "My wife
was an immature woman. I'd be in the bathroom taking a bath
and she would walk right in—and sink my boats."

— "Who *says* I don't do my exercises regularly in the mornings?" demands an indignant Jackie Gleason. "Immediately
after awakening, I always say sternly to myself, "Ready, now.
Up. Down. Up. Down. And after three strenuous minutes I
tell myself, 'Okay, Boy. Now we'll try the other eyelid.'"

*   *   *

A stunt man was offered a hundred dollars for a one-day
task of portraying a savage gorilla in a TV drama. It took him
so long to perfect his makeup that he didn't bother to remove
it at the lunchtime break. The bartender at the bistro next
door was favored, therefore, by a visit from one mighty fe-
rocious gorilla. He never batted an eyelash: simply handed the
gorilla a price list of drinks for sale and called to his assistant,
"Keep an eye on the peanuts."

*   *   *

I've often been asked what contestant, of all the thousands
I've encountered on the TV panel show, "What's My Line?" I
remember most clearly. Without any question, it was a chap
who worked at one of New York's summer recreation centers.
No sooner had we guessed his occupation and shaken hands
with him, than he walked into the arms of six cops who were
waiting for him in the wings.

It developed that the misguided lad was wanted in six different states for stealing automobiles. The minute his face was
reproduced on the TV screen every police station in New York
was alerted and went into action!

*   *   *

The people who dig up occupations to puzzle the panelists
on "What's My Line?" have come up with some dillies in the
past few seasons. For instance: a lady cow washer; a seller of

paper panties for lamb chops; a lady who crocheted pockets for pool tables; a jelly bean polisher; a boxing glove stuffer; a painter of dots on dice; and a man who made false teeth for chickens—as an aid to their digestion!

*　*　*

"What's My Line?"'s famous moderator, John Charles Daly, has invested some of his hard-earned dollars in two interesting new business ventures: 1. A company producing toothpaste with particles of food mixed in for people who haven't time to eat between tooth brushings, and 2. A tobacco company's new cigarette package that includes plastic ear plugs for buyers who are tired of hearing why they should quit smoking.

*　*　*

A TV tour of New York City was scheduled for shooting early one midweek morning, with the first scenes penciled in from the very center of the George Washington Bridge, spanning the Hudson. The cameraman picked that very morning to oversleep. When he awakened, he took one look at the clock, threw a coat over his pajamas, climbed into a pair of bedroom slippers, and dashed out of the house. "Get me up to the George Washington Bridge as fast as you can make it," he implored a passing taxi driver. "New York end or Jersey end?" asked the driver. "Neither," said the cameraman. "I've got to get to the center of the bridge." The driver took a quick look at his prospective fare's anguished face and peculiar attire, and shoved him out of the cab. "You don't need a driver, buddy," he announced. "You need a good psychiatrist!"

*　*　*

At one of those infrequent periods when Bob Hope wasn't feeling up to the rigors of the incredible schedule he sets for himself, his regular doctors told him that among other things he'd have to give up for a time at least was his beloved game of golf. Outraged, Hope kept looking until he found a doctor who told him he could play eighteen holes any time he wanted to. "Thanks, Doctor," exulted Hope. "Just for that I'll remember you in my will." "In that case," the doctor assured him, "play thirty-six!"

Hope confesses that when he took Jayne Mansfield along with him to entertain Armed Forces personnel in the Pacific area, he made her wear a special dress for the tour. It was made of two hundred yards of barbed wire. . . . When the troupe entertained on the deck of a big cruiser, Jerry Colonna pretended to be one of the sailors on the vessel. "What's your job?" Hope demanded. "I polish the brass," explained Colonna. "I've got the shiniest captain in the fleet."

✼   ✼   ✼

Touring Army bases one Christmas season, Hope found himself in South Korea, with an audience composed largely of native soldiers who didn't understand a word of English. Fortunately, a Korean major volunteered to translate the comedian's monologue.

The performance was a riotous success. When he left the stage, Hope enthused, "That old routine of mine never got half that many laughs before. Thanks for your wonderful translating job."

The major registered acute embarrassment. "You talked so fast," he admitted, "that I lost you completely after your first three sentences. I was telling the boys a few stories of my own."

✼   ✼   ✼

How badly do they cut fine old films so they can be shown on TV with all the commercials intervening? Here's what Bing Crosby has to say on the subject: "I won't swear they're chopping the footage out of old movies on TV, but I saw *Road to Bali* the other night and Hope and I weren't even in it!"

✼   ✼   ✼

An autograph hound buttonholed Milton Berle outside of Sardi's and gushed, "I haven't stopped crying, Uncle Miltie, since you quit your regular program on TV." "Confidentially," answered Berle, "neither have I."

✼   ✼   ✼

A teenager came home from a party at 3 A.M. and woke up his parents. "Come clean," he demanded angrily. "Which one of you left the TV set turned off?"

* * *

Having problems with events, humanity-wise? Well, we hold these truths to be as plain as the nose on your face – everybody's equal and has got some rights. Try INDEPENDENCE, and you'll get, _absolutely free_, life, liberty, and more happiness than you can catch...

A thought for today proposed by an editor of *Changing Times*: "Without a den or place of refuge, a man can achieve neither tranquillity nor greatness. Jefferson wrote the Declaration of Independence in a serenely quiet room in Philadelphia. The soaring ideas that went into it evolved during hours of reading and contemplation in a secluded library where not a sound could be heard. Had it been a TV-guest-family room, the U.S. today might still be a colony!"

* * *

A television star told his regular barber he wanted a particularly good haircut one morning. "I'm flying to England tomorrow and I'm going to be introduced to the Queen!" The barber was unimpressed. "In the first place," he commented, "English weather is terrible at this time of the year. In the second place, flying across the Atlantic is no bargain with these winter storms raging. In the third place, you won't like the food over there. And in the fourth place, you won't really meet the Queen. There will be about five hundred people at the same time and she won't even know you're there!"

The television star made the trip, nevertheless, and in due course was back in the same barber's chair. "In the first place," he reported, "the weather in England was superb. In the second place, the plane rides both to and fro were so smooth I never felt a tremor. In the third place, I loved the food so much I gained fifteen pounds. And in the fourth place, there were only two other visitors at Buckingham Palace when I met the Queen. And do you know what she asked me? She asked me, 'Who on earth gave you that horrible haircut?'"

LEGIT

Eugene O'Neill, America's greatest dramatist, was the son of the famous matinee idol, James O'Neill. When Gene O'Neill was eleven, his father sat him down for a heart-to-heart talk. "Son," said James O'Neill, "I'm not going to tell you not to smoke, because I know you will. Nor will I tell you not to drink, because I know you'll do that, too. You'll also gamble and chase women, if you're a son of mine, so I'd be a fool to say 'Don't do that, either.' But now I want you to listen carefully to your father: one at a time, Gene, *one at a time*."

*   *   *

A would-be dramatist, who had been pestering the great Flo Ziegfeld for weeks to read his new play, was struck by a hit-and-run driver one afternoon directly in front of the old Ziegfeld Theatre with the manuscript tucked tightly under his arm.

When the man was carried into the theatre, Ziegfeld reluctantly produced a bottle of brandy from his private stock. Then he suggested a headline for the newspaper account: "Foul Play Suspected."

* * *

A great star, now a grandmother but still beautiful, dropped into Sardi's West for a snack with a lovely young thing who just had graduated from Vassar. The star's manager, at another table, took one look at the youngster and sent over a note which read, "Who is that ravishing kid?" The star answered, "Me."

* * *

A summer stock company was doing *Springtime for Henry* one week, with *Arsenic and Old Lace,* featuring Boris Karloff, scheduled for the week following.

In the middle of Act 2 of *Springtime for Henry,* a bat suddenly whooshed out of the eaves and brushed the face of the male lead. Very calmly that resourceful gentleman waved the bat away and said very clearly, "No, no, you fool. *Next* week. *Next* week."

The bat flew away and the relieved audience applauded madly.

* * *

The visiting star at another summer theatre boasted to the local manager: "I'm so popular in New York, they're going to name a new cigar after me." "Yeah?" yawned the manager. "Well, I hope it draws better than you do!"

* * *

Play producer Max Gordon recalls in his nostalgic memoirs the time he was readying that famous revue, *The Band Wagon,* which starred Fred and Adele Astaire, Frank Morgan, and Tilli Losch. The score was written by Arthur Schwartz and Howard Dietz, who phoned Gordon in great excitement at 2 A.M. one night to tell him, "We've just written a sure hit song. It's called 'I Love Louisa.'" "Fine," chortled Gordon. "Let me hear it over the phone." Schwartz banged it out on the piano and Dietz warbled the lyrics. Gordon was delighted. "Boys," he told them, "you're wonderful. It will be a pleasure to go broke with you."

One morning Gordon instructed his secretary to locate a certain brash comedian who was working on the road. She returned to report, "You're too late. He died last night in Kansas City." To which Gordon sighed, "He always did!"

*   *   *

The author of one of Broadway's reigning hits is investing his royalties in Wyoming cattle. Asked why, he explained, "There are two reasons: one, it's a favorable tax setup, and two, cows don't ask for free tickets."

*   *   *

The late Sir Cedric Hardwicke liked to tell of an evening in Dublin's famous Abbey Theatre, where Irish playwright W. B. Yeats was trying to create the lighting effect for a glorious sunset. For hours he had the electricians trying all kinds of color slides and combinations. Suddenly he saw exactly what he wanted. "That's it," he cried. "Wonderful! Hold it, hold it!" "We can't hold it, sir," answered the chief electrician mournfully. "The bloody theatre's on fire!"

*   *   *

Playwright William Inge was interviewing a wistful girl who sought a part in his next play. "I've played the lead this season in an important production off-Broadway," she told him. "Whereabouts off-Broadway?" inquired Inge. "Peoria," explained the girl.

*   *   *

An ambitious Yale student got a job with a summer theatre and came home to report triumphantly, "I've snagged my first part! Next week I'm going to play a husband who's been married for thirty years!" "Good start," approved his father. "Just you stick to it, and you'll get a speaking part yet!"

*   *   *

Theatrical producer Jed Harris tells of a time when he and the late George S. Kaufman were seeking a young juvenile actor for a part in their Broadway production *The Royal Family*. Kaufman heard that there was a promising young actor named Guido Nadso trying out in a new play in New Haven,

and took a train there to look him over. Sadly he sent a telegram to Jed Harris at midnight. All he said was "Nadso Guido."

One of Kaufman's biggest hits was *The Cocoanuts,* which he
wrote for the Marx Brothers. Late in the run, Groucho tried
to insert a joke of his own, but Kaufman would have no part
of it. "I'll bet they'd laugh at it," insisted Groucho. "Don't forget they laughed at Bell and his telephone." Demurred Kaufman, "Not at matinees!"

A brazen, ill-mannered chorus girl once berated Kaufman for
"overlooking" her in casting his new play. Very properly annoyed, Kaufman asked, "How old are you?" "Eighteen," said
the girl. "Oh, no! You must be more than eighteen," countered
Kaufman coldly. "Nobody's neck could possibly get that dirty
in eighteen years."

Kaufman's lovely wife, Leueen MacGrath, persuaded him
one day in the twilight of his brilliant career to go with her to
a famous antique shop. While she was examining numerous
treasures, Kaufman stood by, so obviously bored to distraction
that an executive of the shop asked him, "Isn't there anything
we can show *you,* Mr. Kaufman?" The playwright responded
sourly, "Yes. What have you got in the way of second-act curtains?"

*   *   *

Harpo Marx's first professional stage appearance was in the
basement of his flat off Second Avenue in New York. The play
was *Quo Vadis Upside Down,* a travesty written by Harpo's
uncle, Al Shean (of Gallagher and Shean). The admission price
was one cat!

It appears that there was a mouse plague in the neighborhood, and store proprietors were paying a penny apiece for
cats. So Harpo (aged twelve) and an older brother named
Groucho decided to cash in on the demand. Harpo recalls that
the performance grossed seven cats at the box office, but that
the troupe netted only four cents in profits. Three cats got
away.

*   *   *

That superb playwright—and gentleman—Robert E. Sherwood once signed another theatre great—George M. Cohan—to star in a new play he was producing. To get his signature on the dotted line, Sherwood had to make a firm commitment with Cohan for ten weeks.

The play, unfortunately, proved to be a clinker, and folded after one dismal week on Broadway. Cohan took his check for ten weeks without a word. Many years later, however, Sherwood, out of a clear blue sky, received a check back from Cohan covering the nine weeks for which he had not played. Attached to the check was a note reading, "Dear Bob: I couldn't go out with this on my mind."

The next day George M. Cohan died.

*   *   *

Outside of business hours, old John D. Rockefeller occasionally betrayed flashes of a certain sly humor. There was the evening, for instance, in the twilight of his life, when he was taken for his first look at an edifice he had authorized: the then brand-new Radio City Music Hall.

Mr. Rockefeller was taken to the back of the very top balcony—a spot from which the mammoth stage looks something like a postage stamp. A herd of trained elephants was going through its paces when John D. focused his attention on the performance. He shook his head after a moment and chided his general manager: "What do you mean by putting mice on the stage of my beautiful new theatre?"

*   *   *

Happy Memories: When Ed Wynn played a waiter in *Manhattan Mary* and a customer demanded lamb chops au gratin. Wynn shouted to the kitchen, "Cheese it, the chops." . . . When Eddie Cantor told a pair of worn-out acrobats, who invariably closed the show in the old vaudeville houses, "Boys, if you ever expect to get anywhere in this profession, you'll have to dream up a new finish for your act." "New finish!" echoed one of the acrobats indignantly. "Nobody's ever waited to see the old one yet." . . . When Lou Holtz told about the law firm of Button, Button, Button, and Button taking in a new partner named Zipper. "Yes," explained Mr. Z., "I've replaced one of the Buttons." . . . When a druggist stopped Bobby Clark to ask, "Did that mudpack I suggested improve your wife's appearance?" Bobby's answer was, "It did for a couple of days, but then it wore off." . . . And when, in Frank Craven's *The First Year* the lady of the house, preparing dinner for an important guest, asked the new maid, "Did you seed the grapefruit?" The maid's answer was, "Oh yes, ma'am, I seed 'em."

✷ ✷ ✷

There's a special niche in Hades reserved for oafs who rush onstage in the middle of somebody else's act to read special messages, but the house manager of a theatre in northern Michigan certainly was justified in interrupting a performance of *Annie Get Your Gun* to implore, "Will the owner of a car with license plate number M-3177 kindly go out and move it. It is parked over an open manhole, and the worker in it wants to go home for supper."

✷ ✷ ✷

The man at the box office for the musical hit *Fiddler on the Roof* received an unusual phone call one morning. "I bought seats G-108, 110, and 112 yesterday for the Saturday matinee," he reported in an agitated voice, "and my cocker spaniel just ate G-110."

✷ ✷ ✷

Jimmy Durante recalls the night his father first saw him acting behind the footlights. Jimmy rushed offstage to ask his father, standing in the wings, "Well, Pop, how'd ya like my work?" The father, whose name, incidentally, was Barthelmeo Durante, answered cautiously, "Lissen, boy, let's not get in an argument."

✷ ✷ ✷

Play producer Josh Logan's mother Susan, who comes from the Deep South and reveres its every tradition, was taken aback a bit when, early in World War II, the son of a fine old family she knew was drafted. She rallied, however, when she heard that he was receiving his basic training at Fort Bragg, North Carolina. "How nice for him to be in that part of North Carolina," she nodded, "at rhododendron time!"

* * *

Never, insists Alexander King, have there been audiences quite so skeptical and hard-boiled as the lonely men who used to crowd into the old-fashioned, bawdy burlesque shows of the twenties. He remembers one night when the strip-tease queen at a theatre in St. Louis grew a trifle too animated, and lost what passed for her costume entirely. While the audience sat stunned for once, and the stripper stood momentarily frozen in her tracks, one beefy spectator in the twelfth row jumped to his feet and yelled derisively, "IT'S A FAKE!"

* * *

My Fair Lady, that incomparable musical, has now been played in over thirty different translations in as many different countries. One of the most intriguing is its translation into Papiamento, a polyglot language of Aruba. In those parts it goes by the name of *Laizo Porko Sushi*, a literal translation of which, any hep Aruban will tell you, is *Liza Dirty Pig*.

* * *

A Broadway agent, lunching at Sardi's, overheard a famous producer of musicals bemoaning the fact that he couldn't find a beautiful redhead to play the lead in an upcoming show. The agent rushed over to the producer and assured him, "I have the perfect girl for the part."

"Great!" enthused the producer. "Get her over to my office on the double."

"She won't be able to see you today," explained the agent. "First she'll have to get her hair dyed red."

* * *

A star of a new musical smash, assured that a three- or four-year run in New York was in the bag, leased a swank duplex apartment on Sutton Place, and had a complete repainting and redecorating job done on it. To give the very independent painter added incentive, the star slipped him a pair of tickets in the third row center—seats that were practically unobtainable even from speculators.

The first of the following month the star was staggered by this item in his bill from the painter: "Wednesday night: four hours' overtime watching customer sing and dance: $36."

* * *

A Broadway producer who has a genius for feuding with six critics, eight stars, and eleven authors and directors at the same time, insisted that one number in a new musical trying out in Boston be eliminated forthwith. "It's awful," he cried.

The author and composer disagreed. "We think," they dared say, "it's the funniest number in the show."

Finally, the producer allowed them to leave the number in when the show moved on to Philadelphia. "It's just to shut you up," he explained. "The audience won't laugh once."

But the audience *did* laugh. In fact, it all but fell in the aisles. The author rushed triumphantly to the producer and demanded, "Do you hear them howling?" The producer came up with the stopper of the month. He grumbled, "They don't mean it."

4. *Animals Galore*

DOGS AND CATS

Dog lovers will be interested in the story of a poodle in Connecticut who objects so violently to the telephone that each time it rings, he jumps up on the desk and bites through the wire. After replacing the wire several times—in places the supervisor foolishly figured the poodle wouldn't be able to get at it—a new strategem was called into play. The phone bell was replaced by a chime. Now, every time the phone chimes the poodle races to see who's at the door.

If we know poodles, however, this new trick will work out just so long. That pooch will have things figured out inside of another two weeks!

* * *

A city dog met an acquaintance at a friendly curbstone. "What's your name?" inquired the acquaintance. "I'm not quite sure," admitted the city dog, "but I think it's Down Boy."

* * *

Swift & Company is about to launch a new dog food called "Arf." The slogan, dreamed up by a young genius at the Earle Ludgen Ad Agency, is "The Only Food Dogs Can Ask For by Name."

* * *

Late December scene on Madison Avenue: a lady admonishing a cocker spaniel pulling desperately on his leash, "No, no, Stanley! Those are *Christmas* trees!"

* * *

Two poodles were watching a couple of exuberant teenagers doing one of the wild new dance routines. "Hmphh," sniffed one poodle, "when I act like that, they give me worm pills!"

* * *

A starlet sought to purchase a sweater for her poodle, but didn't know the exact size. "Bring him in and have him fitted," suggested a clerk. "I couldn't do that," protested the starlet. "It's for his birthday—and I want to surprise him."

* * *

A rabies scare in the suburbs prompted the town fathers to decree a special inoculation for all dogs in the neighborhood. Several society debutantes volunteered assistance. One of them looked up brightly when rare book expert Dave Randall led in his pedigreed boxer, Lord James Boswell. She opened her record book and inquired, "Name, please?" Randall answered, "Lord James Boswell." Visibly impressed, the debutante continued, "And the dog's name, M'lord?"

* * *

Congressman Mike Kirwan tells about a man who picked up his mongrel pup one day, brushed him carefully, tied a ribbon around his neck, and started down the street with him. "Where are you taking that mutt?" asked a friend. "I'm going to enter him in the dog show," said the man.

"You'll never win a prize with an animal like that," hooted the friend. "I know," nodded the man, "but think of the contacts he'll make!"

* * *

A sheepdog at Provincetown fell insanely in love with another sheepdog. Into her ear one night at Balliston Beach he whispered, "Mary, I cannot live another day without you. . . . You are Mary, aren't you?"

* * *

A lady's big Labrador dog refused to accompany her from the supermarket, and she had to drag him into her car. Back home, the dog refused all commands—and even failed to greet his master—whom he adored—when the latter returned from his office.

Just then a friend phoned the nonplused couple. "Do you

realize," asked the friend, "that your Labrador dog is still waiting for you at the supermarket?"

* * *

There's a student at Iowa State who figures he can make a million dollars if he can teach his poodle to talk. "You're on the wrong track," his roommate assured him. "Who'd pay a million dollars for a talking dog?" "Nobody," admitted the student, "but I bet I could find a half dozen dog food outfits who'd pay me a million just to keep him quiet!"

* * *

Actor director Romney Brent owns a cat whose nocturnal adventures dictated an operation at the local vet's. Back home to recuperate, the cat was steeped in gloom. Mr. Brent's maid put her finger on the trouble. "Mr. Brent," she declared, "I'm afraid that poor cat misses himself!"

* * *

Arlene Francis, my Mount Kisco neighbor, claims she was visiting an authoress named Zsa Zsa Horntoot when a cat strolled in and asked if anyone had seen the Sunday newspaper. He was handed the paper and left.

Arlene, for once, was almost speechless. "Incredible," she managed to gasp. "A cat that reads!"

"Don't let him fool you," said Zsa Zsa Horntoot. "He only looks at the comics."

* * *

A few words from cat-lovers:

"A cat can be trusted to purr when she is pleased, which is more than can be said about human beings."—*William R. Inge.*

"To keep their shape without getting muscle-bound from exercises, women ought to try stretching like cats. You never see a muscle-bound cat!"—*Corinne Calvet.*

"If a man could be crossed with a cat, it would improve man, but it would deteriorate the cat."—*Mark Twain*.

* * *

My own favorite cat story involves two intrepid young husbands whose wives traipsed off for a summer vacation and left them in the city to keep house together as best they might.

One evening they purchased a four-pound sirloin steak, and left it on the kitchen table while they repaired to the library for a few libations. What with an extra dividend or two, they were weaving a bit when they re-entered the kitchen, but not too discombobulated to overlook the fact that their four-pound steak had disappeared.

A frantic search proved unproductive, but then one of the men noticed that a cat under the sink was licking his whiskers with an uncommonly satisfied air. "I'll bet," he exclaimed, "that cat has eaten our four-pound steak."

"One way to find out," said the other grimly. He seized the cat by the scruff of the neck and deposited it on the bathroom scale. Sure enough, it weighed exactly four pounds.

"Well," he announced triumphantly, "there's our four-pound steak all right. Now where the hell's the cat?"

* * *

Many years ago, Westbrook Pegler, emphasizing the point that expectation of success is often more gratifying than realization of same, wrote about an elderly gentleman in a Gulf Coast resort who went about leading a soft-eyed, gentle old greyhound on a leash.

"Nice dog you have there," people would say. "Is he a racing dog?"

"He was," the man would reply. "He was a very fine, fast-racing dog, too—but one night he caught the rabbit. After that dogs like this lose interest. They discover that the thing they have been chasing so hard is just a phony, and they just lie down from then on and watch the other dogs run. If this dog could talk, he'd be saying, 'Go ahead, you fools: run yourselves ragged for just a mess of hair and sawdust!'"

* * *

Every Girl Scout in little Mary Higgins' Spokane troop was given ten dollars' worth of cookies and assigned the task of selling as many as possible by the following Friday. Results varied all the way from $1.15 to $7.70—until Mary bounced in and planked two five-dollar bills on the table.

"Girls," beamed the leader, "Mary has sold every last one of her cookies! Tell us how you did it, Mary. Did you sell a box apiece to everybody on your block?"

"I did not," said Mary. "I sold them all to the very first gentleman I called on. His dog bit me."

* * *

There is an imaginative couple up Roxbury way in Connecticut who have a cat and a dog. Nothing unusual in that, granted. But wait. The name of this particular cat is "Dog." And the name of the dog is "Cat." The animals answer to their names unfailingly. It's the neighbors who are confused!

* * *

A cat in Kansas City proudly exhibited a basket full of twelve new kittens. "Considering the fact that I didn't know a soul in this neighborhood four months ago," she purred smugly, "I don't think I've done too badly."

HORSES

Frances Parkinson Keyes tells about a Cajun horse-trading wizard west of New Orleans who gave a prospective customer a big buildup on a nag he wanted to sell and concluded, "That horse is not only the most beautiful and speediest in the whole parish, but he is one great actor as well. When you go down to the paddock to see him, just watch that old devil act like he's gone lame!"

* * *

Jack Benny has a story about a race track habitué who was down to his last two bucks. A sympathetic redhead said, "I know an old Irish trick to change your luck. I'll pull out one hair from my head. Wrap it around the two dollars before you place your bet and see what happens."

What happened is that the gent put the two dollars on a 100 to 1 shot—and won! When he repeated the process successfully on the next three races, he ecstatically proposed to the girl, "Love Boat, with your hair and my selections, we're an unbeatable combination. Let's get married!"

They were wed, and for the next five years the hair pulling and wagering were faithfully continued. So today she is totally bald and he's shining shoes outside of a Jamaica race track.

* * *

The sports editor of a crusading newspaper got a phone call just before the bulldog edition went to press. "What do you mean, you can't make a buck at the race track any more?" demanded the caller. "I made over ten thousand dollars at Belmont this afternoon." "Who are you?" countered the editor. The caller answered, "I'm a horse!"

* * *

Two married men were comparing notes on their respective wives. "I took mine out to the race track for the first time Saturday afternoon," boasted one, "and she won four races." "Remarkable," admitted his friend. "My wife gets winded after one watusi."

* * *

Taken to a race track for the first time, a very conservative lady was persuaded to bet five dollars on the daily double—and she won! As she was raking in her loot at the pari-mutuel window she shook a warning finger at the payoff clerk, and said sternly, "Young man, I hope this will be a lesson to you!"

* * *

An inveterate race track gambler died, and one of his pals called another devotee of the horses on the phone. "I've got to go to poor Al's funeral," he reported, "but I can't remember the name of the cemetery." "So who cares what the name is," shrugged the friend. "Take the Midtown Tunnel and it's the third one on the way to Aqueduct."

* * *

Back from attending his first Kentucky Derby in Louisville, Art Buchwald estimated that he consumed about two hundred mint juleps, heard "My Old Kentucky Home" sung almost as often, and was made an honorary colonel of at least thirty impressive organizations. He didn't quite get to see the Derby itself, but just before he left, the greatest honor of all was bestowed upon him. They made him an honorary horse.

* * *

Herman Levin, one of the shrewdest judges of horseflesh in Shubert Alley, came home from Aqueduct one evening with self-satisfaction written all over his face. "I licked them today, boys," he exulted. "I licked them in the first race, the second race, the third race, the fourth race, the fifth race, the sixth race, and if I'd had a nickel left, I'd have licked them in the seventh race, too."

* * *

There was once a racehorse, avers Ira Gershwin, who in three years on the track had never finished better than sixth.

Finally the owner told him, "I've stabled and fed you long enough, you no-good palooka. Today I give you your last chance. I've signed a famous jockey to ride you. The other horses in the race are worthless. If you lose this time, I promise you that by five o'clock tomorrow morning you'll be pulling an ice wagon."

The race began. At the clubhouse turn, our poor horse was dead last. The jockey resorted to his whip. The aggrieved horse turned his head and snapped, "Cut that out, will you? I gotta be up tomorrow morning at five o'clock!"

* * *

Mourns comedian Joe E. Lewis, "Did I have a great Derby winner last year! But she wouldn't go to Louisville with me."

* * *

Martin Gabel, racing expert, was visiting the stable of Alfred Vanderbilt when he noticed one nag prancing around his stall with the arrogance of a Derby winner. "I notice," remarked Gabel, "that he's 70 to 1 in this afternoon's feature race. What's he got to be so high-hat about?" "Not so loud," cautioned Vanderbilt. "He thinks he's the favorite."

WHO'S ZOO

A Midwest zoo boasted a lion that was known far and wide for his fierce roars and majestic mien, but old age began to cramp his style, and the directors bought a very young lion as insurance.

The young lion was placed in a cage adjoining the old lion's. At five o'clock sharp a keeper appeared and tossed twenty pounds of fine, red beefsteak into the old lion's cage. All the new lion got, however, was a bunch of grapes and a banana.

The young lion was outraged. "I don't mean to hurt your feelings," he told the old lion, "but maybe you are responsible for my getting a raw deal instead of raw meat. How can an up-and-coming, self-respecting lion be expected to do his stuff on a diet of grapes and a banana?"

"You are the victim of a crisis in the city's finances," sighed the old lion. "The budget for this zoo now allows for only one beaten-up lion and that is I. They've had to inventory you as a monkey."

* * *

Books about lions, incidentally, are very much in fashion these days. One of the most fascinating is *Ibamba* by Wynant Hubbard, in which the reader will discover, for example, that:

1. Most lions have a definite sense of humor.

2. Female lions moan piteously with rage and grief when their mates are killed.

3. Male lions go for cheap perfume in a very big way.

4. Lions whistle like birds! (Mr. Hubbard swears to this.)

5. A lion bellowing on a misty night can be heard eight miles away.

* * *

In *A Midsummer Night's Dream* William Shakespeare observed, "A lion among ladies is a most dreadful thing"—and for centuries not even a horse could be found who would say him "Neigh." And yet, here in 1965, in a fashionable cocktail lounge, a very lusty lion sat lapping up the juice in obvious content with three very busty ladies, who also were feeling no pain.

"Gad," exclaimed a bedazzled barfly, "get a load of that lion. He's almost human!"

"You can say that again," nodded the bartender. "Wait till you see him laugh his way out of paying for the next round!"

* * *

An out-of-town member of one of the most exclusive and hoity-toity clubs on Fifth Avenue was glancing listlessly over the evening stock exchange tables when a remarkable sight met his eyes. Feebly clutching the arm of a passing attendant, he wheezed, "Do my old eyes deceive me, or do I perceive two penguins strutting up and down this supposedly sacred chamber?" "Of course they're penguins," nodded the unperturbed attendant. "Where else do you think they'd feel comfortable in tails at five-thirty in the afternoon?"

* * *

Zoologist Rowland Taylor has discovered how penguins keep their feet warm—even when they're standing all day on a cake of solid ice. It seems that they just rear back on their well-padded tails and keep their tootsies off the ice entirely. Dr. Taylor adds that this is a hereditary instinct: penguins born and raised in the sun-bathed San Diego zoo still sleep with their toes in the air.

* * *

A little boy brought a canary in a cage to the local chiropodist. "It hasn't sung or made a sound in a week," complained the boy. "But what do you expect me to do about it?" grumbled the chiropodist. "Well," said the boy, "mom says you're a good chiropodist. Make the canary chirop."

* * *

Legend has it that lovebirds are so devoted that when one dies, the other soon dies, too, of a broken heart. Conscious of this, a pet owner resorted to a clever stratagem when one of his lovebirds gave up the ghost.

He propped a mirror inside the cage of the surviving lovebird, who, seeing his image, chirped happily, snuggled against the mirror, and lived happily for years.

Then one day a careless maid upset the cage, and it crashed on the floor.

The poor lovebird died—of a broken mirror.

* * *

At a children's pet show this fall, a duck won the title "happiest pet." When the pets lined up for awards, said duck broke loose from his young mistress and in a trice ate up his competition: a frog, two worms, and a cricket. The judges thereupon awarded the "happiest pet" a second title: "most hungry."

* * *

A carnival performer was aboard an Ohio train when the conductor asked, "What are you carrying in that wicker basket?" "Pigeons," said the performer. "I thought so," said the conductor. "You can't ride with them in here. Rules specifically forbid pigeons in passenger cars."

The performer's plea that these were specially trained pigeons availed him naught, so he reluctantly pried open the car window—no mean feat by itself—and eased the pigeons out.

"Okay, I hope you're satisfied now," said the performer to the conductor, "but believe me, your superiors are going to hear about this when the train gets to Cleveland."

"Cleveland?" repeated the conductor. "This train goes to Cincinnati."

"Holy smoke," exclaimed the performer. Then he leaned out of the window and hollered to his vanishing pigeons, "Hey, fellows! Cincinnati. CINCINNATI!"

* * *

Newly elected public officials should bear in mind Hubert Humphrey's story about the customer in a pet shop who toyed with buying a parrot on display. The bird was absolutely quiet for several moments, and the customer finally asked a sales clerk, "Does this parrot ever talk?" "Indeed he does, ma'am," the clerk assured her, "but he doesn't wish to be quoted."

* * *

A vaudeville act that stumped the experts for years was called "Hans, the Educated Horse." Hans, a swaybacked fugitive from a glue factory, was billed as a "mathematical wizard." Let's say that a man in the audience called out "What's six times seven?" Hans would tap four times with his left forefoot, twice with his right: 42. If the problem was "Divide 96 by 3,"

Hans would tap three times with his left foot, twice with his right: 32.

The solution was simple, once it was discovered. Hans had been trained to tap each foot until signaled by a barely perceptible crooking of a finger by his master to stop.

❖ ❖ ❖

Mrs. Gottrod, out to bag some big game in the jungle if it was the last thing she did, fired her rifle one day, turned to her guide with a satisfied air, and declared, "There! I just know I hit something that time. Run and find out the name of the animal I shot."

The guide was back in a few moments to report, "He says, ma'am, that his name is Sylvester."

❖ ❖ ❖

Marston Bates, in his fascinating book, *Animal Worlds*, points out that periodically, even without man's interference, certain species have gone down to defeat, and become extinct. Man has hastened these processes immeasurably. Take the case of the musk-ox. Defending themselves against wolves—

their natural enemies—musk-oxen developed a technique of forming a tight circle with their calves in the center. This worked just fine against the wolves, but then man with his weapons came along—and the musk-oxen, in their tight circles, made a perfect target for the spear, and then the rifle.

*   *   *

An official of the Philadelphia Zoo should embarrass litter-bugs with his report that, when careless visitors drop paper cups and containers into the otters' pool, the praiseworthy animals gather up the trash and put it in a neat pile.

*   *   *

Bill Sutherland reminds us all that when two cows stand with their heads to each other's tails, switching flies offen each other, that's cow-operation. And when nags do it, that's horse-pitality.

*   *   *

Animals have their domestic troubles, too, it seems. Consider the case of the exasperated centipede who told her husband she was sick and tired of waiting on him hand and foot, hand and foot, etc. And there was the hen that observed the undisciplined behavior of her youngest chick with obvious disapproval. "If your father could see you now," she cackled disgustedly, "he'd turn over in his gravy."

*   *   *

Up in Connecticut there lives a retired film director who has realized a lifetime ambition: he's writing a novel and raising chickens on the side, and since he has been thus engaged for only a month or so the period of bitter disillusionment has not yet set in. To prove to himself he was through for good with his old Hollywood routine, he even threw out the can of film that had won him a cluster of Oscars back in the forties.

Among the other livestock acquired by the ex-director was a goat which he had named, over my vehement objections, "Mr. Cerf." Mr. Cerf saw the can of film come sailing out of the upstairs window, and promptly had it for dinner.

The next morning, another goat inquired wistfully, "How

was the prize-winning picture that you ate last night?" "It was nothing to write home about," admitted Mr. Cerf. "Frankly, I enjoyed the book a lot better."

* * *

Lorrain D'Essen has become famous for supplying animals of every description to capricious TV directors, fashion photographers, and advertising salons. Her pets include llamas, kangaroos, tiger cubs, pigs, and wombats. They all live peacefully together in Mrs. D'Essen's private home.

The largest semipermanent guest Lorrain D'Essen ever entertained was a miniature bull named Mortimer. Mortimer slipped often on the smooth floors, and became self-conscious and moody if anybody laughed at him.

There was a 300-pound baby elephant in the house one night, too. Jackie Gleason wanted him for a TV show. Lorrain bundled him into a taxicab (no Cadillac being available that night) and the driver became so intrigued with his unusual passenger that he ran right through a red light and almost bowled over an irate cop. "Whassa big idea?" snarled the cop. "You blind or sump-thing?" "Not at all, officer," pleaded the cabbie. "It's just that I got this here elephant in the back seat. . . ." The cop was too flabbergasted to give him a ticket.

Another time, Lorrain supplied a camel named Loomey for a promotion at Macy's Department Store. Loomey made a great big hit with the customers, but lost face (and a return engagement) by chewing up Chairman Jack Straus's new Panama straw hat.

For an Arthur Treacher TV show, she produced Bertha, a hoity-toity White Leghorn chicken who demanded her own dressing room, and broke up rehearsals by cackling continuously till she got it. Treacher referred to Bertha as "the most edible actress" he ever worked with.

There are tricks in every trade, and Lorrain D'Essen has had to learn a new one every day. A piece of shrimp, for instance, in an actor's ear will persuade a cat to kiss him there or "whisper" to him. A lion will roar angrily if talcum powder is shaken on his mane. Cooked liver cut into tiny chunks looks exactly like canned dog food on camera, and dogs never hesitate to gobble it down greedily.

Jordan, a pony in a Broadway musical, learned one trick all by himself. Jordan showed his teeth menacingly every time the show was running late.

* * *

The AOMC, which stands, of course, for the Animal-of-the-Month Club, announces the following irresistible selections:

1. A nearsighted whale who fell in love with a U.S. submarine and followed it clear around the world. Every time the sub fired a torpedo, the proud whale passed out cigars.

2. A tiger in the Central Park Zoo who abhorred captivity. "I've discovered a way to escape," he confided to his cagemate, "and tonight's the night." "I'd think twice before I risked anything like that," warned the other tiger. "They say that at night this park is full of juvenile delinquents."

3. A taxidermist's pet monkey. He suffered from mounting apprehension.

4. An elephant who lumbered into a saloon. "We're not allowed to serve intoxicating liquids to pachyderms," announced the bartender. "Who wants intoxicating liquids?" countered the elephant. "I just came in for the peanuts."

5. An angleworm in Altoona, who was sunning herself in the grass one morning when a hoity-toity caterpillar inched by. "Hmph," sniffed the angleworm, "I'd give plenty to know how she got that fur coat!"

6. A father mosquito who supervised a trial flight of his two young sons over the beach at Elberon, New Jersey. "What a wonderful age we live in," he sighed happily. "When I was young, the only places you could sting those girls were on the hands and face!"

7. An otter in the London Zoo who took it upon herself to watch over a baby weasel and a newborn anteater. On her cage they've hung a sign reading: "Department of Otter Confusion."

8. A giraffe who had a wild affair with a swordfish. The result: the darndest looking tree surgeon you ever saw.

9. A preoccupied porcupine who backed into a cactus plant and mumbled, "Pardon me, darling."

10. A rooster in Ottumwa, Iowa, who is without doubt the laziest in America. He's never crowed once; he just waits for another rooster to crow—and then he nods his head.

* * *

A pig and a chicken, alleges W. R. Grady, were promenading down a Fort Worth thoroughfare when the chicken suddenly proposed, "Let's stop in at yonder beanery and eat some ham and eggs." "A thoughtless and repugnant suggestion," was the pig's reaction. "Kindly remember that for you a dish of that sort is a mere contribution. For me it means a total commitment."

* * *

A proud eagle, waxing romantic one moonlit spring evening, suggested to his mate, "I'd like to hug and kiss you while we're soaring through space." "Why not?" nodded his wife. So off they flew into the wide blue yonder, where the eagle's ardor knew no bounds. Back in their nest later, the male eagle asked, "Did you enjoy the trip?" His mate smoothed her wings and exclaimed happily, "IT'S THE ONLY WAY TO FLY!"

5. Battle of the Sexes

GIRLS

What is a girl? A discerning student at M.I.T. obliged with this "chemical analysis." "Thought to be a member of the human race. Seldom found in natural state. Surface coated with paint and other chemical compounds. Has low freezing point, but is also highly explosive. Extremely active when in vicinity of opposite sex. Chiefly ornamental. Probably the most powerful seducing agent known. Illegal to own more than one specimen."

* * *

Richard Condon offers this explanation of the origin of kissing: "The cave man found that salt helped him survive the fierce summer heat, also that he could get the salt by licking a companion's cheek. Then he discovered that the process became more interesting if the companion belonged to the opposite sex. Next thing you know, everybody forgot all about the salt."

* * *

Warning broadcast by Tom Poston: "Beware of the girl who runs her fingers through your hair. She's probably after your scalp!"

* * *

Goody Ace was present in a beauty parlor in Beverly Hills when a very pretty girl refused to allow the operator to restore a blonde glow to her naturally dark hair. "Your hair really needs touching up," insisted the operator, "and I assure you we can do it every bit as well as they do it back East." "Impossible," sighed the pretty girl. "I may be here in Beverly Hills, but my roots are in New York."

* * *

A young Southern belle asked her mother, "What do you give a man who has everything?" Her mother answered unhesitatingly, "Encouragement."

The Lass Roundup . . .

1. The Sioux City siren who treats her gentlemen callers like dirt. She hides them under her bed.

2. The Beverly Hills bride who made a slight change in the wedding ritual. She kept the bridal bouquet and threw the groom away.

3. The Syracuse strip-tease artiste whose manager propelled her on stage every evening with the same admonition: "Get out there, kid, and show them what you're made of!"

4. The Minneapolis minx who simpered to her friend: "You look like a million, my dear—and I mean every day of it."

5. The daughter of a country auctioneer who dazzled a hardened old city slicker. She would smile, wink, and nod to him, and he would smile, wink, and nod back. After the auction

he discovered he had purchased a pair of mules, a churn, and an electric milking machine.

6. The young lady who had been trying to land a cautious beau for three solid years. In a chop suey parlor she saw her opportunity. He asked her, "How would you like your rice, my dear, fried or boiled?" She answered, "Thrown."

7. The pretty airline stewardess who whispered to her assistant in flight, "Careful, Toots, if you have to carry anything up front. They've got the automatic pilot on."

8. The beautiful but nearsighted fashion model who spotted a many-legged black thing slithering across her bathroom floor and clobbered it with the heel of her shoe. Finally she summoned courage to look at the insect at close range—and discovered she had ruined one-half of a pair of ten-dollar false eyelashes.

9. The loser in a beauty contest who was coldly appraising the face and figure of the girl who just had been declared the winner. "I wonder where she got those looks?" pondered a chaperone. "From her father," stated the loser unhesitatingly. "He's a plastic surgeon."

10. The young co-ed from Kansas State who knows precisely what she wants. Her English professor was elaborating one day on the advantages of acquiring a large vocabulary. "Say a word out loud to yourself five times," he advised, "and it will be yours for life."

Our heroine closed her eyes and whispered, "Walter, Walter, Walter, Walter, Walter."

* * *

A beautiful young lady in the Park Avenue sector has been squired this season by a variety of eligible men-about-town. They bring her home to an exclusive apartment house, where she bids her dates farewell, and is then ushered inside by an obsequious doorman. Her date is no sooner out of sight, however, than the obsequious doorman kisses the young lady warmly and sends her off via the subway to her real home. He is her father.

* * *

"Why won't you buy me a mink coat?" pouted a luscious young thing at a hockey game. "I'm very, very cold."

"Since you know the answer," growled the hockey enthusiast, "why do you ask the question?"

* * *

Fashion tip from a Kansas weekly: "Girls will be wearing the same thing in brassieres this year that they wore last year."

* * *

Just before the opening of a new campaign, the coach of a Big Ten basketball team had a glorious dream. He dreamed that a beautiful, wealthy co-ed lured him to her dormitory— where he met her brother, who was seven feet tall.

* * *

The father of a teen-age daughter found her redheaded boy friend with a coke in one hand and a huge slab of apple pie in the other. "I'm mighty glad to meet you, Clifton," declared the father. "I've noticed you in our budget for some time."

* * *

A chorus girl friend of John Straley asked him if he could find a stage job for a beautiful friend. "What are her measurements?" asked the statistically minded Straley. "They're 26-32-85," replied the chorus girl. "Holy smoke," gasped Straley. "What is your friend doing now?" "She poses," said the girl, "for pyramids."

ROMANCE

Alaska seems to be one of the many places where the course of true love does not run too smoothly. A long way from Nome, a young gallant took his adored one for a ride on his dog sled. In due course he hollered "Mush," then she hollered "Mush," and while they were mushing somebody stole the dog sled.

❉ ❉ ❉

Mr. Jones patted his daughter's hand fondly, and told her, "Your young man told me today he wanted you as his bride, and I gave my consent." "Oh, Papa," gushed the daughter, "it's going to be so hard leaving Mother." "I understand perfectly, my dear," beamed Mr. Jones. "You just take her with you."

❉ ❉ ❉

In Pinsk, an ambitious young man called upon a marriage broker and allowed as how he would take unto himself a bride —if the dowry was big enough. "I've got just the girl for you," enthused the broker. "Her name is Olga, and she has a dowry of twenty-five thousand rubles. Unfortunately, she has only one leg." "No," said the young man.

"Aha," smiled the broker. "How about Natalie? A fifty-thousand-ruble dowry, but she can't see or hear." "No," said the young man. "Maybe you'll have Petrushka," urged the broker. "A hundred thousand rubles is her dowry—but I'm sorry to say she's insane." "Absolutely not," said the young man—but then, wistfully, he inquired, "Have you a client, maybe, who has only one leg, can't see or hear, and is insane all at one time?"

The marriage broker nodded sagely, and folded up his list of prospects. "I can't do business with you," he admitted. "You're too much of a dreamer."

✻ ✻ ✻

Shirley MacLaine has figured out the Seven Lively Arts of Making a Man Say Yes: 1. Find him. 2. Fascinate him. 3. Flatter him. 4. Feed him. 5. Fuss over him. 6. Fondle him. 7. Frame him. And oh, yes—if none of these does the trick, adds Shirley, forget him!

✻ ✻ ✻

"Did you follow my advice about kissing your girl when she least expects it?" asked a senior of a young fraternity pledger. "When?" echoed the pledgee, applying a piece of raw beefsteak to a very black eye, "I thought you said WHERE!"

It Must Be Love . . .

"The way women go about finding magnetism in impossible men is appalling."—*Michael Arlen.*

"If a woman wants to hold a man, she has merely to appeal to what is worst in him."—*Oscar Wilde.*

"There are no oaths that make so many perjurers as the vows of love."—*Rochebrune.*

"In love there is always one who kisses and one who offers the cheek."—*French Proverb*.

"The magic of first love is our ignorance that it can ever end."—*Disraeli*.

* * *

Don Lindsay tells of a young man who confided to his mother at an inopportune moment that he proposed taking unto himself a bride. "Wotsa dees?" screamed Mother. "Who's agon' love you like Mama? Who's agon' starch-a your socks? Who's agon' make-a you lasagna?"

"Wait a minute, mom," pleaded the son. "Why are you talking like that? You're not Italian!"

* * *

The last remaining "bachelor girl" in a big office appeared radiantly one morning and began to pass out cigars to all and sundry. "What's the big idea?" chorused her cohorts. Proudly she displayed a diamond ring and exulted, "It's a boy—six feet tall and weighs 190 pounds."

* * *

The fellow who makes exaggerated statements—a movie press agent, for example—is rarely taken seriously by anybody. Dean Leys, of Roosevelt University, cites the case, for instance, of a chronic exaggerator who lost his girl with this ill-advised note: "My Irreplaceable and Indispensable Treasure: I would climb the highest mountain for you, swim the widest river, battle the wildest animal barehanded. Nothing will ever keep me from your side. (Signed) Your adoring Charlie. P.S. I'll be over Saturday night if it doesn't rain."

* * *

Observes Jim Backus: Many a man owes his success to his first wife—and his second wife to his success.

* * *

And Bob Melvin pinpoints a girl who's broken every date she's had. She goes out with them.

* * *

An anxious young suitor inquired of the proverbial younger brother the whereabouts of his beloved. "Keep your shirt on," counseled said young brother. "She's upstairs working on her acceptance speech."

* * *

A short, short story from the University of Texas:
Oh, Brad, let's not park here.
Oh, Brad, let's not park.
Oh, Brad, let's not.
Oh, Brad, let's.
Oh, Brad.
Oh.

* * *

A wealthy but rather staid banker from Oklahoma brought a beautiful young bride home with him from New York. "She's the last word to me," enthused a friend. "How did you manage to meet her?"

"There was nothing to it," boasted the banker. "I just opened my wallet and there she was!"

* * *

Mary Lou's caller drove his own foreign sports car but his conversation left plenty to be desired. "Your new boy friend hasn't got much to him," grumbled Mary Lou's dad. "What does the lad do, anyhow?" Mary Lou explained, "He inherits."

* * *

The young foreman on a building job reported for work one morning sporting a magnificent black eye. "I gave my fiancée a beautiful diamond bracelet for her birthday," he explained sheepishly, "and now it turns out she wants to keep it."

* * *

In Anniston, Alabama, reports S. Himmell, a lass rummaging in an attic trunk came upon a yellowing letter her father had written to her mother in his courting days. Laboriously the daughter copied the letter word for word, signed a masculine name to it, and mailed it to herself. Then she showed it to her father.

The resultant explosion shook the house. "This lovesick loon," roared the father, "is the biggest idiot I ever heard of. Keep him out of this house or I'll break him in two. We're not going to have a simp like that in this family—and the sooner the ding-busted, fatheaded lunatic knows it, the happier I'll be."

When he discovered the trick, the father reacted the way all fathers do. "I knew what you were up to immediately," he insisted. "Your ma and you were hoping so obviously I'd fall for the gag, I decided to give you both a good time."

* * *

A pert Southern miss was outraged when she received a letter from her beau at Baylor with several X's at the bottom. "The skunk," she muttered darkly. "I'll teach him to double-cross me!"

* * *

Papa Shrecklich wasn't too impressed with the girl Junior brought home for dinner. "I thought you said your girl's legs were without equal," he jeered while she was out of the room. "Not at all," hedged Junior. "I said they were without parallel."

* * *

A sailor spotted a greeting card which expounded this sentiment: "Here's my heart and soul for the only girl I ever loved." "Just the card I'm looking for," the sailor enthused to the sales clerk. "Give me two dozen."

* * *

A local Romeo's face appeared in the window of his beloved's bedroom. "Get a move on," he whispered hoarsely, "and let's get this eloping business over with."

"Ssh," cautioned his Juliet. "Papa'll hear us and spoil all our plans."

"I wouldn't worry about that," smirked Romeo. "He's down on the ground holding up the ladder."

o o o

George Jessel remembers the time a prominent actor and a
beautiful girl approached a hotel registration desk and signed
in as Mr. and Mrs. The clerk inquired, "Double or twin beds?"
The actor turned to his companion and asked, "Would a double be all right, dear?" She answered, "Yes, sir."

MATRIMONY

Very few people alive today seem to recall the evening
Adam came stamping into Eve's kitchen to complain, "Confound it, you've put my pants in the salad again!"

o o o

When anybody asked the late Jim Thurber, "How's your
wife?" he generally countered with, "Compared to what?"

o o o

Julius Pretzfeld, inveterate newspaper reader, usually pe-
rused two of them, from front page to last, at the breakfast
table, thereby annoying Mrs. Pretzfeld very thoroughly. One
evening she asked him casually, "Julius, did you notice anything unusual about me at the breakfast table this morning?"
"Why, no, my dear," replied Mr. Pretzfeld. "Ah ha," cackled
Mrs. Pretzfeld, "I wasn't there!"

o o o

A young bridegroom followed his gal into their shining new
kitchenette. "What is my snookums doing in here so long?" he
inquired. His worried bride explained, "I rinsed the ice cubes
in this hot water and now I can't find them."

o o o

Overheard by Alfredo Macitado in a Rio de Janeiro hotel:
"And just when I was able, finally, through my relentless logic,
to convince her of the absurdity of her argument—she hauled
off and socked me!"

* * *

"I accept your proposal of marriage," said a maiden coyly, "provided, of course, my pappy gives his consent. He loves me madly, and he's mighty tough and choosy, so be careful how you approach him."

Thus warned, the suitor charged into pappy's study and blurted out, "I want to marry your daughter." "Go ahead, and blessings upon you, young man," beamed pappy. "By the way, what did you say your name was?"

* * *

"The boss," reported Mr. Henpeque to his aggressive wife, "turned out to be a real lamb when, like you told me, I demanded a raise. . . . He said, 'Baaah.'"

* * *

Two college alumni who had roomed together for four years met for the first time since graduation at their fifteenth reunion. One of them sported a beard that made Mitch Miller look clean-shaven. "I'd never have known you with those whiskers," laughed his old pal. "Did you lose a bet or something?"

"I presume that you refer to my beard," said the hairy one loftily. "If you must know, I hate the darn thing."

"Then why don't you shave it off?" asked the friend.

"Because," was the logical reply, "my wife hates it even more than I do."

* * *

The bride kissed her husband warmly upon his return from the office and sympathized, "I can tell by your face that you've had one of those frustrating days where everything possible went wrong. What would you say to a round of vodka martinis, followed by a fine thick steak, French fries, a tossed salad, and some fresh peach cake?"

"Not tonight, darling," begged the bridegroom. "Let's just have dinner at home."

* * *

A wise word of caution from Vince Rivers: "That argument you won from your wife isn't over yet!"

* * *

Sign discovered by the milkman on the doorstep of a suburban ranch house: "Please leave two bottles of cream and my wife alone."

* * *

A young bride's face fell when she noticed twin beds in the bridal suite. "What's biting you?" inquired her solicitous bridegroom. "Nothing really," she assured him, "but I certainly thought we were going to get a room all to ourselves."

Ten Wives to Look Out for . . .

1. Mrs. Jones was jubilant. "I've finally cured my husband of biting his nails," she declared. "Land sakes," said her neighbor. "How?" "I hide his teeth."

2. From under the handsomely decorated Christmas tree a wife called to her husband, "Here's your most important present. It took me weeks to find just what I wanted." "I'll be right in to look at it," said the husband. "No, wait," cautioned the wife. "I've got to put it on first."

3. Mrs. Fraunces had a hard time locating her spouse at a big party, but finally spotted him, ecstatically festooned over a limb of a tree in the garden. "It's our signal to bid you adieu," she told her hostess. "My husband is beginning his imitation of Spanish moss."

4. Mrs. Ambruster was just picking out a neat, pearl-handled, six-barrel revolver when she saw her husband ambling into the store. "Don't bother wrapping that revolver," she instructed the clerk. "Here he comes now!"

5. A frowning doctor told Mrs. Gumbach, "Frankly, I don't

like the looks of your husband." "Neither do I," nodded Mrs. Gumbach, "but he's good to the children."

6. At a big Hollywood wing-ding, scribe Mike Connolly overheard a wife solicitously murmur to her spouse, "What did I say to annoy you, dear? It may come in useful again some time."

7. The coroner shot a sympathetic glance at the widow dressed in black, with tears streaming down her face. "Can you recall your husband's last words?" he asked gently. "Indeed I can," sobbed the distraught widow. "He said, 'Don't try to scare me with that shotgun. You couldn't hit the side of a barn.'"

8. It was a cruel, cruel wife who told her husband, "You sure made a prize fool of yourself tonight. It's a good thing those people don't realize you were sober!"

9. Mrs. Wimdinger watched silently as long as she could stand it while her middle-aged husband ogled a striking brunette in a tight-fitting, revealing cocktail dress. Then she hissed in his ear, "I'll bet the sink in her kitchen is well-stacked, too!"

10. A fantastically henpecked husband finally did something on his own initiative. He dropped dead. His nagging wife mourned her loss—and the fact that she had nobody left to badger. A visitor sympathized, "How you must miss dear Wilbur." "Yes," sighed the widow wistfully. "It seems but yesterday that he stood at that very door, holding it open until two flies got in."

And Ten Husbands . . .

1. A mousey little man was hailed into court for beating up his wife—a formidable, Amazonian creature. The judge, trying to conceal a certain amount of admiration, demanded, "What came over you?" The little man explained, "Well, Your Honor,

she had her back to me, the fire poker was handy, and the back door was open. So I took a chance!"

2. Somebody made the mistake of asking Joey Bishop how his wife could cook. Bishop grimaced, grabbed the inquirer by the arm, and implored, "Tell me: How can anyone burn lemonade?"

3. "My wife," boasted a well-to-do jeweler, "has only one extravagance. She just loves to spend money."

4. Complains the husband of curvaceous Zsa Zsa Horntoot: "My wife is like Noah. When she packs for a weekend she takes two of everything."

5. In Hollywood, a luncheon companion of Tony Randall's had this tale of woe to impart: "I thought I was set for life with a healthy bank balance, a beautiful home, and the love of a passionate and wealthy woman. Then, wham! One evening my wife walks in!"

6. At a Coney Island boardwalk cafe, a rather disheveled individual disclosed that he had been married eight times. "Are you married now?" he was asked. He answered angrily, "Do you think I'm a sucker?"

7. "Look at the shabby old frock I have to wear," grumbled Mrs. Black to her husband. "If one of your office friends came to call, he'd think I was the cook." Replied Mr. Black, unperturbed, "He'd change his mind if he stayed for dinner!"

8. A salesman in a swank leather goods store suggested to a male customer, "Can I interest you in a beautifully embossed letter opener?" "You cannot," responded the customer firmly. "I'm married to one."

9. "Why," Ardie Deutsch was asked, "did you send that brand new pressure cooker to the rummage sale?"

"It may look like a pressure cooker to you," explained Deutsch, "but in the hands of my wife, it's a secret weapon. Last Wednesday she shot a pot roast into outer space."

10. Peter Lind Hayes met an old gaffer at the Winged Foot Golf Club who boasted, "My wife and I were married fifty-five years ago today—and we still hold hands." Then he added, "If we didn't—we'd kill each other!"

* * *

The parents of two badly spoiled brats suddenly came to their senses and sneaked off to Florida for a genuine rest—by themselves. Sunning on the beach, the wife murmured happily, "It's wonderful to get away from the kids, much as I love them, for just a few days, isn't it?" "Sure is," agreed the husband, "but just to make me feel at home, darling, would you please throw a few handfuls of sand in my face?"

* * *

"Paw," said Mrs. Simpson over her knitting one evening, "it's time you spoke a piece to our son Wilbur. 'Pears to me he jest plain don't want to get hisself married." "Don't worry 'bout our Wilbur," soothed Mr. Simpson. "He'll marry fast enough when the wrong girl comes along."

* * *

Winter autoists will appreciate a cartoon from a Northwestern weekly that shows a weary husband who has just dug a fifty-yard patch through a six-foot snowdrift from his garage to the road. As he is about to open the garage door with a sigh of relief, his wife calls out from the kitchen, "Oh, I forgot to tell you, dear. I took the car over to mother's yesterday before the storm started."

* * *

One housewife was describing her troubles to another on the terrace of a Catskill resort. "It's impossible," she complained, "for me to satisfy my husband with my cooking. Take last week, for example. I buy him a fine twelve-pound rabbit. Monday I give him rabbit steak. Tuesday, rabbit's feet. Wednesday, barbecued rabbit spare ribs. Thursday, rabbit hamburger. Friday, rabbit goulash. And do you think all these delicacies satisfy him? No, ma'am! Saturday morning he just glares at me with those big, pink eyes!"

"It says in the paper," a wife reported to her husband, "that a man on the next block throttled his mother-in-law this morning." "Hm-m-m," mused the husband. "Sounds like a practical choker."

❋   ❋   ❋

An inquisitive youngster asked his father one evening, "Dad, what was the most money you ever earned in one year?" "Ask your mother," replied Dad from behind his newspaper. "I forget what I told her."

❋   ❋   ❋

As they stepped out into the bracing winter night, and left the noisy, overheated cocktail party within, a wife faced her husband squarely and demanded, "Elmer, did anybody tell you in there that you were ordained the life of the party—the greatest wit, the greatest raconteur, and the greatest lover boy in town?"

"No, dear," admitted the puzzled husband. "I can't say anybody did."

"Exactly," said the wife grimly. "Now tell me this: Just where did you get the idea?"

* * *

A prisoner serving a twenty-year sentence in a Wisconsin jail fell to reminiscing with a fellow inmate of the fun he and his wife used to enjoy at the seaside burying each other in the soft, white sand. "I suppose," he concluded whimsically, "the proper thing to do when I get out of here is to go back and dig her up."

* * *

Bill Feather clipped this out of a Chicago column: "Wouldn't it be wonderful to have a marriage license that expired every few years like a driver's license?"

* * *

Four staid, successful Minneapolis business moguls invested jointly in a hunting lodge deep in the Northern woods, and thither they were wont to repair for a fortnight twice a year. "Roughing it is what we want," they would tell their wives, "no hot water, no modern conveniences—and above all, no women!"

One September the four deserted ladies decided to surprise their husbands and followed them to their woodland lair. They were stopped at the gate, however, by a wizened old guide. "You gals better beat it quick if you know what's good for you," he advised. "This time these fellows brought their wives with them!"

* * *

Matrimonial bliss in Hollywood: At dinner one evening producer Billy Wilder's lovely wife Audrey (Wilder is responsible for *Some Like It Hot, Irma La Douce,* and a dozen other screen triumphs) announced blithely, "Darling, do you realize this is our anniversary?" Wilder poised a fork in midair and reproached her, "Please—not while I'm eating."

* * *

A marriage counselor was having trouble determining the cause of discord between a young husband and wife who insisted on talking at the same time. Finally establishing a semblance of order, he demanded of the wife, "What is the main block to your getting along together?" Grimly she ordered her husband, "You tell him, hon." "Ah," interrupted the counselor. "There's hope for your marriage when you still call him 'hon.'" "That," explained the wife coldly, "happens to be his name: Attila the Hon."

* * *

Asked one elderly lady of another at a Darien dinner party, "Doesn't it embarrass you to see your husband flirting so shamelessly with all the young unmarried daughters of your old friends?" "Oh, I just let him have his innocent pleasure," said the wife tolerantly. "He's like a puppy chasing automobiles. He wouldn't know what to do if he caught one. He just wants to bark at them a little."

* * *

"My wife," a sad-eyed husband told his doctor, "is getting to the stage where I think we'll have to move in with help of some kind. She bursts into tears at the drop of a hat. This morning she wept for an hour because she saw a dog with a broken leg."

"That's not so bad," nodded the doctor. "Many women are particularly sensitive about the suffering of animals. I think my own wife might cry at the sight of a dog with a broken leg."

"You didn't let me finish my story," said the husband. "This particular dog was in a box of animal crackers."

* * *

A whimsical Oklahoman who signs himself "Elisha J. Unlikely" submits the story of a cowboy who brought his bride to Chicago for a honeymoon. The bride had read a great deal about kidnapers before she arrived, and was afraid to be left alone in their hotel room. So when the cowboy left to look up some old pals, he locked her in the room, and took the key with him.

Hours later, after a delightful—and liquid—get-together with his friends, he suddenly remembered his bride. "Holy cow," he cried, jumping to his feet. "You gotta excuse me, boys. I done left Sally Lou locked in a room all night and I ain't neither fed nor watered her!"

* * *

To conclude this section on a gentler and more sentimental note, I quote this heartwarming ad from the classified section of a dignified metropolitan paper:

"I am responsible for all debts and obligations of my wife, Selma, both present and future, and am delighted to be the

provider for a woman who has borne me two fine children,
listened patiently to all my gripes, and with an overabundance
of love and care made the past fifteen years of my life the
happiest I have known. On this, our fifteenth wedding anniversary, I am proud to express my gratitude publicly."

6. *"It's Only a Game"*

BASEBALL

The official baseball records include the names of twelve
rank amateurs who participated in a single major league game.
The date was May 18, 1912, and the team they engaged in
combat was the Philadelphia Athletics.

This unusual turn of events was precipitated by the Georgia
Peach, Tyrus Raymond Cobb. On the afternoon of May 17,
1912, Tyrus took exception to the heckling of a fan in the
grandstand, climbed up to where he was seated, and socked
him in the jaw. For this act, Cobb was fined and suspended,

and the whole Detroit team, in sympathy with their illustrious center fielder, walked out on strike.

That's when the Athletics' management engaged the sand-lotters to substitute for the Detroit Tigers. Several thousand fans turned out to see what would happen when a big league ball team played a bunch of rank amateurs. They saw plenty. The Athletics made twenty-six hits and nosed out the amateurs, 24–2. The strike was settled that night.

* * *

One day when Ty Cobb was at the height of his career, a kid from his own home town in Georgia joined the squad and naturally came to Cobb for counsel. "I guess what's kept me tired so far is being a horse's aid," he opined. "Whaddya mean, a horse's aid?" asked Ty. "Wal," drawled the lad, "I git up every morning at four and fetch water and feed for the horses. Then I curry them and give 'em a morning workout. Then I clean out the stables all afternoon. After giving them supper I play phonograph records to keep them feeling happy-like and do other little chores till the owner lets me go home nights about eleven."

"Son," said Ty Cobb, "I've got news for you. A horse's *aid* you're not."

* * *

Al Lopez, stellar pilot of the Chicago White Sox, once caught for the Brooklyn Dodgers, and tells of a later year when the Brooklyn team brought up a young left-hander who had a world of stuff, but less control than is generally expected even from southpaws.

"I'll tell you how wild that young fellow was," enthuses Lopez. "One evening they sent him out to pitch batting practice at Ebbets Field, and he hit a man in the eye who was watching TV in a bar at Coney Island!"

* * *

The most famous double-play combination in baseball history must be the heroic Tinker, Evers, and Chance trio that brought pennants to the Chicago Cubs early in the century.

Nor will oldsters forget Giant-rooter F.P.A.'s ode to these stalwarts:

"These are the saddest of possible words:
Tinker to Evers to Chance.
Trio of Bear Cubs and fleeter than birds:
Tinker to Evers to Chance.
Thoughtlessly pricking our gonfalon bubble;
Making a Giant hit into a double;
Words that are weighted with nothing but trouble:
Tinker to Evers to Chance."

Incidentally, the name of the third baseman who completed that famous Cubs' infield was Harry Steinfeldt. See how many old fans remember *that*!

* * *

In the days when Babe Ruth was hanging up his home run records, General Pershing once visited Yankee Stadium, and press photographers persuaded him and the Babe to pose together for a few pictures. Babe was not given to much small talk, but he did feel that this occasion warranted a special effort on his part. So he draped his arm around General Pershing's shoulder and asked amiably, "Say, kid, you was in the war, wasn't you?"

* * *

One baseball record established by the New York Yankees' peerless outfielder, Joe DiMaggio, probably will stand for many years to come. He hit successfully in fifty-six consecutive games. His string was almost broken some games earlier when his own brother Dom, wearing the livery of the Boston Red Sox, robbed him of a sure triple with a wonderful catch against the center-field wall. DiMag got his needed hit on his next and last time at bat, but still was shaking his head over brother Dom's catch when he came back to the clubhouse. "This speaks well for the integrity of the game," he remarked, "but the kid sure didn't have to rub it in that way—especially when he's coming to my house for dinner tonight!"

* * *

Frank Frisch recalls one game with the old Boston Braves in which the great Dizzy Dean had struck out another of Joe DiMaggio's brothers, Vince, twice. In the ninth inning, Vince came to bat for the third time. After taking two called strikes, he popped a puny foul behind the plate. "Don't catch it," Dean screamed to the catcher. "Let it drop!"

Manager Frisch stormed out of the dugout, hollering, "What's the big idea?"

"I bet a guy ten bucks I'd fan DiMag three times today. This is my last chance." And then, while Frisch still fumed, Dizzy burned a third strike past DiMaggio at the plate and collected his ten-spot.

* * *

For one Fourth of July doubleheader, the owners of the St. Louis Cardinals baseball club (then known as the Gashouse Gang) hired a band. Dizzy Dean ran out to center field to con-

fer with the leader, with the result that when the trio of um-
pires appeared for action, the band struck up "Three Blind
Mice."

One of the umps pointed a finger at Dizzy and told him,
"I ain't got no proof of who done this, but I got eight to one it
wasn't nobody else but you!"

* * *

Bob Feller, famous pitcher of the thirties for the Cleveland
Indians, was dragged to a five-hour-long opera one evening.
"How did you like it?" he was asked later. "I'm not sure,"
admitted Feller. "I dozed through the first four innings."

* * *

Birdie Tebbetts tells of the spring day he asked a raw baseball rookie to name his best playing position. The rookie answered, "Kinda bent over, like this."

* * *

A second-string catcher on the Los Angeles Angels once set
out in hot pursuit of a Pasadena millionaire's daughter. Weeks
later his manager asked, "Howya doing, Buster, with that society babe?" "Not so good, Rig," admitted the catcher. "So far
it's no hits, no runs—and no heiress."

* * *

Joe Garagiola, onetime big league catcher, has become an
accomplished after-dinner speaker, though his name is frequently misspelled in the banquet programs. Governor Faubus
had occasion to question Joe's name. "In the hills where I was
born, " averred Faubus, "we would take a name like that, get
two girls' names out of it, and have enough left over for three
boys."

Joe Garagiola says he played football, too, when he was a
boy—until he nearly drowned in one game. Joe was playing on
a field so uneven that it was covered with mud puddles. He
was thrown for a loss on one play—right in a puddle, face down,
and the entire opposing line fell on top of him. When they

untangled the mess, Joe was about to go under for the third time. After that, he stuck to baseball.

* * *

There's been a lot of grumbling about the time it takes these days for a game of big-league baseball to be played, what with pitchers posing as statues for minutes at a time, adjusting their caps, pants, belts, socks, and what have you, and managers calling conferences at every turn of a television camera. The president of one of the leagues sent a secret memo to certain officials asking for suggestions as to how play might be speeded up. The likeliest suggestion came from one cynic on the *Journal-American:* "Play only eight innings instead of nine."

* * *

Allie Reynolds, one of the all-time great pitchers for the New York Yankees, hit only one home run in his long major league career. "It was off Early Wynn in Washington," recalls Reynolds. "I didn't see it good, so I ran all the way. When I galloped by second, I saw the third base coach holding up his hands, so I thought he meant me to go back. I slid back into second base! It was pretty embarrassing, especially since it was the opening day of the season and the President of the United States was in the stands!"

*　*　*

In Minneapolis, a sportswriter interviewed a hard-boiled young pitcher recently added to the roster of the Minnesota Twins. "You're a tough hombre, all right," conceded the scribe. "I bet you wouldn't give your own mother a decent pitch." "Why should I?" countered the pitcher angrily. "She batted .297 with Sacramento last season."

*　*　*

Willie McCovey, the slugging first baseman and outfielder of the San Francisco Giants, likes his nine hours of sleep every night. A newspaper man phoned him very early one morning and asked, "Did I awake you, Willie?" McCovey admitted drowsily, "Some."

*　*　*

At a recent wedding in San Diego, each of the five hundred guests was given a sachet of rice, handsomely ribboned, to shower the bride and groom as they exited. All but one of the guests untied the lace bag immediately. The one who didn't— a lad of eleven—obviously proposed to throw the rice in the original package. "What's the big idea?" demanded his father. "It's my first chance," explained the boy, "to test a pitch Sandy Koufax taught us at school Wednesday."

*　*　*

At a banquet honoring stars of the Los Angeles Dodgers' all-conquering baseball team, a pitcher noted for his smoking fast balls reminded the audience, "Behind every successful ballplayer stands a woman." Leo Durocher brought down the house by adding, "Yes, and she'd better be wearing a well-padded catcher's mitt."

*　*　*

Max Kase has a great collection of stories featuring the one and only Yogi Berra. One day the Yankee catcher (now a Met, heaven help him) was asked what he'd do if he found a million dollars. "If the fellow who lost it was poor, I'd return it," answered Yogi. Another time he showed up only fifteen minutes late for an appointment instead of his usual thirty. "See," he exulted to the friend who awaited him, "I'm earlier late!" Probably the best Berra anecdote is apocryphal. It concerns the day he saw a little girl falling out of a window of a house across the street. From sheer force of habit, Yogi rushed over like a gazelle and caught the youngster in his arms before she hit the pavement. But then—still out of force of habit—he threw her to second base!

BOXING

An interesting sidelight on the ethics of the prize ring turns up in a reminiscence of Kid McCoy, a popular champion of his day. McCoy was matched one night with a dangerous contender who happened to be stone deaf. McCoy only became aware of his opponent's affliction near the end of the third round—but then he acted promptly and without hesitation. He stepped back a pace and indicated in pantomime that the bell had sounded, marking the end of the round. Actually, it had not. "Thanks," muttered the deaf opponent, and dropped his hands—whereupon Kid McCoy immediately knocked him out.

❀   ❀   ❀

Murray Robinson tells about a time when John L. Sullivan, burly heavyweight champion, was downing a few beers in a Bowery saloon. A skinny little runt who had had a few too many staggered up to the champ and challenged him to a fight. John L. picked him three feet off the ground by the back of his coat, and grumbled, "Listen, you—if you hit me just once —and I find *out* about it . . ."

❀   ❀   ❀

James J. ("Gentleman Jim") Corbett, popular heavyweight who won the championship from John L. Sullivan in 1892, held the crown for four and a half years, when he was dethroned by Bob Fitzimmons, then was cut to ribbons in an attempted comeback against Jim Jeffries.

Later Corbett became a sportswriter, and distinguished himself by consistently picking the wrong man in fight after fight. "I'll bet you never picked a winner in your life," jeered a fellow scribe one evening. "Oh, yes, I did," answered Corbett very seriously. "The time I fought Jeffries, I picked him to win after the first round!"

* * *

A Los Angeles middleweight boxer was held up the other night and robbed of ten dollars. Asked why he surrendered his wallet without a murmur, he explained, "Shucks, I don't fight no more for them small purses."

* * *

Bernard Gimbel, the dry goods tycoon, won his title as Number One Fight Fan fairly and squarely at the famous Dempsey-Tunney "long count" heavyweight embroglio in Chicago. The victorious Tunney was protected after his victory by a phalanx of police, but somehow or other Bernie Gimbel wangled his way into the dressing room. "The next thing I knew," reports Tunney, "there was Bernie, fully clothed, including raincoat and hat, standing happily under the shower with me, talking a mile a minute about the fight."

* * *

Rocky Graziano, ex-middleweight champion, was asked in a TV interview recently, "Were you ever afraid of an opponent?" The great man pondered momentarily, then blurted, "Naw, I was too stupid!" Later Rocky insisted that he once sent Sugar Ray Robinson reeling to the mat. "He tripped over my body," explained Rocky.

* * *

A prizefighter, having heavy going in his first important fight, was floored in the second round by a punch right on the button. He looked from the mat at his trainer with glazed eyes. "Let the referee count," yelled the trainer. "Don't get up till eight." The fighter nodded and asked weakly, "What time is it now?"

* * *

Saddest prizefight story of the month comes from Red Smith, who overheard a battered, about-to-be-knocked-out preliminary fighter gasp to his manager between rounds one and two, "If I had that bum's right hook I'd moider him!"

* * *

In Philadelphia a strip-tease queen asked Cassius Clay what he did just before a big fight commenced. "I pray that everything will come off all right," declared Cassius. The strip-tease queen nodded sympathetically and giggled, "Me, too."

* * *

Out on his feet after eight rounds against an infinitely superior prizefighter, a glass-eyed gladiator was implored by his manager, "Don't give up now, Eddie boy! You got a no-hitter going!"

BRIDGE

In an amusing book called *The Mad World of Bridge,* Jack Olsen tells about a player who was determined to signal his partner that he violently disapproved of his opening lead of a heart. The usual way to indicate this disapproval is to put a very low heart on the trick—but this player's lowest heart was an eight—and he knew his partner would consider that card a direct invitation to continue in the same suit.

What to do, what to do? The resourceful player found a solution. He deliberately dropped his entire hand on the floor, and as he stooped to retrieve the scattered cards, he remarked clearly, "Don't wait for me. I'm playing a very low heart."

* * *

Both the Warrens and the Smithers were vulnerable in a hotly contested bridge game, when Mrs. Warren felt a hand grasping her leg.

She calmly put her cards face down on the table and announced, "If that's my husband, I bid four spades. If it's you, George Smithers, I'm going to punch you in the nose."

* * *

In Palm Beach, a socialite told bridge authority Charles Goren quite seriously, "My wife loves the game of bridge passionately. It gives her something to occupy her mind while she's talking!"

* * *

Mrs. Axelrod, reading the evening newspaper, called out to her husband in the TV room, "They found an old hen in Ardsley today with two hearts." "I know," called back Mr. Axelrod. "I played bridge with her Sunday night."

* * *

At the Hillcrest Country Club in Beverly Hills, the afternoon bridge games are taken very seriously. George Burns tells of one hand where he and his partner bid seven spades, vulnerable. One of their opponents had recently recovered from a heart attack. After some deliberation, he took out a nitroglycerin tablet, placed it under his tongue, looked at his cards again, and said with a deep sigh, "I double."

* * *

If you are playing bridge, what do you think the odds are against your picking up thirteen cards in the same suit? They are precisely 158,753,389,899 to 1! And in poker, the odds against your picking up a pat royal flush are 649,739 to 1!

*   *   *

Twenty ladies, engaged in an all-female duplicate bridge tournament, were making such a racket that just past midnight, a policeman called to warn them that a complaint had been called in. Later that night the still-seething hostess grumbled, "I wonder who was nasty enough to make that complaint." Confessed her husband complacently, "I did."

FISHING

A stranger stopped his car to watch the strange behavior of a fisherman on a riverbank. First he hooked a big pike, but threw it back. Then he landed a beautiful, large trout, but threw it back, too. Finally he reeled in a tiny perch, and with a grunt of satisfaction, deposited it in his bag.

The stranger couldn't resist calling out, "Why on earth did you throw those two big ones back and keep this tiny one?" The fisherman explained tersely, "Small frying pan."

*   *   *

A ten-year-old boy was instructed to take care of his kid sister while his parents went to town on business, so he allowed her to accompany him on a fishing expedition. "I'll never do that again," he told his ma that night. "I didn't catch a thing." Ma said, "I'm sure she'll be quiet next time if you just explain to her." "Oh, it wasn't the noise," explained the boy. "She ate the bait."

*   *   *

With nary one fish to show for his day with rod and reel, an amateur fisherman stopped at a market on the way home and thoughtfully bought a dozen trout. He then ordered the fish man to throw them to him one at a time. "When I tell my wife,"

he explained to the mystified fish man, "that I catch fish—
I catch them!"

* * *

An impatient angler had tried four varieties of bait without
a single bite. Finally, in disgust, he drew in his reel, and threw
a handful of coins into the stream. "Okay," he hollered, "go and
buy something you *do* like!"

* * *

An avid fisherman was dragged away from his beloved Minnesota lakes and taken on a tour of Europe by his determined
wife. Back home he announced that the summer had been
pretty much wasted, but that Venice at least had proved tol-
erable. "What attracted you most there?" he was asked. "The
Lido or St. Mark's?" "Neither," said the great traveler. "What
tickled me most was that I could sit in my hotel room and fish
right out of the window."

* * *

The late President Hoover in his book, *Fishing for Fun and
To Wash Your Soul*, declared that one of the surest ways to
make political forecasts is to determine how the candidates

feel about fishing. He gave as an example President Coolidge. "Coolidge," he said, "apparently had not fished before election. Being a fundamentalist in religion, economics, and fishing, he began his fish career for common trout with worms. Ten million fly fishermen at once evidenced disturbed minds. Then Mr. Coolidge took to a fly. He gave his Secret Service guards great excitement in dodging his backcast and rescuing flies from trees. There were many photographs. Soon after that he declared he did not choose to run again."

* * *

President Hoover had a copy of this "Fisherman's Prayer" framed and hung in his study at the Waldorf Towers:

God grant that I may fish
Until my dying day!
And when it comes to my last cast
I humbly pray,
When in God's landing net
I'm peacefully asleep,
That in His mercy I be judged
As good enough to keep.

FOOTBALL

From Coach Buck O'Neill of Hamilton College comes a delectable football story of a climactic encounter years ago between Hamilton and its arch-rival, Colgate, in which the Colgate eleven was making damaging and consistent gains through the center of the Hamilton line. O'Neill finally sent in a substitute, Miller, for the varsity center, Doyle—and things immediately took a decided turn for the better.

After the game, Coach O'Neill warmly praised Miller for his key role in Hamilton's last-minute victory. "Thank you for the kind words, Coach," replied Miller, "but I really don't deserve all the credit. You see, when I went in, Doyle never came out."

* * *

"I'm not saying that the football players at so-and-so University are semi-literates who get paid under the table," grumbled a man whose own team had just been shellacked by the squad under discussion. "I'm simply telling you that the first time that 240-pound fullback of theirs won his varsity letter, somebody had to read it to him."

*　*　*

After two big-name football coaches had been chivvied into resigning by alumni of a big Eastern university who considered anything but an all-winning season a disgrace, the late Herman Hickman agreed to take the job. "What are you going to do about those pesky alumni?" he was asked. "My intention," Hickman announced, "is to keep them sullen but not mutinous."

*　*　*

Held up in the middle of nowhere by a blizzard, Coach Hickman had to eat dinner in a run-down, fourth-rate roadside diner. So he only ate three orders of ham and eggs and four slabs of apple pie. As he brushed the crumbs from his ample paunch, he remarked contentedly, "Gentlemen, let's face it: There is no such thing as bad food!"

*　*　*

There's a very homely girl in Ann Arbor who always seeks seats directly behind the goal posts at football games. It's the only time, she explains, that she sees men running right at her.

*　*　*

"Our coach," boasted the second assistant manager of the varsity football team, "thinks of everything. Today he ordered waterproof pants for the entire squad."

"Waterproof pants!" echoed the assistant manager's date with surprise. "Why, the big babies!"

*　*　*

At Georgia Tech, they're still talking about a football game where the visiting team was clinging to a precarious lead, 14–13, with only a minute or two to go. The coach of the team in the lead sent in a new quarterback with instructions to run out the clock by use of simple running plays only. The new boy, however, had dreams of glory and when he spotted one of his backs apparently in the clear, he uncorked a forward pass in that general direction.

Out of nowhere the home team's speediest back flashed into the picture, intercepted the pass, and was off for paydirt —but to the amazement of the onlookers, the substitute quarterback who had made the pass overtook him and brought him down on the five-yard line. Seconds later, the final whistle blew.

Later that evening the Georgia Tech coach grumbled to the coach of the winners, "I'll never understand how that sub quarterback of yours ever overtook the fastest boy on our squad."

"It's simple," was the reply. "Your boy was running for a touchdown. Mine was running for his life."

* * *

Mrs. George Allen, wife of the famous pal of F.D.R., Truman, and Eisenhower, read in the paper about a modest Navy football coach who, following the first Navy victory over Army in years, quietly left the train in Baltimore on the way back to Annapolis so his team could get all the huzzahs when it arrived home.

Allen nodded and said, "That's exactly what I would have done under similar circumstances." "The heck it is," hooted the knowing Mrs. Allen. "You'd have put the *team* off at Baltimore!"

* * *

Duffy Dougherty, renowned college football coach, remembers a wire he received from thoughtful alumni on the eve of a game that would decide the Big Ten championship. It read, "We're 100 per cent behind you, Boy, win or draw."

Dougherty boasts of Michigan's most understanding wife. "When I get home," he relates, "she's put out my slippers, robe, and lots of hot water. She knows I hate to do dishes in cold water."

GOLF

Golf was a rugged pastime in the United States in those distant days before electric carts and portable bars took the spirit of adventure out of an eighteen-hole round.

Mark Twain, for instance, was once playing a twosome with no less a personage than Woodrow Wilson when the future President cut under a drive and sent a shower of turf in all directions. Striving to conceal his embarrassment, Mr. Wilson remarked heartily, "I hope you're enjoying our links here, Mark."

Twain spat the dirt out of his teeth, and answered diplomatically, "I'll say this for them, Woodrow. They're the best I ever tasted."

* * *

Two weekend golfers out Grand Rapids way had their morning ruined by a couple of slowpoke females playing in front of them. To cap the climax, they caught up with one of the females on the fourteenth fairway stretched out in the sun, arms behind her head, while her companion thrashed about in the deep rough. "Don't you think you might at least help your friend find her ball?" snarled one of the men.

"Oh, she's got her ball," said the female dawdler with the sweetest of smiles. "She's looking for her club."

* * *

There's an old girl at an Eastern club who's getting mighty hard of hearing as she nears her eightieth birthday. Her memory isn't so good either—especially when she's toting up her score. Nevertheless, she negotiates eighteen holes every blessed morning.

On the ninth green, recently, her caddie said, "I guess I can put you down for a ten on that hole."

"What's that you said?" she demanded. "Speak a little louder, please—and make that a seven!"

*   *   *

It was after 9 P.M. when Matt Coggins arrived home from the golf club, listing slightly to port, but he had an airtight alibi. "The guy I was playing in the semi-finals of the Class C Tournament," he told his wife, "dropped dead on the eleventh hole. From then on it was hit the ball, drag my opponent, hit the ball, drag my opponent, all the way back!"

*   *   *

Bob Hope overheard two sunbaked old biddies at the nineteenth hole discourse as follows: "Your husband seems to be scoring better now that he has a new stance." "That's not a new stance. That's a new husband."

*   *   *

Near the end of a tense golf match, one of the contestants, very temperamental, was thrown off his game when his caddie developed a severe attack of hiccoughs. On the seventeenth hole, he sliced his drive clean out of bounds, and growled fiercely at the caddie, "That was on account of you and your blank blank hiccoughs." "But I didn't hiccough then, sir," protested the caddie. "That's just the point," screamed the player. "I had ALLOWED for it!"

*   *   *

Morey Amsterdam tells about the first time two pinochle addicts attempted a round of golf. Mr. L. shot the first hole in 47, nosing out Mr. G. by two strokes. As they approached the second tee, Mr. L. mused, "You know something, Mac, this golf has interesting possibilities. What do you say we play for a nickel a hundred?"

*   *   *

"I picked up a golfing companion at the first tee," reported a West Florida vacationist to his wife, "but he was so bad he even lost his ball in the washer."

*   *   *

Poem for the golfing season penned by St. Paul's well-loved
Ben Ridder:
> The minister took seven putts upon one green
> And uttered not a word profane.
> But where he spat, ere exiting the scene,
> No blade of grass will ever grow again.

* * *

Slammin' Sammy Snead tells of one temperamental golfer
who hit four balls in succession into a pond on a three-par water hole. Enraged, he threw his bag of clubs into the pond,
too, and stamped off to the locker room where he set fire to his
clothes and slashed his wrists. Anxious friends summoned an
ambulance. As he was being carried out to it on a stretcher
he spotted old Horace, a member of his golf foursome, watching the proceedings. "Hey, Horace," he croaked weakly, "what
time do we tee off tomorrow?"

* * *

A golf foursome was playing on a course where the first three
holes parallel an interstate highway. As the foursome trudged
down the third fairway, a limousine drove along the road, and

stopped abruptly. Out hopped a beautiful girl in full wedding array. "Horace! Horace!" she sobbed, throwing her arms around one of the players. "Why have you left me waiting at the church?" "Now, now, Natalie," he said sternly. "Remember! I said *if it rained!*"

* * *

An avid golf enthusiast, anxious to get out to the links as quickly as possible, joined a funeral procession, whizzed through a succession of red lights, and eventually turned off into a side street. A motorcycle cop was right behind him, however. "No soap, buddy," said the unfeeling voice of the law. "Back in line! I saw you join that funeral procession. Now stay in it."

The poor golfer ended up at the cemetery, where the cop made him remain for the entire service.

* * *

"Why don't you play golf with Lew any more?" asked a wife one evening. "Hmph," snorted her husband. "Would you play with a sneak who puts down the wrong score and moves his ball when you aren't looking?" "I certainly would not," asserted the wife. "Well," said the husband, turning back to his paper, "neither will Lew."

* * *

Nat Wartels, a two-handicap golfer, stopped in at a sporting goods store just off Times Square and bought a dozen golf balls. "Shall I wrap them up?" asked the clerk. "Don't bother," said Wartels. "I'll just drive them home."

* * *

In the locker room, golfer Arnold Palmer told about a twosome involving the town's leading priest and rabbi. The priest made a little silent prayer before each putt and began sinking them from all corners of the greens. Obviously shaken, the rabbi said, half-jokingly, "If you taught me to say that little prayer, do you think my putts would start dropping, too?" "Not a chance," the priest assured him. "Why not?" demanded the rabbi. "Because," said the priest, "you're a terrible putter."

*   *   *

A golf neophyte teed his ball for the fifth time, swung violently, and watched with jubilation as a small object whirled away at a 45-degree angle.

"I got that ball off at last," he chortled.

"Mister," sighed the caddie, "that's your wristwatch."

7. *God Bless America!*

COMMUTERS

A commuter, anxious to catch his train, hailed a farmer standing at the edge of the road, "Is it okay with you, pop, if I take a shortcut across your field? I got to catch the 8:45."

"Go ahead, young feller," replied the farmer, "but if my new bull sees you, you'll catch the 8:15."

* * *

Henry Albritson is a dapper, law-abiding citizen of Mount Kisco with a deceivingly bland manner. Aboard a wretched commuter local one morning, a burly stranger squeezed in next to Mr. Albritson in a "non-smoking" coach, lit a foul-smelling stogie, and asked condescendingly, "My smoking won't bother you, will it?"

"Not at all," Mr. Albritson assured him, "so long as my getting sick won't bother you."

* * *

A wealthy commuter in Westchester was showing a Japanese visitor his estate, and saved for the *pièce de résistance* a brand new Japanese garden he just had installed. The Japanese visitor was properly impressed. "It's marvelous," he exclaimed. "If we only had something like it in Japan!"

* * *

There's a man in the Chicago Weather Bureau named Charles Fairskies! Furthermore, Mr. Fairskies received this message recently from a suburbanite in Glencoe: "Dear Mr. Fairskies: I thought you'd like to know that I have just shoveled eleven inches of Partly Cloudy off my driveway."

* * *

A new resident in a New England town was invited to join the volunteer fire brigade. "I'll do it," said the newcomer reluctantly, "but I must warn you that I'm not as young as I used to be, and I don't expect I'll be much good climbing up a ladder." "Don't let that worry you," the chief assured him. "Nine time out of ten, by the time we get there, there's nothing to lean a ladder against."

* * *

One midsummer morning a commuter announced to his wife at breakfast, "It's too nice a day to go to the office."

"Good," said the wife, "but don't think you're going to play golf. There are a lot of things that need doing around the house."

"Golf was the farthest thing from my mind," protested the husband. "Now would you mind passing the putter?"

* * *

Item from the obituary column of a Westchester gazette: "Hammond Wilson of North White Plains was accidentally killed yesterday when a bullet ricocheted while he was endeavoring to shoot a rabbit in his vegetable patch. Surviving are his wife, four children, and one rabbit."

* * *

At a country auction, Mrs. Peggy Weidman won a rare old handblown whiskey bottle with a bid of twenty-two dollars. An old farmer had watched her bidding with mounting disbelief. Now, as her bottle was delivered to her, he leaned over to take a closer look at it. "Gosh a'mighty," he gasped to his wife. "It's *empty!*"

* * *

Mrs. Heimerdinger had a dim opinion of the way her neighbor, Mrs. Nussbaum, kept house. "I'll tell you what a mess her place is in," reported Mrs. Heimerdinger to bridge cronies with obvious relish. "While I was having a cup of coffee with her yesterday afternoon, her telephone rang—and she couldn't find it!"

* * *

A bright young Madison Avenue man looked in vain for a seat on the crowded 5:15 train, then pushed his way to the last car and called out, "This car has developed a flat wheel and will be detached from the train. Please move up to cars ahead."

With nasty remarks about the railroad, the disgusted occupants of the car cleared out and the bright young man, very satisfied with himself, sat down, opened his newspaper, and waited—and waited.

Finally a conductor appeared. "You were the clever gent who announced this car wasn't going?" he inquired. "Yep," nodded the clever one. "Well," said the conductor, "it isn't. You were so convincing they just uncoupled the car."

* * *

Two bald-headed husbands, in their early fifties, were exchanging confidences at their country club. "As usual," sighed one, "I came home pooped from the office last night—and as usual my wife wanted to go to the movies or the theatre. I reminded her that we were plagued with a jurisdictional strike, that our new fall line was giving us trouble, and that I was far too exhausted to go chasing around all evening."

The other husband nodded sympathetically, then asked, "And how was the show?"

DRIVERS, MALE AND OTHERWISE

A Pennsylvania legislator, with time hanging heavy on his hands in Harrisburg one evening, came upon a disintegrating, dog-eared pamphlet published just after the turn of the century that set him up for hours. It had been published by a no-doubt worthy outfit that called itself the Farmers' Anti-

Automobile Society, and recommended several rules that motorists on rural roads would do well to follow.

One rule suggested that a car owner, propelling his vehicle after dark, should stop every mile, send up a warning rocket, and then wait for ten minutes to make certain that the road ahead was clear before advancing.

"If a horse is unwilling to pass an automobile," the Society declared on another page, "the driver should take the machine apart as rapidly as possible and conceal the parts in the bushes."

(Just as I finished getting this anecdote down on paper, author Truman Capote came tootling up to our house in a Jaguar geared to do 150 miles an hour. What a sixty years these have been!)

* * *

A speeding car came to a screeching halt at a busy crossroad, barely avoiding a little old lady who, having a green light in her favor, was ambling quietly from one side of the avenue to the other. The old lady didn't seem either frightened or annoyed. She merely smiled at the driver, and pointed to a pair of baby shoes suspended from his rear-view mirror. "Young man," she demanded, "why don't you put your shoes back on?"

* * *

An arthritic mountaineer came into a small and totally unexpected inheritance and decided to buy a second-hand jalopy to ease the burden of his declining years. The cheapest he could find in all Missouri was $235, but the dealer reminded him, "You get five good tires thrown in free; they haven't gone more'n forty thousand miles." "Forget the tires," said the mountaineer. "I don't want any on my car. When I'm auto riding I want to know it."

* * *

A slick college senior, out with his steady in his roadster, headed for the side of the turnpike the minute they were beyond the city limits. "But, Jerry," she protested, "why stop here where everybody will see us? There are so many nicer places down the road a way." "Here we stay," said the swain firmly. "I believe in love at first site."

* * *

An automobile manufacturer confided to some drinking companions in Detroit that his engineers have built a car that can go ninety miles an hour and come to a dead stop in exactly ten feet.

"When are you going to put it on the market?" he was asked.

"We're waiting," explained the manufacturer carefully, "until we can figure out a way to keep the driver from going through the windshield."

* * *

The day after a sedate schoolteacher bought a second-hand sedan she drove it back to the dealer's yard.

"What's wrong?" asked the dealer anxiously.

"Nothing at all," said the teacher sweetly. "I just want to return these things for the dear little old lady you told me owned the car before you sold it to me. She left this plug of tobacco in the glove compartment, and this half-empty bottle of gin under the seat."

* * *

A mortified lady motorist was hauled before a village justice of the peace by a motorcycle cop who announced, "Judging by the way this here woman handles a car in traffic, I don't think she can see very well."

The justice didn't look too surprised. "We'll just give her the little old eye test," he said. "Lady, please read the third line of that chart on the wall."

"Without hesitation, the lady spelled out, "Y-M-P-J-C."

"Perfect," approved the justice. "Now let's hear the line at the very bottom."

"I would like to purchase," read the lady, "some tickets for the Policeman's Pageant and Field Day."

"Better still," boomed the justice of the peace. "How many?"

Short Circuits

"What mileage you can get out of these new economy model cars," boasted a young man just back from his honeymoon trip. "My bride and I had to stop at more gas stations than our car did!"

Val Carmichael writes that his motoring problems have been miraculously reduced since he found a way to stop his wife from being a back-seat driver. He stuffed her into the trunk.

Jack Paar is heartily in favor of shorter taxicabs. "When they knock you down," he explains, "they don't stay on you so long."

An inquisitive little girl asked her mother, "What happens to an automobile when it gets too old and banged up to run?" Mother answered grimly, "Somebody sells it to your father."

Nothing improves your driving, points out Madelaine Hurlock, like being followed by a policeman.

In Kentucky, a harassed motorist kept looking in his rearview mirror, wondering why a light truck was tailing him so persistently. He finally alighted to discover that the truck had no driver, and had been hooked to his rear bumper since he had backed into a parking space a hundred miles away in Cincinnati.

"What I hate most about women drivers," explained Harvardite Mike Frith, "is how they turn out to be men after you've criticized their driving to your girl friend."

Joyce Mizzari defines "perambulator" as last year's fun on wheels.

A complete biography in six words: GIN, SPIN, DASH, CRASH, NURSE, HEARSE.

Art Carney took his car into a Westchester garage for a tune-up and was handed a bill for $120. "Hey," protested Carney, "who did this tune-up? Leonard Bernstein?"

Old Man Babcock was inching his dilapidated jalopy down Main Street when a traffic officer signaled him to halt. "Don't worry, pop," said the officer reassuringly. "I just want to see what it feels like to put my foot on a running board again."

And let us not overlook the story of the woman who told her husband, "Be an angel and let me drive." He did—and he is.

* * *

From upstate New York comes the tale of the motorist who was tootling merrily westward on the Thruway. When he passed a sign reading "Twenty Miles to Buffalo," he was smiling happily. He was still in the pink when he flashed by the sign reading "Ten Miles to Buffalo." Only minutes later, however, he was discovered sitting dazed and battered, holding his head, at the roadside, his shiny new automobile a sorry wreck. "What happened?" demanded the first state trooper to arrive upon the scene. "I didn't heed that last sign," mourned the wounded motorist. "I covered the ten miles—and the damn buffalo rammed right into me."

* * *

Mrs. Wimpfheimer was ambling unconcernedly in her new convertible in the left-hand lane of a parkway, when, without warning, she suddenly made a sharp right turn and collided with another car.

"Blank, blank, blank!" roared the other driver. "Why the blank, blank didn't you signal?"

"Don't be absurd," countered Mrs. Wimpfheimer loftily, "I ALWAYS turn here."

* * *

A workman who was extremely fond of garlic boarded a bus in a Southern city, and plumped himself down next to a very haughty, sour-faced lady. She immediately became aware of the garlic fragrance, and observed icily, "It's a wonder they don't run a special bus for persons who insist on eating garlic." The workman answered cheerily, "They do, lady. You're on the wrong bus."

* * *

A motorcycle cop stopped a driver who was hurtling up the West Side Drive of Manhattan at breakneck speed, and gave him a ticket. "I clocked you doing seventy-five miles an hour," said the cop grimly. The driver nodded cheerfully, then asked, "Couldn't you make it ninety an hour, officer? I'm trying to sell this car."

* * *

Traffic officer (to pedestrian just bowled over by a hit-and-run driver): "Did you get that driver's number?"

Pedestrian: "No, but I'd recognize my wife's laugh anywhere."

* * *

A traffic cop flagged a lady doing eighty-five on a crowded thruway and dodging from lane to lane. He examined her license and returned it with this quizzical observation:

"Your license seems to be valid, Madam. Now would you mind telling me how the heck you got it?"

* * *

A foreign roadster rounded a corner on two wheels, knocked down a policeman and four pedestrians, and finally wrapped itself around a telephone pole. A sweet young thing climbed out of the wreckage. "Yippee!" she cried. "That's what I call a kiss!"

* * *

A New York traffic cop's attention was drawn to a lady motorist who was calmly driving down the wrong side of an avenue. He stopped her and inquired testily, "Don't you know what that white line in the middle of the avenue is for?"

The lady considered carefully, then hazarded, "Bicycles?"

* * *

A motorist paused at a roadside snack bar and ordered coffee and doughnuts. A few moments after he had been served, he called over the pleasant-faced young woman in charge and said, "I can tell you something about yourself. You have a small son who plays in the kitchen with a toy automobile."

"You're absolutely right," gasped the young woman. "You must be a mind reader."

"No, no," insisted the motorist. "Just put me down as the fellow you served a toy tire for a chocolate doughnut."

* * *

A New Yorker drove all the way to California without incident, but once within the city limits of Los Angeles, found himself hopelessly confused in the complex of overpasses, underpasses, and clover leafs of the Freeway system. Finally he pulled up alongside a man who had a lady and four children in the car with him.

"Mister," implored the New Yorker, "can you help me out? I've been trying to get to the Civic Center for six hours and I wind up at this spot every time."

"You're asking the wrong man, brother," replied the man with the lady and the four children. "I ain't even got home from my honeymoon."

* * *

A San Diego matron, driving a spanking new Mustang, turned too sharply at an intersection, reports Neil Morgan, and neatly ran over the left foot of a cop directing traffic. A shrill plea from his whistle brought her to a stop. Helpfully, she flipped into reverse and backed toward the officer.

"I knew it!" he roared in anguish. "Now you got the other one!"

*　*　*

A co-ed reported to police that she had been struck by a ship in the middle of a state highway. She was driving innocently along, it seems, when a speedboat broke loose from its trailer.

*　*　*

Heard about the eager young bridegroom who came home and found his wife knitting tiny things—seat covers for their Volkswagen?

*　*　*

A taxi driver in Chicago got his comeuppance from a habitual lady back-seat driver. "Haven't you got more sense than to leave that window open?" she scolded. "It's blowing my husband's hair too much."

"How far can a little wind blow a man's hair?" scoffed the driver.

"The last little bit," she replied, "blew it about three miles."

*　*　*

Bob Campbell overheard a Brentwood beldame gurgle happily, "I had my first driving lesson today. I think I did very well, too—but, my goodness, that ignition key is tricky."

*　*　*

A Mrs. Miller, of Des Moines, explained how her car had swerved off the road in the dark:

"I was following the white line, and the white line turned out to be a skunk."

*　*　*

A La Jolla pedestrian couldn't duck fast enough, and was struck amidships by a big, mangy dog who came loping over the crest of a hill and catapulted him into a ditch. He barely had arisen and started to dust himself off when a girl in a miniature foreign sports car hove into view and knocked him down again.

"The dog didn't hurt me a bit," he reported later, "but that tin can tied to his tail darn near killed me."

*　*　*

Cornelia Otis Skinner had a nerve-wracking experience when she saw a little boy stroll into the path of a convertible driven by one of the young ladies in her company.

She screamed, snatched him up under her arm, and jumped with him to safety on the curbstone.

He turned out to be a midget of forty, smoking a pipe, and with a quaint and extensive vocabulary.

*　*　*

A Wall Street broker was interrupted in the pursuit of his duties by a phone call from his eight-year-old son.

"Mama ran over my bicycle when she was backing her car out of the garage this morning," wailed the boy.

The unsympathetic father replied, "How many times have I warned you not to leave your bicycle in the middle of the front lawn?"

*　*　*

Albuquerque, New Mexico, is generally regarded as a respectable, law-abiding community, but the other day when a police officer asked Rosemary Collins to show her driver's license after a traffic violation the culprit only laughed at him. Nor was there a thing he could do about it. Rosemary had climbed into a car, and put it out of gear. The car then rolled downhill into another car—a police lieutenant's in the bargain. Rosemary was two years old.

FARMERS

A stingy old lady on an upstate farm hired a new hand, and followed him all the first day to make sure he didn't waste a moment. When dinner time came round, he noted with disgust that the entire bill of fare consisted of a couple of very thin slices of meat loaf, bread, tea, and a very small spot of honey in the center of the table on a big platter.

"I see, Ma'am," observed the new hand coldly, "that you keep a bee."

* * *

Squire Klopfer was constantly annoyed by motorists who scooted past his front porch at an average speed of eighty miles an hour. The wily squire put a stop to that nonsense with a large sign that has slowed drivers down to a very slow crawl. The sign proclaims, "Please proceed with care. Nudist camp crossing just ahead."

* * *

Two gabby matrons in a New England town were gossiping endlessly on a party-line telephone when they were suddenly interrupted by the unmistakable sound of a receiver being slammed down on the hook. "Well, how do you like that?" snorted one of the talkers indignantly. "Somebody's hung up on us!"

* * *

Harry Golden tells about the Carolina farmer who sold a Yankee an old mule. "What's the mule's name?" asked the Yankee.

"I don't know his name," admitted the farmer, "but I call him Bill."

* * *

Little Oswald toddled out to a field his Pa was plowing to report, "There's a strange man at the house. I dunno what he wants."

"Son," the father told him, "if it's the landlord, he wants his rent. If it's the banker, he's come to foreclose the mortgage. And if he's a traveling salesman, you run home fast as your legs will carry you—and sit in your maw's lap till I get there!"

* * *

Two sour-visaged farmers liked to complain about conditions together. "Never did see hay grow so short as mine this summer," sighed one. "You think yours is short," scoffed the other. "I had to lather mine to mow it."

* * *

The noted minister, Dr. Harry Emerson Fosdick, summering in Maine, recalled a romantic interlude that occurred there a few years back. The local blacksmith, only five feet one for all his muscles of steel, fell in love with a girl who towered fully a foot above him. Diffident for months, he proposed marriage to her one night in a sudden burst of courage, and was promptly accepted. He climbed on top of his anvil and kissed the girl rapturously. Hours later, walking home through a pasture, he asked if he might kiss her again. "No," she decided. "Let's not overdo our sparking."

"Shucks," said the disappointed blacksmith. "If I can't kiss you no more, I might as well stop lugging this anvil."

* * *

A farmer took a train for his very first visit to New York. He alighted at Grand Central and was led through an underground passage to the Roosevelt Hotel. He had dinner in the Grill, and then relaxed in the newsreel theatre in the Terminal. The next day he bought gifts for the family in Grand Central shops and took a train back to the sticks.

"Well, Paw," asked his wife, "how did you like New York?"

"It was wonderful," enthused Paw, "but why didn't somebody tell me it had a roof over it?"

* * *

In Wappingers Falls, a farmer was trying to sell a broken-down old horse to a city fellow. After walking him slowly around a field, he remarked, "Got a handsome coat, hasn't he?"

The city fellow listened to the old horse breathe for a moment, then replied, "I like his coat all right—but not his pants."

* * *

You've heard a lot about farmers' beautiful daughters, but Squire Kislik was one farmer who had himself a beautiful wife. When she went home to visit her parents, all the joy departed from his life, and when she finally wired she'd be home on the 5:50, he hitched up his bay stallion, and set out to fetch her at the station in a fever of anticipation.

The stallion had been cooped up in his stall for days and was rarin' to go. He wheeled into the turnpike at fifty an hour, and began picking up from there. Farmer Kislik turned white with fear, and when they just missed ramming into Deacon Lapolla's Stanley Steamer, he finally hollered to the stallion:

"You gol durn fool! Who do you think got that telegram? You or me?"

* * *

The Guggenheim herd in Sands Point includes one cow who's mighty hoity-toity. "Go ahead," she was heard mooing to the dairyman one evening. "Milk me! See if I give a dram!"

*　*　*

The proprietor of a small village drugstore was called out one sleepy summer morning, leaving the establishment temporarily under the sole management of a very old, and very uneducated porter. "Just answer the phone if it rings, Jim," instructed the proprietor.

The phone rang. "Hello," said the porter.

"Do you have streptomycin and aureomycin?" asked a voice at the other end. The porter scratched his head, then said, "Ma'am, when I said 'Hello' I told you everything I know!"

*　*　*

A farmer's wife went stark raving mad one morning. As she was being led away by attendants from the nearest asylum her husband scratched his head in perplexity and muttered, "I'm danged if I kin figger what's gotten into the old girl. She ain't bin out of this kitchen in thutty-two years!"

*　*　*

George Heister writes about the rancher who couldn't keep his hands off his beautiful young wife. Finally had to fire every one of them.

*　*　*

In Kansas, they seem to relish the story of a small-town wife who accompanied her husband to Topeka for a cattlemen's convention. She wore a homemade blouse of which she was inordinately proud, for on it she had embroidered every cattle brand she knew.

A veteran cattleman watched her with something akin to awe as she approached the registration desk. Then he cackled loudly to a friend, "Get a load of that critter, Tom! She's sure changed hands a lot, hasn't she?"

*　*　*

Why do rich society ladies have so many more neuroses and mental disturbances than farmers' wives? The following story, contributed by Jim Donaldson, may contain the key:

Mrs. Smith had raised nine children on a Michigan farm, fed them and the farmhands, done all her housework, and helped with outdoor chores. She'd never been ill a day in her life. A doctor implored her to reveal her secret.

"I constantly see young women," the doctor said, "who have one or two children, and whose homes are full of gadgets to lighten work, but who suffer from nervous exhaustion or psychosomatic aches and pains. How is it that you managed to go through all these years and never have a nervous breakdown?"

"You know, Doctor," said the hardworking woman, wistfully, "I've always wanted to have a nervous breakdown. But every time I was about to get around to it, it was time to fix somebody a meal."

GARDENS ARE TO NAP IN

It's just twelve years since I bought a house in the country and I confess that when we moved in I couldn't tell an oak tree from a willow. Now, of course, I can—just! A rose was a rose was a rose to Gertrude Stein, but roses aren't always roses to me. I call them as I see them. And sometimes I see them as geraniums.

I never have known anything about gardening and probably I never will—nor am I ashamed of the fact. I am just an underprivileged city boy in that respect. Lawns, trees, flowers, hedges—they're all beautiful and I love them—so long as there's somebody else around to take care of them. For me, gardens are to nap in.

In our household, the "somebody else" is a rare Scottish gentleman who is just about perfect in his job. Before he came with us an Army colonel with whom he had been associated for a decade called me on the phone. "I want to tell you three

things about Mac," said he. "First: he's the greatest gardener I
ever met. Second: he's the kind of manager we dream of finding in the Army. You can go off on a two-year trip publishing
and lecturing to your heart's content and when you get home
you'll find everything just the way you left it—or better. Third
—and most important of all—if Mac wants to do things one way
in the garden and you want to do them in another—SAVE
YOUR BREATH."

It's all worked out in dreamy fashion. Not only do I never
want to do things in the garden in another way than Mac's; I
don't *know* any other way. So we agree perfectly. My only
contribution came when I discovered that rabbits and squirrels
were eating five out of every six ears of corn we were growing
and that those we did manage to smuggle to the dinner table
were averaging us about two dollars apiece. "I've thought of a
new method of getting corn," I told Mac—who registered polite disbelief. "It's called the A&P system," I continued. Mac
approved at once. He definitely does not like rabbits and squirrels. In the space we formerly grew corn we now play bad-
minton. It's a big saving.

A noted columnist in his day who *did* cultivate a garden was
Franklin P. Adams (remember his caustic wit on that classic
radio program, "Information Please"?). F.P.A. concentrated

on raising peonies—probably just so that he could pun, "If you take care of the peonies, the dahlias will take care of themselves."

Another flower grower in the metropolitan area always bought her seeds at a great big department store south of Forty-second Street. One day she came charging into that store's complaint department seething with rage. It seems that a few months previous she had buried her husband and purchased several packages of carnation seeds with which to decorate his grave. Then she flew off to Paris to pull herself together.

The day after her return, she visited her husband's grave. It was decorated all right—but not with carnations. It was one full bed of ripe rhubarb.

"I don't know what she was screaming so about," protested the manager of the department store's complaint department later. "We were perfectly willing to refund the price of the seeds."

The most avid—and horrifyingly articulate amateur gardener I know boards my train one station down the line every summer weekday morning. According to him, he has such a green thumb they asked him to lead the St. Patrick's Day parade this year. When he isn't snipping away at his plants, he is supervising the pruning and spraying of his trees. His favorite time for spraying seems to be when his wife is serving drinks to guests in the garden. I can testify personally that tree-spray-on-the-rocks will never replace the martini.

To distract my friend one day I told him about the unfortunate tree surgeon who fell out of his patient, but he didn't think this was funny, having fallen out of a tree himself only an hour before. He soon rallied, however, threw a copy of Rachel Carson's *Silent Spring* angrily aside, and proposed, "Let us spray."

The most fashionable gardener I know is having a problem this year with her front lawn. "The trouble with grass," she complains, "is that it comes in only one color."

There are three standard, made-to-order garden jokes that sprout every spring as regularly as the trees and flowers.

Number One is about the gardener who did nothing but

hoe, hoe, hoe—and if you think that's funny, you've never worked in a garden yourself.

Number Two cites the suburbanite whose garden was such a success one year that his neighbor's chickens won first prize at the local poultry show.

And Number Three reports the cautionary message that a cynical seedsman has imprinted on the back of every packet he sells: "Don't throw away this packet when it's empty and you have finished planting your garden. Probably it will be just the right size for storing your crop."

A story *I* like to tell concerns a lonely little widow in Los Angeles who had one pleasure left in life: every morning a gentleman left a rose for her. "It's from his garden," she explained to a visitor one day. "Here he comes now." Sure enough, the gentleman handed her a beauty. "I grew this one just for you," he said with a gallant bow.

The visitor left with the donor of the rose, who then explained sheepishly, "I've never been in a garden in my life. I buy her a rose in the florist shop across the street every morning. It gives her such a happy look for a few moments."

And now I'm off to a garden myself. Madison Square Garden.

HILLBILLIES

Bob Burns loved telling stories about an uncle and aunt who picked on each other continuously for forty years. Uncle was an old gadabout; Aunt was a homebody. Uncle had one particularly hectic week: on Monday night he went to a lodge meeting; Tuesday night to a Salvation Army rally; Wednesday night to a church meeting; Thursday night to a YMCA lecture. On Friday night, his wife saw him reach for his celluloid collar and demanded tartly, "Where you headed this evening, playboy?"

*   *   *

A mountain lad was very late for school one morning, but his excuse was deemed adequate. "Maw woke up Paw at three in the morning," he explained, "because she heard a noise in the hen house. Paw grabbed his shotgun and ran outside. He pointed it at the hen house and waited for something to happen. Something happened, all right. Our old hound dog came up behind Paw with his cold nose, and we've been cleaning chickens ever since."

*   *   *

The villagers in a remote Arkansas community got their best laugh in ten years when a damyankee erected a tool shed and hired a night watchman to guard the tools and supplies therein. "As though," they jeered, "any sane man in these hills would steal anything to work with!"

*   *   *

A revenue agent, hot on the trail of a West Virginia whiskey still, suddenly heard a shot, and something grazed his left sleeve. Undaunted, the agent continued forward, whereupon a second shot whistled through his coattails. When a third bullet, neatly puncturing his slouch hat, still failed to halt him, a voice from the woods sounded.

"One more step, mister," it warned grimly, "and I begin takin' aim!"

*   *   *

An itinerant preacher in the Blue Ridge Mountains shook an old reprobate and thundered, "Are you ready for the Judgment Day?" "Mebbe yes, mebbe no," said the old rep cagily. "When's it coming?" "It might come this very day," warned the preacher. "Then again, it might come tomorrow."

By this time the old reprobate was registering genuine concern. "Don't tell my old woman," he begged. "She'd want to go both days."

*   *   *

After the biggest hillbilly wedding the Blue Ridge Mountains region had celebrated since the Hatfield-McCoy feud, one stalwart admitted to the bride's father, "I didn't like the way that bridegroom dragged himself to the altar. He acted like he had lead in his pants." The bride's father answered grimly, "He did!"

*   *   *

A fable from the North Carolina back country: The revenue agents found a number of trails leading into the deep forest. Reinforcements were brought up, and several agents were put on each trail. At a given signal, they all crept forward. Miles into the woods they discovered that all trails converged on one little cabin, where a bearded man sat working. Was he making moonshine whiskey? Not at all. He was building a better mousetrap.

*   *   *

Help was mighty tough to come by in an out-of-the-way Missouri town, and "Pop" Miller, who ran the biggest—in fact, the only—motel thereabouts was reluctant to part with his night clerk, despite the fact that said clerk was a hopeless kleptomaniac.

"Pop" Miller finally solved his problem. Over the desk in the lobby he hung this sign: "Leave your valuables with our night clerk. He'll get them anyway."

*   *   *

A Kentucky backwoods lad took unto himself a wife and off they went to Louisville for their honeymoon. When they got back home, a friend told the bridegroom, "We hear you treated your bride awfully good."

"Well, sir," admitted the bridegroom, "the first day I was pretty tough with her, but after that I couldn't look her in the face for a week. By then, I could see a little out of one eye."

DRINKERS

Two darling old ladies were having lunch in the dining room of a residential hotel. "I've forgotten the name of it," one of them told the waitress, "but we both want one of those appetizers my nephew bought me here last week. In a little glass you get a green olive, covered by a perfectly delightful clear white sauce."

* * *

A young bride in distress called her father and wailed, "I'm afraid I've married a drinking man. All last night Oscar kept mumbling in his sleep, 'No, Sidney, no. I don't care if it's free; not one more drink for me.'"

Interrupted the father wistfully, "Did Oscar happen to mention any address?"

* * *

The bride-of-a-month tittered nervously as she passed the cocktails at the first formal dinner party she hosted. "I do hope these martinis will hit the spot," she quavered. "We ran out of olives, so I had to pour a spoonful of olive oil into each glass."

* * *

Mr. Sneedle, wont to imbibe at least four martinis with every lunch, was not too spry when he wobbled back to his office. His secretary found a way of protecting him, however. She told callers sweetly, "Can Mr. Sneedle call you back later? He's still out from lunch."

* * *

Two inebriated gents were weaving their way down a railroad track. "Golly," complained one, "this is a long flight of steps." "I don't mind the steps so much," countered the other. "It's the low railings that get me."

* * *

The town drunk tried to get to bed without disturbing his wife, but heard her clomping downstairs the moment he shut the door. He made a dive for the library, reached for a book, and was sitting under the lamp when his wife collared him. "Hello, darling," he mumbled a bit indistinctly. "I thought I'd catch up a bit on my reading tonight."

"You did, did you?" she replied grimly. "Well, you just shut that valise and come up to bed."

* * *

An imaginative bartender in Tel Aviv has invented a new cocktail he calls a Little David. Imbibe two and you goliath down.

* * *

An attendant in the Manhattan D.A.'s office recalls a wild night during Prohibition days when twenty-five of the town's top bootleggers were rounded up in a surprise raid. As they were being arraigned, the judge asked each one his occupation. The first twenty-four promptly replied, "Real estate broker." The twenty-fifth stanchly declared, "Your Honor, I'm a bootlegger."

Surprised, the judge permitted himself a laugh and inquired, "How's business?" The answer was, "It would be better if there weren't so darn many real estate brokers around."

* * *

W. C. Fields, never known as a teetotaler, was suffering from a really stupendous hangover one morning at the Paramount lot. "Let me fix you a Bromo Seltzer," suggested his director. "Oh, no, not that," groaned Fields. "I couldn't stand the racket."

* * *

A big fire in a Midwestern brewery caused a temporary beer shortage in those parts, and every bar and grill had to go on a quota. The proprietor of one roadside retreat called to plead for an additional shipment "toot sweet." "It's an emergency," he declared. "But you've had your quota for the week," the brewery superintendent pointed out. "I know I have," answered the caller, "but what about my customers?"

* * *

Mike Connoly started off the new year by reporting, "I slept like a log last night. I must have. I woke up in the fireplace."

* * *

Maybe you're not on the mailing list that has been receiving this touching *Ode to a Martini Drinker:*
Starkle, starkle, little twink
Who the deuce you are I think.
I'm not under what they call
The affluence of incohol.

I'm not as drunk as thinkle peep
I'm just a little slort of sheep.
Tee martoonis make a guy
Feel so dizzy, don't know why.
So pass the mixer and kill my fup,
I've all day sober to Sunday up.

*   *   *

Swifty Morgan, a statistician of great renown, looked up from the financial page and announced, "It says here that freight car loadings are going down, but that the sale of Scotch whiskey has gone up. This means only one thing: More people are getting loaded than freight cars!"

*   *   *

Two extremely intoxicated celebrants at a college reunion sought still another bottle to imbibe—and found one in the garage of the motel where they were registered. One took a long swig and gulped, "This is powerful stuff," and passed it to the other, saying, "Maybe you'll know what it is." The other sampled the liquid, and gasped, "Holy mackerel! You've been drinking *gasoline*." "I know that, stupid," grumbled the first, "but what kind—regular or high-test?"

      ✿   ✿   ✿

Gene Sherman was proceeding peacefully down Sunset Strip in Beverly Hills when he saw a gray-haired old lady of seventy-five or eighty peering intently into a doorway. As Sherman hesitated, she tapped his arm and quavered, "Is this place a restaurant or a saloon?" "It's a saloon, ma'am," Sherman warned her, "and one with a very unsavory reputation, too." "Oh, thank you, young man," said the old lady—and went in.

      ✿   ✿   ✿

Once upon a time there was a terrible, terrible week when Jackie Gleason didn't touch a single drop of liquor. Gleason's friend Toots Shor took this as a personal affront, but Gleason blamed it all on his doctor. "He's put me off the stuff for life," he explained sadly. "Foofel and poofel," scoffed Shor. "I'll send you to *my* doctor. He'll let you drink all you want."

The next day Geason was still on the wagon. "Didn't you go to see my doctor?" demanded Toots. "I went," nodded Gleason, "but I couldn't get in. The office was too crowded."

      ✿   ✿   ✿

A finicky wine connoisseur took unto himself a bride. "She was Wellesley '53," he explained to a fellow imbiber. "You'll recall that's a very fine year for women."

      ✿   ✿   ✿

A minister dropped into a strange barber shop for a quick shave and had the misfortune to choose a chair presided over by a barber who was suffering from an acute hangover. His breath nearly asphyxiated the poor minister, and then, to cap the climax, he took a huge nick out of the minister's chin. "You see," said the minister reproachfully, "what comes from drinking intoxicating liquor?" "Yep," agreed the barber cheerfully. "It sure makes the skin tender."

      ✿   ✿   ✿

From San Francisco comes the story of three Chinese gentlemen who stepped up to a local bar. The first one ordered a
Mai Tai sour, the second a Hoong Wong on the rocks. The
third, however, declared, "Nothing for me, thank you. I'm
pulling the rickshaw."

*   *   *

A great big grizzly bear wandered down from the woods
at Lake Louise, Canada, one afternoon and shambled into a
saloon. There a well-oiled patron exuberantly put his arms
around the bear and proclaimed, "Look at us, men!" The bear
was having no part of this, however. He picked up the patron
and very accurately threw him through the entranceway into
the street.

The drunken one picked himself up at length, and mumbled
disconsolately, "Isn't that just like a woman? Give her a fur
coat and she thinks she owns the world!"

INDIANS

We've all learned in our youth about the supposedly simple-
minded Indians who sold Manhattan Island for twenty-four
dollars and a lot of glass beads. Waste no sympathy on said
aborigines, counsels Don Russell in his *Book of the American
West*. "Those Indians," he asserts, "were somewhat in the same
position as the confidence man who sold the Brooklyn Bridge
for ten dollars. They didn't own Manhattan Island at all. They
chanced to be there for a weekend's fishing!" So it was Peter
Minuit and his fellow Dutchmen after all who were the ones
taken in by that famous transaction!

*   *   *

An old—very old—scout swears he once heard a forceful
squaw tell Sitting Bull, "Well, don't just sit there—do something!"

*   *   *

Big Chief Pokum's favorite squaw promised to make him a new bead necklace but when the time came for the annual conclave of the tribe, it wasn't finished. Chief Pokum expressed his disappointment in no uncertain terms, but his mate reminded him, "School teacher always tell me I be heap slow beader."

* * *

Two Indians were having their first look at water skiing. Asked one, "Why boat go so fast?" Answered the other, "Lunatic on string chase 'em."

* * *

From Phoenix comes the story of a wise old Indian chief who led his son to a tall hilltop and pointed to the densely populated valley below. "One day soon," prophesied the chief, "all this land will belong to the Indians again. White men all go to the moon."

TEXANS

Before she hit the jackpot as a novelist, a now-famous Texas lady applied for the job of school teacher in a sparsely settled county adjoining the one where she had been reared. The school board president was relaxing on his front porch. "I know your family, Miss," said the president. "Is it true that one of your cousins killed a man and your father bribed enough witnesses to save him from the chair?" "Yes, sir," admitted the applicant. "I'm not denying it."

"Is it also true," he continued, "that another of your cousins killed her husband and is now serving a term in the penitentiary?" "No, sir," blurted our heroine. "She's out! They sent her up for five years, but she got out in three for good behavior. But," she added, "with all those facts, I don't suppose you'll want me to teach in your system."

"Lady," he assured her, rising to his feet, "you're the very one we *do* want. You can't hold your head above nobody!"

*   *   *

A Texas billionaire indulged himself with a new whim this season. Back from a New York trip that included a visit to its teeming East Side tenement district, he constructed back of his twenty-eight-room ranch house a replica of a slum area block, complete with pushcarts, manholes, bagel and pizza parlors, fire hydrants, and assorted debris. "This is the latest thing up in Manhattan," he boasted to his friends. "They call it a stickball court."

*   *   *

The famous Lon Tinkle tells about a West Texas cattle raiser who was asked what he did between the time he alighted from his air-conditioned automobile and got into his air-conditioned ranch house. Replied the Texan, "I run like hell."

Dr. Tinkle also claims he ran into an effeminate stevedore in Galveston who refuses to unload anything but hairpins.

*   *   *

Colonel James Cokesbury Albright, the pride of Dallas, says that when it comes to gallantry, Texans cannot be beat. He cites as an example a rough old gaffer from the oil fields who was just preparing to dig into a succulent piece of roast pig at a barbecue when someone careened into him from behind and knocked his plate to the ground. In a rage he bellowed, "You hawg! You want all the space there is?" and then he perceived the offender was the dignified wife of his host. Without a second thought he amended his statement, "Lady hawg, that is, Ma'am."

*   *   *

While making a personal appearance in Tulsa, Art Linkletter was persuaded by a wildcatter to invest five thousand dollars in drilling a new oil well. Some weeks later he received this telegram: "Struck ketchup at 6000 feet. Drilled into hamburger stand abandoned during dust storm in early thirties. Estimate we need five thousand more to locate mustard. (Signed) Your Partner."

* * *

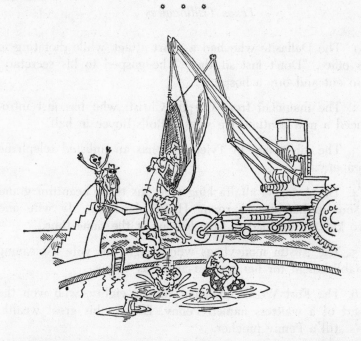

A millionaire's daughter came home to Dallas to find that her father had a small surprise for her: a brand-new home with forty bedrooms, three tennis courts, a nine-hole golf course, and an Olympic swimming pool. Cavorting in the pool when she came by was an assortment of handsome, bronzed young athletes. The daughter clapped her hands delightedly, and cried, "Oh, Daddy! And you've stocked it just for me!"

* * *

A Tulsa family man, delirious at the imminent arrival of his first baby, set a new record between his bungalow and Tulsa General Hospital. He made the five-mile trip through heavy traffic in eight minutes flat.

Arrived at the hospital, he discovered, however, that, in his excitement, he had made one slight mistake. He had forgotten to bring along his expectant wife.

Texas Trillionaires . . .

1. The Dallasite who had a heart attack while dictating in his office. "Don't just sit there," he gasped to his secretary. "Go out and buy a hospital."

2. The magician from Corpus Christi who has just introduced a new routine. He saws a Rolls-Royce in half.

3. The oil tycoon in Tyler who has an unlisted telephone company.

4. The Amarillo alfalfa king who has three beautiful grand pianos in his rumpus room. His explanation: My wife and two kids all decided to take lessons at the same time.

5. The Austin moneybags who bought his wife a cleaning establishment for her anniversary—Las Vegas.

6. The Fort Worth financier, turned eighty, who won the heart of a waitress named Penny. Despite his great wealth, he's still a Penny pincher.

7. The Galveston magnate who pulled in a fish he thought was too small to take back to the club. So he persuaded two attendants to help him throw it back in the Gulf.

8. The sturdy son of a Bonham benefactor who came down to breakfast one morning and declared, "What a day! I feel like a million dollars." His mother, deeply concerned, cried, "Darling! What makes you so depressed?"

9. The El Paso rancher who's so rich he doesn't even know he's got six kids going through college.

10. The San Antonio hostess whose new mansion is so fantastic it has staggered even jaded Dallasites. "How many bathrooms did you say your new residence has?" inquired publisher Ted Dealey. The hostess answered modestly, "I can seat fourteen."

* * *

An expansive Waco character arrived at a Montana dude ranch with a great big motor launch tied down to his trailer. "Sorry," said the amused ranch foreman, "there's not a drop of water within a hundred miles." "I know," nodded the character. "The lake is arriving tomorrow."

* * *

A man from Texas, visiting in Alaska, was the butt of considerable humor about the fact that Texas was now only the second largest state in the Union. "True, true," conceded the Texan, "but wouldn't you half-frozen galoots up here like to have some of our herds of cattle? Everywhere you look in Texas, you see the finest, healthiest, most expensive cattle ever bred."

"Okay," joshed an Alaskan. "You've got a few head of mangy cattle. But you've got nothing like our majestic, towering, snowclad mountains up there."

"Not now," shot back the Texan, "but we did have, son. We had 'em before our cattle trampled 'em down!"

* * *

President Lyndon Johnson recalls a time when his fellow Texan, the late House Speaker Sam Rayburn, visited President Truman just after the latter had been sworn in. Said Mr. Sam, "You're now in the most powerful office on earth, Harry, and people are going to keep unpleasant things from you if they can. Pretty soon they'll have you believing you're the smartest man in the world. And you and I know, Harry, that *you're not!*"

8. The Great Society

RAGS TO RICHES

Rags . . .

John D. Rockefeller, never considered exactly a spend-thrift, was accosted outside his office by a smooth-talking panhandler who announced, "Mr. Rockefeller, I hoofed it thirty miles down here just to meet you, and everybody I met assured me you were the most generous man in New York."

Mr. Rockefeller thought this over for a minute, then asked quietly, "Are you going back by the same route?" "Probably," said the panhandler. "Aha," nodded J.D., "in that case you can do me a great favor. Deny the rumor."

✻   ✻   ✻

Into a supermarket strode an emaciated man, obviously
suffering from severe malnutrition, accompanied by five bedraggled, woeful little children. Even the hardhearted manager was touched. "Here," he volunteered. "Take this cart.
Load it up with stuff for you and the kids. And tell the cashier
I said there's to be no charge. It's on the house."

The father loaded the cart, then sought out the manager
again. "Looks like you're all set," approved the manager. "Feel
a little bit better now?"

"I do not," snarled the father. *How about my green trading
stamps?*

✻   ✻   ✻

His progress impeded by a derelict with the familiar whine,
"Kinyu spare a quarter for a poor man to get a cup of coffee?"
a busy magnate handed over a dollar saying, "Here, get yourself four cups," and hastened on his way. Next day the derelict
was waiting on the same corner. "Say," he snarled, "aren't you
the wise guy that slipped me a dollar for four cups of coffee?
You big bum—I couldn't sleep a wink all night!"

✻   ✻   ✻

Myron Cohen tells about a chronic borrower who begged
an old friend to lend him a hundred dollars. "I'll pay it back
the minute I return from Chicago," he promised. "Exactly
what day will you return?" probed the wary friend. Shrugged
the borrower, "Who's going?"

✻   ✻   ✻

Characters: an old tramp and a young bride. Scene: the
young bride's backyard. Young Bride: I'll give you a big slice
of the very first cake I ever baked if you'll chop some firewood
for me. Old Tramp (after one bite of the cake): Tell you what
I'll do, lady. I'll eat the firewood and chop the cake.

✻   ✻   ✻

Art Buchwald tells of two old friends who met for the first
time in years. One obviously had prospered; the other looked

terrible. Proposed the prosperous one: "Al, you've got to come to work for me. I've got a good job for you. Now cheer up—and here's fifty dollars on account. Get some food for your family and have a jolly weekend."

Al turned up for work Monday morning looking worse than ever. "I haven't eaten for five days," he confessed.

"What happened to the fifty bucks I gave you?" demanded his friend.

"Well," said Al, "when I showed it to my wife and kids they all smiled the first time in two years. And so, since we all looked happy for a change, we went to a photographer's and had our picture taken!"

* * *

Marvyn Carton, the sailing expert, was returning home from his yacht club when a bedraggled individual stopped him to beg for a quarter. His explanation, "I need it for the parking meter!"

* * *

John Straley tells of a hobo who was sitting on a curbstone in a fashionable neighborhood, munching contentedly on a homemade sandwich. Along came a supercilious lady with an equally supercilious poodle. Both sniffed disdainfully—but the poodle picked up interest when he spotted the sandwich. "Shall I throw the doggie a little, Ma'am?" asked the hobo.

When the lady gave her condescending consent, the hobo seized the poodle by the collar and sent it sailing over a nearby hedge. "Thank you, Ma'am," he said. "If the doggie comes back, I'll be happy to throw him a little more."

*　*　*

Mrs. Dillenberg, on the veranda of the Comfort Arms, remarked, "I gave a bum ten dollars today." Her companion inquired, "What did your husband have to say about that?" Mrs. Dillenberg admitted, "He said thank you."

To Riches . . .

A millionaire, recalling the days when he was just beginning to claw his way up the ladder, mused, "Once I was living in California, while my parents were still in Michigan. I had just saved enough money to buy myself a bicycle when I heard my mother was sick. I jumped on my bike and pedaled all the way back to Michigan, only to be told that California air was the one thing that could save my mother's life.

"Gentlemen, I was equal to the occasion. I carted the bicycle over to my mother's bed, let the California air out of the tires —and she lived to the ripe old age of ninety-six."

*　*　*

A social climber in St. Paul has lost interest in his family tree. He paid a researcher two hundred dollars to dig up information about his ancestors. Now he's had to give the researcher a hundred dollars more to keep him quiet.

*　*　*

Miss Something-or-Other from away down South appeared at a cotillion in a new gown which, her beau informed her, looked just right on her. "Sho' nuff?" she purred. Blushing, he replied, "Sho' does."

* * *

Tony Randall tells of the post-debutante who called up her boy friend to advise him, "We'll have to postpone our marriage for a little while. I've just eloped with another man."

* * *

An oculist had prescribed expensive new glasses for a rich patient, and, meeting him soon after at Carnegie Hall, asked if the change had proved helpful.

"The new specs are just fine," beamed the patient. "My wife likes the frame, they fit well behind the ears, and for distance, they can't be beat. There's just one tiny flaw I might mention, however. I still walk off the wrong end of ferryboats."

* * *

A cautious suburban socialite makes it a point to tell all weekend guests when they check in, "If we get to drinking Sunday afternoon and start insisting that you stay over until Tuesday, *please* remember that we don't mean it!"

* * *

Along with the Cabots and the Lodges, the Adams family has dominated Boston Back Bay society for generations, and Charles Francis Adams was one of the most dignified and unapproachable of them all. A disturbing factor was another Charles Francis Adams, who owned the Boston Bruins hockey team, a race track, and other sporting interests. The socialite grew increasingly wrathful as he kept getting phone calls intended for the sports promoter. One night he was called to the phone at 3 A.M. and came clomping back to bed in a fine rage. "What's the trouble?" asked his wife. "Nothing to speak of," answered Mr. Adams curtly. "The Bruins' goaltender has been thrown into jail."

* * *

Cleveland Amory knows one very proper—and well-heeled —Bostonian who never saw asparagus growing until she was past fifty. The sight obviously unnerved her. "Why," she gasped, "I always thought that the cook braided the ends!"

* * *

"You Bostonians are always so loyal," taunted a Midwestern matron, "yet I notice that neither your father, your brother, your sister, or you yourself married a Bostonian." "Of course not," answered Amory smoothly, "we feel we have to spread the culture."

* * *

Two venerable members of a fashionable club were examining a new wall plaque in the card room. "The faults of our brothers," it read, "we write upon the sand. Their virtues we inscribe on tablets of love and memory."

Just then a loud crash was heard from the lobby below. "What's that?" exclaimed one member.

"Probably," said the other, "a truck delivering another load of sand."

* * *

One of the greatest New Year's Eve parties ever given in New York was hosted by the late editor of *Vanity Fair*, Frank

Crowninshield. Printed invitations read, "Admit Bearer and One Wife."

* * *

A couple prominent in the Social Register attended a masquerade party at a Long Island country club. After dinner, the wife developed a headache and elected to go home. Her husband so obviously was having a high old time, however, that she gave him a special dispensation to stay until the festivities were concluded.

At home, she recovered so rapidly that she decided to go back to the party, but sneakily put on another costume—her notion being that she might discover how her husband was comporting himself.

Back at the masquerade, she saw him sitting alone behind some potted palms. She disguised her voice and asked him if he'd like to dance. One thing led to another, and what with a full moon shining overhead, the two soon found themselves romancing in the back seat of a parked car. Finally she disentangled herself, and returned home to await her erring spouse.

When he finally came home he complained that his feet were sore from dancing. "You mean you never left the dance floor?" she asked sharply. "Only toward the very end of the evening," recalled hubby. "Our old club bartender complained that he never got in on the fun, so I loaned him my costume and took his place behind the bar."

* * *

Joe Mankiewicz tells of another fancy dress ball that was given in Rome when he was there for a couple of weeks producing *Cleopatra* with Elizabeth Taylor, Richard Burton, and Rex Harrison. A chap well known in international society decided to attend the party as a wolf, but decided he was too tired at the last moment. "I know how you've been looking forward to this gala," he told the lovely young thing he had been squiring all season, "so why don't *you* go as the wolf?"

She liked the notion well enough to discard the costume she had originally intended wearing, and set forth as a reasonable, if well-filled facsimile of Walt Disney's Big Bad Wolf. When she came home, however, her costume was in tatters. "What happened?" asked her anxious protector. "I don't know exactly," admitted the young lovely. "Who the heck were Romulus and Remus?"

* * *

"Are you quite sure," asked a customs official loudly of a lady on the dock, "that you have nothing to declare?" "Absolutely sure," insisted the lady. "Am I to understand, then," continued the official much more loudly, "that the fur tail hanging from under your dress is your own?"

Maid to Order . . .

1. Before an important dinner in UN circles, a new maid was cautioned by the hostess, "Remember to serve from the

left of each guest, and to clear the dishes away from the right. Is that clear?" "Yessum," nodded the maid. "You superstitious or something?"

2. Another new maid was asked by a Bar Harbor blueblood, "Do you know anything of my wife's whereabouts?" "Yes, sir," was the respectful reply. "I put them in the wash."

3. A proud Washington hostess instructed a maid taken on as an extra for a big diplomatic cocktail party, "Dress modestly —and don't wear any jewelry." The maid nodded, "Thanks for the warning, Ma'am."

4. A resident in a swanky midtown apartment-hotel noted that appreciable inroads were being made into his supply of bourbon by persons unknown. Very carefully, he made a small pencil mark on the label of the bottle on his side table opposite the current level of the liquid.

Returning home that night, he found this note from the chambermaid: "Please don't put any more pencil marks on this bottle, because I don't want to have to put water in such wonderful whiskey."

*　*　*

Mr. Sinsheimer was showing off his new eighteen-room duplex apartment to his less fortunate boyhood friends who still lived on the crowded Lower East Side. In the midst of the tour, an elegant butler appeared and announced, "Refreshments are being served in the Louis XIV dining room." "Thank you," nodded Mr. Sinsheimer. "Where is it?"

*　*　*

A prominent sportsman who practiced farming as a hobby fed a lot of torn-up racing forms to his chickens. The next morning he found them laying odds.

*　*　*

Trelawney was outraged to discover that his favorite club had passed a law allowing members to bring their wives into the sacred premises one evening a month. "Darn females barging in everywhere," he grumbled. "Besides, the rule is unfair to bachelors like myself. Is it all right if I bring a girl friend?"

The chairman of the house committee pondered deeply, then answered tentatively, "I hardly think anyone would object—provided, of course, that she's the wife of a member!"

* * *

The dignified London Tatler describes an anguished moment at a great dinner given by socialite Mrs. Ronnie Greville for the Foreign Secretary, Sir Austen Chamberlain, and his wife.

Mrs. Greville's butler, unfortunately, had been partaking very liberally of the cocktails and wines intended for the guests. Reluctant to make a scene, Mrs. G. handed him a note which said, "Leave the room at once. You are drunk."

The butler nodded gravely, and promptly handed the note, on a salver, to Lady Chamberlain.

* * *

Out in New Mexico they tell of a rancher who suddenly struck it rich and decided it was time his son learned some manners. The boy, tutored by a refugee from Harvard, got along famously with his new course in etiquette until the rancher decided to throw a big party in honor of his boy.

Decorators came all the way from Dallas to fix up the ranch

house and all the guests took their dinner coats out of the moth-balls. Everything went well until one guest made an insulting remark about the young heir, who jumped up in a rage and went for his adversary.

That's when the rancher pulled back his boy by the seat of his pants. "Doggone, boy," he exclaimed, "how often do I have to tell you? Put down that knife and go after him with your fork!"

* * *

Sylvia Kaye tells of a Palm Springs matron who has her desert mansion redecorated every winter. The precise shade that each room is to be painted is an obsession with her. Last fall she covered ping-pong paddles with the exact colors she wanted and left them for the painters to match.

When the job was finished, the painters had done such a faithful job that the gratified matron gave them a substantial bonus. "Best painters I've ever found," she enthused. They departed without telling her that they had made numerous mistakes, but had carefully covered them up by repainting the ping-pong paddles to match the walls.

* * *

P. G. Wodehouse, extolling the virtues of the once perfect, but now practically extinct English butlers, tells about one who presided over a mansion in Ireland. One day a gang of Sinn Feiners descended upon the place, and battered down the front door with axes. Inside the butler awaited them to tell them austerely, "His Lordship is not at home." They wrecked the house from cellar to attic, and finally set fire to it. On leaving, they found the butler still standing statuesquely in the hall. Flames were everywhere, and ceilings were crashing down, but the butler stopped the mob to ask, "Who shall I say called, gentlemen?"

* * *

A gouty old plutocrat sat cutting coupons in his club and grumbling about current political goings-on. "Blast those

Democrats," he rasped. "Do you think the Republicans are really any better?" asked a fellow member. "Not at all," admitted the plutocrat. "Blast them, too!" "Then what *are* you in favor of?" persisted the fellow member. The plutocrat's eyes gleamed. "The *feudal* system, sir," he cried, and tottered off to dinner.

* * *

That eminent man-about-town, Jack Baragwaneth, told about a day when one of the fabulous Du Pont clan came from Wilmington to New York for three important engagements. He kept the first two all right, but then, for the life of him, couldn't remember whom he was to meet on the third. No one to indulge in long-distance calls, he telegraphed home base, "Unfortunately have forgotten name my four o'clock appointment. Please advise." Back came this reply: "Name of your four o'clock appointment is J. P. Morgan. Your name Du Pont."

THE GAMING TABLES

A young writer who hit the jackpot this year with a surprise best-seller, and a subsequent six-figure sale of the property to Hollywood, allowed at a cocktail party as how he was contemplating a trip to Nevada. "I've invented a system for beating the roulette wheel," he announced, "that I believe is infallible."

Director Anatol Litvak, no stranger to the gaming tables himself, cooled off the young writer's enthusiasm somewhat by reminding him, "Nevada welcomes all gamblers with open arms when they blow into the state. But for gamblers *with a system*, my boy—they send an airplane!"

* * *

A customer beckoned the bartender in a Grand Bahamas gaming room. "Can you change a fifty-dollar bill?" he inquired. "My wife's playing the slot machines." "Sure thing," nodded the bartender. "How do you want it?"

"Humph," mused the customer, "shall we say two bucks in quarters—and the rest in drinks?"

*　*　*

A big chicken farmer from Oregon went to Puerto Rico one weekend and won ten thouasnd dollars in a hotel casino. "Turn the chickens loose," he ordered his wife by long distance, "and join me for a trip around the world."

Six months later the two of them were back in the U.S.A. and broke. "Well," sighed the farmer, "it's home to Oregon for us, I guess." "To recoup our losses?" suggested the wife. "No," said the farmer, "to re-coop our chickens."

*　*　*

The town's most notorious deadbeat boasted at the weekly poker game, "I give the little woman a check regularly every Saturday night so she can put it aside for a rainy day." "That's nice," commented one of his many creditors sardonically. "She can sew them all together and make a rubber raincoat."

*　*　*

Dean Martin tells of a gambler in the wide-open Capone era in Chicago who ran a slightly crooked roulette wheel. In fact, the house couldn't lose even if the players had every number covered. "If that happened," explains Dean, "the pill would jump off the wheel, hop out the door, and roll down Michigan Avenue."

*　*　*

One time the gambler was warned that the heat was on, and urged to take it on the lam. "I'll go on a huntin' trip," said the gambler. "Good idea," approved his mouthpiece. "Where'll you go?" "Milwaukee," said the gambler. "*Milwaukee?*" echoed the mouthpiece. "What the heck you gonna hunt in Milwaukee?" "Oh," said the gambler, "cats, dogs—whatever they got there!"

It Could Only Happen at Las Vegas . . .

This story comes from Bob Smith, television's famous Mr. Howdy Doody, who told it to me one morning in a TV studio:

A Brooklyn baker worked so hard and turned out such superior bread and cakes that at the age of fifty-five he was able to sell out his business for seventy thousand dollars. With seventy crisp, new thousand-dollar bills stashed away in his pocket, he and his wife boarded a plane for California, set on living the rest of their lives in peaceful retirement.

Over the Nevada desert, the plane developed minor engine trouble, and the passengers were told, "There is no danger whatever, but we're playing it safe and putting down at Las Vegas. We'll be grounded for approximately three hours; you may dine at any hotel you choose as guests of the airline. May we caution you, however, that if you choose to gamble, you're strictly on your own."

"Gamble," scoffed the baker to his wife. "Anybody who plays against those odds ought to have his head examined!" But the lure of the gambling tables was too much and he decided to risk a thousand-dollar bill on the roll of the dice.

Alas! The thousand dollars soon melted away, and the baker, now intent only upon recouping his losses, lost his head completely. He also lost his entire seventy thousand dollars.

The poor man headed unsteadily for the public washroom, but he didn't even have the ten cents that would gain him admission to that sanctuary. A fellow passenger from the plane understood his plight and pressed a dime into his hand.

"You're very kind," said the baker. "I've never borrowed a penny from anybody in my life, but I will take this coin with the understanding that I reimburse you at the first opportunity." He thereupon insisted upon writing down the man's name and home address.

Somebody, however, had left the door to the washroom ajar and when the baker came back to the lobby he still had the borrowed dime in his pocket. On an impulse, he put it into a slot machine and pulled the lever. He hit the jackpot! There followed one of the most amazing runs of luck ever seen at Las Vegas. The baker went back to the tables, doubled and redoubled his bets, and by the time he and his wife boarded the plane for Los Angeles, he had over a hundred thousand dollars in his pocket!

In California, the baker and his wife soon discovered that a life of idleness was not for them. They started another bakery, and because they knew their business so thoroughly, prospered from the start. In a few years, their assets were up in the millions.

One day the baker told his well-satisfied sales staff about his unnerving experience in Las Vegas. "This whole business— everything I've built up here in California," he said, "I owe, as you can see, to one man. I will leave no stone unturned to find out who he is."

"But I don't understand," interrupted the sales manager. "You told us yourself that the man who loaned you that dime gave you his name and address."

"He's not the one I'm looking for," explained the baker. "The man I want to find is the one who left that washroom door ajar!"

THE LECTURE CIRCUIT

"The human brain," opines William Nichols, "is a wonderful thing. It starts clicking the instant you are born and never stops until you are called upon to speak unexpectedly at a public gathering."

*   *   *

A Denver elocution teacher told Stan Peckham to practice speaking with pebbles in his mouth. "I was doing fine," recalls Peckham, "until one day I got the hiccups. I broke two mirrors and the picture window."

*   *   *

Judge Miles McDonald tells of the self-made millionaire, a pompous egomaniac, who hired a ghost-writer to turn out speeches and articles for him. He not only underpaid said ghost-writer, but subjected him to a continuous shower of criticism and abuse. The ghost-writer finally had his revenge. He provided his employer with a long speech to read at a very important conclave. The employer read the first ten pages of the speech in booming, confident tones, but when he turned to page eleven—in the middle of a sentence—he found only these words, printed in red: "FROM HERE ON, YOU OLD GOAT, YOU'RE ON YOUR OWN!"

*   *   *

Harry Hershfield, scheduled to be guest of honor at one of the innumerable banquets he attends, stood in front of a mirror in the washroom, straightening his black tie and adjusting his dinner coat. Pinching his cheeks to bring out the color, he asked the attendant, "How many great men do you reckon there are in New York City today?" The attendant answered solemnly, "One less than you think."

*   *   *

Harry Truman still splutters angrily when he recalls the evening he was guest speaker at a banquet in Des Moines. The coffee had been passed and the master of ceremonies turned to the former President to ask genially, "Shall we let them enjoy themselves a few moments longer, Harry—or should we have your speech now?"

* * *

A noted philosopher was delivering a speech in a California auditorium when a severe earthquake suddenly shook the building to its foundations. As big chunks of plaster began falling from the ceiling, the chairman made a dive for the shelter in the basement, pausing only to remark to the philosopher, "It is increasingly evident, Professor, that our premises will not support your conclusions."

* * *

Edmund Whitman, former V.P. of the United Fruit Company, confided to newshawk John Fuller that he won't consider his life complete until he's asked to deliver a June Commencement Day address at a respectable college. He's got his whole speech prepared already. It will go like this: "Gentlemen of the graduating class: I have only two thoughts to leave with you as you march forth from these cloistered halls: (1) There is no such thing as a free lunch. (2) You will never go broke taking a profit. I thank you."

* * *

The late President Henry Noble MacCracken of Vassar College once delivered a lecture in an Albany high school that neither he nor the audience ever forgot. There were to be accompanying lantern slides on "Campus Life," but by mistake, the pictures put into the slide box depicted scenes on a big dairy farm near Vassar.

Prexy MacCracken opened his talk by saying, "I'd like you to look at a picture of Matthew Vassar, who founded our college in 1861." Onto the screen came a picture of a great Holstein bull. A roar went up. The embarrassed MacCracken clicked the signal, and began again, "And here are some of our beautiful Vassar students." Out came a herd of cows, climbing over each other in their haste to get into green pastures.

By this time the audience was so hysterical that the poor college president had to call off the speech. The students went tottering off to green pastures of their own.

*　*　*

On a lecture tour, silver-tongued Norman Cousins found himself aboard a crowded Pittsburgh bus, when a young lady boarded same, laden with two large bundles and a howling baby. She took a quick look around, then deposited the baby squarely upon Mr. Cousins' lap.

Surprised, Mr. Cousins inquired, "Why, may I ask, did you pick me?"

"You have a kind face," replied the young woman without hesitation, "and besides—you're the only person wearing a raincoat."

*　*　*

A lecturer was instructing a ladies' club gathering on "What's Wrong with the Movies Today."

"The one I saw last night," he concluded, "is the worst yet. It includes murder, rape, arson, cannibalism, and perversion. If anything will justify censorship, this vile picture will do it. Now then, ladies, have you any questions?"

"Yes," cried three ladies in the audience simultaneously. "Where's it playing?"

*　*　*

Governor George Romney tells about the guest of honor at a banquet who discovered at the last moment that his upper plate had cracked. "You'll have to cancel my speech," he told the toastmaster. "Nonsense," said the latter. "Here's a spare upper I have in my pocket."

The guest of honor inserted the plate in his mouth, and essayed a few words with disastrous results. "No good," he announced, pulling out the plate. "It doesn't fit."

Like a magician taking rabbits out of a hat, the toastmaster produced a second plate, which didn't fit either, and then a third plate, which was exactly right.

The guest of honor made a fine speech, received an ovation, then turned gratefully to the toastmaster. "It was a lucky break for me," he said, "that you happen to be a dentist."

"Dentist nothing," said the toastmaster. "I'm an undertaker."

* * *

Rushing to redeem his hat and coat after a lecturer had overstayed his allotted time on the podium by a full forty minutes, a sore-bottomed but silver-tongued auditor consoled other disgruntled patrons with this reminder:

> It's never so bleak
> But it couldn't be bleaker:
> There might have been
> A second speaker!

And then he added these lines by R. Cheney:

> Charm and wit and levity
> May help you at the start;
> But at the end, it's brevity
> That wins the public's heart.

* * *

George Jessel, making one of his innumerable after-dinner orations, noticed with chagrin that his audience was growing rather restless. "Take it easy," he assured the wrigglers. "Like Lady Godiva on the last lap of her historic ride, I am drawing near my close."

* * *

And then there was the lecturer who announced that he had made a speech that would not be forgotten for a long, long time. "My audience," he added, "was composed entirely of elephants."

MEN OF LETTERS

Not every letter in the morning's mail is a bill, an advertisement, or a summons to some boring banquet at fifty dollars a head. It only seems that way! Comb the haystack carefully and once in a blue moon you'll discover a needle like the following (mailed to a hundred friends by an obviously overworked Wall Street broker):

"Dear Bennett: Perhaps you have heard of me and my nationwide campaign in the cause of temperance. Each year I make a tour of the South lecturing on the evils of drink.

"On these tours I have been accompanied by my friend and cashier, Mr. Oswald Shucat. Oswald is a pathetic case, a man of good family and excellent background whose life was ruined by excessive indulgence in whiskey and gin.

"Poor Oswald would appear with me at my lectures, sitting on the platform, drooling and besotted, staring popeyed at the audience while I would point him out as a horrible example of what drink would do.

"Now poor Oswald has died. A mutual friend has given me your name and I wonder if you would care to accompany me on the fall tour this year in his place? Yours in hope, Aloysius Drybone."

* * *

Letters Magazine printed this revealing exchange of notes between a patient's wife and the doctor who had been treating him.

1. "Dear Doctor: My husband was for years the perfect mate and father. Since consulting you, however, he has become a hopeless gadabout, critical of my housekeeping and our children, an ogre about bills, vain, arrogant and unfaithful. It is my belief that you have been giving him hormone shots which have entirely changed his personality. Mrs. A. Jones."

2. "Dear Mrs. Jones: In answer to your letter, I have not been giving your husband shots of any kind. I have simply had him fitted with contact lenses. Dr. Shallbe Nameless."

* * *

How does a man tell his wife that he has accepted an important new job in another city—necessitating his leaving his family temporarily behind?

Here, in essence, is how one Virginia gentleman broke the news to his wife:

"You may believe me, my dear, that far from seeking this new appointment, I used every endeavor in my power—but in vain—to avoid it. Not only was I reluctant to part with you and the family, but I was conscious that the new trust might be too great for my capacity. How well I know that I would find more real happiness in one month with you than I shall in my new post, though my stay be seven times seven years!"

It was via this letter that Mrs. George Washington learned

that her husband had been appointed Commander-in-Chief of the American Army.

* * *

John Fuller, of *Saturday Review*, quotes this communiqué from an author in Maine to her publisher, who had neglected to report on a manuscript she had submitted to him several weeks before:

"GENTLEMEN:
     I have sent you a manuscript
     which you have failed
     to consider, and I think you are
     a big jerk, and I mean
     the biggest. I also think
     when it comes to stupidity
     you deserve all there is
     in the book. You're not known
     for your astuteness and judgment
     but I *do* know your total idiocy,
     which is beyond man's reason.
     I cannot express what I think.
     If prizes are to be awarded for

imbecility, you surely deserve
the very biggest, and the greatest
prize; and there is no doubt
you richly deserve this top award.
P.S. If you decide to accept my novel, please read only every
other line."

◦   ◦   ◦

Ingenious and persevering fellows, these post office authorities! One of them, according to Bill Feather, came upon a letter addressed to:
Wood.
Mr.
Mass.
and promptly and correctly delivered it to:
Mr. Underwood
Andover,
Mass.

◦   ◦   ◦

Dave Sherwood, of St. Cloud, Minnesota, sent me a copy of this letter, which a local merchant received (with a check enclosed):

"Sir: I understand you desire to have me pay my account in full, but the present condition of my bank balance makes that impossible. My shattered financial status is due to federal laws, state laws, county laws, corporation laws, liquor laws, mother-in-laws, sister-in-laws, and outlaws.

"Through these 'laws,' I am compelled to pay a business tax, amusement tax, school tax, gas tax, water tax, sales tax, and income tax. My brains are taxed most of all. I am required to carry fourteen different forms of insurance and my wife discovers one more charity a day to which I must contribute.

"My business is so governed that I'm no longer sure who owns it. I am inspected, suspected, disrespected, rejected, examined, re-examined, summoned, fined and confined until I provide a constant source of revenue for everybody but myself and my legitimate creditors.

"Fortunately, the wolf that comes to my door daily just had pups in my kitchen. I sold them—and here's ten per cent of what I owe you. I'm afraid you won't be so lucky next month. Faithfully, etc."

❊ ❊ ❊

Teacher Berenice Hoffman, of New York, had an eight-year-old student named Susan who could read faster and more intelligently than any other kid in the class, but she was a chronic dawdler and couldn't seem to get to school on time in the morning. To punish her, her mother decreed that Susan could not borrow another single book from the school library.

Reader Susan chafed under this restriction for a week, then happily presented this note to teacher Hoffman: "Susan has been on time to school now five mornings straight, so you can let her have all the books she wants. Love, My Mother."

❊ ❊ ❊

A school teacher in the Southland received a form letter from a loan company that began, "Because you are a teacher you can borrow $100 to $1000 by mail." His reply began, "Maybe I can borrow this money because I am a teacher, but I couldn't pay it back for the same reason."

❊ ❊ ❊

Aristides Perkins, Harvard '22, hired a new salesman who could talk a mile a minute. Two weeks later the salesman sent in his first order—a whopping one—with this note attached: "Dear Boss: I seen this outfit which they ain't never bought a dime's worth from us, but the owner's daughter kinda took a shine to me and I sold them twenty thousand dollars worth. Next stop: Sinsinate." The next letter arrived two days later: "Dear Boss: Sinsinaty is my erster. Here's an order for ninety thousand, C.O.D."

Letter number three went out from Aristides Perkins to all.

his other salesmen. It enclosed carbons of the new man's two notes and orders and this comment from Mr. P.: "We bin spendin' too much time here it seems tryin' to spell insted of tryin' to sell. Lets watch them sales. Read our new mans letters, and then I want you should go out and do like he done. Sinserley, Aristides Perkins."

* * *

The Missoula Lumber Company has achieved noteworthy results with this rather offbeat collection letter to delinquent accounts: "It has been said that a man who squeezes a dollar never squeezes his wife. In looking over your account, it has occurred to us that your wife is not getting the attention she deserves."

* * *

A cute, freckled little girl in Iowa was given a sizable speech to memorize for the school's graduation program. Two days before the big event, however, the elocution teacher received this note from the little girl's mother:

"I'm sorry to say Audrey will not be able to recite Friday morning. Our goat ate her speech."

RESTAURANTS AND HOTELS

Graybeards who cry in their champagne for the good old days are particularly depressed by the passing of a building on the corner of Fifth Avenue and Forty-fourth Street, New York, that once housed the establishment of society's favorite restaurateur, Louis Sherry.

Here, at the turn of the century, the most dazzling debs of the year made their bows in society and their fathers hosted "stag" dinners topped off by "Jack Horner" pies—huge concoctions, decorated in whipped cream that, when cut open, revealed a covey of nymphs in their birthday suits.

Capitalist C. K. G. Billings, self-styled "American Horse King," staged a banquet at Sherry's on March 28, 1903, that, to quote historian Grace Mayer, "reached uncharted heights in planning for the discomfort of his guests."

Mr. Billings was bent on publicizing his newly opened two hundred thousand dollar stable at 196th Street and Fort Washington Road, now Fort Tryon Park.

He converted the grand ballroom of Sherry's into a woodland paradise by means of ten thousand dollars' worth of full-scale scenic props, artificial foliage, potted palms, and a tanbark floor covering, borrowed, at Mr. Sherry's insistence, from the Barnum & Bailey Circus.

Thirty-six mystified horses were conveyed up to this bosky dell by freight elevators, and the guests, appropriately attired in white ties and tails, gingerly climbed aboard when Mr. Billings chirruped, "Tally Ho!" Only one fell off. Miniature tables had been attached to the pommels of the horses' saddles, and apprehensive waiters dressed as grooms served course after course to the miserable company.

The horses ate right along with their riders—out of oat-filled troughs thoughtfully decorated with gold foil.

* * *

Sherry's bitterest rival was Monsieur Delmonico, who was doing a land office business diagonally across Fifth Avenue. Both were gifted with the patronage of the prize playboy of all time, "Diamond Jim" Brady, who boasted an income of a million dollars a year, and spent it cheerfully on diamonds, pretty girls—and food.

Brady had thirty sets of diamond studs, and sometimes wore several sets at a time. "Them as has 'em, wears 'em," he explained. He was a Gargantuan eater, thinking nothing of putting away at a single sitting four dozen oysters, six lobsters, two steaks, and an entire tray of French pastry.

Small wonder that he tipped the scales at close to three hundred pounds. Sherry hailed him as "the twenty-five best customers I ever had."

*   *   *

To gauge the diminishing purchasing power of the dollar, it is necessary only to recall that less than fifty years ago such fashionable New York hotels as the Waldorf, Biltmore, and Plaza were serving free lunch to their bar patrons, and that thousands of well-heeled businessmen ate their noonday fill at the cost of two schooners of ten-cent beer!

The menus were varied, too. An old ad for the Knickerbocker Hotel offered free chicken salad, lobster Newburg, cold corned beef, Virginia ham, and even chafing dishes.

*   *   *

World War I put an end to that nonsense. True, the late cinema star, Norma Talmadge, spotted a restaurant in the thirties that still advertised a ten-course dinner for forty-five cents, but when she asked her husband of the moment, George Jessel, how they could afford it, he explained glibly, "The music is terrible."

*   *   *

This year prices have reached a point where a Detroiter, experimenting at a highly touted new restaurant, told the waiter, "I'm not very hungry, so I think I'll try your ten-dollar dinner."

"Very good," noted the waiter. "Will you have your coffee black or with cream?"

"I'll decide that," said the Detroiter, "when I've finished my dinner."

"Pardon me, sir," corrected the waiter. "Coffee *is* our ten-dollar dinner."

*　*　*

Earl Hall, of Mason City, ordered a ham sandwich at a fancy new restaurant and got a bill for three dollars and fifty cents. "I've got to wire my readers back home," chortled Hall. "According to this bill, every pig in Iowa is worth six thousand dollars!"

*　*　*

During the Saturday night rush at a popular Long Island inn, one of the parking attendants was summoned to help check hats and coats in the jammed-up cloak room. In his first quarter of an hour he dented nine overcoats.

*　*　*

Near O'Hare Airport in Chicago there's a motel with one of those African shrunken heads behind the bar. The sign that adorns it reads, "He asked for credit."

*　*　*

A real estate agent was showing a very blonde, very well-developed female through a luxurious penthouse atop a resort hotel. "Now in this wing," said the agent, "we have the master bedroom, bath, and den."

The blonde interrupted suspiciously, "And den what?"

*　*　*

Claude Terrail, proprietor of the luxurious La Tour d'Argent Restaurant in Paris (it overlooks the Seine and is a "must" for all American tourists) has his own explanation for the superstition about having thirteen at a table. "The reason is," he says, "that most people have sets of only twelve knives, forks, and dinner plates."

✸ ✸ ✸

A customer had been trying in vain to get some service in a crowded midtown restaurant one lunchtime. Finally he beseeched the majordomo, "Can't you change my table, please? I'd appreciate something nearer a waiter."

✸ ✸ ✸

A restaurant proprietor told his wife happily, "Well, I finally found out today what's been happening to all those oysters we've been missing in the kitchen. That fool new cook has been putting them in the oyster stew."

✸ ✸ ✸

Mr. Weybright came home from the office one evening with a horrendous tale of the lunch he had eaten. "The restaurant looked inviting," he said, "so I tried it for a change. Sure enough, the soup, salad, and beef were delicious. But the pie was inedible and the coffee was slop. Do you know what I discovered? The place had changed hands right in the middle of my meal."

✸ ✸ ✸

"The world's two greatest point-killers," declares Don Quinn, "as everyone must know, are waiters and telephones. Most of us have experienced that shattering moment, when, lunching with somebody we want to make sure realizes we have a great sense of humor, we've crept up to the punch line of our very best story, only to have the waiter barge upon the scene, demanding, 'Who gets the roast beef hash?'"

✸ ✸ ✸

Overheard at an East Side restaurant:
"Hey, waiter, this sauerkraut isn't sour enough."
"Mister, that isn't sauerkraut. It's noodles."
"Oh, for noodles it's sour enough."

✸ ✸ ✸

Overheard at Sardi's: "Be sure that red wine is imported because I can't tell the difference."

* * *

A family group, dining at Danny's Hideaway, reached the dessert course. The ten-year-old daughter summoned the always-on-the-job Danny, and asked, "What kind of pastry do you have?" Then, before he could answer, she added, "And, by the way, what *is* pastry?"

* * *

A man with a passion for yeast was just receiving an order of same in a health restaurant when a clumsy waiter bumped into him. The powdery yeast went all over his clothes. The title of this sad little tale is "Yeast Meets Vest."

* * *

A high-flying, expensively attired public relations counsel brought his equally haughty date to an expensive restaurant, and boasted loudly all through dinner—especially when the waiter was within hearing distance—of the big deals he was engineering and the important new clients he was acquiring. When he left, his waiter commented to the wine steward, "Did you hear that braggart? He lives in a rear flat of one of my apartment houses. Tomorrow, first thing, I'm going to double his rent!"

* * *

In search of a snack at his private refrigerator (this story comes from G. A. Houdershal, of York, Pennsylvania), the longtime tenant of a residential hotel could find nothing but a dog biscuit. He bit into it tentatively, liked it, and the next morning told his wife to put in a large supply.

Mr. Binswanger, local restaurateur who was the source of supply, observed, "You don't need so many biscuits for a dog as small as yours." "They're for my husband," she corrected him. "These biscuits are strictly for dogs," grumbled Mr. Binswanger. "They'll kill your husband."

Six months later the wife admitted that her husband indeed

was dead. "I told you those biscuits would kill him," Mr. Binswanger reminded her. "It wasn't the biscuits," said the wife.
"He was killed chasing cars."

*   *   *

Myron Cohen knows a waiter who suffered a severe cramp
and was rushed to the hospital. As he lay doubled with pain
on an emergency ward table he grabbed a doctor hurrying by
and implored, "Help me, help me. I'm dying." "Sorry,"
snapped the doctor. "This isn't my table."

9. *It's a Good Life!*

CHRISTMAS STORIES

The Christmas issues of some of our big magazines have to go to press so early these days that the poor writers usually have to compose their tales of Yuletide cheer in the middle of an August heat wave.

* * *

On a sun-drenched beach at Atlantic City, in the closing hours of a Miss America Pageant, Mitch Miller, waxing nostalgic, suddenly sighed, "Oh, for those good old Christmases—when whiskey came in ordinary bottles!"

* * *

Florenz Ziegfeld always bought Christmas trinkets for his beautiful Follies girls early in the season—but paid for them, if at all, very late. One day he instructed his treasurer to hop over to Tiffany's to buy a diamond bracelet for his leading lady.

"But why Tiffany's?" asked the treasurer. "I know where we can pick up a bracelet wholesale for a thousand dollars less."

"What's the difference?" inquired Ziegfeld cheerfully. "I'm not going to pay for it anyhow."

* * *

An intrepid jurist named Manges paid a visit to Kris Kringle's workshop at the North Pole recently, and promptly named old Santa's helpers "Subordinate Clauses."

* * *

In a crowded department store last holiday season, a man dropped a shopping list his wife had given him, and spent several anxious moments retrieving it from under the feet of the jostling throng. Not until he was out on the sidewalk did he discover that the trampled-upon paper he had snatched up was not, alas, his shopping list, but a printed reminder the executive office evidently had passed out to every store employee. It read, in big, red, capital letters: "Remember: try to sell last year's merchandise first!"

* * *

A ten-year-old boy insisted that his father tell him exactly what he wanted as a Christmas gift. "If you don't tell me," the boy explained, "how will I know how much money I have to borrow from you?"

* * *

An ingenious toy store proprietor in a suburban shopping center decided last holiday season to present Santa Claus in a full-size replica of an Eskimo igloo. Furthermore, he provided a shiny red sleigh to transport delighted youngsters to the igloo. One eight-year-old girl didn't relish the idea at all, but was persuaded by her mother to climb into the sleigh nevertheless. Just before the sleigh rounded the last turn before the igloo, the little girl panicked, and hopped out of the sleigh, leaving her mother alone to complete the journey. Santa Claus regarded the embarrassed mother with a twinkle in his eye and commented, "Some people never give up, do they?"

* * *

A wife, to her intense dismay, came down with a virus attack on the very day the town's biggest department store opened its mammoth pre-Christmas sale. Tearfully she persuaded her very reluctant husband to go in her place, and purchase a few items she had marked in the store's newspaper ad.

"If you have trouble fighting your way to the counter," she reminded her husband at the last moment, *"act like a lady!"*

* * *

Harassed by a surging mob on the last shopping day before Christmas, a clerk shook her head sadly and paused while writing down an impatient customer's address. "It's a madhouse, isn't it?" sighed the clerk.

"Not at all," replied the customer haughtily. "It's my private residence."

* * *

Ed Condon writes jubilantly that his wife has at last completed knitting a pair of socks for him originally intended for a 1964 Christmas present. "They're magnificent," adds Condon, "but just the least bit tight under the arms."

* * *

Returned home from the Christmas holidays, a blithe young bachelor found two notes awaiting him. One, from a prosperous girl friend, was in his mailbox. It read, "There was no answer when I rang, so I left your Christmas gift in the mail chute." The second note was in the mail chute. It read, "Thanks a million for the wonderful bottle of Scotch. (signed) Your Mail Man."

* * *

In old Vienna, when the Hapsburgs still reigned, recalls Vincent Starrett, the good burghers had so much food to consume at Christmastime, and so many waltzes to dance, that parties, starting on Christmas Eve, sometimes lasted seventy or eighty hours. Retiring late on December 28, an exhausted host could take comfort in the thought that a Viennese Christmas came only three days a year.

Parting guests, incidentally, were given a ripe apple and a knife. Everyone bisected his apple at once, and if he managed that without cutting through a single seed, it meant that a wonderful New Year lay ahead for him.

*　*　*

Diplomats and heads of state exchange costly holiday gifts, too. David Ben-Gurion, destined to be the head of an Israeli state not yet in existence, once visited a wealthy Eastern potentate who presented him with a magnificent full-blooded Arabian stallion. Ben-Gurion was unimpressed.

"I hate gifts that can eat," he said.

*　*　*

A Westchester prep school presented its annual Christmas Nativity play last year, and assigned the role of innkeeper to a promising new student. In early rehearsals, he delivered his line, "There is no room at the inn" perfectly, but in the dress rehearsal he was overcome with brotherly love and when he opened the door, called out, "Welcome, welcome!" "No, no," cried the director. "You're ruining everything. You must recite your line as it was given to you!"

The contrite young actor promised to do just that, but when the curtain rose for the evening's performance, the director had certain apprehensions. And how justified they proved to be! When the visitors knocked loudly on the door our young innkeeper pulled it open and declared, "There is no room at the inn—*but*, gentlemen, come in and have a drink, anyhow!"

* * *

Carl Goerch recalls a Christmas program in a school outside Raleigh, North Carolina, that had an unrehearsed finale. Two groups of parents, unbeknownst to each other, had persuaded a Mr. Willet (weight 212) and a Mr. Hopper (weight 236) to give the kiddies a happy surprise by bursting into a party dressed as Santa Claus. The Santas arrived simultaneously.

"What do you think you're doing here?" asked Mr. Willet menacingly.

"I'm Santa Claus," maintained a slightly unsteady Mr. Hopper.

"Like heck you are," cried Mr. Willet, "and besides, you're plastered."

Mr. Hopper picked up a loose guitar and broke it over Mr. Willet's noggin. The kids whooped with joy. Mr. Willet thereupon uncorked a Sunday punch that knocked Mr. Hopper flat. The kids were delirious. Fortunately, the principal had once been a football star. He threw out Mr. Willet and Mr. Hopper and for the rest of the evening played Santa Claus himself. May all your Christmases be equally eventful and joyous!

HAPPY ENDINGS

Here are a few little stories that will, I think, make the world seem a little bit brighter.

1. There lives an obstetrician in Dayton who has two fixed charges. He sends patients a bill for either one hundred or two

hundred dollars. "Do you look up your patients' financial rating before you decide on your charge?" he was asked one day by a friend.

"Not at all," answered the doctor. "I base my fee on the first question the father asks when I come out of the delivery room. If he asks, 'Is it a boy or a girl?' he gets a bill for two hundred dollars. But if he asks, 'Is my wife all right?' I only bill him for one hundred dollars."

2. In Montreal, the same sleek limousine stands in front of the same exclusive club every afternoon. Promptly at four a down-at-the-heels old derelict lurches by, nods to the chauffeur at the wheel, and announces loftily, "I won't be using the car this afternoon, Fergus. A walk home will do me good." "Very well, sir," says the chauffeur respectfully, tipping his cap.

One afternoon a reporter demanded of the chauffeur, "That can't be your boss—or is it?" "My boss?" echoed the chauffeur, "I don't even know who he is. But he always says the same thing. It obviously makes him feel good—so what have I got to lose?"

3. A bus was bumping along a back road in the South recently. In one seat, a wispy old man sat holding a bunch of fresh flowers. Across the aisle was a young girl whose eyes came back again and again to the old man's flowers.

The time came for the old man to get off. Impulsively he thrust the flowers into the girl's lap. "I can see you love them," he explained, "and I think my wife would like for you to have them. I'll tell her I gave them to you."

The girl accepted the flowers, then watched the old man get off the bus and walk through the gate of a small cemetery.

4. An old lama in India, given to long hours of stroking his chin and meditating in silence, one day turned up at the retreat with a big drum he had borrowed from a neighborhood boy. "I had no idea you could play the drum!" exclaimed a fellow monk. "I can't," chuckled the lama, "but now—neither can the boy!"

5. A young miner was badly injured in an explosion and hovered between life and death in a hospital ward. His anxious

mother begged so earnestly to see him that the doctor waived rules and conceded, "All right—but put on a nurse's uniform so the boy won't know it's you. Otherwise, the excitement might prove fatal."

The mother tiptoed into the ward and put her hand softly on the fevered brow of her delirious boy. He relaxed, smiled through his bandages, and whispered hoarsely, "Thank you, nurse; that feels as good as mother."

6. An ancient king decided to honor the most worthy of his subjects. Candidates appeared from all over his realm. One was lauded for his wealth, another for his knowledge of the law, a third for his powers of healing the sick. In the wake of this illustrious company, however, came a stooped, shabbily dressed old woman, from whose dim eyes shone the light of understanding and love.

"Who is this woman?" asked the King. "What has she done to earn her entry into company like this?"

"You have seen and heard all the others," said his minister. "This is the one who was their teacher when they were young."

The King descended from his throne and placed the wreath of honor on her brow.

7. Writes Stephen Still, from Melbourne, "I could tell from the bus driver's greeting when the blind lady climbed aboard that she must be a frequent passenger. She sat down directly behind him and they carried on an animated conversation as he drove.

"When we reached the woman's stop the driver got out and escorted her through heavy traffic to the other side of the street. When he returned to his seat I noticed the woman still standing where he had left her. 'She won't budge till she knows I got back safely,' he explained. He honked his horn three times, the woman waved, and off we drove. 'I feel good,' said the driver. I answered, 'So do I.'"

8. One of the greatest mayors New York ever had was Fiorello La Guardia—"The Little Flower." Every New Yorker remembers the day Fiorello read the funny papers over the radio—with all the appropriate excitement and inflections—

when a strike kept the Sunday journals off the stands. They remember too his squeaky fulminations against the "crooks," and "tinhorns" in our town, and his weekly radio sign-off, "Patience and fortitude."

One time the ubiquitous mayor chose to preside in a Night Court. It was bitter cold outside. A trembling man was brought before him, charged with stealing a loaf of bread. His family, he said, was starving. "I've got to punish you," declared La Guardia. "The law makes no exceptions. I must fine you ten dollars."

But The Little Flower was reaching into his own pocket as he added, "Well, here's the ten dollars to pay your fine—which I now remit." He tossed the ten-dollar bill into his famous sombrero.

"Furthermore," he declared, "I'm going to fine everybody in this courtroom fifty cents for living in a town where a man has to steal bread in order to eat. Mr. Bailiff, collect the fines and give them to this defendant!"

The hat was passed and an incredulous old man, with a light of heaven in his eyes, left the courtroom with a stake of $47.50.

A-HUNTING THEY DID GO

Invited by millionaire tool manufacturer J. A. Wilkie to join him on a safari vacation, author Don Weldon promptly flew to Southern Rhodesia where the party was already in progress. A jeep, a Portuguese chauffeur-interpreter, and two native guides were waiting to take Weldon to the camp where his host was hunting elephants. After a three-day trip into the heart of darkest Africa, they reached a clearing where Wilkie was "roughing it" in a mammoth aluminum trailer—specially designed, stocked with delicacies, and shipped over for the holiday—with forty native cooks, butlers, and miscellaneous servants in starched white uniforms to attend his every whim. Weldon's waggish greeting was, "Dr. Livingstone, I presume!"

* * *

Woodland idyll: A hunter lost his bearings and wandered about the forest in a daze. Suddenly he spied another man. Dropping his rifle, he threw his arms about the other's neck and chortled, "Boy, am I glad to see you. I've been lost in these woods for three days!"

"Restrain your enthusiasm," cautioned the other sourly. "I've been lost here a week."

* * *

Sign outside a deluxe Adirondack hunting lodge: "If you have a chance to bag a moose near the lodge, be sure you don't shoot the fellow milking it."

* * *

"My, my," reminisced a bogus old party at a sportsmen's dinner. "The tigers I shot in my day in the wilds of Africa!" "Very interesting," interrupted a disgusted listener, "but there do not happen to be any tigers in Africa." "Of course not," agreed the old party without batting an eyelash. "I shot them all."

VACATION TIME

In the Mountains . . .

"Spend your vacation in your own backyard," suggests Bill
Vaughan, "and your friends will know the kind of man you
are: sensitive, introspective, home-loving—and broke."

*   *   *

The late Fred Allen's suggestion for lazy vacationists: de-
tachable blisters for folks who abhor sun-bathing; self-wetting
bathing suits to make diving into a rough surf unnecessary;
and shoes with built-in pebbles for people who prefer having a
beer on a cool porch to hiking through the poison ivy in the
woods.

*   *   *

A young minister was vacationing in the White Mountains
when he learned that a lady guest of the hotel, recently arrived from Boston, was gravely ill. Anxious to cheer her up he
paid a courtesy call, murmured a wish for her speedy conva-
lescence, and concluded, "I should like to say a brief prayer for
your recovery before I leave."
The sick lady rallied at once, and snapped, "That will be
quite unnecessary, young man. I am being prayed for in Boston."

*   *   *

Stan Holworthy's pretty little wife had been picking on him
all the way up to Lake Placid, so as they stepped into the
crowded hotel elevator with all their baggage, he squared accounts. He threw his arm around her and inquired in a very
loud voice, "What did you say your name was, honey?"

*   *   *

Jackie Gleason dropped in at a summer resort in the Catskills where business was so phenomenal that the management
turned away a young unmarried doctor.

* * *

On the porch of Tannenbaum's Manor, a stout lady earnestly assured the occupant of the next rocker, "My husband holds an extremely responsible position. No matter what goes wrong, he's responsible."

* * *

Eddie Fisher was writing a letter in the library of a hotel in the Catskills when he sensed the presence of a kibitzer behind him trying to read what he was putting down. So, after signing his name to the letter, Eddie added in a postscript, "I can't say more in this epistle because a nosey stranger is snooping over my left shoulder."

Whereupon the kibitzer drew himself up and demanded haughtily, "Who's snooping?"

* * *

Mr. Campbell finally has discovered a foolproof system for keeping relatives from dropping in for weekends in his mountain hideaway. "I borrow money from the rich ones," explains Campbell happily, "and lend it to the poor ones. None of them come back."

* * *

After British humorist Ronald Searle returned home from his first comprehensive American tour, he reported, "I asked a mountaineer in West Virginia who was 103 years old how he passed his time. He told me that in winter he mostly sleeps, in spring he chases some likely female cousin around the rocks, in the summer he makes moonshine whiskey out of potato peelings and coffee grounds, and in the fall he drinks it."

* * *

Explaining why his first night at a mountain hotel had been a sleepless one, Mr. Wartels told the room clerk, "That honeymoon couple occupying the next suite were arguing until 5 A.M. about their wedding. They couldn't agree on where to have it."

*   *   *

A penniless Jewish lad immigrated to the U.S.A. in the steerage in 1905, and worked his way westward. Now, sixty years later, he was living in great luxury at Aspen in the Rockies.

"Only in America could this happen," he exulted at a testimonial dinner in his honor. "Sixty years ago I didn't have a penny to my name. Today I'm a senior partner in the great Denver House of Nussbaum and McCarthy. And this, my friends, is the most wonderful part of all: *I'm McCarthy!*"

At the Seashore . . .

Jack Kofoed swears he saw this happen in the dining room of a swank Palm Beach hotel. A clumsy waiter spilled a whole plate of soup on the white jacket of an outraged guest. The manager rushed up immediately and purred, "Give that coat to me, Sir. I'll have it sponged immediately and returned to you absolutely spotless before you've finished your meal."

Five minutes later, the waiter who had spilled the soup poked the guest indignantly on the shoulder, and demanded: "Don't you know you're not allowed in this dining room unless you're wearing a jacket?"

*   *   *

Mrs. Appleby had talked her husband into taking her to Florida for a winter vacation, and here they were after dinner in Miami Beach one evening, looking up at a full moon, hidden from other tourists by a big potted palm.

A young man and his girl sat down near them, and not realizing they were being observed, fell into each other's arms. Whispered Mrs. Appleby to her husband, "Oh, Luther, he doesn't know we're here, and he's going to propose. Shouldn't you whistle and warn him?"

"Why should I?" objected Mr. Appleby grimly. "Nobody whistled to warn me!"

*   *   *

Nick Morgan tells of a bather on a chilly, overcast morning who ordered hot coffee from a beachside snack bar.

"Cream or sugar?" asked the waitress.

"It doesn't matter," shivered the bather. "I'm going to pour it on my feet."

* * *

A young toddler at a crowded beach reported tearfully to a lifeguard that he was lost. "Why didn't you hang on to your mother's bathing suit?" asked the lifeguard. The toddler explained, "I couldn't reach it."

* * *

Walter Evans was spending his first hours at one of those fashionable seaside hotels that advertise off-season rates of six dollars a day—with a steak dinner included. When he asked the waitress for his steak, however, she announced, "The steak is all over today."

"All over what?" asked the puzzled Mr. Evans.

The waitress explained, "With."

* * *

An astonishing conversation, allegedly overheard at a Miami Beach luxury motel, involved two girls friends who met accidentally after a year of separation. "So what's new?" asked one. "A terrible thing," answered the other. "My doctor just told me I seem to be turning into a man." The first girl nodded absentmindedly and inquired mildly, "So what else is new?"

* * *

Two red-hot mamas were acquiring a suntan on the sands of Montego Bay. "See that girl in the bikini over there?" whispered one. "She's my daughter-in-law. In one year she turned my poor son into a pauper." "That's nice," said the other. "A boy or a girl?"

* * *

Jack Benny believes that the waiters at Miami Beach's swanky Fontainebleau Hotel are the classiest and most cultured he's ever encountered. "Of course," he adds, "most of them were guests of the hotel when they arrived a week earlier."

*　*　*

At an elegant hotel in the Bahamas a prosperous merchant was urging his wife to complete her toilette.

"Should I wear my Dior dress or the one from Mainbocher?" she asked. "Wear the Dior," he said.

"And my hat—should it be the one from Mister John or the Lily Daché?" "The Mister John," he said.

"And my fur coat—should it be the chinchilla or the sable?"

The husband's patience was exhausted. "Wear anything you please," he shouted, "but for Pete's sake, come on downstairs for breakfast!"

*　*　*

The purchaser of a spanking new pleasure boat was not averse to female companionship on his moonlight cruises. The way he'd lure a debutante aboard the boat was to assure her, "You'll be crazy about my new boat, and you must come out on it with me. Incidentally, I wonder if you know that I named it after you."

No girl could resist a pitch like that! It was only when she came to the marina and saw the boat bobbing at the landing that she realized she had been had. The letters on the stern read "AFTER YOU."

*　*　*

A wealthy New York garment manufacturer was persuaded to try his skill at skin diving. Equipped with all the latest paraphernalia, he was lowered to the bottom of the sea, and was poking gingerly about when he spotted his arch-competitor flailing about in nothing but a bathing suit.

"Morris," cried the garment manufacturer. "What are you doing here without a diving helmet?"

Morris replied sourly, "I'm DROWNING!"

*　*　*

A man who believes in logic is H. Allen Smith. "It is a known fact," says he, "that most major hurricanes along the Atlantic Coast occur in August and September. The solution is therefore simple. Do away with August and September."

*   *   *

Then there were the two crystal ball gazers who were marooned in their seaside home by a hurricane and forty-foot waves crashing in from the sea. "You know," said one, "this storm reminds me of the one in 1988!"

10. *Not According to Webster*

relish such a... served before or be courses of a meal. [t. F: aside ... (the main body of the) work]

cow¹ (kou), *n., pl.* **cows**, (Archaic) **kine. 1.** the female of a bovine animal, esp. of the genus *Bos*, that has produced a calf and is usually over three years of age. **2.** the

"DEFINITIONS"

Upheld too long to damyankee joshing about the way the English language is spoken south of the Mason-Dixon line, Winston McCord of Baton Rouge, Louisiana, strikes back justifiably with a few definitions he compiled while visiting the Greater New York area:

Oily: The opposite of late.

Sore: Viewed: "I sore it in *Try and Stop Me.*"

Dare: "Not here, stupid—dare."

Verse: Barbara Cook's got a good one.

Use: A pronoun: "Where use going, Al?"

Ax: To query: "I wanna ax you something."

* * *

Possibly Mr. McCord had been musing over definitions like these, published in his own home territory in *The Dixie Dictionary*—which sells for "50 cents: Yankee money."

Auto: "I auto go to work, but Ahm tared."

Barn: "I was barn in Kentucky."

Balks: "Pass me that match balks."

Did: He's did.

Gull: A young female human.

Rat Cheer: Lay it rat cheer (not there).

Yawl: Yawl come to see me soon.

(The pamphlet also warns strangers to always say, "Pass them grits," since there is no such thing as one grit.)

* * *

From a long list of definitions being circulated surreptitiously in Washington's huge Pentagon Building:

A program: An assignment that cannot be completed by a single telephone call.

Consultant: Any average man more than fifty miles from home.

To activate: To make carbons and add more names to a memo.

To implement: To hire more people and wangle additional office space.

Reorientation: Getting used to working again.

Committee: The unwilling, recruited from the unfit to do the unnecessary.

* * *

A little girl, fond of dismissing any problems with an airy "It's nothing," was asked finally just what she thought "nothing" meant. Her imaginative definition was, "Nothing is like a balloon with its skin off."

* * *

Another budding Webster is Norman Collins. He defines a family swimming pool as "a small body of water completely surrounded by other people's children."

* * *

And here are some other definitions you'll find in no standard dictionary:

Acoustic: What you use when you shoot pool.

Adolescence: When a girl begins to powder and a boy begins to puff.

Alimony: The fee a woman charges for name-dropping.

Aloha: A Pullman berth.

Anatomy: Something everybody has—but it looks better on a girl.

Anecdote: A revealing account of an incident that never occurred in the life of some famous person.

August: The month you can't open the car window you couldn't close in February.

Bachelor: A man who has faults he doesn't know about yet.

Banjo: Let's not invite Joseph.

Basso profundo: A deep-thinking fish.

Bath mats: Little dry rugs that children like to stand beside (*John Ciardi*).

Bust truster: A man who is sure his girl doesn't wear falsies.

Caddy: A lad who stands behind a golfer and didn't see the ball either.

Carbuncle: An auto collision.

Career girl: One who'd rather bring home the bacon than fry it.

Coincide: What you do when it starts raining.

Conscience: A little gimmick inside you that makes you tell your wife before somebody else does.

Conservative: One who believes that nothing should be done for the first time.

Debate: It lures de fish.

Desk: A trash basket with drawers.

De trop: A forward pass.

Deuce: The unkindest cut of all.

Dogma: A canine female parent.

Egoist: One who is always me-deep in conversation.

Experience: The only thing most people get out of life.

Forger: A man who gives a check a bad name.

Gladiator: What the cannibal said after he ate the female explorer.

Guest towel: A small square of absorbent linen completely surrounded by useless embroidery.

Heredity: Something you subscribe to wholeheartedly when your son's report card shows all A's.

Hoosiery: Stockings made in Indiana.

Inflation: Something that cost $10 to buy a few years ago and now costs $20 to repair.

Intuition: The instinct whereby a woman can tell she's right whether she is or not.

Jaywalking: An exercise that brings on that rundown feeling.

Kindergarten teacher: One who should know how to make the little things count.

Knob: A thing to adore.

Minor operation: One performed on somebody else.

Money: Jack of all trades.

Monologue: A conversation between a real estate promoter and a prospect.

Officer: A cop whom you can talk out of giving you a ticket.

Operator: An employee who takes the padding out of his shoulders and puts it in his expense account.

Pedestrian: A chap who knows what the lady motorist is driving at.

Pessimist: A man who's always building dungeons in the air.

Pharmacist: Man in a white coat who stands behind a soda fountain and sells ball-point pens.

Platonic lover: One who holds the eggshells while somebody else eats the omelette.

Procrastinator: Man with a wait problem.

Reno: The city of otherly love.

Repartee: What a person thinks of after he becomes a departee (*Sid Skolsky*).

Slang: Language that takes off its coat, spits on its hands, and goes to work (*Carl Sandburg*).

Small fry: A one-dollar steak.

Sneezing: Much achoo about nothing.

Taxidermist: A man who knows his stuff.

Theory: A hunch with a college education.

Toothache: A pain that drives you to extraction.

Violin: A bad hotel.

Wallflower: A girl without a gent to her name.

Wife: A person who can look in a bureau drawer and find the husband's tie clasp that isn't there.

Will power: The ability to eat *one* salted peanut.

11. Only on Sundays

A young minister, just out of divinity school, was assigned a parish in a tiny Blue Ridge community in Virginia, where he promptly was called upon to perform a wedding ceremony for a mountain couple.

He did his part beautifully, and the bridegroom told him, "Parson, it's easy to see you're going to be a big hit in these parts. I'd like to start you off real good too, but I'm sorry to say I ain't got no money to give you. Tell you what I'm gonna do. I got an ole houn' dawg I was aimin' to sell for ten dollars—and I'm gonna let you have him for five!"

*　　*　　*

Taken to church for the first time, a four-year-old girl was mystified when the entire congregation kneeled. "What are they doing?" she asked her mother. "Ss-s-h," cautioned the mother. "They're praying." "What?" exclaimed the four-year-old. "With their clothes on?"

*　　*　　*

The services of one congregation in West Palm Beach always include a group reading of the Twenty-third Psalm. One Sunday a visitor with a shrill, penetrating voice got about ten words ahead of the rest at the beginning and maintained her lead doggedly to the very end.

At the end of the services, one resident member asked another, "Who was that irritating lady who was always by the still waters while the rest of us were lying down in green pastures?"

*　　*　　*

A clergyman once assured his congregation, "Every blade of grass is a sermon."

Two days later, as the clergyman was moving his lawn, a member of the congregation passed by and nodded approvingly, "That's the stuff, Reverend! Cut your sermon short!"

*　　*　　*

Baptist minister Carl Winters, of Oak Park, is one cleric who appreciates the value of humor. "I definitely try," he says, "when I preach, to make people laugh. And while their mouths are open, I put something in for them to chew on."

*　　*　　*

St. Peter gazed solemnly at twenty-seven wives, just arrived, and seated before him. "Now, girls," said St. Peter kindly, "I want every one of you who ever was untrue to your husband on earth to stand up—and remember, no fibbing. I have ways of checking up on you, you know."

Sheepishly, twenty-six of the wives rose to their feet, but the twenty-seventh steadfastly remained seated.

St. Peter nodded, and put in a phone call to the devil. "Satan," he said, "I'm sending down twenty-seven untrue wives to you—and I advise you to be particularly careful of one of them. She's stone deaf."

*   *   *

Jerome Beatty's nephew announced he was going out on the lawn to play ball with God.

"How do you play ball with God?" asked Beatty.

"It's easy," explained the nephew. "I just throw the ball up in the air and God throws it back down to me."

*   *   *

A minister in Evansville had fallen into the habit of placing his sermons on the pulpit about an hour before the church service. One young rascal discovered this habit, and one day, before the congregation convened, he neatly detached the last page from the manuscript.

The minister delivered his sermon in ringing tones, and read the last line of what was now the final page: "So, Adam said to Eve . . ." Searching in vain for the following page, the minister made a mental note to give his secretary what for, cleared his throat nervously, then concluded his sermon weakly, "So, Adam said to Eve—there seems to be a leaf missing!"

*   *   *

When Bishop Stephen Bayne, Jr., was appointed executive officer of the Anglican Communion, he was asked as he embarked for London how he regarded his new duties. "I am rather like a mosquito in a nudist camp," admitted the bishop with a wry smile. "I know what I ought to do, but I don't know where to begin."

*   *   *

A venerable bishop got tired of receiving pleas for aid from the pastor of one of his most impoverished parishes, and wrote to the pastor, "These pleas must stop. I can do nothing more for you." For a full two months, not another word was heard from the chagrined pastor. Then, one day, the bishop got another letter from him. It read, "This is not an appeal. It is a report. I have no pants."

*   *   *

After extraordinary displays of patience, the parents of a three-year-old tomboy had taught her to say grace before meals. Then one day they heard her carefully reciting the prayer while she was taking her bath.

"This isn't the time to say grace," called in her mother. "You do that just before you eat."

"I know," called back the youngster cheerily. "I just swallowed the soap."

*   *   *

To stress his conviction that the people of today are too commercial and material in their outlook, a British bishop cited a question asked of a London stockbroker by his precocious offspring. "Father, why is it that so many churches have plus signs on them?"

* * *

Brian James tells of a well-heeled tourist who dropped into a tiny village church in Essex County, England, for the Christmas service. Before it began, he buttonholed the rector and said expansively, "I mean to give you a handsome contribution. I only hope you'll put on a good show today." The rector answered quietly, "It won't be a bad one. It's been running now for almost two thousand years!"

* * *

Cartoon in a religious weekly depicts an usher passing a collection plate at a church wedding. The caption reads, "I admit, sir, it's a bit extraordinary—but the bride's father insisted on it."

* * *

Rear Admiral George Dufek, one of the first Americans to actually reach the South Pole, was surveying the ice-capped landscape there at lunchtime one day with Father Linehan, geophysicist from Boston College. In his hamper, the admiral found ham and roast beef sandwiches. "None for me," said Father Linehan regretfully. "It's Friday, you know."

Admiral Dufek is not the man to be stopped by a thing like that. "If you'll step about fifteen paces to the left," he suggested, "it will still be Thursday." Father Linehan did just that and enjoyed the sandwiches immensely.

* * *

Two clergymen were talking animatedly at the corner of Madison and Fiftieth when a third man of the cloth appeared. The first two looked pleasantly surprised. One stuck out his hand and exclaimed heartily, "Well, speak of the devil . . . !"

* * *

Dr. Lee Fairchild recalls the story of the village priest who told his congregation, "Next Sunday I propose to give a sermon about liars. I suggest that before then you all read Chapter Seventeen of St. Mark's."

Came the following Sunday, and the priest began, "Will all those who obliged me by reading Chapter Seventeen of St. Mark's please raise their hands." Every right hand in the congregation shot up.

Observed the priest, "There happen to be only sixteen chapters in St. Mark's. I will now deliver my sermon on liars."

*   *   *

A beatnik wandered into church, and on the way out, told the Reverend, "You were swinging, Daddy-o. You were way out."

"What was that again?" inquired the Reverend, knitting his brow.

"I mean," amplified the cat, "I dug your jive. I read you so good I put ten big fish in your collection plate."

"Ah," beamed the Reverend, grasping the beatnik's hand. "Cool, man. Cool!"

*   *   *

The Reverend Andrew Poole tells about a fellow clergyman who was invited to a child's fashionable birthday party. Arriving tardily, he heard sounds of jollity in the rumpus room, and told the maid, "Don't announce me. I'm going to surprise them." He thereupon dropped to his hands and knees and crawled into the rumpus room, barking like a dog.

Looking up, he found six adults staring at him incredulously.

He had come to the wrong house.

*   *   *

Have you heard about the new sport developed by Fathers Clancy and Hallorhan behind their Pawtucket parish house? It's played with rackets and a shuttlecock. They call it goodminton.

*   *   *

Things weren't going too well in the first-year Sunday school class. Nobody seemed able to recall the identity of St. Matthew. Nor did they do any better with St. Mark. Finally the teacher said hopefully, "Surely somebody will remember who Peter was?"

A small boy in the last row came to the rescue. "Teacher," he piped, "wasn't he a wabbit?"

* * *

Copy of a prayer discovered by a correspondent in a room at a Long Island inn:

"Lord, Thou knowest better than I know myself that I am growing older.

"Keep me from getting too talkative, and thinking I must say something on every subject and on every occasion.

"Release me from craving to straighten out everybody's affairs.

"Teach me the glorious lesson that occasionally it is possible that I may be mistaken.

"Make me thoughtful, but not moody; helpful, but not bossy. Thou knowest, Lord, that what I want most is a few friends at the end."

* * *

E. H. Taylor tells this tale at the expense of Bishop Bompas, the first Anglican missionary to venture into the Yukon.

The good bishop discovered a tribe of Indians who had never recorded a baptism, a confirmation, or a marriage service. The bishop soon rectified this situation, baptizing and confirming everybody in sight, and winding up by uniting every beaming couple in holy wedlock.

Later the tribal chief told Bishop Bompas that his tribe hadn't had so much fun in a month of Sundays. "And what part of the ceremonies," asked the bishop, "did you enjoy most?" "The marriage service," replied the chief, happily. "We all got new wives!"

* * *

An unscheduled transcontinental airliner was definitely in trouble: one engine out, and the others backfiring, but the passenger in seat 9-A took some comfort from the fact that the priest sitting alongside him seemed quite undisturbed. "Do you think we'll get down safely, Father?" asked the passenger. "I certainly hope so," said the priest. "But what can we do if these other motors conk out?" persisted the passenger. "I can't answer that," admitted the priest. "You see, I'm not up in administration; my department has always been sales!"

* * *

They tell about a fifteen-year-old boy in an orphans' home who had an incurable stutter. It was agony for him to talk to strangers.

One Sunday the minister who came out regularly from town was detained, and the boy, to the surprise of the people in charge, volunteered to say the prayer in his stead. He did it perfectly, too, with the proper reverence and not a single stutter. Later, he explained, "I don't stutter when I talk to God. He loves me."

* * *

An enthusiastic minister, who liked to wave his arms to emphasize salient points in his sermons, had trouble keeping his shirttails in his trousers, and got into the habit of stuffing them in surreptitiously whenever he had the opportunity. One Sunday, while preaching away, he fished around behind his back in the usual way, and found more material than usual to push out of sight. He persisted manfully, however. At the close of his sermon he discovered that he had about half of a United Nations flag stuffed into his pants.

* * *

The late and great Pope John one morning granted a private audience to a newly appointed bishop, who complained that the complexity and responsibilities of his new office prevented him from sleeping. "The very same thing happened to me in the first few weeks of my pontificate," Pope John reassured him, "but then one day my guardian angel appeared to me in a daydream and whispered, 'Giovanni, don't take yourself so seriously.' And ever since then I've been able to sleep!"

12. *The Professions*

ARTISTS

Along about the year 1500 or so, an irreverent Italian legend has it, a young girl in Milan beseeched a famous artist she knew to paint her portrait. "I'm far too busy," he is purported to have told her. "Why not ask that fellow Da Vinci across the courtyard, Mona? He needs the business!"

* * *

Le Gallidaut, a meek, undersized Parisian sculptor, had never fashioned anything longer than a woman's hand, so everybody was mildly surprised when he turned out nothing less than an elephant in marble.

"But Le Gallidaut," marveled his oldest friend, "how could you sculpt such a perfect likeness without a model?"

"There was nothing to it," explained Le Gallidaut airily. "I simply chipped off every piece that didn't look like an elephant."

* * *

Dan Melnick, rising young theatrical and TV producer, and his wife, Linda, who is a daughter of composer Dick Rodgers, are in the process of acquiring a first-rate collection of modern paintings, abstractions, and expensive pop art.

A few weeks ago, a lady arrived at the Melnick home to bind a new rug. She gazed intently at the paintings on the wall, clucked appreciatively, and announced: "Nice pictures you've got here. Who's the artist in the family?"

* * *

Speaking of abstractions, a little boy in Arizona was stopped cold by one at an exhibition of local talent. "What's *that?*" he asked his mother. She explained, "It's supposed to be a cowhand and his horse." The little boy cut right to the heart of the matter. He asked, "Well, why ain't it?"

* * *

A business tycoon who painted for diversion got short shrift when he asked a young lady of his acquaintance to pose for him in the nude. "I'm not a model, I'll have you know," she said haughtily. "That's all right," soothed the tycoon. "I'm not an artist."

* * *

A wealthy dowager, very *avant-garde*, had her portrait executed by a new painter whose technique consisted of splattering great blobs of paint on the canvas. "It's the best I've ever done," he announced when he delivered the finished portrait, "although I'm not entirely satisfied with how your nose turned out."

"Why don't you change it?" asked the dowager.

"Frankly," admitted the painter, "I can't find it."

* * *

At an art class in California a young model slipped out of her clothes, then covered her face with shame. "I'm so embarrassed," she confessed. "I forgot my teeth."

* * *

While a Greenwich Village sidewalk artist was munching a hot dog, some rascal painted a mustache on his portrait of Elizabeth Taylor.

"What are you going to do about it?" the artist was asked after he had surveyed the damage.

"Raise the price," said the artist.

* * *

The owner of a picture gallery on Fifty-seventh Street tells of a night when Pablo Picasso supposedly caught a burglar red-handed in his château in southern France. The burglar tore loose from Picasso's grasp, but the artist later assured the police he could draw a rough sketch of the intruder.

On the basis of the drawing, the police promptly arrested the minister of finance, a visiting lady columnist from New York, a Univac machine, and a replica of the Eiffel Tower.

* * *

A friend once brought Picasso three paintings to sign. Picasso refused, declaring that all three were palpable fakes. "But," protested the exasperated friend, "I saw you paint these pictures with my own eyes." Picasso's unabashed answer was, "I can paint fake Picassos just as well as anybody."

* * *

A fabulously wealthy Argentine playboy dropped in to a famous Paris art gallery with his wife one blustery December day and bought all the Picassos, Gauguins, Klees, Hans Hofmanns, and Jackson Pollocks in sight. "Well, that's done," he told his wife happily. "Now that the Christmas cards are out of the way, let's get started on the real presents we've got to buy."

* * *

Salvador Dali, the eccentric artist, can come right down to earth when occasion warrants. At the Stork Club recently, for example, he was heard earnestly assuring a beautiful young hat-check girl, "Never take a fur coat from an amorous customer, my dear. A fur coat is like a painting by me: you have to explain both to your mother."

* * *

A water color specialist found an old Indian squaw in New Mexico who struck him as a perfect model for a painting. Promised sufficient wampum, she agreed to pose, but after remaining absolutely still for a half hour, she began to squirm. "Be patient," urged the artist, "I'll soon be finished." Ten minutes later she started wriggling again. "I thought Indians were patient and stoical," grumbled the artist. "What makes you so nervous?"

"Well, for one thing," explained the Indian squaw, "I'm sitting on a swarm of bees."

DENTISTS

On Madison Avenue, a lady patient descended upon society dentist Ed Pullman's office for the fifth time to command him to grind down her false teeth again. "I tell you they don't fit," she insisted. "Okay," said Dr. Pullman reluctantly. "I'll do it one last time. But by every test, they should fit your mouth perfectly as they are."

"Who said anything about my mouth?" snapped the lady. "They don't fit in the glass."

* * *

If the American Dental Association is on the ball, it will give serious attention to John Fuller's suggested slogan for the tooth-pullers of our nation: "Nothing dentured, nothing gained."

* * *

Arlene Francis, backstage before a "What's My Line?" broadcast, was talking about a man who began his professional career as a dentist, later became an internationally renowned brain surgeon. "How did he ever make so radical a change?" wondered Dorothy Kilgallen.

Explained Arlene, "His drill slipped."

✿ ✿ ✿

Dr. Villard closes his clinic each day at six, and pauses on the way home for a Daiquiri cocktail—or two—at a Madison Avenue bar. One afternoon he noticed that the barkeep was sprinkling the top of his cocktail with grated hickory nuts. "Is that a new fad?" asked Dr. Villard. "Not at all," the barkeep assured him. "That is simply a hickory Daiquiri, Doc."

✿ ✿ ✿

They sneeze, insists Irene Keepin, thisaway:

A dentist: Ah chew.

A R.R. engineer: Ah choo-choo.

A travel agent: Where choo?

A banker: Cash shoo.

A dancer: Ah cha-cha choo.

✿ ✿ ✿

A world-wise ten-year-old, asked to write a school paper on "Care of the Teeth," came up with these three basic rules:

1. See your dentist at regular intervals.
2. Brush your teeth after every meal.
3. Watch out for shovers at the drinking fountain.

DOCTORS

An elderly lady in Baltimore was a hopeless hypochondriac who called her doctor at all hours of the night to complain about imaginary aches and pains. The doctor finally had to tell her, "If you wake me up once more in the middle of the night with one of these cock-and-bull stories, Mrs. Hilliard,

I'm going to have to ask you to transfer your business to another doctor."

Two weeks later, however, the poor lady fell down a flight of stairs, breaking a leg, four ribs, and suffering a concussion into the bargain. The doctor examined her from head to foot, shook his head approvingly, and said, "Well, Mrs. Hilliard! At last you're beginning to get the real hang of it!"

❊　❊　❊

"The time has come," Dr. Nudnick told his patient, "to wheel you to the operating room. Don't fret about the outcome. I've lost my last eleven patients straight, and if there's anything at all in the law of averages, you'll pull through. Is there anything I can do for you before we start?"

"There certainly is," said the patient grimly. "You can help me on with my shirt and pants."

❊　❊　❊

"I don't get it," declared one pretty girl as she divested herself of her garments. "I tell the doctor my sinus is bothering me, and he asks me to strip." A nude redhead with a satchel on her lap replied, "My case is even more puzzling. I'm here to tune the piano."

* * *

A hypochrondriac was discussing his various ailments with a doctor he had encountered aboard a transatlantic liner. "Take the matter of kissing my wife," he proposed. "The first time I kiss her, I feel very warm and perspire. But the second time, I am chilled and shiver with the cold. How do you explain that?"

"Before you answer, Doctor," interrupted the hypochrondriac's wife, "you should know that the first time he kisses me it's July and the second time it's January."

* * *

Dr. Morris Fishbein tells about a nurse who was given three demerits. She was absent without gauze.

* * *

A trustee of Lenox Hill Hospital has dug up a copy of the 1888 rule book for the School of Nursing at that superb institution. One of the startling statements in the 1888 compendium made it clear that "any nurse who smoked or had her hair done at a beauty shop gave the director of nurses good reason to suspect her worth, intentions, and integrity."

Among other duties that nurses in 1888 were expected to perform were mopping floors, cleaning chimneys, trimming wicks, and fetching coal. Hours were from 7 A.M. to 8 P.M., except on Sunday, when they were off between noon and 2 P.M.!

As an incentive, nurses who performed faultlessly for a period of five years were given an increase of five cents a day— providing there were no outstanding hospital debts at the time!

* * *

Overheard at a mountain resort: "I'll tell you how good my son, the doctor, has become after one year of practice: in three weeks he cured that rich Mrs. Teitelbaum of fourteen hundred dollars!"

* * *

In a pleasant little town in northern Westchester, there's an elderly doctor whose battered jalopy is the subject for considerable merriment to the young fry who hang out in front of the new supermarket.

The good doctor remains unperturbed by their jibes. "Yes, boys, this car is getting mighty old," he told them amiably one morning. "It's also fully paid for. If you'll check with your parents, you'll discover most of you ain't!"

*   *   *

A middle-aged matron in Scarsdale startled the clerk in a dairy when she ordered twenty-four quarts of milk. "Oh, I'm not going to drink them," she explained. "The doctor told me to take a milk bath, and I figure it will take twenty-four quarts to fill the tub." "Pasteurized?" asked the clerk. "No," said the matron. "Just up to my neck."

*   *   *

A new patient appeared in a doctor's office to explain, "Doctor, I'm disturbed. A week ago I came home to find my wife in the arms of another man, who talked me into going out for a cup of coffee. The next four nights, exactly the same thing happened." "My good fellow," said the doctor, "it isn't a doctor you need; it's a lawyer." "No, no," insisted the patient. "It's a doctor's advice I want. I've got to know if I'm drinking too much coffee."

*   *   *

Dr. George Stevenson, of the National Association for Mental Health, offers these suggestions for calming tensed-up nerves:

1. Don't bottle up anger. Find some way of venting it, such as sawing wood or taking a long hike.

2. Find a sympathetic ear. Putting vague fears into words helps ease them.

3. Listen to the other fellow's troubles. Everybody has plenty of them. They'll put your own in better perspective.

4. Practice "giving in" on some points. Always insisting on having your own way takes a high toll.

5. Turn your back on your problems for a while. A trip, a show, or above all, an amusing book can give your jangled nerves a valuable respite.

* * *

The whole neighborhood shook from the explosion in the rear of the town's oldest pharmacy. The pharmacist himself staggered out, his glasses broken, streaks of black besmirching his white uniform. "Lady," he implored a customer who was wiping debris from the soda counter off herself, "would you please ask your doctor to copy off that prescription again—and this time I hope he'll PRINT it!"

* * *

Have you caught up with the story of the Las Vegas transient who awoke with bad pains in his stomach one night and put in a hurry call for the house physician? That gentleman gave him a quick examination, folded up his stethoscope, and said, "I'll give you four to one you have acute appendicitis."

* * *

A sweltering midsummer afternoon had famous gynecologist "Sunshine" Rodgers in a swivet. Noticing his foul humor, a sympathetic patient asked, "These hot August mornings getting you down, Doctor?"

"Not these hot August mornings at all," scowled the good doctor. "It's those cold nights last November!"

* * *

In Ohio there lives a medical student who spent his summer vacation building up his sadly depleted cash reserve. He worked as a butcher in the daytime and was a hospital orderly at night. Both jobs, of course, involved wearing similar white uniforms. One evening he was instructed to wheel a patient on a stretcher into surgery. The patient, a stout, very frightened lady, looked up at the student and let out an unearthly scream. "My God!" she wailed, "it's my BUTCHER!"

* * *

"You certainly seemed fascinated by that medical magazine in my waiting room," observed a doctor as he prepared to examine a patient. "Indeed I was," agreed the patient. "The issue you have out there announces the discovery of ether."

* * *

A man with a very sore throat indeed went to the home of a doctor and rang the bell. The door was opened by the doctor's wife. In an almost inaudible croak, the man inquired, "Is the doctor in?" In a conspiratorial whisper, equally low, the doctor's wife answered, "No. Come on in."

* * *

Nancy Parks reports the meanest doctor in Flatbush. He keeps his stethoscope in the deep freeze.

* * *

A husband wandered nervously about a doctor's waiting room while his wife underwent a complete checkup inside. After some time the doctor stuck his head out of the door, summoned the husband, and said, "To be blunt, I don't like the looks of your wife."

"Neither do I," responded the husband, "but she's great with the children."

* * *

The laziest man in Westchester County fell off a couch and had to be taken to the doctor's in an ambulance. A doctor examined him and reported, "I'm afraid I've got some bad news for you, sir. You will never be able to work again."

"Thank you, doctor," said the lazy one. "Now what's the bad news?"

* * *

A Cleveland doctor, reports Jerome Beatty, recently treated a young girl for an angry, infected insect bite on her right lower leg. She phoned the following day to say that the pain and itching were gone, but the calf was purple. The Cleveland doctor promptly told her, "I never saw a purple calf. . . ."

* * *

A couple of newspapermen were having a cold soft drink at the corner drug store one afternoon when a pretty girl, neatly dressed, came in and asked the pharmacist to read a letter for her. It was obviously a rather intimate letter, too, because the girl blushed while she listened, and gave the pharmacist a hug and a kiss before she rushed happily out of the store.

"Don't think she's an illiterate," the pharmacist hastened to explain to the newspapermen. "Matter of fact, she's a senior at Radcliffe. But her boy friend is a doctor—and only a pharmacist like me can make head or tails of his handwriting."

* * *

"I note," murmured a young doctor to a very pretty nurse, "that 317 isn't chasing you any more. How did you bring it off?"

"It was simple—once I thought it through," laughed the nurse. "I took the tires off his wheelchair."

* * *

In a chic Park Avenue office, a doctor gave a socialite a checkup, then asked, "Have you been living a normal life?" "Indeed I have," the socialite told him warmly. "Well," said the doctor, "I'm afraid you'll have to cut it out."

* * *

Margery Bartlett tells about a stranger in town who was lured by a doctor friend to a dance at a deaf and dumb institute. "How the dickens do I ask a deaf and dumb girl to dance?" he asked the doctor. "Just smile and bow to her," explained the experienced doctor. It worked. The stranger picked out the prettiest girl on the floor, smiled and bowed to her, and away they went. After a full hour he was still dancing with her, happy as a clam at high tide, when a tall, dark man suddenly approached the girl and said, "Darling, when are you going to have a dance with me? After all, I'm your fiancé." "I don't know, dear," sighed the girl, "I can't seem to get rid of this poor deaf and dumb fellow."

* * *

Joe E. Lewis tells about a surgeon who had imbibed a few too many before he showed up in the operating room. Presently he told the nurse, "It's okay to wheel the patient out." "But, Doctor," she protested, "we haven't wheeled him in yet." "Indeed," declared the surgeon icily. "Then what do you think I've been doing the past ten minutes?" "I *know* what you've been doing," said the nurse. "You have amputated a leg of the operating table."

* * *

Miss Edna Ferber sent flowers to a sick friend in the hospital recently, enclosing a card that made the recipient feel better on the instant. It read, "If loving thoughts are a comfort, my dear, you are lying on cream puffs."

*   *   *

"Wouldn't you know it?" sighed Dr. Busby. "The worst blizzard in years and at 3 A.M. the patient who lives farthest from the Thruway gets sick and I have to go see him."

Through the snowdrifts Dr. Busby fought his way to the side of the stricken man. After examining him, he shook his head gravely, and ordered, "Get your lawyer, your family, and your friends over here on the double!"

When he got back home, Dr. Busby told his wife the instructions he had given. "Poor fellow," she sighed, "is he really that sick?" "Not at all," grinned Dr. Busby. "He'll be perfectly well in twenty-four hours. But I was darned if I was going to be the only sucker out on a night like this!"

*   *   *

Victor Borge urges caution in the use of those new rejuvenation pills. "Take the case of a cousin of mine in Copenhagen. He took some pills guaranteed to make him fifteen years younger and they all but killed him. You see, he was only twelve at the time."

*   *   *

The young doctor's very first patient was a beautiful maiden with entrancing curves. "Steady, boy," the doctor admonished himself, but the stethoscope kept slipping from his fingers.

"What's the trouble?" whispered the girl softly. "You seem rather nervous."

"Not at all," the doctor assured her, then added, "Once more now, if you please. Deep breathely."

* * *

Old Dr. Boosey, general practitioner in Gooseleg Falls for nigh on fifty years, was dozing peacefully on the veranda of the Mansion House when a young man hailed him loudly, pumped his hand, and declared, "I want to thank you for your invaluable treatment."

"Never saw you in my life before," harumphed Doc Boosey. "You can't be a patient of mine."

"Me? Certainly not," agreed the young man cheerfully. "My uncle was your patient. And I'm his sole heir."

* * *

A young mother, being examined by her doctor, made no effort to control her son, who, despite the remonstrances of the doctor's secretary, was raising cain in the waiting room. Finally, a crash of bottles disclosed the fact that he had reached the doctor's cabinet of supplies. "I hope," simpered the mother, "that Billy's mischievous ways are not distracting you." "Not a bit," replied the doctor grimly. "Besides, he'll be quiet in a minute when he gets to the next shelf. That's where I keep the poisons."

* * *

Doctor's explanation to a three-hundred-pound patient: "These pills I'm prescribing for you are not to be swallowed. You just spill them on the floor twice a day and pick them up one at a time."

* * *

The inmates at a well-run loony bin chipped in and bought the new doctor a great big red balloon. "It's to show how much better we like you than the doctor who preceded you," explained the spokesman of the inmates. "Somehow you seem more like one of us."

* * *

A man who often confused himself with Young Lochinvar cherished a number of interesting ideas about the lovely young nurse who took care of him for some days at a local hospital. "Honey," he confided to her one morning, "I've fallen so deeply in love with you that I don't want to get well." "Don't worry," she assured him. "You won't. Your doctor, who happens to be engaged to me, saw you kissing me last night."

*   *   *

Two doctor cartoons have given me a special laugh recently. One, in the *Journal of the American Medical Association*, shows a newly graduated surgeon sawing the arm off a patient. "What kind of an operation do you think you're performing?" asks a nurse. "Operation!" gasps the surgeon. "I thought this was an autopsy." Another, mailed in by a thoughtful reader, depicts an obviously delighted medic standing over a patient on the operating table and telling the other doctors: "Gentlemen, this is Mr. Hellman, author of the best-selling *All Doctors Are Quacks. . . .*"

*   *   *

The classic doctor story is about the fine old country doctor who had neither time nor inclination to dun patients for payment. He died in his second-story office one morning, and one of his few worldly possessions was the wooden sign that had stood on his lawn for fifty years or more.

His loyal patients would have liked nothing better than to buy him an imposing tombstone, but they were just as poor as he was. After his funeral therefore, they uprooted the wooden sign and lovingly planted it on his grave. It read, "Dr. Farnum, upstairs."

BOTH SIDES OF THE LAW

The time was the cocktail hour, the scene the club car of a transcontinental train, and the cast of characters composed entirely of well-heeled legalites bound for their annual convention in San Francisco.

Every lawyer had a case to tell about, of course, but now Mr. Richards of New York had the floor—and indeed had had it for a full half hour. He wound up in a blaze of oratory. "Masterful as you will agree my defense was," he asserted, "the jury, inflamed by newspaper headlines, brought in a verdict of guilty and my client got twenty years in the clink."

Lawyer Brown of Louisville was the first to congratulate lawyer Richards of New York. "Not only was that a magnificently told story," he boomed, "but I can safely say it's the first case lost aboard this train in over eight hundred miles."

* * *

The rising young comedy team of Allen and Rossi have come up with an ingenious plan to relieve New York City's appalling traffic problems. They propose nothing less than making *every* crosstown street in Manhattan one way in the *same* direction —going west. "What good would that accomplish?" they were asked. "What good?" echoed Allen and Rossi. "Put the plan into operation on Monday—and by Wednesday the whole problem will be New Jersey's!"

* * *

A distinguished judge had a wife who was just a bit too fond of the grape. At a party one afternoon at the mayor's mansion, he reproved her, "My dear, that's the seventh time you've gone up to the bar and asked for another whiskey sour. Doesn't it embarrass you?"

"Why should it?" she answered happily. "I just explain I'm getting them for you."

* * *

Myron Cohen tells about a fellow who was having a running battle with his landlord. "I'll tell you how I keep *my* landlord in line," volunteered Myron. "You just do the same."

Three weeks later Cohen got this note from his friend: "I took your advice, and I expect no more trouble from that dirty landlord. Sincerely, Joe Schwartz. Sing Sing Cell Number 208."

* * *

Roommates at Vassar both had boy friends at Columbia Law School, which worked out very nicely for weekend parties. Suddenly, however, the ardent love letters of both law students ceased, and the girls had to content themselves with dry, non-committal little notes. "What's the matter with you two goons?" the girls demanded one Saturday afternoon. "Don't you love us any more?" "We do, we do," insisted one of the law students, "but, you see, we're studying breach of promise cases this month."

* * *

Donlin was on his way home through a dark alley when three thugs attacked him. Donlin fought like a wildcat, but finally was overcome and robbed of all the change in his pocket —thirty cents, to be exact. "You're a fighting feller," grunted one of the thugs with something like admiration in his voice, "but why would you be wanting to put up such a battle for a measly thirty cents?" "Sure," confided Donlin, "I thought yez wanted the ten dollars I've got hidden in me shoe!"

* * *

A Yale professor was toddling nervously along a dark back street of New Haven when a tough-looking character suddenly accosted him. "Would you be gracious enough," suggested the sinister character, "to lend material assistance to a forlorn, unfortunate fellow who is out of employment? All I've got in the world is just this here loaded pistol."

* * *

A clumsy shoplifter was nabbed pocketing a wristwatch in a jewelry shop. "Give me a chance," he pleaded. "I'll pay for the watch." When a bill was made out for him he turned pale. "This is more than I planned to spend," he quavered. "Can't you show me something less expensive?"

* * *

Stickup men become more sophisticated daily. Take the gunman who suddenly popped up at the paymaster's window of a mammoth assembly plant and barked, "Never mind the payroll, bud. Just hand over the welfare fund, the pension fund, the group insurance premiums, and the withholding taxes."

* * *

Two prisoners on the rock pile suddenly started slugging each other. A warden pulled them apart and asked the aggressor, "Why did you attack this man?" The prisoner's surly explanation: "He called me a dirty number!"

* * *

Defendant Nails Epstein, convicted for his ninth robbery, pleaded for mercy, whining, "I just finished a term of ten years, Your Honor." His Honor decreed promptly, "You are hereby sentenced to twenty more. One good term deserves another."

* * *

In a small town in Maine, the sheriff doubles as the vet. In the middle of one cold night he received an emergency call. "Do you want me as sheriff or vet?" he inquired. "Both," came the agitated reply. "We can't get our dog's mouth open—and there's a burglar's rear in it."

* * *

A short biography, submitted by Serena Babbitt: 1. High chair. 2. High school. 3. High stool. 4. High finance. 5. High hat. 6. "Hi, Warden."

* * *

In a busy suburban bank, a mean-looking hombre silently slid a note to the paying teller which read, "Put every dollar in your cage into a bag and don't open your mouth or I'll shoot." The teller obediently slid back the bag of money with a note of his own, which read, "Straighten your necktie, sloppy. Your picture is being taken."

* * *

"Hello! Is this Police Headquarters?" came an anguished voice over the telephone. "This is the Old Maids' Home. Send a riot squad quick! A burglar has broken in!"

"Okay, okay," soothed the lieutenant at the desk. "Who's this speaking?"

"It's the burglar," answered the terrified voice.

* * *

A chronic bad check passer suffered his greatest indignity recently. He received a call from his Red Cross blood bank. It seems his blood bounced.

* * *

Clancy, traffic cop at a busy Main Street corner for twenty years, celebrated his birthday just a bit too riotously and had to call the station house to say he was so ill he couldn't report for duty. The chief urged him with unexpected understanding just to go back to bed and sleep it off. "The chief is getting soft in his old age," reflected Clancy contentedly. Of course, he couldn't know that at that very moment the chief was telling his sergeant with a chuckle, "Poor Clancy's got one beaut of a hangover. Wait 'til he realizes this is his day off!"

* * *

A pretty stenographer brought a paternity suit against her very uncomfortable boss. The judge listened to the mass of most incriminating testimony, and when the time came to announce a verdict, pulled a cigar out of his pocket and handed it to the defendant. "Congratulations," said the judge. "You have just become a father."

* * *

Judge Jacob Brande tells of a young lawyer who had just passed his bar exams and was representing his first client in a city court. He put his brand-new overcoat and brand-new hat on a bench in the courtroom, and, obviously nervous, stepped forward before the judge to do or die.

The judge was a wise and kindly man. He peered at the fledgling lawyer over his glasses and remarked dryly, "Young man, I gather that this is your very first appearance in this court." "It is, sir," quavered the young lawyer. "I thought so," nodded the judge. "Now before we get started, get ahold of your coat and hat and put them where you can keep your eyes on them!"

* * *

"What do you do for a living?" asked the judge.
"I'm night orderly at the hospital," lied the prisoner.
"Thirty days for pan-handling," said the judge.

* * *

A mugger invaded a delicatessen shop, pointed a gun at the proprietor, and demanded, "Give me all your money." The proprietor quavered, "To take out?"

* * *

Patrolman Michael Conlin was banished to a beat in the darkest and dreariest part of town. His sin? He inadvertently arrested a man climbing into a taxi in a convict suit, only to discover that said man was an irascible judge on his way to a fancy dress party.

Patrolman Conlin has learned his lesson. "That's the last time," he swears, "I'll ever book a judge by his cover."

* * *

Alan King asked a veteran city judge, "How do you usually decide a case?" The judge answered, "First, I read the facts of the case. Then I listen to the plaintiff. Then I render my verdict." "Don't you listen to the defendant, too?" demanded the astonished Mr. King. "Never," insisted the judge. "That would get me all mixed up."

* * *

The police finally caught a bank robber red-handed in a corruption-ridden city. This not-so-clever robber was attempting to hold up the bank with a sawed-off shotgun. Unfortunately for him, he had sawed off the wrong end.

* * *

A police teletype was registering "wanted" notices and an operator at the station house read the reports into the radio microphone. This one brought conversation to a halt: "Lefty Loomis. Height: 5:9. Eyes: brown and blue. Hair: blond and dark brown. Nose: flat and bulbous. Mustache: yes and no. Marks: jagged scar on one chin." "This Loomis clown," muttered Sergeant Epstein, "sounds like he's got two heads." "That's right," nodded the operator, "he has." "Hmm," pondered Sergeant Epstein. "Not much to go on except the scar."

* * *

"Nails" Flanagan's wife turned up for the first time in months to see him on visitors' day at a federal penitentiary. "Nails," she said earnestly, "you been in this jail now for two full years and the children are starting to ask questions." "Yeah?" mumbled Nails suspiciously. "What kind of stuff do they want to know?" "Mainly," said Mrs. Flanagan, "where you stashed the loot."

* * *

When Ronnie Anville won his fourth straight breach of promise suit, he told reporters jubilantly, "These cases never bother me. No dame has been able to pin anything on me since I was ten months old!"

* * *

"I've got a skunk in my cellar," wailed a housewife over the phone to the police. The officer receiving the call assured her, "Nothing to get excited about. Just make a trail of breadcrumbs from the basement to the yard and wait for the skunk to follow it outside."

An hour later, the housewife was back on the phone, more frantic than ever. "I did what you told me," she announced. "Now I've got *two* skunks in my cellar."

* * *

The defendant in a big fraud case showed signs of panic on the witness stand. His high-priced lawyer, seeking to restore his confidence, told him in a stage whisper, "Take it easy, man. All you've got to do is tell the jury, in my words, exactly what happened!"

* * *

A crook high on the list of "most wanted" by the police of twenty states sneaked up the stairs of an ornate suburban mansion and headed for a cache of diamonds and pearls, when from the bedroom a shrill voice was heard:

"What do you mean, I spend too much money on clothes? That chinchilla you're always yapping about is four years old. I haven't had a new evening dress in months. Your partner's

wife spends more on herself in one week than I do in two years.
. . . Blah, blah, blah. . . ."

The crook tiptoed out of the house and rejoined his accomplice on the lawn. "It's no use," he sighed. "I can't go through with it. It's too much like robbing my own home."

* * *

The victim of a bus mishap had just collected fifty thousand dollars in damages in court, but his jubilation ended abruptly when his lawyer announced that he intended to keep 70 per cent of the sum for himself. "You're a damnable extortionist," blustered the accident victim. "Don't forget I'm the man who was involved in the accident." "Agreed," nodded the lawyer, "but it was my legal know-how and power of persuasion that won the case for you. Any imbecile can get knocked down by a bus!"

* * *

A Milwaukee judge, inspecting the state prison at Waupun, needed a shave, so took a chair in the prison barbershop. The barber lathered his face, then suddenly recognized him as he was stropping the razor. "Say, you're Judge So-and-So," he growled. "You sent me up here for twenty years!"

The judge, who never lost his presence of mind, jumped up from his chair and exclaimed, "By Jove! What a coincidence! I'm up here to get a pardon for you!"

* * *

The Detroit Athletic Club *News* printed a cartoon recently that had lawyer members chuckling. It showed a legalite about to read a will to a roomful of beady-eyed relatives. The legalite opened the session by confiding, "Before I read this will, I'd like to announce my engagement to Miss Hudson in the second row."

* * *

A recent Supreme Court ruling prompted this story from Herb Stein in California: A group of schoolchildren were kneeling on the floor just before class was to begin. The teacher walked in, and deeply concerned, asked, "What are you children doing kneeling on the floor?" Replied one of the youngsters, "We're playing marbles." "Oh, that's just dandy," said the teacher, relieved. "I was afraid you were praying!"

MUSICIANS

M. Tippit was at one of those parties where the host made a reluctant offspring play the violin for helpless guests. The offspring, visibly seething, snarled, "Folks, I hereby dedicate the piece I've selected to my former music teacher—who chickened out."

◦ ◦ ◦

At the conclusion of one of his most triumphant concerts before a packed house in Carnegie Hall, pianist Sergei Rachmaninoff was asked by a critic, "What sublime thoughts were passing through your head as you sat down at the piano to begin your concert?" Rachmaninoff answered frankly, "I was counting the house."

◦ ◦ ◦

Sir Thomas Beecham, internationally famous orchestra conductor, adamantly refused to hire female musicians. "If they're pretty," he explained testily, "they distract my male musicians. If they're not pretty, they distract me."

◦ ◦ ◦

During composer-conductor Igor Stravinsky's first tour of the United States, his command of the English language was sketchy, to say the least.

One day in Milwaukee, the first violinist made the same ghastly mistake three times at a rehearsal. Stravinsky never ceased addressing the miscreant in the most polite terms.

Later a friend complimented him on his control. "How you

could speak so politely," he marveled, "when you obviously were seething in rage inside beats me."

"Ah," explained Stravinsky in his native tongue, "that is because I have learned only polite phrases in English. You should have heard what I was calling him under my breath in Russian!"

* * *

That eminent composer and band leader, Duke Ellington, who understandably is not displeased when disciples refer to him as "The American Bach," often quotes that same Bach in his casual conversation. The Duke once was heard to remark, speaking about piano playing, "As Bach says, if you ain't got a left hand, you ain't worth a hoot in hell."

* * *

Jascha Heifetz once spent a summer vacation in Lake Placid, in the Adirondacks. The lady in the cottage next door practiced piano regularly for an hour each morning, Heifetz or no Heifetz. What's more, she played terribly.

One day a stranger appeared at her door and said, "I'm the piano tuner." "I didn't order any piano tuner," expostulated the lady. "You didn't," agreed the piano tuner, "but Mr. Heifetz did."

* * *

Mrs. Glogauer, fat, rich, and fortyish, was about to give her first recital after years of arduous vocal lessons. The audience was large, if unenthusiastic, consisting of Mr. Glogauer's employees, who had been ordered to attend—or else.

"Oh," wailed the jittery Mrs. Glogauer, "if I only could learn what to do with my hands while I'm singing."

"Why not," suggested Mr. Glogauer wearily, "just hold them over your mouth?"

* * *

A famous opera star rests up between acts at the Met by performing Yoga exercises. "There's one person who gets a bigger kick out of this than I," he told a fellow artist, "and that's my little boy. I heard him explaining to a friend this morning, 'It's great when Daddy stands on his head. I grab all the money that falls out of his pockets and my dog licks his face.'"

* * *

Victor Borge once confessed to Irving Berlin, "Every time I stop telling jokes to an audience, and sit down at the piano to play a little Mozart, I hear a voice whispering in my ear: 'Don't play it!' the voice says, 'For heaven's sake, don't play it!'"

"Do you recognize the voice?" asked Berlin.

"I certainly do," Borge assured him. "It's Mozart."

* * *

John Rosenfeld tells about the lady musician who was fired in disgrace from a nationally famous orchestra. "We had a concert date in Dallas," she explained tearfully, "and I forgot my harp."

* * *

Theme song of the Association of Nearsighted Citizens: "I've Lost My Glasses—So I Wonder Who's Kissing Me Now."

* * *

A college student explained how he picked up a few dollars each week working as an extra in the opera. "All I do," he laughed, "is carry a spear—and keep my mouth shut." "But after a hard day of classes, all that extra work!" gushed an elderly lady. "How do you keep awake?" "That's the least of my worries, lady," said the student. "The fellow behind me carries a spear, too!"

* * *

According to expert Sigmund Spaeth, a tabulation of the three songs most often sung by Americans would include neither "The Star-Spangled Banner," nor "Home Sweet Home," nor "Dixie." Number One, in fact—and by a wide margin—is "Happy Birthday to You." Number Two is "For He's a Jolly Good Fellow." And Number Three is "Auld Lang Syne."

* * *

"Often a song that fails completely is given a brand-new title by its composer and publisher and then promptly scores a smash hit," notes Louis Sobol. "Make Me a Star," for instance, renamed "Blue Moon," quickly made the Hit Parade. Other temporary flops that followed a similar pattern were: "Turkish Tom Tom" changed to "Dardanella," "Smile and Show Your Dimple" renamed "Easter Parade," "If I Were on the Stage" changed to "Kiss Me Again," and "I Have No Words," republished as "Something to Remember You By."

* * *

Along about 1930, a young man named Irving Caesar wrote the lyrics for a song he hoped would make him famous. It was called "Louisville," and wasn't very good. The point of this story, however, is that Caesar persuaded a composer named J. Fred Cootes to set the words of "Louisville" to music—and Cootes' melody was very good indeed.

In fact, Cootes remembered the melody some four years later when another lyricist named Gillespie popped up with lyrics that impressed everybody in Caesar's office. The words of the new song and the melody written for "Louisville" fitted together like ham and eggs, or Scotch and soda—and the result was published just in time for the holiday season of 1934. It has sold over a million records and copies of sheet music every year since, and promises to go on for many years more. The song: "Santa Claus Is Coming to Town."

✿ ✿ ✿

The audience was still applauding the first number rendered by the Wappingdale Falls Marching and Chowder Club band when the trombonist leaned over and asked the flute player, "What number do we do next?" "The Washington Post March," answered the flute player. "Holy cow," gasped the trombonist. "That's what I just finished playing!"

✿ ✿ ✿

Morris Fishbein tells of a man who bought his wife a piano for Christmas, but by Valentine's Day had persuaded her to switch to a clarinet. "How come?" asked a friend. "Well," was the explanation, "when she's playing the clarinet, she can't sing."

✿ ✿ ✿

After Carl Sandburg had played his guitar for a TV show recently, the director apologized for all the sneezing and coughing that had been done by the audience. "They didn't do it on purpose," said Sandburg indulgently. "They're like the little boy who sneezed in church, and was reprimanded by his mother. The boy explained, 'I didn't sneeze the sneeze, mama; the sneeze sneezed me.'"

✿ ✿ ✿

A draftee from Kansas was sent to Honolulu and was enraptured by the supple hula dancers he encountered there. He wrote to his father, "I've got to tell you, Dad, that those girls sure know to shake hay while the son pines!"

✿ ✿ ✿

In his amusing autobiography, *What Time's the Next Swan?* Walter Slezak tells how his father, the famous opera star Leo Slezak, was put on a strict diet when his weight became alarming. For a week he howled that he was being starved, then suddenly began accepting his meager fare with amazing serenity. His dog betrayed him by taking a stand at Slezak's desk, holding a rigid point, and barking like mad. Mrs. Slezak investigated and found inside the desk a two-foot-long Hungarian salami.

For showing up his master, the dog was renamed Judas Iscariot.

* * *

Famous novelist William Styron has a four-year-old daughter who fancies herself as a connoisseur of fine music. She was listening intently to Leonard Bernstein leading his orchestra on TV one morning when her father inquired, "Do you know what they're playing?" The daughter answered haughtily, "I'm not sure, but I suspect it's one of those symphonies by Boat-Haven."

* * *

Karl Haas, Director of Fine Arts at Station WJR, Detroit, has a rare sense of humor. Asked to prepare a program to entertain sick students at Wayne University, he labeled the concert, "Music for Ill Literates." A morning TV program of rock 'n' roll selections he listed as "Music to Steal Hubcaps By."

* * *

Teachers as well as parents have their problems with teenagers. Harold Dunn, for instance, who teaches music in Jefferson City, Missouri, submits these five excerpts from classroom essays:

Joseph Haydn was born in 1732, and soon became the father of classical music. Later, at the age of twenty-eight, he got married. Haydn had a lot of will power. He died in 1809 and is still dead.

Bach was the most famous composer in the world and so was Handel. Handel was half German, half English, and half Alsatian. He was rather large.

Chopin had many fast friends. Among the fastest was Miss Sand.

Paganini was a famous fiddler. He fiddled with many of the greatest singers in Europe.

Requiems are usually played for sad occasions like funerals

and marriages. Fugues are also popular. The most popular fugue was the one between the Hatfields and the McCoys.

* * *

Jack Benny recalls a day in his youth when he was practicing on his violin in old Waukegan, Illinois. A dog stood outside the window howling his head off. Benny's father stuck his head inside the door and implored, "For Pete's sake, Jack, play something that dog doesn't know!"

* * *

How long will the Beatle craze last? The Beatles themselves know how quickly idols of the teen-agers can topple, but they are not too concerned. "When it's over and done with," reflected Ringo Beatle unemotionally, "I imagine we'll have nothing to do but sit on the deck of our yacht—and sulk."

* * *

At Carnegie Hall, in New York, a famous pianist took a final bow, then retired moodily to his dressing room, barring old friends and autograph hunters. He had given a slipshod performance and knew it. "Cheer up," counseled his manager. "We all have our off days. You had one coming to you."

The pianist finally was consoled, and he and his manager went to a nearby Russian tea room for refreshments. There one of the pianist's bitterest rivals appeared suddenly and cried, "Dear boy! You were magnificent tonight! You outdid yourself."

The pianist paled visibly and whispered to his manager, "Damnation! Was I *that* awful?"

❋ ❋ ❋

Art Buchwald tells of the day an ambitious and aggressive mother conned the great pianist, Artur Rubinstein, into listening to her ten-year-old son murder a nocturne by Chopin. At the conclusion of the massacre, Rubinstein announced, "Madam, that is undoubtedly the worst piano playing I ever heard." Whereupon the mother nodded happily and told her son, "You see, stupid? Now will you give up those expensive piano lessons and try out for the Little League baseball team?"

PSYCHOANALYSTS

At the conclusion of a first—and most painful—session with a brand new patient, a psychoanalyst cleared his throat and murmured, "Now about weekly bills and where they're to be sent. . . ." "Ah," interrupted the patient. "I see you are concerned about my credit rating. Don't you worry about a thing, Doctor. You're going to get every penny I ever owe you or my name isn't Napoleon Bonaparte!"

❋ ❋ ❋

Another glassy-eyed character who was convinced he was Napoleon burst into an analyst's study, thrust his hand inside his vest, and announced, "It isn't myself I've come to see you about, Doctor. It's my wife Josephine. She thinks she's Mrs. Margolies!"

* * *

"You've got to straighten out my husband," said a wife to a Park Avenue psychiatrist. "He thinks he's a jet plane." "Bring him here Thursday at two," suggested the psychiatrist. "That time is impossible," said the wife. "He's got to appear in court that afternoon—for flying low over Flatbush."

* * *

A new patient, signing up for treatment, confided to a psychiatrist, "I'd better tell you before we begin that I suffer from marked suicidal tendencies." "Very interesting," nodded the psychiatrist. "Under the circumstances, I'm sure you won't mind paying me in advance."

* * *

Heard about the sheep who simply couldn't get to sleep at night? In despair, he sought a psychiatrist, and told him, "You simply have to find a way for me to fall asleep nights—and please, Doctor, NO WISECRACKS."

* * *

A new patient from a publishing house informed his analyst, "I have just finished writing a play called *The Taming of the Shrew.*" "My dear fellow," sympathized the analyst, "*The Taming of the Shrew* was written by William Shakespeare." "That's a coincidence," mused the patient. "They told me the same thing when I wrote *Hamlet.*"

* * *

Paul Pearlman relays a story about a weirdie who wandered into a psychiatrist's office and stuffed tobacco into his left ear. "Obviously you need me," said the doctor. "I sure do," agreed the man. "Got a match?"

* * *

A proud but disturbed gentleman who had convinced himself he was General Robert E. Lee was brought by relatives to a famous New Orleans brain specialist. After a year, however, the specialist had to admit he could provide no cure. He gave up the case and submitted his bill. "General Lee" paid it promptly—in Confederate money!

* * *

Molly Berg has a neighbor whose husband became convinced he was a cannibal. The distressed wife finally persuaded him to visit a psychiatrist. Molly met him on the way home. "Nu?" she inquired, "What's the fancy psychiatrist like?" "Delicious," beamed the husband.

* * *

Then there's the worried lady who called her doctor to report, "My husband has suddenly gone off his rocker. He seems to think he's George Washington."

"When can I see him?" asked the doctor.

"Just take a look out of your window," said the lady. "He's out in your backyard chopping down your cherry tree."

* * *

"Now," said a head doctor to his new patient, "we're going to find out just what makes you tick."

"That won't be enough," mourned the patient. "I also want to know what makes me chime every quarter of an hour."

* * *

A desperate man sought an analyst. "I've developed a phobia," he reported, "that is ruining my business. Crowds make me violently ill." "What's your business?" asked the analyst. The patient answered, "I'm a pickpocket."

* * *

"My poor husband," moaned a woman to the town's leading psychoanalyst. "He's convinced he's a parking meter." The analyst regarded the silent, woebegone fellow holding the wife's hand, and asked, "Why doesn't he say something for himself? Can't he talk?" The wife said, "How can he—with all those dimes and nickels in his mouth?"

13.   *The Printed Word*

AUTHORS

What must be one of the most cynical remarks ever made—as well as a frightening insight into the mental attitude of a world-famous author—was a comment of Somerset Maugham. Said Maugham aciduously, "It is not enough that a writer succeed: his friends must also fail!"

* * *

Other authors on authors:
"I don't understand how two men can write a book together. To me that's like three people getting together to have a baby."
—Evelyn Waugh.
"No man but a blockhead ever wrote except for money."
—Samuel Johnson.
"An author is a fool who, not content with having bored those who have lived with him, insists on boring future generations."
—Montesquieu.
"The good writing of any age has always been the product of someone's neurosis. We'd have a mighty dull literature if all the writers who came along were a bunch of happy chuckleheads."—William Styron.

* * *

The author of two fantastic best sellers remarked at a literary cocktail party, "I went over to the Cannes Festival on the *United States* and came back on the *Queen Elizabeth*." From the rear came the audible whisper, "Boat-dropper!"

* * *

The wife of one of America's most distinguished authors sued him for divorce recently, claiming that she could no longer stand his clomping around the house day after day. "I married him," she explained, "for better or for worse—*not* for lunch."

*　*　*

It is not unusual for an author to disdain his publishers, but William Makepeace Thackeray was more vociferous on the subject than most—possibly because his masterpiece, *Vanity Fair*, had been turned down by eighteen publishers before one was found willing to take a chance on it. Thackeray found himself, with a friend, in the drawing room of a publisher's home, awaiting the publisher, one morning. The carpet in the room was of a gaudy design of red and white. When the publisher appeared, Thackeray announced, "We have been admiring your carpet, sir. It is most appropriate! You wade in the blood and brains of authors!"

*　*　*

In a fascinating book called *The Fine Art of Literary Mayhem,* Myrick Land describes a variety of bitter feuds and vendettas in which world-famous authors climbed down from their ivory towers and exchanged insults that left everybody concerned gasping for breath.

The great historian, Thomas Carlyle, for instance, characterized the poet Algernon Swinburne as "sitting in a sewer and adding to it," and dismissed none other than Ralph Waldo Emerson as a "hoary-headed and toothless baboon." Henry James, rallying to Emerson's defense, deprecated Carlyle as "that same old sausage, fizzing and sputtering in his own grease." Most vitriolic of all was George Bernard Shaw, ready always to take on all comers. He once infuriated Henry Arthur Jones, reigning London playwright of his day, with such a string of insults that Jones counterattacked Shaw in a public letter beginning, "The Nag Sedition was your mother and Perversity begot you; Mischief was your midwife, and Misrule your nurse!"

* * *

Who says great writers and thinkers are undependable? Viscount Hailsham recalls the morning philosopher Immanuel Kant suddenly remembered he had proposed marriage to a lovely neighbor—and been accepted. He hastily donned his best clothes and rushed over to his prospective bride's home—where he found to his intense disappointment she had left town—some twenty years before.

* * *

From the moment Sherlock Holmes became a byword in England, his creator, Arthur Conan Doyle, was pestered by people of all kinds demanding solutions of problems that perplexed them. A lady who sat next to Doyle at a large dinner, for instance, annoyed him greatly. "Mr. Doyle," she asked so loudly that all other conversation at the table ceased, "there has disappeared from the inside of my country home within a single week one broom, one box of golf balls, a left riding boot, a dictionary, and six tin plates. What would Sherlock Holmes do in a spot like that?" "Very simple," snapped Conan Doyle.

"Sherlock Holmes would tell you that you keep a goat in your home."

* * *

Edith Wharton, author of such great books as *Ethan Frome* and *The Age of Innocence,* was no heroine to her hoity-toity relatives, who considered writing books no fit occupation for a young lady of quality. One uncle up in Newport, in fact, admitted that he rated Miss Wharton slightly more erratic than another unfortunate relative who "spent his last years sitting on a marble shelf in the happy illusion that he was a bust of Napoleon."

* * *

In the days when everybody was reading *Little Women,* Bronson Alcott, high-living and work-disdaining father of authoress Louisa May, regularly dropped into the offices of her publisher in Boston, Little, Brown and Company, in search of cash. "Just charge it against Louisa's royalties," he would suggest grandly. Finally, his daughter had to call a halt; thereafter he was given cash only when he could produce a written authorization from her.

Today, framed at Little, Brown is one of Miss Alcott's notes, reading "Please give my pa $50." Pa had thoughtfully crossed out the "$50" and made it read "$100." Nobody knows whether or not he got away with it.

* * *

Mark Twain was something of a practical joker. A seedy old acquaintance met him at the Hartford railroad station one morning and begged, "Help me once more. Treat me to a ticket to New York." "I'm pretty low on funds myself right now," answered Twain, "but I'll tell you what I'll do. You stow away under my seat and I'll hide you with my legs."

The acquaintance agreed. When the train pulled in, he scrambled under Twain's seat. When the conductor came around, Twain presented two tickets. "The second one," he explained loudly, "is for my friend cramped up under my seat here. He's a bit on the eccentric side—and this is the way he likes to ride."

* * *

When the great Irish poet and dramatist, William Butler Yeats, won the Nobel Prize in 1923, a group of his admirers in Dublin insisted upon giving a banquet in his honor. Yeats, a very shy, introspective man, writhed with embarrassment as speaker after speaker sang his praises. He sank lower and lower in his chair on the dais, but was suddenly revived when the chairman presented him with a check for twenty-five hundred pounds—over ten thousand dollars in those days—the gift of several wealthy gentlemen present. Yeats rose to his feet, stared at the check for a moment, then startled his audience by remarking, "Twenty-five hundred pounds, eh? I must say that's damn little for all the lies I've had to listen to this evening!"

* * *

Hesketh Pearson recalls an evening he spent with the
George Bernard Shaws. While G.B.S. told one story after an-
other, Mrs. Shaw sat silently doing needlepoint. "What are
you working on so diligently?" whispered Pearson to Mrs.
Shaw. "What difference does it make?" she whispered back.
"It's just that I've heard these stories of his five hundred times,
and if I didn't do something with my hands, I'D CHOKE
HIM!"

*   *   *

Minneapolis sage "Mox" Lindquist met an old friend who
had taken up story writing as a career. "Have you sold anything yet?" asked Mox. "Yes," nodded his friend. "My dress
suit, some furniture, and my watch."

*   *   *

A distinguished author who summers in Provincetown received a note there from a schoolgirl which read, "I have chosen
you as my favorite author. Please write me immediately in
not less than three hundred words and tell me why."

*   *   *

Writers are famous procrastinators, and seize on any kind
of excuse to put off getting down to work.

Novelist Graham Greene found a brand new way of pro-
crastinating. A friend visited him at his English country estate and reported, "Every day Graham would disappear
mysteriously for hours from the house. When I finally asked
what he was up to, he explained that he could not write another word until a certain combination of numbers—987—appeared to him by accident. He was spending hours by the
roadside waiting for those numbers to pass on a license plate.

"Well, it's a poor country road, and there are not many motor cars. So Graham didn't write a single word for the entire
week."

*   *   *

A distinguished novelist was complaining at the Overseas
Press Club one evening that his wife had been driving him

batty for ten years and more. "Why don't you give her the air?" asked a sympathizer. "I can't," mourned the novelist. "She's the only typist I know who can read my damn handwriting."

*　*　*

With censorship battles raging throughout the land, it might be interesting to read what two famous writers had to say on the subject.

Noted George Bernard Shaw: "All censorships exist to prevent anyone from challenging current conceptions and existing institutions. All progress is initiated by challenging current conceptions, and executed by supplanting existing institutions. Consequently, the first condition of progress is the removal of censorships."

And Eugene O'Neill noted: "Censorship of anything, at any time, in any place, on whatever pretense, has always been and always will be the last cowardly resort of the boob and the bigot."

*　*　*

One of Noel Coward's Jamaica acquaintances was bemoaning the fact that the ranks of his old friends were being depleted at an alarmingly accelerated rate. "Two funerals this week alone," he sighed. Coward assured him grimly, "Personally, I'm delighted now if they last through lunch!"

*　*　*

Bill Saroyan, of *Daring Young Man on the Flying Trapeze* fame, returned one day in triumph after he had made a fortune, to the San Francisco grocery store where he had clerked briefly in his youth. Everybody crowded around to hear the famous man give his views on life and love. Later the proprietor of the grocery story was asked, "What was the most important thing Saroyan said?" The proprietor answered testily, "He didn't say *anything* important. All he did was eat up my fruit."

❖ ❖ ❖

Honor Tracy, witty and brilliant Irish author of *The Straight and Narrow Path,* was not too pleased with the looks of the English edition of her succeeding effort. She sent the London publisher a copy of the ever-so-much handsomer American edition of the book with a note reading, "As the cock said to the hens when he showed them an ostrich egg, 'I am not disparaging; I am not criticizing. I merely bring to your attention what is being done elsewhere.'"

❖ ❖ ❖

Frank Sullivan, beloved sage of Saratoga, consented to an interview recently, what with the local racetrack closed for the season and a birthday coming up. "What do you think of American women?" began the interviewer. "They should be torn down," said Mr. S. briskly, then added, "Oh, pardon me, that's my answer to what do you think of the newfangled New York skyscrapers. As for American women, I'm not sure there are any nowadays. Everybody wears pants and how is a fellow with astigmatism and myopia going to tell which are women and which are men?"

Mr. Sullivan also commented on the state of American belles-lettres. "It's in a state of flux," he opined. "This chap Katherine Anne Porter seems a good bet, and so does this other chap, Walt Whitman. As for the Russians," he concluded, in no uncertain terms, "they'll never amount to anything until they get rid of the Czar."

* * *

Shortly before his death, William Faulkner, one of America's greatest authors, told me that editor Albert Erskine was the finest literary craftsman whom he ever had met. "When he approves a manuscript of mine," said Faulkner, "I know it's ready for the printer."

"Coming from you," I said, "that is a great, great compliment. Have you told that to Erskine? I know how delighted he would be."

"No, I haven't," admitted Faulkner with a slow smile. "In my book, when a race horse is running good, Bennett, you don't stop him to feed him a piece of sugar!"

* * *

Faulkner enjoyed the reputation for being a prodigious imbiber of bourbon whiskey, but his brother John reveals that many of his most celebrated binges were just playacting. He would get word to his family in Oxford, Mississippi, that somebody must come and fetch him. The "somebody" almost always was his mother, a gallant, indomitable wisp of a woman who knew her son Bill merely wanted to be fussed over.

Once she tricked Faulkner by serving him iced tea with just a dash of whiskey to lull him. When he stammered that he was sozzled, and couldn't get out of bed, she told him calmly he had been drinking tea for ten hours straight. The sheepish Mr. Faulkner rose silently and trudged off to work.

* * *

A young novelist began his speech at a Book and Author luncheon by quoting from a letter he had recently received: "You are the finest young writer in America today. You combine the skills of O'Hara, Faulkner, Hemingway, and Michener. Furthermore, you are the handsomest man I've ever encountered."

The audience was obviously taken aback by the young novelist's conceit—until he added, "Incidentally, the letter is signed 'Mother.'"

* * *

Jean Kerr, wife of drama critic Walter Kerr, notes that when a collection of her old magazine articles was published in book form under the title of *Please Don't Eat the Daisies*—and promptly zoomed to the top of the best-seller lists—her mother wrote to her saying, "Darling, isn't it marvelous the way those old pieces of yours finally came to the surface like a dead body!"

❈ ❈ ❈

Poet John Ciardi cherishes this note received from a young admirer, whose name he thoughtfully refuses to disclose: "Dear Mr. Ciardi: I think your new book of poems for children is very funny. I read it in church. I thought it was much better than the sermon. P.S. Please don't tell my daddy about the sermon because he's the minister."

❈ ❈ ❈

Have you heard about the astronaut who buttonholed a famous novelist at a cocktail party and told him, "I read your new book while I was in orbit last week. *Couldn't put it down!*"

A PLEA FOR THE UNKNOWN WRITER

Like the Broadway theatre, the book business today is suffering from a rash of "me-too-ism" that has the country in its grip. Every visitor to New York wants to see the same few smash-hit shows and spurns the broker who tries to sell him tickets for a play that his neighbor has not boasted of seeing when *he* visited the Big City. By the same token, people are buying books today not because they have a particular message, but because their neighbors are reading them or at least displaying them on their library tables—or because they are Number One, Two, or Three on national best seller lists.

This insistence of the American public to read and see what everybody else is reading and seeing has proved a bonanza, of course, for the few fortunate authors of the smash hits and best sellers, but what about the authors—just as deserving and

often more so—whose plays and books have not hit that magic circle? More important still, what about the authors who are totally unknown and have just seen their very first novels appear in print? If nobody will give these newcomers a hearing, how are they ever going to get started on the road to success?

I cannot emphasize the difficulty a publisher encounters today in getting a hearing for a new writer. There are exceptions to the rule, of course; maybe once or twice a year an unknown hits the jackpot, but for every *To Kill a Mockingbird, Goodbye, Columbus,* and *Catch 22,* there are at least a hundred extremely good first novels that not only sell fewer than two thousand copies, but that are never given as much as a one-paragraph review in leading literary journals and book sections. Booksellers do not even want to stock a couple of copies of these first novels, despite the fact that they have full return privilege from the publisher. How often have I heard them say, "First, you create a demand for the book and then I'll order copies. Meanwhile, I don't want to clutter up the shop with books nobody has ever heard of."

It's disheartening to tot up the number of the shining literary American greats of the past generation who have disappeared from the scene in recent years. Just think of the stars who have died in that brief span: Theodore Dreiser, Thomas Wolfe,

Sinclair Lewis, Willa Cather, Edna St. Vincent Millay, and within the past three years Ernest Hemingway, James Thurber, and William Faulkner. In the theatre, we have lost Eugene O'Neill, Robert Sherwood, Moss Hart, and George S. Kaufman. This is but a partial list. How are we going to develop replacements for these great stars if we don't encourage our promising newcomers?

This, then, is an urgent plea to every reader of this brief piece: the next time you go to a bookstore in search of something to give a sick friend or to take for yourself on a vacation, let a clerk whom you trust persuade you to buy a book by somebody who has never had anything published before. Then, if you like what you have read, beat the drum for your discovery. Tell people about it. Help, possibly, to launch another Hemingway or Faulkner on the road to fame!

BOOKS

Richard Armour, wise to the ways of the literary hucksters, notes:

> The publisher riffles the lukewarm review
> To find him a bookselling blurb
> Consisting of adjectives three or two
> To one paltry noun or verb
> Though many the words of another stripe,
> A flattering few he frisks.
> What he wants, he prints in a bold, black type,
> What he doesn't, he asterisks.

* * *

Two venerable gentlemen met on the veranda of a New England inn one summer's day in the eighties. One of them spiced his conversation with so many elaborate quotations that the other grew curious and interrupted with, "What did you say your name was, my good sir?" "Bartlett," was the answer. "John Bartlett."

* * *

An Eskimo sat in his igloo, reading a Shirley Temple Fairy Tale collection to his little boy. "Little Jack Horner sat in a corner," began the father, when the son interrupted him to inquire, "Daddy, what's a corner?"

* * *

Sidney Harris, acidulous Chicago critic, won the undying enmity of a fat, prolific lady novelist with a one-sentence review of her newest potboiler. "Miss Black's new book," noted Harris, "is underwhelming."

* * *

The day after the late Lloyd Morris's *Postscript to Yesterday* was published, the noted critic, Orville Prescott, gave it a glowing review, and Morris's agent rushed over to read it to him. "Prescott says the book obviously was written by a great gentleman of leisure." At that moment, Morris, having parted company with an incompetent servant the day before, was on his hands and knees scrubbing the kitchen floor.

* * *

An ambitious book salesman was endeavoring to sell a Los Angeles retailer a hundred copies of a handsome new gift edition of Elizabeth Barrett Browning's *Sonnets from the Portuguese*. The retailer snorted, "What do I want an item like that for? There aren't a hundred Portuguese in this whole neighborhood!"

* * *

In Bermuda, a formidable lady spent an hour poring over the stock of a book shop near the Salt Kettle House. After rejecting numerous suggestions, she finally decided, "Oh well, I'll take this Ian Fleming paperback." The clerk gave her a startled look, and then said gently, "But, madam, this is the book you brought in with you."

* * *

The type in some of the mammoth new paperbacks gets smaller and smaller and one anguished reader has struck back at his tormentors.

"I propose," he writes, "that these typographical monstrosities henceforth carry this legend on the last page:

'A NOTE ON THE TYPE IN
WHICH THIS BOOK WAS SET.

The type in which this book was set is known, quite unfavorably, as one-half point Myopia, and was designed in 1622 by that noted sadist, Feodor Astigmatism. It bids fair to become one of the most heartily disliked faces this side of Fidel Castro. It is perfect for engraving the complete text of *The Brothers Karamazov* on the head of a pin.'"

＊　＊　＊

Authors of books intended to make readers laugh spend more time on dedications than do their more serious confreres. Here's the dedication Carl Winston came up with for his titilating *How to Turn a Million into a Shoestring*: "I should be remiss, indeed, if I failed to acknowledge my indebtedness to the People's Bank of Bridgeport, the Connecticut Light and Power Co., the New England Telephone Co., Sears Roebuck, Casey Fuel, the West Redding Market, the Internal Revenue Department, and another creditor whose name is Morris H. Legion. The total is $17,886.05. Hi, Fellows!"

＊　＊　＊

A few other inspired book dedications:

Inez McEwen dedicated her *So This Is Ranching* to "My infant grandson, the only gent on whom I've been able to pin anything."

Mark Hellinger dedicated one of his volumes to the bargain basement of a department store, for designing "underwear that doesn't bind while seated at a typewriter."

Vice President Tom Marshall dedicated his memoirs to "President Woodrow Wilson, from his only Vice."

Franklin P. Adams inscribed one volume of verse to his

"Loving wife, but for whose constant interruptions, this book would have been finished six months earlier."

* * *

Officials in New York's Public Library receive a lot of strange requests in the course of their work, but this one from a recent arrival from Tokyo just about takes the cake:

"Sir or Lady: To look for of see to make me a dictionary of thirty thousand words in double from Japanese to English. If no in your book warehouse, I have great need for he now, so interest another warehouse deposit please and see with price how to cost. If no is nowhere twenty five thousandth you give and to you send money in check of bench. Inrespectfully yours . . ."

* * *

A salesman stepped gingerly into a publisher's office and asked the receptionist, "Is His Nibs in a good mood this morning?" "I never saw him in a good mood," admitted the receptionist. "I've only been here three years."

* * *

"If you had occasion," asks Vincent Starrett, "to send a letter to the following characters of history and legend, what addresses would you write on the envelopes? 1. Sherlock Holmes; 2. Solomon Levi; 3. Dr. Manette; 4. Alice's Right Foot, Esq.? Here are the answers: 1. 221-B Baker Street, London; 2. 149 Salem Street, New Haven; 3. 105 North Tower, Bastille, Paris; 4. Hearthrug, near the Fender, with Alice's Love."

* * *

Critic J. Donald Adams, in an idle hour, jotted down the names of ten world-famous books whose authors are virtually unknown today. How many of them do you think you can recall?

Here are the books: 1. *The Swiss Family Robinson;* 2. *Quo Vadis?;* 3. *Black Beauty;* 4. *Baron Munchausen;* 5. *Lorna Doone;* 6. *The Four Horsemen of the Apocalypse;* 7. *East*

Lynne; 8. *Elsie Dinsmore;* 9. *The Covered Wagon;* 10. *Ben Hur.*

The authors: 1. Johann David Wyss; 2. Henryk Sienkiewicz; 3. Anna Sewell; 4. Rudolf Erich Raspe; 5. Richard D. Blackmore; 6. Vicente Blasco Ibáñez; 7. Mrs. Henry Wood; 8. Martha Finley; 9. Emerson Hough; 10. Lew Wallace.

* * *

George Hecht of the Doubleday book shops thought he had heard about everything until a rather brassy young lady sashayed into the Fifty-second Street branch and announced, "I'm looking for a good mystery story to read this evening while waiting to jump out of a birthday cake."

* * *

A distinguished English scholar named George Ordish is working on a history of the Incas, and he went all the way to the Vatican Library in Rome for a look at a book he heard would provide special illumination on the subject. Unfortunately for Mr. Ordish, the head librarian in the Vatican reported that the volume wanted was missing. "Yes, it's too bad," sighed the librarian. "Our records show that the book you wanted to examine has been missing since 1635!"

* * *

One hears a great deal of talk these days about so-called "pornographic" literature, but who is to be the judge of what books really deserve banning on that score?

D. H. Lawrence, observes critic John Hutchens, considered Charlotte Brontë's *Jane Eyre* pornographic, though it is now recommended to high school students. On the other hand, Lawrence cried "Unfair" when his own *Lady Chatterley's Lover* was banned. When Thackeray edited the *Cornhill Magazine*, he rejected a manuscript by Elizabeth Barrett Browning. Why? It contained the word "harlot"! Pornography's all-time best seller, *Fanny Hill*, hasn't one word your maiden Aunt Emma could blush at. On the other hand, Chaucer's *Canterbury Tales* has dozens of them.

In other words, as George S. Kaufman once remarked in a review of ancient Asian wars, "One man's Mede is another man's Persian."

* * *

Early in 1936, the late Wendell Willkie, then President of the Commonwealth and Southern Corporation, attended a convention in Atlanta, Georgia. One of the delegates told him, "Remember meeting my wife the last time you were here? Well, she's written a novel, and a publisher has accepted it. If it sells enough to earn five thousand dollars, we are going to buy a new house." "Good for her," enthused Mr. Willkie. "Although I never have done anything like this before, I'm going to write a letter over my signature to every stockholder urging him to buy a copy of your wife's book."

He was true to his word, and for years thereafter laughingly demanded some of the credit for getting the book off to a rousing start. The name of the book was *Gone with the Wind*.

* * *

Norman Kline is one literary light who believes firmly that the title of a book can mean the difference between a rousing best seller and a dismal failure. What might have been the fate, he asks, of seven all-time favorites, had they been named: 1. *Moby Richard;* 2. *This Side of Paramus;* 3. *Farewell to Feet;* 4. *Happiness Is a Hot Dog;* 5. *Gulliver's Trips;* 6. *Treasure Peninsula;* and 7. *Canoe of Fools?*

* * *

A notorious gangster decided to give his mother a leatherbound Bible for a birthday gift, but felt a bit conspicuous in the shop where he bought it. He handed the Bible to the clerk rather surreptitiously and asked, "Will you please put this in a plain wrapper?"

* * *

Dorothy Parker ended one of her scathing book reviews with a characteristic flourish. "I suppose," she conceded, "that this is another of those young writers who is worth watching. Not reading; just watching."

* * *

In Oshkosh, a cagey bookseller put two copies of *Rabbit Raising for Profit* on his shelf one evening, found six there the next morning.

᛫ ᛫ ᛫

When the late Carolyn Wells earned enough money to buy some long-wanted books for her library, she pasted this plate in every volume: "They borrow books; they will not buy; they have no ethics or religions. I wish some kind Burbankian guy would cross my books with homing pigeons."

᛫ ᛫ ᛫

Jack Fuller discovered a rare two-volume edition of the Essays of Montaigne that evidently never had been opened, since the pages were still unsliced. "Oh, yes," nodded the bookseller, "this is the uncuttest kind of all."

᛫ ᛫ ᛫

Mrs. Healy was the kind of reader who couldn't resist sneaking a look at the ending of a book before she was halfway through it. One day she began reading the dictionary, and true to form, turned to the last page before she got down to the last of the words beginning "*ad.*" "Hah," she exclaimed triumphantly. "Just as I thought. The *zebra* did it!"

MAGAZINES

A would-be fiction writer in Wyoming submitted a story some time ago to the editor of a big magazine. The editor read the story with some interest, then wrote the man who had submitted it, "I thought the story you sent us was excellent. I always have thought so. Unfortunately, I promised Bret Harte that I would only publish 'The Luck of Roaring Camp' under his own name." The editor figured that would shut up the plagiarist once and for all—but he was wrong. Back from him came another letter to the editor, reading, "You were a darn fool ever to have made him such a promise!"

✿ ✿ ✿

A brilliant young editor on a big national magazine received steady promotions and salary increases for years, and seemed headed inevitably for the post of editor-in-chief. Then, unaccountably, he fell out of favor with the capricious owner and was banished to a minor post abroad. In his indignant wire of resignation to the owner, he demanded, "Why did you keep me on tiptoe so long if you weren't going to kiss me?"

✿ ✿ ✿

This letter is framed and hung on the wall behind the desk of Herbert Mayes, brilliant Pooh-Bah of *McCall's:* "SIR: My wife was about to divorce me until she read your touching article about the evils of a broken home. Now she says she is going to stick to me through thick and thin. Please cancel my subscription."

✿ ✿ ✿

Harold Ross, founder of *The New Yorker* Magazine, received a letter one morning from a famous short story writer. Engraved on the letterhead were not only the author's name and address but laudatory quotes from summaries of the writer's work.

Ross stewed about this for a week, then had some letterheads of his own printed just so he could answer the famous short story writer in similar style. Ross had *his* name and address engraved on each sheet, plus these two quoted tributes to himself: 1. "A splendid fellow"—John Wilkes Booth; 2. "Among those present was Harold Ross"—Account of a murder trial in the New York *Journal.*

✿ ✿ ✿

One of the probably apocryphal stories concerning a running feud between Editor Ross and his star but temperamental contributor, Alexander Woollcott, concerns the time Woollcott turned in a "Shouts and Murmurs" column for *The New Yorker* a little too dripping with schmaltz and purple prose. Ross sent it back to Mr. W. with this note crayoned across the margin: "What you need, Woollcott, is a good, stiff ride on the subway in the rush hour."

◦ ◦ ◦

Cruelest blow dealt a doughty magazine editor came from a mere wisp of a girl—a very pretty one, too—who submitted a short story in longhand. "Your story's first-rate and I mean to buy it," the editor told her cheerily, "but we had the devil's own time deciphering your handwriting. Why didn't you type the story?" "Type it?" jeered the girl. "Do you think I'd waste my time writing stories if I knew how to type?"

◦ ◦ ◦

The editor of a brand-new digest magazine wired a famous author in Switzerland offering him five thousand dollars for a "definitive article on the significance of the idealistic split between the Soviet and Red China." The writer accepted the assignment. "Fine! Fine! Go to it," enthused the editor, "but please remember to confine your article to fifteen words."

◦ ◦ ◦

A woman submitted a torrid love story to a popular magazine and awaited word in vain from the editor for several weeks. Finally she wired, "Please report on my story immediately as I have other irons in the fire." An answering wire—collect—read, "We have considered your story and advise you to put it with the other irons."

NEWSPAPERS

In the middle 1830's, Richard O'Connor points out, there were fifteen daily newspapers circulating on the streets of New York—as opposed to six in 1965. But those papers of the 1830's had little to offer their readers in the way of news or features. A murder was dismissed in a few lines if it was mentioned at all. Court actions, misbehavior by socialites or celebrities, and business misfortunes were absolutely taboo. One man changed all this. James Gordon Bennett, whose irreverent

New York *Herald* was introduced on May 6, 1835, soon set a new pattern that was the direct forerunner of the kind of newspaper we're accustomed to reading today.

Before they had to emulate Bennett to escape bankruptcy, however, his competitors labeled him "an obscene vagabond," "a leprous slanderer," "a profligate wretch," "a pestilential scoundrel," and "a vile nuisance." They capitulated when the *Herald's* circulation soared to fifty-one thousand—against thirty-six thousand for his three principal rivals combined!

* * *

In his youth, James Gordon Bennett was a reckless gadabout. His wild driving of a four-horse tally-ho once caused a crash in which one of his loveliest companions, Miss Jennie Jerome, was injured. Fortunately, she recovered—and went on to marry Lord Randolph Churchill. One of her sons was Winston Churchill.

Bennett was as vain as he was capricious. He demanded personal credit for every triumph earned by his staff; when any employee was accorded public recognition on his own, Bennett sacked him. One day Bennett demanded by cable that a list be given him of all the men on the *Herald* staff the managing editor considered indispensable. A list of his fourteen best men was promptly supplied. Bennett immediately fired every one of them! He told his secretary, "I will have no indispensable men in my employ."

Stupidity of this sort left Bennett and his *Herald* an easy victim when newspaper giants like Hearst and Pulitzer appeared upon the New York scene.

* * *

This clipping from what he claims is a leading New Hampshire newspaper has been turned up by an eager young Harvard upperclassman: "Jared Hemp, one of the oldest residents of Pewter County, N.H., celebrated his ninety-seventh birthday at his home yesterday. When interviewed, Mr. Hemp was winding his watch. 'Yes, I still wind my own watch,' he said with a twinkle in his eye. 'I attribute my virile old age to my constant use since I was a boy of licorice lozenges and to my never wearing a collar. This gave me adequate saliva and health-improving neck-play.' Mr. Hemp entered the business of making lasts at the age of eleven and has lasted ever since. He has fourteen children, all of whom are in jail."

* * *

Damon Runyon landed his first newspaper job in Denver, Colorado. He waited in the anteroom of the city editor while an office boy announced his presence. The office boy reappeared and said, "The boss wants you to send in a card."

Runyon had no card—nor did he ever have one after he became famous—but he did have a pack of playing cards in his back pocket. He carefully extracted the ace of spades and told the office boy, "Give him this!" The city editor not only hired him, but treated him to lunch.

* * *

Lester Markel, for many years the brilliant but crusty editor of the Sunday Magazine section of a big newspaper, often made contributors rewrite an article several times before he blessed it with his O.K. He admitted at a staff conference, "We once asked England's great economist, Barbara Ward, to rewrite a piece five times." "Right," chimed in Markel's assistant, "and you printed all five versions."

* * *

One of the reasons Bob Considine has more friends than almost anybody else in the newspaper business: he was overheard explaining to a first-time visitor at his apartment: "Millie and I have four children, two of whom we adopted. I forget which two."

A Few Classified Ads Culled from Small-Town Dailies and Weeklies . . .

1. "Will the mother whose little boy laid his half-sucked lollipop on a mahogany end table please come in again? She can have the end table for exactly one dollar, with the lollipop still intact."

2. "Attractive kitten seeks position purring in a nice little girl's lap. Will also do light mouse work."

3. "For sale: diamonds: $3; microscopes: $2.75."

4. "Will the party who picked up the black cocker spaniel puppy Friday on the boardwalk either return him or come back and get the heartbroken four-year-old boy he belongs to?"

5. "Send for a box of our homemade soap. It doesn't lather. It doesn't float. It contains no secret ingredients. It is designed solely to keep you company in the tub."

6. "Wanted: smart young lady to act as deceptionist." . . .

7. "For sale: 38-foot cruiser. A beauty equipped with two bailing pumps. May be seen by appointment. Bring diving helmet."

8. "Will the lady who saved $90 on electric washer I advertised in last week's *Gazette* please get in touch with me? It was the drier my wife wanted to sell."

9. "For sale: modern house with 4 bedrooms, 3 baths and rumpus room in cellar. Extra attraction: the family next door is building a swimming pool."

10. This plaintive classified ad was inserted in a Missouri gazette by the minister of a Presbyterian church: "Wanted! Men, women and children to sit in slightly used pews on Sunday morning."

* * *

A gentleman's umbrella was pilfered at a town meeting in the Midwest. After spending twice the price of the umbrella in ads for its recovery, he still had not gotten it back. His ad was worded:

"Lost from town meeting last Friday: a black silk umbrella. The gentleman who took it will be handsomely rewarded by leaving it at number seven, National Bank Building."

A high-powered copywriter sniffed, "No wonder your advertisement produced no results," and rewrote it as follows:

"If the man who was *seen* taking an umbrella from the vestibule at Friday's town meeting does not wish to get into trouble and have an indelible stain cast upon his Christian character, which he values so highly, he will return it *at once* to number seven, National Bank Building. *He is well known.*"

Next day the man who had lost the umbrella found twelve of them propped up in his anteroom.

* * *

The late Arthur James Pegler was a newspaper reporter in the grand tradition, a rootin' tootin' daredevil of a man, who risked his own life a hundred times to bring home a good story.

Once, Pegler was held up by a blizzard in Iowa. Seeking refuge in a farmhouse, he discovered that the owner had just passed away; the widow asked him to sit up with her husband's body while she went off to make the funeral arrangements. Pegler dropped off to sleep. When he awoke, the "corpse" was observing him critically. "You're dead!" gasped

Pegler. "Heck, no," was the reply. "It's just my fits. The old woman has tried to bury me three times before this!"

Pegler always said this was the one moment in all his wild life as a reporter that he was terrified. He also tried to persuade his son Francis not to follow in his footsteps. "Be anything but a newspaperman," he counseled son Francis, who later changed his name to Westbrook, and did not take his father's advice.

* * *

Jack Fuller has come up with a new game called "Reporters and Newspapers." Examples: Brown from the *Sun;* Cutt from the *Blade;* Justice from the *Tribune;* Left at the *Post;* Noyes of the *Bugle;* Plato of the *Republic;* and Lowering of the *Standard.* The one I like best is Alice of the *Mirror* (the London *Mirror,* that is). I'm sure readers of *Laugh Day* can come up with more of the same!

* * *

John McPhaul tells of a morning when a Washington businessman dropped in at a Chicago newspaper office endeavoring to collect a $150 debt owed to him for many a long day by one of the featured columnists on the paper. He failed in his mission, but for his pains he did get this attention in the columnist's next outpouring: "Mr. So-and-So, the well-known Washington banker, is in Chicago for a few days looking after some of his permanent investments."

* * *

A sadder but wiser newspaperman in Buffalo is looking for a new job. He lost his old one when the chief auditor spotted this item on a big expense account tab he tried to get away with: "Dinner with the sports editor of the Congressional Record: $46."

* * *

At a Westchester country club, a member told the owner of a big metropolitan newspaper, "Say, I owe you a vote of thanks. Your paper proved just the thing to stop my two kids from raising the devil this morning." Obviously pleased, the newspaper owner inquired, "What particular article did the trick?" "No article at all," explained the father. "I just rolled up your paper and whacked them with it."

❋   ❋   ❋

No approver of all the newspaper mergers that have studded the history of American journalism in recent years was the late James Thurber. "One day," predicted Thurber dourly, "we're going to end up with just one newspaper for the entire country —and *the whole front page will have to be devoted to the name.*"

14. *Punsters on Parade*

If it's true, as many pun-dits aver, that the more ludicrous the buildup, the more shattering is the pun, Don Addis, of Hollywood, richly deserves first place in this staggering compundium for his story of the lad who was counting on his Uncle Al to take him to the circus.

Came the big day, however, and his mother told him that Uncle Al had flown to Australia to see the Davis Cup tennis matches. "I didn't know Uncle Al liked that game so much, Mom," mourned the lad. "Oh, but he does," she assured him. "Many's the time I've heard Alfred laud tennis, son!"

* * *

Last New Year's Eve, recalls William Travis, of Birmingham, a neighbor of his, named Early, gave a costume party, and to in-

sure its success mailed invitations far in advance. Two eager
guests, dressed as an old man and a dazzling young girl, to
represent May and December, showed up for the party on
Halloween. "You've pulled the boner of the year," scoffed the
host. "Not at all," corrected the masqueraders. "We're two
months, Early."

*   *   *

Playing golf at the Century Club, the curvaceous Mrs.
Manges hit a niblick shot fully thirty yards beyond the second
green. "What did I do wrong?" she asked her husband, a prominent attorney. "You didn't dig deep enough," he explained.
"You only took af-fadavit." (The penalty for this sort of thing
at most clubs is two strokes and distance.)

*   *   *

In an obviously enchanted forest near the home of Mrs.
Mary O'Brian, in San Bernardino, lived two families of amiable, hard-working gnus, who often enjoyed picnicking together.
Each family boasted one young mischief-maker, however,
though each mother was convinced her own little gnu was the
innocent dupe of his evil friend.

"You should punish that rascally brat of yours," shrilled one
mother finally. "A sound spanking might do him some good."

"Spank *my* son, indeed," huffed the other. "Why don't you
go paddle your own gnu?"

*   *   *

Nominated for the worst of the year: the story of the three
Indian squaws who were admitted to the maternity ward at
the same time. Chief Wampum, head obstetrician, assigned
one to a buffalo hide, the second to an elk hide, and the third
to a hippopotamus hide (now where did he get hold of *that*
one?). At any rate, the squaws on the elk and buffalo hides
each produced a six-pound son. But the squaw on the hippopotamus hide mothered healthy, six-pound twins. All of
which proves, of course, that the sons of the squaw of the hippopotamus equal the sons of the squaws of the other two hides.

* * *

John Hutchens reports that a man intent upon reading up on locusts (there's a new plague of them due, we're told) was annoyed by the cost of books covering the subject, and declared forcefully, "What this country needs is a good five-cent cicada."

* * *

Miss Beatrice Lillie managed to remember she was a punster, too, even when a waiter spilled a whole cup of coffee on her costly new evening gown. "Go," Miss Lillie told the crestfallen waiter, "and never darken my Dior again."

* * *

A man, later identified as Tunis Conquy, was walking down a Southern road one day when, caught in an unexpected downpour, he sought shelter in a farmhouse. The friendly folks there invited him to join them for dinner. Said the hostess, "The meat on the plate on the left comes from a North Carolina piggie; the ham on the other plate comes from a little piggie from South Carolina. Which do you prefer?"

Whereupon Mr. Conquy replied (what a way to repay fine old Southern hospitality!), "Either one, Ma'am. Any pork in a storm."

Punsters by the Score . . .

1. The fire chief who responded to a call from a lingerie shop, but found no sign of a blaze when he got there. His official report read, "falsie alarm."

2. The poet who insists that a pond on his farm is the smallest body of water in the U.S.A. He's named it Lake Inferior.

3. The crow who perched himself on a telephone wire. He wanted to make a long distance caw.

4. The snake charmer who wooed and won a lady undertaker. One of their most cherished wedding gifts was a set of towels, marked—how else?—"hiss" and "hearse."

5. The effeminate Indian who checked in at the Waldorf. He registered as "homo the brave."

6. The Eskimo who stabbed himself with an icicle. He died of cold cuts.

7. The San Antonio restaurateur whose pie list suggests "remember the alamode."

8. The exasperated bus rider who suggests the Chicago Transit Authority adopt the slogan "no bus oblige."

9. The talkative musician who can't hold on to a job. Every time he opens his mouth he puts his flute in it.

10. The advice-to-the-lovelorn editor who insists "if at first you don't succeed, try a little ardor."

11. The commuter whose Volkswagen broke down once too often. So he consigned it to the Old Volks Home.

12. The bookseller who was dawdling over a second cup of coffee one Sunday A.M., reading *The Canterbury Tales*. His

wife demanded, "What have you got there?" He answered, "Just my cup and Chaucer."

13. The Broadway publicity man who bought a new electric typewriter and crawled under the desk with the extension cord to plug it in. A client caught him in the act. "You press agents," he chortled. "Always looking for a plug."

14. The baseball star who made his debut as a singer at one of the Playboy clubs. "Tonight," he quavered, "I'm like a girl who flirts with the butcher. I'm playing for big steaks."

15. The poker shark who once had an extraordinary run of big hands—and was smart enough to quit before his luck changed. "Not another hand, gentlemen," he announced firmly, as he cashed in his chips. "I intend to fold my tens and silently steal away."

16. The impetuous young man who deliberately threw three pairs of trousers into the furnace one Sunday, then told his wife, "No longer can you accuse me of being a stick-in-the-mud, unwilling to take a chance. I have just burned my breeches behind me."

17. The two hundred-pound lady who always insists she's on a diet, though none has ever spotted her observing it. Her husband calls her "the wishful shrinker."

18. The police captain, regarded as something of an egghead by subordinates, who was shown two sets of fingerprints of a suspected robber. "These can't belong to the same man," objected the captain. "They're whorls apart."

19. The Pennsylvania farmer with relatives in East Germany who heard that a food package he had sent them had never arrived. Putting a brave face on things, he assured them, "Cheer up! The wurst is yet to come."

20. The promoter of a big flower show in Pennsylvania, who, told that a postponement was necessary because the ex-

hibits could not be installed on time, explained to his backers, "We simply were caught with our plants down."

* * *

"Cheerful people," declares Dr. Wilbur Abercrombie, "resist intestinal diseases better than gloomy ones."

What the doctor obviously means is that the surly bird catches the worm.

* * *

"Don't let the word 'paronomasia' throw you," advises good old Dr. John Fuller. "All that it means is an old-fashioned pun."

Dr. Fuller therupon gives a few examples, such as the missionary who was seized by cannibals, tied to a post, and jabbed with daggers so that the savages could drink his blood. After a week he told the chief, "Look: I'm tired of being stuck for the drinks."

Fuller also identifies Hawaii as "the place where men make passes at girls who wear grasses" and claims that what Sir Lancelot *really* asked Lady Guinevere was, "Who was that last knight I saw you out with, Lady?"

Then there was the great composer Bach, who, whenever he worked away from home, developed a prodigious appetite. So every time he went any place he packed a valise with six sandwiches, three apples, some cheese, and a selection of cookies. This became known as a Bach's lunch.

Well, at least we now know what a paronomasiac is!

* * *

A youngster found a salamander in his backyard and put it into a tank with his pet alligator. The alligator promptly swallowed the salamander. "Something awful's happened," wailed the youngster to his mother. "Sally's in our alli!"

* * *

A local district attorney was informed that the cheesemakers of Wisconsin had produced 1.9 million pounds of Limburger in 1958. Said the D.A.: "That's quite a phew."

* * *

Erudite critic Walter Kerr likes to pun as much as the next fellow. He found on the breakfast table one morning a misaddressed invitation to a dinner that had been held four nights previous. "Well," he commented, tossing the outdated invitation over to his wife, Jean, "There's one fete accompli!"

* * *

Mrs. Lanning Humphrey, of Waban, Massachusetts, tells of a wealthy gentleman who took time out from a world yacht cruise to give his crew a Christmas party in port. He went ashore to round up evergreens, victuals, musicians, gifts, and local notables. When he returned to the dock he found all the greens installed—but on the wrong ship. "Ahoy!" he shouted. "You're treeing up the wrong barque."

* * *

An artistic Indian erected a new wigwam and decorated it with costly manufactured baubles, purchased via a mail order catalogue. His neighbors, miffed because the new wigwam was getting too much attention, disparaged his efforts. Sneered they, "Cheap Sioux veneer!"

* * *

Frank Sinatra once engaged a chef freshly imported from Bombay, but after serving the same menu six nights running, he was discharged. Explained Sinatra, "This was one poor guy who got fired for favoring curry."

* * *

Unquenchable punsters have now turned to new color designations for interior decorators to conjure with. What do you think, for instance, of Conquered Grape, Foreseeable Fuchsia, or Enry Iggins Just You White? Then there's Zane Gray, Bipartisan Slate, and World Cerise. See what we mean?

* * *

A nearsighted debutante turned up for a soiree very much under the weather. "I can't see," she mourned. "I couldn't put in my contact lenses because my poodle bit me in the eye this afternoon." "What did he do that for?" asked the hostess. "Heaven knows," admitted the debutante. "Probably he felt like having an eyeball before dinner!"

* * *

There was an unscheduled dustup in a Bagdad harem one day long ago. The sultan barged in unexpectedly—and his sixty-two wives let out a terrified sheik.

* * *

There has come to light an episode in the early life of William Penn that I believe has escaped the attention of many young Philadelphians.

It appears that Mr. Penn had a couple of aunts named Natalie and Ellie who were past mistresses in the art of whipping up a mince pie or an apple strudel. When greedy Quakertown bakers formed a combine and tripled the price of their pastries overnight, Aunt Natalie and Aunt Ellie decided to teach the greedy fellows a lesson. They put *their* delectable pastries on the market at absolute cost—and then proceeded to reduce the price five cents every day.

In no time flat, of course, the good citizens of Quakertown were discussing only one topic: the pie rates of Penn's aunts!

❊　❊　❊

The late Heywood Broun liked to tell about the zoo that imported the biggest yak ever seen in America. Every morning at breakfast time the animal, who was very fond of pancakes with maple syrup, would yawn prodigiously, and get up. Of course you know what song Broun declared this brought to mind? "Mighty Yak Arose."

❊　❊　❊

They say that what Christopher Columbus really told Queen Isabella when he got home from his American tour was: "Well, I bet I'm the first man who ever got nineteen hundred miles on a galleon." . . . Have you noticed how ship news photographers favor clothes-up shots? . . . And Charlie Poore discloses that a highly rated rock 'n' roller was run out of Newport recently. They guitarred and feathered him.

❊　❊　❊

There is an eccentric artist in the south of France who cultivates carp in the natural pool in his garden. When the carp attain full growth, he catches them, skins them, and makes gentlemen's wallets out of the skins. He is, in fact, the only man on the face of this earth who is noted for his carp to carp walleting.

15. Right up the Riddle

The late and unlamented craze for elephant riddles left countless parents, teachers—and elephants—reeling. Lest we forget, I've assembled here ten of what I think were the best of them.

1.

Q. Why do elephants need trunks?
A. Because they have no glove compartments.

2.

Q. What do you call elephants who ride on jets?
A. Passengers.

3.

Q. How do you get six elephants in a Volkswagen?
A. Put three in the front seat and three in the back.

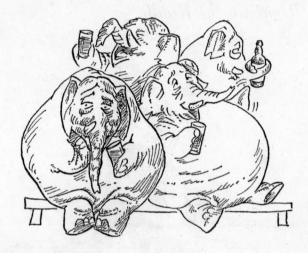

4.

Q. Why do elephants drink?
A. To forget!

5.

Q. What do you do when an elephant sneezes?
A. Get out of the way.

6.

Q. How do you get an elephant out of the theatre?
A. You can't. It's in his blood.

7.

Q. How can you tell when there's an elephant in the refrigerator?
A. The door won't close.

8.

Q. What weighs four thousand pounds and sings?
A. Harry Elefonte.

9.

Q. What do they call a girl who eats elephants?
A. Big Mouth.

10.

Q. What happens when you cross an elephant with a jar of peanut butter?
A. You get either a jar of peanut butter with a wonderful memory or an elephant that sticks to the roof of your mouth.

* * *

Since my riddle anthology ("Riddle-De-Dee": Random House) was published a few years ago, a veritable flood of new ones has come along. The following may be valuable for the student of 2100 who wants to know how the lighter-hearted set was passing its time in 1965:

Q. What's yellow and writes?
A. A ball-point banana.

Q. What's red and goes putt-putt-putt?
A. An outboard apple.

Q. What wallows in mud and carries colored eggs?
A. An Easter piggie.

Q. What do ducks do when they fly upside down?
A. They quack up.

Q. What color is a burp?
A. Burple.

Q. What's the difference between a schoolteacher and a railroad train?
A. The teacher says, "Take that gum out of your mouth"; the train says, "Choo, choo."

Q. Are carrots really beneficial for the eyes?
A. Well, have you ever seen a rabbit wearing glasses?

Q. What does a two-hundred-pound mouse say?
A. "Here, kitty, kitty."

Q. What is green and red and rents for $175 a month?
A. A two-room watermelon on East 62nd Street.

Q. What has a gray skin, four legs, and a trunk?
A. A mouse on vacation.

Q. What has eight legs, wears feathers, and says, "Ba-a-a, ba-a-a, ba-a-a"?
A. An Iroquois Indian quartet singing "The Whiffenpoof Song."

Q. Why did little Mary say, "There's a grape sitting in the bathtub" when it really was a giraffe?
A. Little Mary is color-blind.

Q. What is the most arrogant insect in the world?
A. A cocky roach.

Q. How can a leopard change his spots?
A. By going from one spot to another.

Q. What can a cat do to get fat?
A. Go to a butcher shop and meow for it.

Q. What kind of a waiter never accepts a tip?
A. A dumb waiter.

Q. What's the difference between a radio and a clothesline?
A. A radio draws waves. . . .

Q. What happens when you get stung by a bee and bitten by a mosquito simultaneously?
A. You sting along with itch.

Q. What did Mason say to Dixon?
A. "I suppose we've got to draw the line somewhere."

Q. What's yellow, soft, and goes round and round?
A. A long-playing omelette.

Q. What's black and white and hides in a cave?
A. A zebra who owes money.

Q. What's white outside, green inside, and hops?

A. A frog sandwich.

Q. What sentence of twenty-nine letters contains every one in the alphabet?

A. "Quick-wafting zephyrs vex bold Jim."

Q. How can a person go down Pike's Peak without first going up?

A. By being born at the top.

Q. What weighs six ounces, sits in a tree, and is very dangerous?

A. A sparrow with a machine gun.

Q. What would we have if every automobile in the country were painted red?

A. A red car nation.

Q. Why did the cookie crumble?

A. Because his mother was a wafer too long.

Q. How do you make a rhinoceros float?

A. With two scoops of ice cream, a rhinoceros, a dab of whipped cream, and a maraschino cherry.

16. *Still out on a Limerick*

There was a young maid from Kuwait
Who was rated as tops on a dait.
Though she started out slow
'Twas the lads who cried "Whoa!"
At a point we're not free to relait.

I thought that I had rounded up enough good (and print-able) limericks to last for a lifetime in *Out on a Limerick* (Harper's, $2.95)—but how new ones do keep rolling in! For instance:

1.

Most limericks discreetly called laundered
Are ones where the washer has wandered
Far off from his tub
And neglected to scrub
The lines over which he has pondered.

2.

The latest report from the Dean
Concerning the teaching machine
Is that Oedipus Rex
Could have learned about sex
Alone, without bothering the queen!

3.

Crooned a whimsical King of Siam
To his drinking pal, Omar Khayyam,
"Whoo and toot-toot,
They say you're astute,
But right now you're drunker than I am!"

4.

An imaginary line is the waist:
It never stays long where it's placed,
But rises or slips
From shoulder to hips,
According to popular taste.

5.

The kings of Peru were the Incas
Recognized everywhere as great drincas.
They worshiped the sun
And had barrels of fun
But their subjects considered them stincas.
                  —*Reed Warsham*

6.

A young man down in old Allegheny
Proposed to a typist named Janey.
Groaned his friends, "You can't win:
She's as ugly as sin."
He explained, "But the day was so rainy!"

7.

A Briton who shot at his king
Was doomed on the gallows to swing.
When the rope was made fast
He cried out, "At last!
I'm getting the hang of the thing!"
                  —*David Ross*

8.

There was a young pastor in Kew
Who kept a brown cow in a pew.
There he taught it each week
A new letter in Greek,
But it never got farther than *mu*.

9.

There once was a co-ed, quite dapper,
In psychology classes a napper,
But her Freudian dreams
Were so classic, it seems,
That now she's a Phi Beta Kappa.

10.

There was a young lady named Lynn
Who thought that to love was a sin.
But when she was tight
She considered it right—
So everyone filled her with gin.
                    —*Rosemary Johnson*

11.

A gallant young blade from Duquesne
Went home with a girl in the ruesne
Said she with a sigh
"I wonder when Igh
Shall see such a rain-beau aguesne."

12.

There was a young maid from Kuwait
Who was rated as tops on a dait.
Though she started out slow
'Twas the lads who cried "Whoa!"
At a point we're not free to relait.

13.

An opera conductor named Paton
Conducted a score with his hat on.
By wiggling his ear
His toes and his rear
He contrived to dispense with a baton.
                —*Joseph Rosenthal*

14.

A spendthrifty fellow named Si,
Who charged everything he could buy,
Said, when hailed into court,
With his bank account short,
"The Government does: Why can't I?"

15.

A cute little feminine specter
Got scared when another spook necked her.
She gave such a start
That her bones fell apart,
And it took quite a while to collect her.
                —*Don Augur*

16.

A sweet little miss near Fort Bliss
Told her G.I. 'twas sinful to kiss
When that resourceful young rat
Asked, "You mean, dear, like *that?*"
She said, "Yes, and like *this* and like *this.*"
—*Staff Sergeant George McKeshnie*

17.

There was a young lawyer named Pique
Who was blessed with a prominent bique.
But one mortified client
Grew extremely defiant
And gave that proboscis a twique.

18.

A stylish young gent in St. Pierre
Had a girl friend and oft went to Sierre.
She was Gladys by name
And one eve when he came
Her mother said, "Gladys St. Hierre."
—*Roy Baldridge*

19.

Two starry-eyed, reckless young beaux
Were held up and robbed of their cleaux.
While the weather is hot
They won't miss them a lot—
But what will they do when it sneaux?

20.

History is being made at such a breakneck pace these days
that even Harvard's erudite David McCord seems a bit be-
fuddled. Muses McCord:

There once was a man in the moon,
But he got there a little too soon.
Some others came later
And fell down a crater.
When was it—next August? Last June?

17. *Military Orders*

THE ARMY

General Matt Ridgway was reminiscing at the Pittsburgh Field Club about his days as a cadet at West Point. "I recall the first sergeant in my life," he said with a happy gleam in his eye. "He lined us up and roared, 'Men, I want three volunteers for K.P. duty and that means you and you and you.' I was one of the yous."

* * *

At an infantry officers' training camp, one tough, officious captain was the pet hate of every candidate. Yet at graduation ceremonies, every newly hatched second lieutenant contributed happily for a present to the detested captain.

It was a framed picture of Lassie, neatly inscribed, "With love, from Mother."

*　　*　　*

A one-star general was assigned to training draftees in the hottest, sandiest corner of West Texas. He staggered back from a ten-mile hike at the head of his troops one evening and fell moaning on his bed. "These boots," he announced, "are about to kill me. I swear they're three sizes too small." "Let me get you a new pair," suggested his orderly.

"Not on your life," cried the general. "We have no clear water, women, golf, or movies. Taking off these blank blank boots is the only pleasure I've got left!"

*　　*　　*

Now it can be revealed that canny news correspondents at the various fronts in World War II hit upon a new way of hornswoggling their home offices with inflated expense accounts. Aware that Army censors clipped entire paragraphs out of many letters sent back to the U.S.A., the correspondents would list formidable expenses on their tabs, then carefully cut out the explanations, leaving only the net amounts.

The home treasurers, truly impressed with all the top-secret stuff the censors apparently had cut out, invariably paid the bills without raising an eyebrow.

*　　*　　*

John Toland reminds us of the day a rewrite man in Rome was doing a piece on General Mark Clark and cabled his home office, "How old Mark Clark?" A joker at the home end cabled back, "Old Mark Clark just fine. How you?"

*　　*　　*

A pompous broker was reminiscing interminably about his glorious exploits in World War II. "I hadn't had my wings in the Air Force for a month," he asserted, "when I blew up four ammunition dumps and shot down nine fighter planes." "Ah, yes," sighed the lady next to him wearily. "I presume that's when they decided to send you overseas."

*　　*　　*

When General Patton was in an expansive humor, he liked to tell a story about a valuable officer under Napoleon who developed a brain tumor and had to submit to an emergency operation. The surgeon, maintained Patton, unscrewed the officer's cranium, took out the brain, and laid it on the table.

Just then a messenger arrived with the glad tidings that the officer had been promoted from colonel to general. With a whoop of joy he bounced up from the operating table, slapped on his cranium, and headed for the nearest exit. "Wait a minute," cried the surgeon. "You've forgotten to put back your brain."

"I won't need it now," called back the patient. "I'm a general!"

*　*　*

Shortly after D-Day in World War II, an aviator was dispatched over the Rhineland to drop propaganda leaflets. He didn't check back in at headquarters for three weeks. "Where you been?" demanded his squadron leader crossly. "How could you take three weeks just to dump a load of leaflets over enemy territory?"

"Dump them?" repeated the pilot in a hollow voice. "I thought you wanted me to slip one under every door!"

*　*　*

A V.P. at an aircraft factory, enlarging upon the virtue of initiative to the four o'clock shift, told of the day in World War II when General MacArthur summoned one of his Army engineers and asked, "How long will it take to throw a bridge across this stream?" "Three days," was the answer. "Okay," snapped MacArthur. "Have your draftsmen make blueprints immediately." Three days later the general asked if the bridge was under way. "It's finished," smiled the engineer. "You can send your troop across it this minute if you don't wait for those damn blueprints. They aren't started yet."

*　*　*

At a gay reunion of World War II veterans, the conversation got around to cartoons that had made the nation laugh a bit during the grim days before the tide turned in America's favor at Guadalcanal. It was surprising how clearly some of those cartoons—and the exact wording of the captions—were remembered, almost as clearly, in fact, as the famous pinup of Lana Turner looking back over her shoulder in a white swimsuit.

Favorites: Two goats chewing up top-secret reports at the Pentagon, with one grunting happily, "Best darn propaganda I ever ate!"; a general's hatchet-faced wife collaring him at the door of his home to snarl, "You're not going to go inspecting barracks until you tidy up the mess in your own room!"; the G.I. having a tooth yanked at the dispensary, gasping, "Ouch— Sir!"; and an admiral jumping up from his chair with a shriek of anguish while his aide whispers to a J.G., "I think the admiral's found that Japanese carrier that was missing from his chart."

*　*　*

A crusty professor of comparative literature registered distinct annoyance when a student just out of military service was late for class for the third morning running. "Tell me," rasped the professor, "exactly what did they say in the Army when you sauntered in late like this?"

"Well," mused the unperturbed student, "first they saluted. Then they inquired, 'How do you feel this morning, sir?'"

* * *

In Korea, an ace correspondent, pressed into emergency service at a field hospital, observed a young nun calmly assist in the amputation of a cruelly mangled Chinese soldier's leg. The correspondent, ashen-faced and trembling himself, told the nun, "I wouldn't do that for a million dollars." The nun nodded and said, "Neither would I."

* * *

The lieutenant at a small outpost had a new recruit assigned to keep quarters bright and clean. He was quiet, competent—and always called the lieutenant "Major." A sergeant drew him aside one morning and said, "Soldier, haven't you been in this man's Army long enough to know that one gold bar denotes a looie, not a major?" "If it's all the same to you, sergeant," implored the recruit, "you won those stripes your way; let me earn mine my way."

* * *

Reservists being recalled for active service are griping about shortages in equipment and uniforms. They recall a jest current during World War I: a recruit mourning, "I reported at Yaphank Monday morning, and by Tuesday I had a uniform, hat, shoes, and puttees that fit me like a glove. I don't understand it. Can I be deformed?"

* * *

The raw recruits were lined up for their first review and the colonel stopped before one very sad sack. "Your face is unshaven," snapped the colonel. "Your boots are unpolished. Your tunic is unbuttoned. Who told you you're a soldier?"

Weakly the sad sack replied, "My draft board."

*　*　*

The tough M.D. at a Texas Army post, death on any poor G.I. who reported for sick call, was on his way to a show in town when the motor in his car stalled. Very meekly, he called out to a group of privates lounging in front of barracks, "Hey, fellows! I can't seem to get my car going. Would you know what to do for it?"

"Sure thing Doc," one of the group answered happily. "Paint it with iodine, and mark it 'Duty'!"

*　*　*

Private Goodkind was whistling happily as he cleaned out the cages of the carrier pigeons. "Well!" observed a passing lieutenant, "that's the first time I ever saw a private happy performing a job like that."

"Yes, sir," beamed the private. "This job doesn't bother me a bit. Before I was transferred here I was in the cavalry."

*　*　*

Booked to emcee a vaudeville show at a veterans' hospital, lavish George Jessel sent an orchid ahead of time to each and every nurse. The nurses wore them, too. Georgie had overlooked one detail, however. All the nurses were male.

*　*　*

Outside an Army area that houses parachute troops and test pilots for supersonic planes, there's a sign that reads: "Danger! You are now entering a state thruway. Good luck!"

*　*　*

Captain V. R. Fernandes recalls the day a two-hundred-man Army group arrived to begin training as parachutists in an airborne outfit. A tough major welcomed the already appre-

hensive newcomers with a crisp, "So you're gonna be parachutists, hey? Fine! Your jump training will be conducted in three
stages. The first week, we'll separate the men from the boys.
The second week we'll separate the boys from the idiots. And
the third week we'll let all you idiots jump!"

* * *

In the jungles of Viet Nam, a high-ranking officer was staring moodily into the pitch black night. "You haven't slept in
forty-eight hours, sir," an anxious aide reminded him. "You
need rest desperately." "My work is never done," answered the
officer grimly. "My autobiography is due next Tuesday and
I'm only up to Chapter Twelve."

* * *

A Pentagon official had occasion to call one of our astronauts
recently. The astronaut's young son answered the phone.
"Where's your dad?" asked the big brass. "He's orbiting nine or
ten times around the globe," answered the lad. "He ought to
be home in an hour." "Let me talk to your mother, then," requested the b.b. "Oh, she's out shopping at the bargain center," said the boy. "She won't be home till tonight."

* * *

Because the spectacular goings-on in the world of guided
missiles and space ships is utterly mystifying to me, I had not
realized until I visited Cape Kennedy in person that since 1953
Pan Am is the prime contractor for operations there, with RCA
the principal sub-contractor. As one Cocoa Beach newshawk
explained to me, the whole Atlantic Missile Range operates on
three levels: 1. Pan Am talks with N.A.S.A. (The National
Aeronautics and Space Administration) in terms of billions of
dollars. 2. Pan Am then talks with RCA negotiators in terms
of millions of dollars. 3. Pan Am VIP's then go to their homes
and demand of their wives, "What do you mean, tomatoes have
gone up to thirty-five cents a pound?"

* * *

N.A.S.A. is planning to put a hundred head of cattle into orbit at one time. A. C. Spectorsky points out that this will be the herd shot round the world.

THE NAVY

Sailor Wilhelm shambled into a Navy recruiting office on Tremont Street and diffidently tapped the officer in charge on the arm. "Say, Bud," he pleaded earnestly, "gimme that old sales talk again, will you? I'm getting mighty discouraged!"

* * *

A U. S. Navy supply ship put in for a spell at a Pacific island famed for its voluptuous and scantily clad maidens. One sailor spent a memorable day on shore posing groups of the cooperative beauties, and photographing them with his miniature camera. An ensign watched him silently for some time, then inquired, "Where do you think you're going to get all those films developed?"

The sailor replied, "Films? Who's got films?"

* * *

How to get ahead in the Navy: The Secretary of the Navy was inspecting a recently launched carrier. The entire crew stood at attention. "I suppose," said the Secretary jokingly to the carrier's captain, "you know the name of every man on the ship." "I think I do," was the captain's unexpected reply.

"Aha," smiled the Secretary. "What's the name of the third man from the left there in the rear rank?"

"William Jones," said the captain.

The Secretary addressed the seaman himself.

"What's your name, lad?" he asked.

"William Jones, sir," replied Seaman Jonathan Abernathy.

* * *

"One of my most challenging wartime experiences," recalled a not-too-reliable sea captain, "came in the icy North Atlantic. I was torpedoed and lived for nine days on one can of sardines." "Remarkable," nodded the man next to him at the bar. "How did you keep from falling off?"

* * *

Two attractive girls sauntered down Broadway, with a lone sailor dogging their every footstep. Finally one of the girls wheeled around and announced angrily, "You there, Mr. Fresh! Either quit following us this way, or get another sailor!"

* * *

A young British naval lieutenant, reports John Fischer, commanded his first ship—a frigate—during practice maneuvers. He succeeded in bumping into the admiral's vessel at the very outset of the operation.

The admiral signaled, "What do you propose to do now?"

The lieutenant's answering signal—rapidly to become a British naval legend—was, "Buy a small farm, sir."

* * *

On a U.S. cruiser the officer of the deck asked the starboard lookout, "What would you do if a sailor was washed overboard?" "I'd yell 'Man overboard,'" answered the lookout snappily.

"Good," said the officer. "Now what would you do if an *officer* fell overboard?"

The lookout asked, "Which one, sir?"

＊　＊　＊

There's a winsome lass stationed near the outer gate of a Navy base who's been kissed by so many sailors her lips go in and out with the tide.

＊　＊　＊

At a Navy officers' dance, a young lieutenant's eyes were attracted to a brooch worn by a hostess assigned to him. It depicted a cluster of Naval signaling flags, and the girl explained, "This brooch was a present from my bridegroom. The flags mean, 'I love you.'" The lieutenant held his peace, although he knew full well there was no such word as "love" in the naval signal manual. He could hardly wait to get back to the barracks and dig out his own copy of the manual.

What the flags actually signaled, he discovered, was, "Permission granted to lay alongside."

＊　＊　＊

In a time when all mail from military personnel was heavily censored, the father of a valiant young sailor received three letters, spaced some weeks apart, from his son. Letter One began, "I cannot tell you where I am, but yesterday I shot a polar bear." Letter Two began, "I cannot tell you where I am, but yesterday I danced for over eight hours with a hula girl." Letter Three began, "I still cannot tell you where I am, but yesterday the doctor told me I should have danced with the polar bear and shot the hula girl."

THE MARINES

A hardened Marine veteran, his discharge in sight, signed up for a correspondence course in electrical engineering and was puzzled by one question on the application blank. "How long has your present employer been in business?" it said. The Marine finally answered, "Since 1776."

* * *

Cocky Marine sergeant Timothy McShane, no blushing violet, found a member of his platoon engrossed in—of all things—a hardbound book. "Reading, huh?" marveled McShane. "What's the name of the book, son?" The private answered, "It's called *What Twelve Million Women Want.*" "Hey," cried the good sergeant. "Lemme see that book a minute. I want to know if they got my name spelled right!"

* * *

Newly arrived in boot camp, a volunteer Marine from Long Island received this letter from his mater: "Dear Sebastian: Now that you are on your way to being a hero in the Marine Corps I trust that you will arise on time every morning so that the other young gentlemen in your set will not have to sit at the table and wait for you to come downstairs before they can begin eating their breakfast."

* * *

A nationally famous general in the Marine Corps recently was met at Kennedy Airport by his very fat wife. While they stood waiting for his baggage, a trim, red-headed airline hostess swayed by, and the general beamed. "Hope we fly together soon again, Miss Fenichel," he said. "How do you know her name?" demanded the wife. "It was posted up front," explained the general, "right under the names of the pilot and the co-pilot."

"I see," nodded the wife. "Now tell me the names of the pilot and the co-pilot."

18. *Time Marches on*

BABIES

A young lady at Cook County Hospital in Chicago had given birth that morning to a healthy, strapping baby girl. Some hours later a nurse found her propped up in bed poring through the pages of a telephone directory. She explained that she was looking for a name for the baby.

Said the nurse, "We have a little book here that lists a thousand first names for boys and girls. Let me get it for you." "That's not what I'm looking for," protested the young mother, clinging to the phone directory. "I need a *last* name."

* * *

Great-great-grandmother Johnson studied the newborn babe with obvious satisfaction. "If my memory doesn't fail me," she cackled, "it's a boy!"

* * *

In Paris, a lady on the eve of producing a baby was in a grumpy mood indeed. "What you need," prescribed her husband, "is a bit of diversion. Tonight we're going to the Folies Bergère." "I should say not," countered the wife. "Think of the prenatal influence. Our child might be born stark naked!"

* * *

A noted punster was told by the doctor that his wife had just given birth to quadruplets. Dazed but game to the core, the punster exclaimed, "Four crying out loud!"

* * *

Papa Herlihy marched his five-year-old son up to the maternity ward to give him his first look at his baby brother, born six hours earlier. Said baby brother was howling piteously. The five-year-old studied him carefully, then nodded his head and commented, "No *wonder* Mom hid him under her coat so long!"

* * *

Bessie Moore tells of the Little Rock father who told his seven-year-old son, "Floyd, I have a surprise for you. The stork flew in last night and left a little brother for you. Why don't you write your sister the good news?" The boy wrote as follows: "Dear Sis: You owe me two bucks. It's a boy."

* * *

The newest thing in baby care has been introduced by the wily Parisians. Aboard the ocean liner *France*, in the children's nursery, where the desk of the nurse in charge adjoins the infants' sleeping quarters, a numbered bell tinkles every time a baby's diaper needs changing. Moisture in the linen activates a signal.

* * *

Elbert Sisson's wife was bathing the baby when he heard his four-year-old daughter Clare demanding the scissors. "Not now," answered Mrs. Sisson. "I'm bathing the baby." "I hate babies," announced Clare. "Now you stop saying that," commanded Mrs. Sisson. "Remember *you* were a baby yourself not too long ago."

"I know," admitted Clare, "but I didn't want the scissors then."

*   *   *

"The quickest way to make a tossed salad," suggests Clementine Paddleford, "is to feed vegetables to an eighteen-month-old child."

*   *   *

Delphine Koshland overheard two pert nursemaids in converse in Central Park, as they wheeled their daintily attired charges down the Mall. "Why can't you come with me to Radio City tomorrow?" pouted one. "For the simple reason," answered the other, "that I'm afraid to leave this poor baby alone with its mother."

*   *   *

I am indebted to Rev. Charles Nober, of Syracuse University, for this wonderful definition of a baby: an alimentary canal with a big noise at one end and no sense of responsibility at the other.

BOYS AND GIRLS TOGETHER

Precocious children continue to make cute and quotable remarks at an ever-accelerating pace and, what's more, there
always seem to be a couple of parents, neighbors, and columnists within earshot, pens in hand, ready to record the
remarks for posterity.

Years ago the late Robert Benchley tentatively suggested
that the least the precocious children could do in return was
to set down some of the cute remarks made by their *parents*.
One Alfred Deedee, aged three, of Deedee, D.D., according
to Benchley, actually acted upon this suggestion, but then
the movement died aborning. This was Alfred's memorable
contribution:

"My father asked my mother if she thought he was made of
money. 'I'm not sure what it is you're made of,' she replied,
'but I'm pretty sure it isn't money.' This amused my father so
that he hauled off and whammed her into the china closet,
much to the surprise of the cups and saucers."

Boys . . .

A Milwaukee four-year-old brought a wriggling worm home with him from play-school and deposited it on the dining room table. "What," demanded his horrified mother, "are you doing with that worm?" "I met him on the lawn," explained the boy, "and I thought I'd show him our house."

* * *

Sam Levenson tells about the day his mother collared him just as he was about to drop an empty milk bottle on the noggin of his public school principal from a window in his seventh-story apartment. "Have you lost your mind?" cried his mother, giving him a whack over the ear. "The grocer gives us five cents apiece for empty milk bottles like that."

* * *

A little boy deposited two overdue books on the desk of a public library, and handed his past-due letter, plus the eighteen-cent fine called for, to the clerk. Then he asked, "Please, can I have the letter back? It's the first one I ever got!"

* * *

A young mother looked into the nursery and found her six-year-old son laboriously putting a bandage on his thumb. "What happened?" cried the mother. "I hit it with a hammer," said the boy.

"You poor darling," sympathized ma. "I wonder why I didn't hear you cry." "What was the use of crying?" explained the boy. "I thought you were out."

* * *

An English lad was walking across a village common when he saw a rabbit. "Look, Mum, there goes a rabbit," he exclaimed. "Nonsense, boy," scoffed his mother. "It must have been your imagination." The lad pondered a bit, then demanded, "Mum, has imagination always got a white behind?"

* * *

Nanette Fabray was describing the son of an acquaintance who had "freckles as big as nickels." "Big deal," scoffed her companion. "Lots of kids have freckles as big as nickels." Miss Fabray raised her eyebrows. "With *buffaloes* on them?" she asked.

* * *

"Cyril," said a teacher one bright morning, "do you feel that there is one thing you can do better than anybody else in the world?" "There is," said Cyril firmly after the briefest hesitation. "Read my own handwriting."

* * *

"Now, John," a mother coaxed her seven-year-old son, "you've been horsing around way past your bedtime. It's time to go to sleep." "I just can't, Mom," argued John. "My mouth is still full of words."

* * *

"For ten dollars," proposed Papa Giogrido to his son, "I'll teach you to talk like an Indian." The skeptical son asked, "How?" "See," beamed Papa, "you're learning already!"

* * *

Papa Erskine reacted as expected when his eight-year-old son Cuthbert brought home a report card containing four D's. "Cuthbert," said Papa, "I'll give you an incentive to improve your work in school. Come home with a better set of grades next month and I'll give you a crisp new dollar bill."

The next morning Cuthbert was waiting at the teacher's desk when she came in. "Teacher," he proposed cheerily, "how would you like to make yourself a quick fifty cents?"

* * *

John Drury tells of a south Georgian boy who was taken to Chicago one January and saw snow for the first time. He stared in wonder from his hotel room window at the snow-blanketed street below and cried to his mother, "Look, Ma! Grits all over!"

*   *   *

A sturdy lad asked his father, "Do you know if Mary's lamb followed her to school every day?" "That she did," said Father. "And how," pursued the lad, "did it all end?" "They finally separated," said Father. "The lamb graduated."

*   *   *

A mother and her two adolescent sons were trying to decide what to give Pop for his birthday. "I know," cried the younger son finally. "Let's let him drive the car this weekend!"

*   *   *

A number of five-year-old Timothy's playmates gathered beneath his window and shrilly importuned him to come out and play. Timothy finally appeared at the window and replied, "Can't you see I can't come down now? I'm taking my nap."

*   *   *

One minute little Warren had a big, fat, candied apple in his hand, the next minute it had vanished. "A man took it," he wailed to his father. "Imagine a man mean enough to steal an apple from a kid this size," exploded the father. "What did the man look like, Son?"

Little Warren pointed promptly to a tall, dignified gentleman who was strolling some paces ahead—with a big red candied apple dangling from the seat of his pants!

*   *   *

Young Danny, fooling about in his father's den, succeeded in swallowing a shotgun shell. His frantic mother rushed him to the doctor. "Let's keep our heads about all this," counseled that wise gentleman. "I won't be able to operate until Friday. Meanwhile, keep the boy from jumping around too much—and don't point him at anybody!"

*   *   *

Jim Backus lives near a rich movie tycoon whose overindulged twelve-year-old son ran away from home the other day. The outraged father called over to Backus, "How do you like that? A twelve-year-old brat running away from his mother and father!" "Take it easy," counseled Backus. "Your son is like many other youngsters, rebelling against authority. All twelve-year-old kids at one time or another run away from home."

"What?" roared the movie tycoon. "In a Thunderbird?"

＊　＊　＊

Max Shulman describes the remarkable progress made by the son of a neighbor in Westport. "He began," recalls Shulman, "as an unwanted child, but today, at the age of seventeen, he's wanted in twenty-two states."

＊　＊　＊

An Illinois lady heard an unholy racket in her backyard, and upon investigation, found her young son Michael clinging desperately to the back of a very shaggy sheep dog who was trying with equal desperation to escape. Michael, hanging on to the dog for dear life, begged his mother breathlessly, "Help me hold on to him, Mommy. Can we keep him? He followed me all the way home!"

＊　＊　＊

The teenage son slumped dejectedly in his chair, and his mother anxiously whispered to his father, "What's biting him now?" "It's nothing worth whispering about," said the father resignedly. "He wants to go to the drugstore down at the corner—but the car won't start."

＊　＊　＊

Young Mauruss kept a firm clutch on his first report card from school. "Maybe," he told his dad, "I should explain you the system first. A means wonderful, B means excellent, C stands for all right, and D is what I got."

＊　＊　＊

Little Cyril came home from Town School with a black eye and a bloody nose. "Tsk, tsk," sighed his mother, "you've been fighting again." "Yes," admitted Cyril, "with Pete." "Didn't I tell you," the mother reminded him, "to count to fifty before you became involved in another fight?" "I did," insisted Cyril, "but Peter's mother told him to count to twenty-five."

* * *

A geography teacher had just been explaining to her charges the differences between the frigid, temperate, and torrid zones. At the conclusion of her talk she asked young Andrew what sort of zone he lived in.

Andrew answered, "Brooklyn, 18."

* * *

A Seattle five-year-old smelled a pancake breakfast being readied in the kitchen. "Mom," he called out happily, "my stomach is smacking its lips!"

* * *

Harlan Miller reports that the fourteen-year-old son of one of his colleagues has purchased a little black book for addresses and telephone numbers. On the outside, the lad, no blushing violet he, has confidently written "Volume One."

* * *

A fond grandmother, visiting her family, was freshening up for dinner when her four-year-old grandson brought his puppy in to see her. "I'm busy, dear," she said absently. "Wait for me downstairs." The grandson asked her tearfully, "Grandma, aren't you even going to speak to your granddog?"

* * *

Bob McGovern, of the famous McGovern fighting clan, initiated his four-year-old son into the manly art of self-defense. The very next afternoon the lad ran into the house in a fever of delight. "I did it, Dad! I did it," he exulted. "I hit her!"

* * *

It was his father's birthday, and seven-year-old Timothy Carson insisted on shining his shoes as a gift. Reluctantly Father Carson, already late for the office, took off his shoes and handed them to his son. They were returned in due course—glistening black.

"Great work, Tim," enthused the father—then whispered to his wife, "Well, there goes my only pair of brown oxfords!"

* * *

The playroom of a pampered lad in a lakeshore duplex is filled with cloth animals: lions, tigers, and what-not. One day the lad's mother decided the menagerie needed cleaning, and consigned the animals to the electric washing machine in the laundry. While she was superintending the operation, her phone rang. The boy answered. "Mother is home," he conceded, "but she can't come to the phone right now. She's stuffing an elephant into the washing machine."

There was a pause at the other end of the line and then a man murmured weakly, "I see. I guess I have the wrong number"—and hung up.

And Girls . . .

A five-year-old girl in Wellesley Hills, reports Ernie Heyn, was looking forward with wild excitement to her first day in school. When the great day dawned, she bounced out of bed at seven, and was outside waiting for the bus at eight. She was still enthusiastic when she got home that afternoon.

The next morning, however, when her mother woke her at seven-thirty, the little girl wasn't quite so happy. "What?" she protested angrily. "*Again?*"

*   *   *

An inexperienced nursemaid, taking a baby for a ride in the park, encountered a friend of the family, who peered inside the carriage and observed, "I see the poor little thing has her father's nose."

"Good heavens," gasped the nursemaid. "I thought that was a nipple."

*   *   *

An enchanting but temperamental little girl of eight received a phone call from a schoolmate the other evening. "Please call me back in ten minutes," she requested. "I'm in the middle of a tantrum."

*   *   *

Cuddly Tillie Expresso had the prize excuse of the week for being late to school: "I guess I overwashed."

*   *   *

Hank Meyer took his precocious three-year-old daughter with him into a voting booth. After he had pulled down a number of levers, he asked her, "See how it's done?" "Yes, Daddy, I see," she replied, her eyes shining. "Now where's the gum?"

*　*　*

Danny Kaye was a houseguest of the talented Mills family in Britain when Hayley Mills, then five (how the time flies!) came running downstairs at midnight in a near-panic. "I've got to see mother at once," she told her father. "My heart has stopped!"

*　*　*

Mother to perverse girl who won't eat her spinach. "Try a mouthful of it, darling. Pretend it's mud."

*　*　*

A rising suburbanite started to put on his dinner jacket the other evening, preparing to escort his wife to a country club dance. His young daughter, however, registered disapproval. "Please don't wear that suit, dad," she begged. "It always gives you such a terrible headache the next morning."

*　*　*

Sister Annette writes about the time she took some third-graders in her parish to visit the zoo, then asked them to write a paragraph about the animals that interested them most. Wrote one moppet: "The animal that interested me most was the Warning Stand Back. Every time we looked at it he spit at us."

*　*　*

"Look at that funny man across the street," suggested a little girl to her mother. "What's funny about him?" asked the mother indulgently. "He's sitting on the sidewalk," reported the little girl, "talking to a banana peel."

*　*　*

A Park Avenue matron took her six-year-old daughter up to see a very large stable in the Bedford Hills sector of Westchester. The youngster's attention was captured immediately by a newborn colt. "Look, Mommy," she caroled. "A foreign horse!"

*　*　*

A wide-eyed little girl from the slums was given her first two-week vacation in the country by a big newspaper. Things went tolerably well the first day until it was time for her to retire for the night. Her hostess took her to a lovely guest room with a wide, spotless, cool bed and said, "My dear, this is all yours." To her surprise, the little girl burst into tears. "I want to sleep in a regular bed," she sobbed—"one with five or six people in it!"

*　*　*

A whimsical teacher asked her class, "Would you say that 'trousers' is singular or plural?" Observant nymphet Virginia answered promptly, "Both: singular at the top and plural at the bottom."

*　*　*

John Fischer, erudite editor of *Harper's Magazine*, spotted a beloved child perched precariously on the peaked roof of a barn and asked her what she was doing there. "Her answer," says Fischer, "covered the situation like a horse blanket." She called down, "I'm trying not to fall off."

*　*　*

A ten-year-old girl, described by her doting mother as "temperamental," raised particular tantrums every time she was told it was time to go to bed. "I hate bed," she exclaimed one night. "If I took bed in school it would be my worst subject."

*　*　*

There's an eight-year-old girl up north of Boston whose passionate love of pastries and hamburgers has kept her waistline indecently oversize—and expanding continuously. Her mother keeps admonishing her, "Fat girls find it hard to get husbands! Pull in that stomach of yours!"

The other day the poor girl came home from school bathed in tears. "During Salute to the Flag this morning," she sobbed, "I pulled in my stomach like you always tell me to—and my skirt fell off!"

*   *   *

A tense moment in a fifth-grade Austin, Texas classroom came when a teacher asked, "Who said, 'God's in His heaven, all's right with the world'?" One little girl answered, "Mrs. God."

*   *   *

A very small girl in Atlantic City, whose sunburn had reached the peeling-off stage, was overheard grumbling, "Only four years old, and I'm wearing out already!"

*   *   *

On a TV program in Detroit, a seven-year-old city-bred girl boasted that on her first visit to a farm she had gotten around to milking a genuine cow. "Did you enjoy the experience?" asked the master of ceremonies. "Oh, yes," enthused the little girl, "but I didn't get much milk out of it."

*   *   *

Late for school the third time in one week, ingenious young Malvinia came up with a brand-new alibi. "This time it really wasn't my fault," she told her teacher solemnly. "I was walking behind a slow dog."

* * *

The four-year-old daughter of an advertising executive in Connecticut asked her father how she might catch a bird. "Sprinkle salt on his tail," he advised soberly. That evening she came home with four birds.

* * *

A conscientious father had promised his wife that he would chastise their ten-year-old daughter for repeated digressions, and this time he laid it on good. The surprised little girl took the tongue-lashing in utter silence, then stamped off to the library and pulled a volume of the Encyclopedia off the shelf.

She sat engrossed in this volume so long that the father couldn't resist stealing up behind her to see what she was reading.

The little darling was studying up on poisons.

* * *

Erasmus Hall High School boasts an intriguingly built sophomore who's constantly mimicking Miss Bardot. Classmates have affectionately dubbed her the "Brooklyn Brigitte."

* * *

Jean Kerr tells about a seven-year-old little girl who got into a fight at a friend's birthday party and was sent home in disgrace. And when she arrived home, she found that her cat had been run over on the highway. Completely undone by all this, she burst into tears and wailed, "This is the worst day I've ever been to!"

* * *

On the wall of a building near his residence, Mike Nichols noticed a chalk inscription one morning that read "I LOVE GRILS." The next morning a line had been drawn through this declaration and a new line printed below that read "I LOVE GIRLS." The third day that line had been crossed out, too, and a third line substituted—in letters twice as large. It read, "WHAT ABOUT US GRILS?"

Together . . .

Seven-year-old Peter came home from the little girl next door to report disconsolately to his mother, "Agnes just broke our engagement. She returned my frog."

* * *

Mrs. Gumbiner came back from her canasta party and asked the baby sitter, "Did you bathe the children as I instructed you to?" "Yes, Ma'am," said the baby sitter, "and they behaved like lambs about it—all except the biggest boy. He fought like blazes before I could get him undressed and into the tub."

"What do you mean, biggest boy?" inquired Mrs. Gumbiner. "We have only one son. Which biggest boy?" "The one with a bald spot and eyeglasses," said the baby sitter. "Good heavens," gasped Mrs. Gumbiner, "that's my husband!"

* * *

A distinguished author in Connecticut has an enchanting four-year-old daughter who wants desperately to be older than she is. One afternoon recently she came tripping into her mother's study to announce blithely, "I am now *five* years old." "My dear," corrected the mother, "you know perfectly well you are only four." "No, no," contradicted the daughter, "I'm five. I just met another year coming down the driveway!"

* * *

Young Jonathan returned from school in disgrace, with a note from the teacher explaining that he had put mud in a little girl's mouth. "What made you do a crazy thing like that?" demanded Jonathan's mother. "Well, for one thing," he explained, "her mouth was open."

* * *

A poignant tableau revealed in Yellowstone National Park one day this summer: a father with four unruly kids in tow gazing pensively at a sign reading, "Deposit your litter here." The father sighed, and confided to a bystander, "Don't think I'm not tempted!"

* * *

Fourth-graders in a class for gifted children were asked by their teacher to complete a sentence beginning "Let's be as quiet as . . ."

Here are some of the answers, as reported by William Feather: "A leaf turning colors . . . a feather falling from a bird . . . time passing . . . the first star coming out . . . a gentle rainfall . . . when you pray . . . a butterfly flying . . . a soft breeze."

* * *

A self-satisfied mother, when her offspring went off for his first day in school, sent along this note: "The opinions expressed by this child are not necessarily those of his mother's side of the family."

* * *

A tough teacher asked her third-grade class to write a sentence beginning with the word "than." All but one of the kids was stymied. (Wouldn't *you* be?) The resourceful one's sentence read " 'Than' is a word with four letters."

* * *

At the conclusion of five-year-old Bartlett's first month in kindergarten, his father asked, "Well, have you grown to like the little boys who scared you so at first?" "Yes, I have," admitted Bartlett. "And the girls?" Bartlett assumed an expression of deep disgust. "Oh, come now," chided Bartlett's father, "you at least like Susan, don't you?"

Bartlett's face was a study in shocked disappointment. "*Susan*," he echoed. "Is *she* a girl?"

* * *

H. Allen Smith quotes this paper written for a history class by a fourth-grade genius in Mount Kisco:

"One day when Alfred the Great was wandering around the English countryside, he stopped at the house of a certain lady who was supposed to be baking cakes, but the lease said about that the better."

* * *

Armand Deutsch gleefully came upon this essay on geese by an eight-year-old nature lover: "Geese is a low, heavy-set bird which is mostly meat and feathers. His head sits on one end and he sits on the other. Some geese, when they grow up, has curls on their tails and is called ganders. Ganders don't have to sit and hatch, but just eat and loaf and go in swimming. If I was a geese, I'd rather be a gander."

* * *

And this is an essay about ants by a Kentucky eight-year-old:

"My subjeck is ants. Ants is two kinds: insects and lady uncles. Sometimes they live in holes, and sometimes they live with their married sisters, and they always are in the sandwiches at pikniks. That is all I know about ants."

* * *

From "Doc" Mack in Atlanta comes the story of two Cub Scouts whose younger sister fell into a lake. The two Cubs rushed home with tears streaming down their countenances. "We tried to give her articial respiration," sobbed one to their mother, "but she kept getting up and walking away."

* * *

A tired-looking mother entered a supermarket with her four boisterous youngsters and begged, "Haven't you got some brand of cereal that will sap their energy?"

* * *

From an essay by a ten-year-old scholar in New Orleans: "I hate Fidel Castro for two reasons: (1). He brought communism to Cuba and (2). He invented Castro Oil."

* * *

Another time, Art Linkletter entertained a little girl named Ellen, and a boy of the same age she obviously adored named Stevie. "When I grow up," confided Ellen (all of five) "I'm going to marry Stevie." "That's great," enthused Linkletter. "Do you feel the same way about Ellen, Stevie?" "Nah," scowled Stevie. "Never as long as I live." "Why not?" persisted Mr. L. "Because," explained Stevie with some dignity, "every time I turn around at school, she paints my nose."

* * *

Art Linkletter, waiting for one of his TV shows to start, suggested to the kids who were his guests that day that they draw pictures of what they wanted to be when they grew up. One lad depicted himself as a plane pilot. Another drew himself in the engine cab of a streamliner. But one little girl just handed Art a blank piece of paper. "I want to be married," she explained earnestly, "but I don't know how to *draw* it."

* * *

Herb Stein reminds us that the old-fashioned wall telephone had its advantages. For one thing, the kids couldn't reach it.

* * *

Steve Allen, who has learned by experience, contends that the best way to make your children heed your advice is to find out exactly what they want and then tell them to do it.

* * *

Nine-year-old Peter came home from dancing school to announce that every girl in the class was a clumsy cow. "All they can do," he explained with disgust, "is dance backwards."

* * *

A young lady carted a bundle of wash to a laundromat the other day and registered disbelief when the attendant informed her that it weighed nineteen pounds. "Ridiculous," she snorted—and together they sorted out the dirty wash. That's when she discovered the baby in it, cooing contentedly.

* * *

A solemn youngster with a fantastically high I.Q. keeps asking his socialite mother questions she can't answer—but to keep him quiet, she must give some sort of reply, so she makes things up as she goes along. "Invention," she sighs, "is the necessity of Mother!"

* * *

"A kid is the last container of a genuine sense of humor," maintains Dr. Seuss, author of the all-conquering *The Cat in the Hat*. He continues, "This sense of humor disappears as the kid gets older, and learns to laugh only according to the way the boss, society, politics, or race want him to. Then he becomes an adult. And an adult is an obsolete child."

＊　＊　＊

Katheryn Launtz, of Washta, Iowa, assures us, "A man may have a battered hat and his trousers may be shiny, but if his children have their noses flattened against the window pane a half hour before he is due home for supper, you can trust him with anything you have."

＊　＊　＊

The sheriff's office in a Texas city deserves some sort of Oscar for distributing a wonderfully wise and ironic list of rules titled "How to Raise a Juvenile Delinquent in Your Own Family." You may already have seen quotes from it in your newspaper, but I think it's worth reprinting. Here are a few highlights:

Begin with infancy to give the child everything he wants. This will insure his believing that the world owes him a living.

When he picks up obscene words, laugh heartily at him. Soon he'll acquire a vocabulary that will blow off the top of your head.

Pick up everything he leaves lying around. This will teach him he can always throw off responsibility on others.

Take his part against neighbors, teachers, policemen. They are all prejudiced against your child. He is never wrong.

Finally, prepare yourself for a life of grief, brother. You're going to have it.

CAMPERS

Many of the letters-to-parents-from-summer-campers that pop up in the columns and midsummer "news" items obviously are the brainchildren of professional gag-writers and TV scripters. Some of them, however, must be genuine, and if they're funny, what's the difference?

Here are some of the best of the recent crop:

1. "Dear Dad: We've been taking some pretty long hikes this week. Please send my other sneaker. Walter."

2. "Dear Mom: I left home in such a hurry I think I forgot to hang up the phone. Gwen."

3. "Dear Folks: What is an epidemic? Kerry."

4. "Dear Mommy: Please bring some food when you come to visit me. All we get here is breakfast, lunch, and supper. John."

5. "Dear Mom: Three of the girls in my tent have the dire rear. Chris."

6. "Hear ye, Parents: There are 190 boys in this camp. I wish there were 189. Your loving son, Ronald."

7. "Dear Folks: Yesterday our counselor told us all about where babies come from. You lied to me. Love, Margaret."

8. "Hi, fans! Your worries are over. I'm really growing very ladylike. All we talk about here is boys and sex. Please send me my water pistol and catcher's mitt. Love, Jill."

9. "Dear Parents: Oh boy, is this place wonderful! When I get back to the city, can I go to night camp? Willie."

10. "Dear Ma: Who said it was never hot in Maine? Please mail me some ice cream. P.S. You know what? I think this is a girls' camp. Pat."

* * *

When F. Scott Fitzgerald's daughter Frances was eleven years old, the famous novelist (author of *The Great Gatsby* and *This Side of Paradise*) sent her this capsule of advice while she was in summer camp:

"Darling Scotty: It's okay to worry about these four things: courage, cleanliness, efficiency, and horsemanship. But don't you *ever* worry your pretty little head about popular opinion, dolls, the past, the future, growing up, parents, boys, disappointments—or failure unless it comes through your own fault."

COLLEGE DAYS

A lady who ran a boarding house for students in a New England college town checked in a gangly new student who paid a month's rent in advance. A week later the lady received a note from the new student's mother. "Thank you for taking in my poor, lonesome boy," it read, "and I'll appreciate your keeping an eye on him, seeing that he gets enough sleep and eats enough wholesome food. This is the first time really he's ever been away from home—except, of course, for two years in the Navy."

* * *

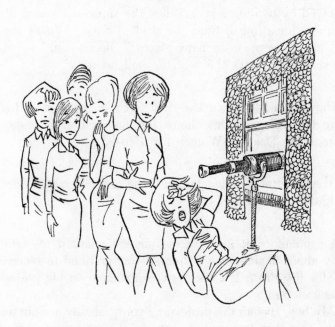

A fraternity house in Michigan went in for a thorough spring cleaning, which involved sending all the window curtains to the laundry. This brought an angry note from the sorority across the road. "Gentlemen," it read, "we must insist that you put back the curtains in your upstairs windows immediately. We are not interested in a course in anatomy."

Back went this note from the fraternity brothers: "Dear Girls: This course is not compulsory."

* * *

Ray Washburne found a student sound asleep in his Williamstown bookshop the other day. Explained the student, "I was just drowsing around."

* * *

In some fashion that I do not understand, a Purdue sophomore swallowed a ping-pong ball and was rushed to the infirmary to have it removed. He bore up bravely while the surgeon made an incision, but began to squirm when this was followed by two more jabs. When the surgeon wielded his instrument for a fourth time, the student cried, "What's the big idea of cutting me in so many places?" "Relax, man," suggested the surgeon. "That's the way the ball bounces."

* * *

They're talking about the rich man's only son who had to leave the college of his choice because of bad eyesight. He mistook the Dean of Women for a co-ed.

* * *

Overheard at a college prom: "She reminds me of Bardot." "Brigitte?" "No, Guy Lom."

* * *

A sophomore at a Southern university, asked to write an essay about Shakespeare's *Hamlet,* was gratified to receive an "A" for his effort, but then was summoned to his professor's inner sanctum.

"My boy," began the professor, "you probably are not aware of the fact that I am a fraternity brother of yours—and spent my undergraduate days in the very house you live in now. What's more, we used to keep a pile of old student essays on hand just as you do today. You have had the bad luck to copy word for word a paper on *Hamlet* that I happened to write myself.

"Now, I suppose you're wondering why I gave you an 'A.' Well, when I turned in that paper, the fool who was giving the course at the time marked it "C-minus." I've always believed it rated an 'A.'"

❈ ❈ ❈

The manager of a motel, reports Bob Sylvester, was asked if he could handle adequately a party of eighty teen-agers. "We have the room," he answered honestly, "but I'm afraid we haven't enough outlets for their electric guitars."

❈ ❈ ❈

There sat a classroom full of bright-eyed Vassar sophomores, the new fashions clearly revealing the cute dimples in their knees. The puritanical visiting lecturer from Boston eyed the girls apprehensively, and murmured, "What, oh what, will the styles be up to next?"

❈ ❈ ❈

Some time ago the superintendent of the Boston Public Library system was visiting a branch where an elderly gentleman had just borrowed a dozen lurid detective stories. "Don't you think," suggested the superintendent to one of the librarians, "that you could improve that man's literary tastes by suggesting that he read an occasional book a bit more meaningful and profound than a mystery?"

"I thought so myself," replied the librarian, "until I found out who he is. That's the president of Harvard University!"

❈ ❈ ❈

"A fool," sighed Professor Wolfe, "can ask more questions than a wise man can answer." One of his students murmured in barely audible tones, "No wonder so many of us flunked your last exam!"

❈ ❈ ❈

A Bowdoin sophomore called to his buddy across the hall, "Hey, Daly, your laundry's back." "Some service," approved Daly. "I only sent it in this morning." "That's right," agreed the sophomore. "The laundry refused to take it."

❈ ❈ ❈

Supposedly it was a Princeton hopeful who started on a shoestring—then worked his way up until he got slapped in the face.

* * *

A student at Oregon State, challenged to include both the words "analyze" and "anatomy" in a single short verse, promptly came up with:

> My analyze over the ocean,
> My analyze over the sea.
> Oh, who will ride over that ocean
> And bring back my anatomy?

* * *

Once upon a time there was a rich man's son who was so slow on the uptake it took him seven years to go through high school—yet he longed to go to college. The father reluctantly agreed to stake him *if* he could answer a few simple questions. The first question propounded by Pop was "What's what?" "I don't know," admitted the son—and was promptly put to work in a menial job at Pop's plant.

Came the time for the son's first vacation, and off he went to the big city to see the sights. In a bar, a very beautiful girl indeed suggested that he buy her a drink or two, and several hours later, to his surprise and delight, he found himself in the girl's apartment. She left him momentarily, then returned in a lovely informal gown. The boy pointed to her hips and inquired, "What's that?"

"What's what?" asked the beautiful girl.

"Holy mackerel," gasped the boy. *"If I'd known that two years ago—today I'd be in college!"*

* * *

There's a freshman up at Dartmouth this year who bids fair to make his mark as a social commentator. His first paper for a philosophy section contained this summary: "Socrates was a famous Greek who went around giving people excellent advice. They poisoned him."

* * *

Co-ed to her studying companion: "What more could any girl want on a cold evening than a warm robe, a glass of milk, a good book to study, and—oh, thank heaven! The phone is ringing!"

*   *   *

Crew coach Darrow looked over a bowlegged freshman and inquired, "So you're aiming to come out for the crew, eh? Ever rowed before?" The freshman confessed, "Only a horse, sir."

*   *   *

A co-ed at Baylor University paraded around the campus with two silver bars conspicuously pinned to her sweater. "I take it," commented an observant English professor, "that you have an army captain for a boy friend."

"No, sir," said the co-ed cheerfully. "Two lieutenants."

*   *   *

In the hallway outside a university library in Tennessee there's a row of hooks with a sign reading "For Faculty Members Only." A campus wit added in pencil below, "May also be used for hats and coats."

*   *   *

"They tell me Stanford is a great college," grumbled the father of a student at that noted institution, "but my son's handwriting seems to get worse and worse up there. Here's a letter that just arrived from him this morning, for instance. I can't even make out how much he wants me to send him!"

＊ ＊ ＊

A Syracuse junior, back from an expensive weekend at Vassar, composed this melancholy couplet:

> Pretty dishes
> Are avaricious.

＊ ＊ ＊

Not unlike many other college athletic departments, the University of New Mexico's was worried by the disappearance of sundry supplies, notably sweat shirts with the University's name emblazoned thereon. Dean Sherman Smith may have been responsible for the stratagem that effectively dissuaded would-be athletes in search of these status symbols. The manufacturer was instructed to mark all new shirts, "U. of N.M. Athletic Department: THIRD STRING."

＊ ＊ ＊

The Dean of the Columbia Graduate School of Journalism, Ed Barrett, tells of a rich trustee who called a college president and said, "Send somebody over to address our home-builders' convention next week, Sam. But please don't send anybody lower than a dean." The prexy answered dryly, "There *is* nobody lower than a dean!"

＊ ＊ ＊

The morning after a big class reunion at a university some fifty miles from New York, an old grad called a friend to ask if he had gotten home all right. "No," complained the friend, "I missed my train and had to doze on a bench in the station for six hours." "You're lucky," nodded the old grad. "I got home."

＊ ＊ ＊

The late and famous editor, Ellery Sedgwick, offered this challenging advice to a graduating class at Amherst: "It is my constant endeavor to persuade young men just starting their business careers that, instead of joining some company organized, successful, and regimented, they should sign up with a leaky ship, scrape down her decks, caulk her seams, refit her sails; for it is on the slipperiest decks that adventure beckons, and a speedier chance provided for rising in the world."

UNDERGRADUATE HUMOR

Every September, "welcome-back-to-the-campus" numbers of countless college comic magazines are pressed into the hot little hands of not-always-receptive undergraduates. Meanwhile the collegiate editors will be chortling loudly, and slapping each other on the back over puns and wheezes they have conjured for the text pages. Any resemblance to puns and wheezes of previous decades will be commented upon only by spoilsport fathers with fiendishly good memories.

It is just possible that some of the following stories will bob up in the months to come. They always have!

1. A pert Vassar junior, emerging from a conference with her renowned old professor of drama and literature, remarked ruefully to a roommate, "That old boy may be eighty, but he's still in there pinching!"

2. A Bradley senior is in the doghouse with his lady love's parents. "I promised to get her home before twelve last night," he admits, "but she had fifteen—and passed out."

3. *Fair co-ed*: Now before we start on this picnic you may as well realize that I neither smoke, drink, nor neck.
Experienced Princetonian: You're quite mistaken.
F.C.: You mean that I do do those things?
E.P.: No, I mean about starting on this picnic.

4. "Tomorrow is Marshall and Mary's wedding—so we bridesmaids are staying in this evening to give Mary a shower."

"Not a bad idea! I guess we ushers will stay home too and wash off old Marshall a bit."

5. "Were you ever troubled with athlete's foot?"

"Once—the time a Michigan State fullback caught me out with his girl."

6. Professor Binswanger defines "teen-age" as the time in life when girls begin to powder and boys begin to puff.

7. U.C.L.A.-ristocrat Rudy Toyt, known as "Hoity" Toyt by envious classmates, says that in his exclusive suburb, there are so many foreign cars, it's two years since anybody's been hit above the knees.

8. *Sophomore:* You like girls, I gather.

Junior: I like girls anybody gathers.

9. A romantic young bride, just graduated from Smith, persuaded her groom to stop the car on their honeymoon to lunch at an inn on the edge of a steep, lovely valley.

When they drove off later, she enthused, "What a wonderful gorge that was, darling!"

"Agreed," nodded the bridegroom, "but I could have done with one more piece of that apple pie."

10. *He:* I hear you neck.

She: Pardon me. I'll be more quiet the next time.

11. They tell of a lad who took so long to get through Harvard that he had ivy growing up his left leg. He met his fate

when he fell out of a speeding airliner. His last words were, "Gad! I guess that wasn't the washroom after all!"

12. An exhilarated U. of Texas promtrotter was driving the wrong way on a freeway. A cop overtook him and hollered, "Hey, you crazy or something? Can't you see those arrows?"

"Are you kidding?" replied the promtrotter gravely. "I can't even see the Indians!"

13. *Professor:* I will use my hat to represent the planet Mars. Any questions?

Student: Yes. Is Mars inhabited?

14. *Groom:* Nothing but toast for dinner this evening?

Bride: Yes, Michael. The bread toasted when the steak caught fire and fell into the chocolate pudding and I had to use the tomato soup to put out the blaze.

15. *From Texas:*
Uncle's health is much improved
Since he had bad things removed.
Purified of lewd desire
He sings soprano in the choir.

16. *From Indiana:*
The thunder god went for a ride
Upon his favorite filly.
"I'm Thor," he cried.
The horse replied,
"You forgot the thaddle, thilly."

17. *From Ithaca:*
She wore her stockings inside out
Straight through the summer heat.
She said it cooled her off to turn
The hose upon her feet.

18. "Hey, little boy, can you direct me to the best movie in town?" "Yeah. For fifty cents." "Isn't that pretty high?" "Not for a movie director."

19. *Sailor:* "Are you nautical?"
Pretty young thing: "No, I'm niceical."

20. "I owe all I have to one woman."
"Your mother?"
"No, my landlady."

21. Aboard a Mediterranean cruise ship:
"What's that white stuff on yonder hill, Steward?"
"That is snow, Miss."
"I thought so—but that creep on the bridge keeps telling me it's Greece."

22. Mary Newlywed had just cooked her first dinner. "It was great," enthused the bridegroom, "but didn't you think the lamb was just a teentsy-weentsy bit tough?" "Come now," chided Mrs. Newlywed. "Let's not talk chop."

23. *Football coach:* Miss Barber, what are you doing with that varsity letter on your sweater? Don't you know you're not supposed to wear that unless you've made the team?
Miss Barber: Well?

25. She was only a chimney sweep's daughter but she soots me fine; a printer's daughter, but I like her type; a hash slinger's daughter, and can she dish it out; a moonshiner's daughter, but I love her still; a lawyer's daughter, so she goes from bar to bar; a real estate agent's daughter, but, oh, what a development!

26. Observation by an indignant faculty adviser: "When I was a kid there was no such thing as juvenile delinquency. We were all hardened criminals."

27. A motorist gave a lift to a beatnik, and after several moments of desultory conversation, asked him, "Is there something bearing down on us from behind?" The beatnik looked, and told him, "Nothing but a dog." So the driver slowed up a bit and there was a terrific crash. While waiting for the ambulance, the driver grumbled, "I thought you told me nothing

was coming but a dog." "Yeah, man," nodded the beatnik. "A Greyhound."

28. "Does a sweater do anything for your wife?"
"Naw. Just makes her itch."

29. "Have you ever been pinched for going too fast?"
"No—but I've been slapped."

30. Ad in a New Haven daily: "Encyclopædia Britannica complete set, for sale cheap, never used. *My wife knows everything.*"

31. "What do you think of the new captain of the crew?"
"He's a gentleman and a sculler."

32. *He:* Do you neck?
She: That's my business.
He: I see. A professional.

33. *Sophomore co-ed:* Are you wearing that skirt to make you look shorter?
Junior co-ed: No—to make the boys look longer.

34. *Visitor:* Where can I get hold of your sister?
Little boy: I wouldn't know. She's ticklish all over.

35. *He:* If you refuse me I'll get a rope and hang myself right in front of your door.
She: No, no! You know how my father detests your hanging around here.

36. *Redlands:* My uncle knew a month before his death the exact date he was going to die.
U.C.L.A.: Did he learn it from a fortune teller?
Redlands: No. The judge told him.

37. *Customer:* Waiter! I just found this hair in my turtle soup.
Waiter: Well, well! So the turtle and the hair finally got together!

38. *Father:* What do you mean, you have to have a new car? Look at all these jalopies parked here on the campus!

Ohio State '67: Pa, you just don't understand. Those are the cars that belong to the faculty.

39. Have you heard about the unfortunate co-ed at the University of Kansas whose nickname is Turnpike? Not a curve in sight!

40. *Student:* How much is a haircut?
Barber: One-fifty.
Student: How much is a shave?
Barber: Sixty cents.
Student: Okay. Shave off my hair.

41. *New bride:* What's worrying you, Joe? Remember your worries now are *our* worries.

Bridegroom: Wonderful, darling. We just had a letter from Syracuse from a girl who's suing us for breach of promise.

42. Letter from a freshman co-ed to her friend back home: "I now weigh 108 pounds stripped, but I'm not sure that the scales in front of the campus co-op store are accurate."

43. *Sue:* When I get down in the dumps, I buy a new dress.
Prue: Oh, I was wondering where you got them.

44. Three men were busy repairing telephone wires. As a Wisconsin co-ed drove along in her convertible, she saw all three climbing poles. "Look at those nuts!" she told her seatmate. "You'd think I'd never driven a car before!"

45. *Movie patron at Chinese movie:* "Usher, I smell punk."
Usher: "That's O.K. Just stay where you are and I won't seat anybody near you."

46. The students of Iowa State have taken to writing ballads in their spare time. Here's one of the soul-searing results:

A bunch of the germs were hitting it up
In a bronchial saloon.
Two bugs on the edge of the larynx
Were jazzing a hay-feverish tune.
While back of the teeth in a solo game
Sat dangerous Dan Kerchoo,
And watching his pulse
Was his queen of the wultz,
The lady that's known as Flu.

47. "Here's an autograph of Mark Twain."
"All I see is an X."
"Well, that's his Mark."
"Where's the Twain?"
"Down at the station."

48. A nearsighted lady pointed to a round object at a Cambridge supermarket and inquired, "Is that the head cheese you're advertising?"
"No, Madam," replied the Harvard clerk politely. "That's his assistant."

49. A group of sidewalk superintendents were watching a new building go up in Austin, Texas, when a luscious co-ed, clad in a tight blue serge dress, ambled by.
For a moment silence reigned while all eyes turned from

one type of construction to the other. Then a learned U. of T. senior piped up, "It'll never work, men. Too many moving parts!"

50. A young man approached a cigar counter behind which stood a cute young thing and inquired, "Do you keep stationery?" Answered the c.y.t. thoughtfully, "Yes, up to a certain point. Then I just go all to pieces."

You have been listening, ladies and gentlemen, to the Voice of the Future.

SUNSET YEARS

Old Mr. Hardrocks sat rocking in his chair at the window of the Union League Club, favoring his young friend O'Connor with an occasional remark. "My wife," he finally grumbled, preparing to decamp, "won't believe I spend my afternoons here. *She* thinks I'm out chasing women. Gad, I wish she was right!"

* * *

"The middle years?" David Savage describes them as "that quiet, peaceful, serene period between completing the children's college education and starting in to help with the first grandchildren." "The middle years," he adds as a clincher, "usually last from three to five months."

* * *

The manager of a Connecticut brokerage office relates how he stepped outside during a blizzard last January to see an elderly gentleman poking with his cane into a piled-up snowbank at the curb. Assuming that the old fellow was blind, the manager suggested, "Can I help you across the street?" "Now why should I want to cross the street?" countered the oldster irritably. "I'm looking for my sports car."

* * *

Vincent Peel tells of a gray-haired lady waiting for a Madison Avenue bus. She was overweight and obviously crippled with rheumatism. Her arms were loaded with packages.

As she prepared to climb aboard the bus, a man behind her volunteered a helping hand. The old lady declined with a sad smile. "I'd best manage alone," she explained. "If I get help today—I'll want it tomorrow."

* * *

On his seventieth birthday, Henry Wadsworth Longfellow wrote this letter to a friend: "You do not know yet what it is to be 70 years old. I will tell you, so that you may not be taken by surprise when your turn comes. It is like climbing the Alps. You reach a snow-crowned summit, and see behind you the deep valley stretching miles and miles away, and before you other summits higher and whiter which you may have strength to climb or may not. Then you sit down and meditate, and wonder which it will be. That is the whole story, amplify it as you may. All that one can say is, that life is opportunity."

* * *

Dr. Robert McMillon, of Winston-Salem, North Carolina, has compiled "A Coronary Decalogue" which contains the following excellent nuggets of advice:

1. Thou shalt not try to be a champion athlete after 50.

2. Thou shalt consider losing thy temper a luxury to be indulged in sparingly.

3. Thou shalt avoid worry. (The government probably will take care of thee.)

4. Thou shalt take regular vacations.

5. Thou shalt keep thy alcoholic intake below the point where it may delude thee into thinking thou art a better man than thou ever were.

6. After a certain age, thou shalt not take unto thyself a young and frisky wife, nor even a reasonable facsimile thereof.

* * *

Old Colonel Beauregard was a devil with the ladies, still charming the daylights out of them at seventy-seven. In fact, on his seventy-seventh birthday he adopted the practice of cutting a notch on his cane to mark each new conquest. That's what killed him on his seventy-eighth birthday. He made the mistake of leaning on his cane.

*   *   *

A rhyming calendar from a Victorian English miscellany:
JAN et, aged, fell ill one day
FEB rile troubles came her way.
MAR tyr-like she lay in bed;
APR oned nurses softly sped.
MAY be, said a lord judicial
JUN ket would be beneficial.
JUL eps, too, though freely tried
AUG ured ill for Janet died.
SEP ulchre was sadly made
OCT aves pealed and prayers were said.
NOV ices with many a tear
DEC orated Janet's bier.

*   *   *

Shortly before his own death, author Ben Hecht wrote a book about departed cronies he remembered best: famous individualists like H. L. Mencken, Charles MacArthur, and Gene Fowler. "There's one thing," wrote Hecht, "that keeps surprising you about stormy old friends after they die: their *silence*. For a while an echo stays in your ear. You hear a laugh, a revealing phrase or two, a certain quality of enunciation. Then—nothing. Another death takes place: VOICES."

*   *   *

The Chinese Reds are trying to stop circulation of a story about a country woman who was found high in a remote mountain wilderness, sobbing beside a freshly dug grave.

"My grandfather was killed on this spot by a man-eating

tiger," she wailed. "My father met with the same fate. And now my only son has been killed here, too."

"Why not move to Shanghai, where there are no tigers?" urged a young Chinese Communist. "No, no," protested the sobbing woman. "I'd rather take my chances with the tigers!"

*　*　*

And from Hong Kong, frighteningly close to Red China's border, comes a poignant tale about a boy named Po-yu. Po-yu misbehaved and cried bitterly when his mother chastised him with a stick. "You never used to cry when I thrashed you," observed his mother. "Why do you cry now?"

Po-yu answered, "When I did wrong and you thrashed me it always used to hurt. But now my mother's strength has ebbed to the point where it hurts no longer. And that is why I cry."

*　*　*

Sick joke from Chicago: a one-legged man died at the ripe old age of ninety-two. His nephew was in court in connection with the will when a well-wisher told him, "I was sorry to hear that you had lost the rest of your uncle!"

*　*　*

A young visitor, anxious to please the late Bernard Baruch, told him on his ninetieth birthday, "My, sir, you're looking well!" Angrily, Mr. Baruch replied, "The fellow who announced that there are seven ages of man was wrong. There are three, my boy. The first is Youth. The second is Middle Age. And the third is, 'My, sir, you're looking well!'"

19. Trade Winds

ADVERTISING

The pretensions and exaggerations of a handful of exhibitionists in the advertising field have put a whole and long-established profession on the defensive. There *are* frenzied account executives who bandy expressions like "Let's toss it around and see if it makes a salad" or "Let's smear it on the cat and see if she licks it off," but most of the advertising folk you'll encounter on Madison Avenue are as sober and conservative as—well, book publishers.

Furthermore, not every advertising man is afflicted with an ulcer, either. A panel recently queried fourteen hundred ad executives on the state of their health for the express purpose of scotching this canard. Only 4 per cent admitted that they suffered from ulcers!

* * *

Making tall claims is no new manifestation of the advertising fraternity. An unearthed clay tablet of Babylon bears an inscription of cattle and feed for sale at "unheard-of low prices." At least one Egyptian papyrus is an advertisement for a health resort. Circus-like wall posters were discovered in the ruins of Pompeii.

* * *

Consider this coffee come-on from the "Publick Adviser," published in London over three hundred years ago:

"In Bartholomew Lane, the drink called Coffee, which is a very Wholesome and Physical drink, having many excellent virtues, closes the orifice of the Stomach, fortifies the heat within, helpeth Digestion, quickeneth the Spirits, maketh the heart lightsome, is good against Eyesores, Coughs, Colds, Rhumes, Dropsy, Gout, Scurvy, King's Evil and many others, is to be sold both in the morning and at three in the afternoon." What that copywriter could have done with *instant* coffee!

* * *

You will hear nothing on television today more jarring than this magazine ad of the 1880's:

Though love grows cold
Do not despair:
There's Ypsilanti
Underwear!

A patent medicine outfit of that day got away with this in the most conservative newspapers:

Lucinda Cordial! Barren wives
It turns to mothers fair
And the fond name of father gives
To husbands in despair.

* * *

The status of the account executive has definitely improved since the day, in the 1890's, when adman pioneer Frank Presby opened his agency in downtown New York. The morning he entered the building as a tenant for the first time he spotted this sign over the entrance: "Peddlers, book agents, and advertising men are not allowed in these premises."

* * *

Frantic copywriters, wallowing in a maze of secret formulas, astounding discoveries, giant economy sizes, and non-irritating filters, spend their days and nights seeking new keys to the public's pocketbooks.

One ingenious soul came up recently with the notion of printing ads backwards on the reverse sides of postage stamps, so that when you licked one, you would involuntarily carry the slogan around on your tongue for the rest of the day.

Unfeeling post office authorities gave him and his idea the heave-ho.

* * *

It's easy—if you know how—to spot a vice president in an advertising agency, states John Straley. "If he stays out to lunch for four hours," says John, "and nobody misses him—he's a vice president."

* * *

On a transcontinental plane trip, somebody asked chewing gum tycoon Philip K. Wrigley why he continued to advertise so extensively when his business already was a fantastic success. "For the same reason," replied Wrigley, "that the pilot of this plane keeps the engines running when we're already twenty-nine thousand feet up in the air."

* * *

David Ogilvy, one of the big men in advertising today, tells of a time when Max Hart, the men's clothing tycoon, summoned his advertising manager to complain that he was using too much copy in his new campaign. The ad manager disagreed violently. "Furthermore," he proposed, "I'll bet you ten dollars I can write a whole newspaper page of solid type and you'll read every word of it." Hart took the bet. "I won't have to write a line to prove my point," the ad manager than declared. "I'll only tell you the headline: '*This page is all about Max Hart.*'"

* * *

A well-known gourmet in the advertising world carries his own tiny, gold-trimmed pepper mill around with him. When luncheon is served at the restaurant he chances to be patronizing, he whips out the pepper mill and grinds elegantly. A sneering rival hails him as "the fastest pepper mill in the East."

* * *

A polltaker up Boston way has perfected an action-guaranteed approach. He smiles sweetly and announces, "Good morning, you unbelievably ugly old ape: we're conducting a survey to see how touchy people are."

* * *

One unattended, itty bitty advertising magnate in the Twin Cities, according to Jerry Beatty, coined the following six unintentional malapropisms in the course of one five-day, thirty-six-hour week:

1. Chafing at the dish.
2. Dropped it like a ten-foot pole.
3. Get on your bicycle and run like crazy.
4. He's just an ignorant ramus.
5. Let's not downgrade this up.
6. There's a dirge of good music on the radio.

* * *

There's a big ad agency on Madison Avenue whose quick-tempered boss fires about five employees a day. Anybody who lasts a full year is secretly awarded a medal by astounded colleagues. One of the v.p.'s of the agency was recalling the day he first worked there. "I didn't mind too much," he sighed, "that my name was printed on the door with chalk—but I did think the wet sponge hanging on the doorknob was rather disturbing."

* * *

Two high-powered advertising geniuses were talking about a third member of the fraternity, whose sudden death had been something of a shock. "What do you think the poor fellow had?" asked one in a properly mournful tone. "Nothing to speak of," sighed the other. "Just a small publishing account and a deodorant client. Nothing really worth going after."

* * *

Charles Brower, of Batten, Barton, etc., warns eager young account executives that if they had courted their wives the way they court prospects, their patter would have sounded something like this: "I can see you are a smart girl: the kind that can't be fooled on value. So you'll notice that I am wearing a three-hundred-dollar suit. That suit, girlie, is only an outward indication of the super-hydraulic, synchromesh, patented double-action heart that beats beneath it. Now listen carefully to something I tell only a chosen few. I am in limited supply. There are a lot of women after me. So for one day only, I'm offering to marry you. But you'll have to hurry—hurry—hurry—before I'm all gone."

*   *   *

A big talent agency was trimming its sales staff and fired two of its most high-powered agents. While they were bemoaning their fate, a cockroach walked across the floor. One of the agents stepped on it.

"I hope you realize," said the other bitterly, "that you have just destroyed our corporate image."

BUSINESS AS USUAL

"When I find myself depressed over present conditions," said Roger W. Babson, "I can, within one hour, banish worry and turn myself into a shouting optimist. . . . Here is how I do it. I enter my history library, close my eyes, and reach for a book, not knowing whether I am picking up Prescott's *Con-*

quest of Mexico or Suetonius's *Lives of the Twelve Caesars*. I then open my eyes and read for an hour; and the more I read, the more sharply I realize that the world has always been in the throes of agony, that civilization has always been tottering on the brink. The pages of history fairly shriek with tragic tales of war, famine, poverty, pestilence, and man's inhumanity to man. After reading history for an hour, I realize that bad as conditions are now, they are infinitely better than they used to be. This enables me to see and face my present troubles in their proper perspective as well as to realize that the world as a whole is constantly growing better."

*   *   *

In *Why Did They Name It?* Hannah Campbell tells how some of America's best-selling products got their names. Maxwell House Coffee, for instance, is named for a hotel in Nashville, Tennessee, where the coffee was so excellent, Teddy Roosevelt declared impulsively, "It's good to the last drop." Mr. Heinz was selling many more than 57 varieties when he registered his trademark in 1896. He just liked the number 57. Camel Cigarettes came along in 1913 when Turkish tobaccos were in vogue. The original camel was a venerable dromedary named "Old Joe" who lumbered through Winston-Salem with a circus just when R. J. Reynolds' were seeking a name for their new brand. Not sure they were right, they put "Old Joe" on their package. The rest is history. And Kodak? It means nothing at all. In Rochester, Boss Man George Eastman's favorite letter happened to be "K," so he invented a name that began and ended therewith.

*   *   *

"One thing you must say for people today," admits Frank Morris. "They're willing to do a day's work. But they want a week's pay first."

*   *   *

Cleaning up his cluttered desk for the first time in months, a successful but careless businessman found wedged into a crack at the bottom of one of the drawers a redemption check for a pair of shoes he had left for repair way back in 1933—thirty years ago. The shop, he knew, still existed, just around the corner, with the same sign on the outside: "Joe Antonio: Shoes Repaired While You Wait." Joe was an artisan of the old school—a man who took intense pride in his work.

More or less as a joke, the businessman presented the check at Joe's, saying, "I know it's thirty years since I left these shoes here, but it occurred to me you just might be able to find them." "Wait here. I go see," said the unsmiling Mr. Antonio. He handed back the check a moment later, explaining casually, "They'll be ready Tuesday."

* * *

The president of a big corporation let his eyes roam over the faces of his board of directors—which consisted of his own son, three sons-in-law, and his good-for-nothing nephew.

"Well, gentlemen," he said, "I suggest you give me all your ideas as quickly as possible—before my two tranquilizer pills wear off."

* * *

An antique shop up Bedford way featured an extensive collection of old snuffboxes. "They were handed down to me," explained the proprietor, "by my dear departed grandmother." "Oh," nodded a customer, "your grandmother took snuff." "Not at all," said the proprietor. "She took snuffboxes."

* * *

The vice president of an electronics firm had to excuse himself in the middle of an important meeting recently. "I hate to leave," he explained to his sympathetic fellow directors, "but my mother-in-law is arriving on the five o'clock broom."

* * *

"America," proclaims Tom Stevens, "is still the land of opportunity where a man can start out digging ditches and wind up as a top executive behind a desk—if he doesn't mind the financial sacrifice." (George Killian defines an executive as a man who leaves his air-conditioned office to drive in his air-conditioned car to an air-conditioned club to take a steam bath.)

* * *

Douglas Watt overheard a distressing conversation at a midtown snack bar. "You're nothing but a bum," upbraided a seedy-looking father. "Yeah?" answered his son. "Who brings home the unemployment checks?"

* * *

A publicist who lived high on the hog was frowning over a huge dinner check placed before him by the maître d' of a famous restaurant. His girl friend kidded him about his worried look. "Don't misunderstand," he assured her. "It's not the size of the check. I'm just trying to figure which client to charge it to."

* * *

Asked why he had lost his job, a worker in a mill explained angrily, "You know what a foreman is like these days: a faker who stands around and watches other men slave? Well, my foreman got jealous of me. Visitors to the plant all thought I was the foreman!"

* * *

On the second floor of a huge cigarette factory the secret formula for the company's most popular brand was concocted —a mixture of tobacco, tar, charcoal, and heaven knows what else. Then the finished product was funneled into a huge steel conveyor to the ground floor where the actual cigarettes were produced and packaged.

One day the top scientist produced a brand new secret ingredient to be added to the mixture, then pointed to the steel conveyor. "Okay, men," he ordered, "put *that* in your smoke and pipe it!"

* * *

A prosperous purveyor of rare orchids on Park Avenue is intoxicated about four working hours out of every five. He now is known as "the petrified florist"!

* * *

A venerable graybeard hobbled in to a credit manager's office to announce, "I'm here to pay the final installment on a baby carriage." "Thank you," said the credit manager, "and how's the baby today?" "Oh, I'm doing as well as could be expected," answered the graybeard.

* * *

A new industrial plant was opened in Chicago, and local stockholders were invited to see a mammoth metal-bending machine. "The first thing to remember about this machine," they were cautioned by the foreman, "is not to get your fingers caught in it."

* * *

Remember when Valentine cards were all sweetness and light, dripping with gooey sentiment? Well, here are a few *current* Valentines, spotted in those immaculate gift card racks that now take up so much space in alleged book shops:

1. A little lady with an obviously disgusted bird on her head. Coos the lady: "A little birdie told me all about you, my Valentine—cheep, cheep, cheep."

2. A not-too-bright-looking young man, with a bouquet of flowers, intoning, "Valentine, I'd like to lay the whole world at your feet—but you're so clumsy, you'd probably trip over it."

3. "Candy is dandy—but remember, My Valentine, that necking won't spoil your teeth!"

4. "Be loved! Be adored! Luckily you won't need sex appeal, charm, talent, or good looks—just three dollars for a small dog."

How could *any* girl in her right mind reject romantic appeals like these?

* * *

The president of a big importing house hired a new secretary the other day and put her to work at once taking down long letters to agents in Hong Kong, Buenos Aires, Rome, Stockholm, and Hawaii. A short time later the girl poked her head in his door and reported cheerfully, "Mission accomplished." "That's quick work," beamed the importer. "Where did you learn to type letters so fast?"

"I didn't," admitted the girl. "I just phoned those agents instead. That's much faster than writing."

* * *

"I'll tell you how ugly my new secretary is," mourned a debonair broker to his luncheon companion. "When I chase her around the desk, I *walk!*"

* * *

A secretary had just been told that she was fired, as of Friday evening, so she spitefully added a few parenthetical comments of her own to one of her boss's standard "alibi" letters. The result:

Replying to your urgent letter about non-delivery of your order of eleven weeks ago, unforeseen circumstances (I was away playing golf) prevented my answering sooner. Your order was marked for personal attention by our sales manager (he lost it) and he is heartsick at having failed you. (He's still looking for it.)

Please forgive us: this will never happen again (till next time). Your friendship means too much to us. (This is no kid-

ding, either. You're one of the few customers we have left.)
Faithfully (like my wife always said before running away with
the head shipping clerk). . . .

    ❉ ❉ ❉

Alan King tells about the secretary who handed her boss a
letter written on heavily perfumed note paper. "This letter
was marked 'Strictly Personal,'" she told him, "but it isn't
very."

    ❉ ❉ ❉

Eager to make good in his new job, Eustace Filligrew arrived at the office at eight-thirty sharp, only to find the curvy,
blonde secretary sitting on the boss' lap.

The next morning he showed up at eight-fifteen. The boss
and the secretary were locked in a tight embrace. As Eustace
tiptoed out of the office, the boss looked up at the clock and
hollered, "Filligrew, if you get in here tomorrow at eight—
you're fired!"

    ❉ ❉ ❉

Ben Cassell lists the four faux pas that lost the beautiful receptionist in his office her job:

1. "Insurance? I'm sure the boss is interested in a new policy. Go right into his private office."

2. "I forgot to tell you yesterday. President Johnson called
from Washington while you were out to lunch and wanted you
to call him right back on a very important matter. I guess it
just slipped my mind."

3. "You may be the boss's son—but you can't make passes at
me like that."

4. "I'm sorry, but you can't go in right now, Mrs. Marshall.
Your husband is dictating to that new red-headed secretary he
hired personally last Monday."

    ❉ ❉ ❉

A prominent midtown dress manufacturer lavishly entertained an out-of-town buyer last week. The very next day he
got an order for three hundred more girls.

    ❉ ❉ ❉

"There's no limit to the amount of work a man can do," insisted Robert Benchley, "provided, of course, that it isn't the work he's *supposed* to be doing at that moment."

*   *   *

Memo pinned on the bulletin board of a paper-box factory:

"To Our Employees:

"The Management of this organization, after due and careful consideration of certain regrettable practices which have recently been brought to its attention, is desirous of again reminding you of the fact—which has, of course, been pointed out on several previous occasions but which nevertheless has apparently been overlooked or ignored by an all-too-preponderant proportion of our present personnel—that all members of this organization should make an earnest, sincere, continuous, and persistent effort to eschew and avoid all excessive wordiness, repetitive phraseology, unnecessarily complicated sentence structure, lengthy, involved, or obscure paragraphs, and other tautological and/or grammatical errors to indite or transcribe an internal communication of any nature whatsoever to one or more fellow employees,

The Management

"P.S. In other words—make it brief!"

✿ ✿ ✿

A very self-confident young man had just submitted to a long series of aptitude tests, and awaited results with lofty unconcern. "I suppose," he told the returning examiner, "I have an aptitude for so many fields that you fellows are a bit confused about it all."

"You have an aptitude for exactly one field," the examiner told him tartly, "and that is any field in which your father holds an extremely influential position."

✿ ✿ ✿

Adam Gimbel tells about a man who went to a clothing store to buy a suit, and was immediately asked his name, address, family history, favorite pastimes, political affiliation, and his wife's maiden name.

"Why all these questions?" he demanded. "I only want to buy a suit." "Ah, my friend," said the salesman silkily. "Before we sell you a suit here, we make sure that it fits your personality and position in life. We send to Australia for the proper blend of wool for you. From France we import just the right lining, from Scotland the buttons you should have. Then five tailors in our shop make it fit you to perfection, regardless of the fittings that may prove necessary."

"Shucks," said the customer. "I need this suit to be married in tomorrow morning."

"Stop worrying," said the salesman. "You'll have it."

✿ ✿ ✿

Colonel Duffy is bemoaning the plight of the mattress tester who got fired for standing up on the job.

✿ ✿ ✿

Mourned the proprietor of a men's clothing emporium, "In our five-story establishment, with sixty fancy clerks, we sold exactly one suit Tuesday. Wednesday we sold nothing at all. And Thursday was even worse than Wednesday." "How could it possibly be worse," demanded a stickler for accuracy. "Because," explained the proprietor, "on Thursday the loafer who bought the suit on Tuesday brought it back for credit."

* * *

Mr. Rinswanger, with eight hungry mouths home to feed, braced his employer for a substantial raise. "For six years," he wailed, "I haven't been able to buy even one suit of decent clothes for myself. Lord how the threads are unraveling in this worn-out coat I'm wearing."

"O.K.," conceded the boss wearily, "You can have a ten-dollar raise. But please, I beg you, don't show me your stringy coat any more. This organization can't afford any fringe benefits!"

* * *

In the dark recesses of a Third Avenue antique shop, Mrs. Hayward asked a clerk, "What is that quaint old figure in the corner worth?" "About two hundred grand," answered the clerk. "He's the proprietor."

* * *

A stout lady in Dayton's approached a lovely young sales-girl and inquired as to the whereabouts of the perfume counter. The salesgirl suggested politely, "Just walk this way, Ma'am." "Hmpfhh," commented the customer. "If I could walk that way, my dear, I wouldn't need perfume."

* * *

A top official at Chrysler confesses, "When we have a tough new problem at the plant and our experts can't figure an easy way to solve it, we put our laziest man on the job. He'll find the easy way in forty-eight hours flat. Then we adopt his method."

* * *

Overheard in an air-conditioned office: "Makes me feel a bit guilty, sitting here in comfort, while the wife and kiddies suffer under the broiling sun at the seashore!"

* * *

A professor from the Harvard Business School was telling his six-year-old son the story of Cinderella. The boy paid flattering attention—particularly when his father came to the part where the pumpkin turns into a golden coach. He interrupted only long enough to ask, "Hey, Pop, did Cinderella have to report that as straight income, or did they let her call it a capital gain?"

＊　＊　＊

Dave Balch, passing a fish store on Vesey Street, spotted two tubs of live soft-shell crabs, side by side. One tub had a sign reading "$2.50 a dozen"; the other a sign reading "$1.50 a dozen." While Balch watched, a crab in the $1.50-a-dozen tub pulled himself up laboriously from among his fellows, attained the rim of the tub, and climbed into the $2.50-a-dozen receptacle.

"That's the sort of thing," opined Balch with great satisfaction, "that can happen only in the U.S.A.!"

＊　＊　＊

Congressman John Lindsay of New York tells about a shop owner with 148 employees who proposed a profit-sharing and pension plan—provided every employee signified his approval in writing. One hundred forty-seven men signed at once, but one maverick refused, thereby nullifying the entire project. For two weeks the holdout persisted, then one day marched into the boss's office and declared meekly, "I've decided to sign." "Good," enthused the boss, "but what finally persuaded you to change your mind?"

Explained the holdout: "This morning the two huskiest members of the union grabbed me by the collar and told me, 'If you haven't signed up by ten-thirty this morning we'll break both your arms, break both your legs, and knock out all your teeth.' Well, Boss, nobody had ever bothered to explain the plan to me so clearly before."

INGENUITY

A young man in a drugstore phone booth left the door of the booth ajar, so the druggist couldn't help overhearing his conversation. "I want to talk to the boss," was his opening gambit. "Please connect me. This *is* the boss? Well, how would you like to hire a new, on-his-toes office boy? You already have one who is entirely satisfactory? No way to persuade you to make a change? O.K., I'm sorry. Thanks anyhow for listening to me. Goodbye."

After the young man hung up the druggist told him, "I couldn't help hearing what you said over the phone just now. I like your initiative and I'm sorry you didn't connect on that job. Better luck next time."

"Thanks," said the young man airily, "but everything is just dandy. That was my own boss I was talking to. I was just doing a little checking up on myself."

*   *   *

When F. W. Woolworth opened his first store, a merchant down the block resented the new competition and hung out a big sign reading, "I have been doing business in this spot for over fifty years." The next day Mr. Woolworth hung up a sign, too. *His* read: "Established a week ago; no old stock."

✿   ✿   ✿

A garage man who owns the first of four closely bunched gas stations on a federal highway leading to the Mojave Desert erected a big sign proclaiming, "This is your LAST chance to fill up before you hit the desert. The three other stations you think you see are mirages."

✿   ✿   ✿

A senior at the University of Minnesota awoke one midnight at the height of a violent storm to find the ceiling of his top-floor room leaking like mad. The resultant puddle next to his bed was rapidly assuming the proportions of Lake Superior.

Our hero was equal to the emergency. He calmly took the proper tool out of his kit and drilled a neat hole in the center of the puddle.

✿   ✿   ✿

A visitor to a Sunset Boulevard confectionery parlor noticed that one salesgirl had a line of customers waiting to be served by her while three other salesgirls stood idle. Later the busy salesgirl explained her popularity. "The other girls scoop up more than a quart of ice cream and then start scraping away. I always scoop up less than a quart and then add to it."

✿   ✿   ✿

An irate gent in a jewelry store demanded a refund on a watch he had purchased there a few days before. "This watch," he asserted, "loses fifteen minutes every hour." "Of course it does," nodded the proprietor. "Didn't you see the sign '25 per cent off' when you bought it?"

✿   ✿   ✿

A young girl who got a job in a bakery was telling her mother of her first day's experience there. "They put me to work taking stock of all the cakes that were left and I just couldn't spell meringue." "What did you do?" asked the sympathetic mother. The girl explained, "Well, there were only seven left, so I ate them."

* * *

There once was a capricious tycoon in downtown New York whose office was overrun with dogs. Never less than thirty assorted poodles, pugs, Pomeranians, and terriers had the run of the premises. Furthermore, every applicant for a job had to run the gamut of these canines before being granted an audience with the boss. The reaction of the dogs was carefully noted. If they liked him, the job was his; if they growled at him, he never had a prayer.

One wily applicant learned of the tycoon's idiosyncrasy in time. He carefully lined the cuffs of his trousers and the inner band of his hat with strips of raw liver. Of course the tycoon's dogs greeted his arrival with wild barks of approval—and he was made office manager on the spot!

* * *

A college graduate wangled his way into a tony publisher's office and asked cheerfully, "Need a good editor?" "I do not." "A proofreader, perhaps?" "Nope." "A sixth assistant secretary?" "No. Sorry, but we haven't any openings at all at the moment."

"Then," said the applicant, "you certainly need one of these." And from his briefcase he produced a neat metal sign reading, "No help wanted."

* * *

"Lackaday," sighed a Chinese businessman in Hong Kong, "I have lent a tricky competitor a thousand gold dollars and he has not given me a receipt. What can I do?"

"Write sternly," suggested his friend, "and demand payment of the two thousand gold pieces."

"Most careless listener," reproved the businessman. "I told you it was only one thousand gold dollars."

"I know," nodded the friend, "and your competitor will indignantly write and tell you so. Then you will have your receipt."

                            *   *   *

Two small brothers, aged eight and three, entered an ice cream parlor, with the three-year-old vehemently announcing, "I want vanilla! I want vanilla!"

The supply of vanilla had been exhausted, and bystanders wondered how the eight-year-old would cope with the situation. He did not hesitate. He ordered two strawberry cones and handed one to his younger brother.

"Here you are," he said cheerfully, *"pink vanilla!"*

INSURANCE

America's big insurance and casualty companies never have been in healthier financial shape, but life remains rugged for their underlings setting out to peddle policies for the first time.

To them are allotted the most unlikely prospects—in the most inaccessible territory—and woe betide the neophyte caught resting his dogs by an agency head. "A man who gets holes in his pants before his shoes," warned one, "is obviously making his contacts in the wrong place."

One foot-weary agent resorted to the telephone, and after 293 prospects had hung up on him, decided to shoot the works. He dialed the richest old coot in town. "I don't suppose," he hazarded timidly, "you're in the market for some additional life insurance."

"It happens that I am," was the astonishing reply. "Would you care to come out here and write a policy for a million dollars?"

"Excuse me, sir," stammered the agent, "I must have the wrong number."

Another agent, more optimistic by nature, came home jubilant from his latest brush with an ornery prospect. "No vague promises this time," he told his wife. "He says he will definitely buy a policy when hell freezes over."

❄   ❄   ❄

The library of the Atlantic Insurance Company boasts the most complete set of marine disasters in the world. "I'll bet," joked a broker, "they even have a record of Noah's Ark." Inquiry proved that somebody at the Insurance Company had an excellent sense of humor, at least, because back came this dossier: "Built about 2448 B.C. Gopher wood, pitched within and without. Length: 320 cubits; width: 52 cubits; height: 35 cubits. Three decks. Equipped to carry animals. Owners: Noah and Sons. Last reported stranded on peak of Mount Ararat."

❄   ❄   ❄

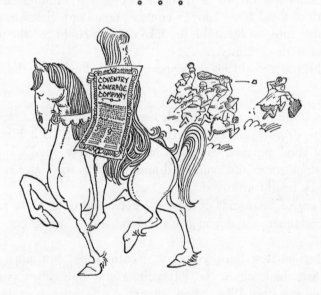

Insurance men will tell you that the most unpopular insurance salesman who ever lived was the killjoy agent who tried to sell a full coverage policy to Lady Godiva.

❄   ❄   ❄

Most people think "Lloyd's of London" is the most famous insurance company in the world. As a matter of fact, Lloyd's writes no insurance whatever. It is merely an association, whose members write policies strictly on their own.

Originally, Lloyd's was a London coffee shop, where marine

underwriters were wont to gather. In 1774, "Lloyd's Rooms" were moved to the Royal Exchange, and there a big bell was installed. For a hundred years, every important event has been announced via the tolling of this bell. It was salvaged from the frigate *Lutine*, sunk off the Netherlands coast in 1799 with a million pounds in gold bars and coins aboard.

Marine insurance is only one facet of the business done by Lloyd's today. Some years ago a professional flea trainer, for example, came to Lloyd's to insure his winsome performers. He was offered a policy, too, but the premium demanded was one hundred dollars a day for every five hundred dollars' worth of fleas! Even Lloyd's couldn't come any closer to a reasonable rate, he was told, because nobody could tell the age of a flea with certainty.

The trainer sold his fleas and opened a burlesque theatre.

*   *   *

An insurance salesman made the mistake of asking a prospect in the dress business how things were going with him. "I'll show you," moaned the dress man. He threw open a door to the stock room and pointed dramatically to rows and rows of dresses neatly arranged.

"Tens of thousands of dresses I got hanging on these racks," he exclaimed, "and you ask me how things are going. They ain't!"

"But what a fine inventory," soothed the insurance man. "Dresses hanging in the loft you've got, but clever partners you've got, too. What about them?"

"My partners?" sneered the dress man. *"They're hanging in the closets."*

*   *   *

The insurance adjustor was indignant. "How come," he demanded of the man who had sent for him, "that you didn't call the police the minute you discovered your car had been stolen?" "Well, for one thing," was the answer, "my wife was in it."

* * *

The formidable wife of a henpecked worm told an insurance salesman, "Let me be sure if I've got this right. You say that if my husband dies within even one year, I'll get the full fifty thousand dollars mentioned on Page One of this policy?" "Absolutely," the salesman assured her. "And within even a month?" "Yes, Ma'am." "And if he dies the day after I sign up?" "Then, Madam," said the salesman, snapping shut his briefcase, "I am confident you'll get the same fifty thousand—but they won't be dollars; they'll be volts."

* * *

An insurance broker in California sent his friends this announcement when his irrepressible sixty-seven-year-old mother graduated from college: "I announce with pleasure and relief that my mother finally nailed down her Bachelor of Arts degree this week. If you think it's tough putting your kids through college—just try your mother!"

* * *

A heavily bearded author invaded a book publisher's office recently, proposing an account of his six weeks on an uninhabited, treeless island without a bite to eat.

"How did you survive?" inquired the skeptical publisher.

"By luck," explained the author. "I had my insurance policy in my pocket. I found enough provisions to keep me going indefinitely."

SALESMANSHIP

An American shoe manufacturer read with interest about the upheavals in Africa, and correctly figured that along with their new freedom and opportunities, the African people would demand luxuries long denied to them.

The manufacturer hastily dispatched two salesmen Congoward to open new accounts. The bad salesman soon cabled back, "Returning next plane. Nobody can sell shoes here. Everybody goes barefoot."

The good salesman cabled, "Request permission open branch office here. Possibilities unlimited. Not a man or a woman in the territory knows what shoes are."

*　*　*

Another quick-thinking salesman is employed by a real estate broker on East Fiftieth Street in New York. The other day a lady on the telephone dialed him by mistake and inquired, "Do you sell maternity clothes in this shop?" "We do not," the real estate salesman told her regretfully, "but possibly I could interest you in a larger apartment?"

*　*　*

Lonesome George Gobel defines a salesman as "a fellow with a smile on his face, a shine on his shoes, and a lousy territory."

*　*　*

A conspicuous case of overselling is reported by Priscilla Platfoot, of Kansas City. A tiny runt of a man came into the emporium where she toils and asked for a job as store detective. "Nothing has escaped my eagle eyes in the past twenty years," he boasted breathlessly. "Why are you puffing?" interpolated the personnel manager. "You sound as though you climbed all seven flights of stairs to get here."

"I did," admitted the aspirant. "I couldn't find the elevators." (He didn't get the job!)

*　*　*

An overeager salesman got his comeuppance from a storekeeper in Maine. "You must remember that in this part of the country, young feller," said the storekeeper, "every want ain't a need."

*　*　*

A fur salesman was driving his wife along a mountain road when a small animal scurried across it in front of him. "What

was that?" he inquired. "A mink," said his wife. "Pfooie," sniffed
the furrier. "What a terrible fit."

IN THE SOUP

The nation's favorite beverage? Is it beer? Corn likker? Soda
pop? No, sir, it's soup!
According to a recent report, just about everybody in the
U.S.A. (approximately nine of every ten of us) has the soup
habit—and more and more of it is coming. Over ten billion
bowlfuls of soup were purchased by America's housewives in
1964.

* * *

No longer need mama slave long hours in the kitchen, or
worry which of her limited number of soup recipes she will
draw upon. Since the Campbells, not to mention the Heinzes,
Liptons, and others have been a-comin', she has only to heat
up some "mongol," "bird's nest," onion soup, bisque of lobster,
or bouillabaisse, and the family is served a treat comparable
with the fare at the most expensive restaurants. No matter
how fancy and infinite the varieties have become, however,
America's allegiance remains rooted to good old-fashioned
tomato soup, the sale of which tops all the others put together.

* * *

The succulent red tomato was unknown until it bobbed up
among the wild crags and rock-ribbed valleys of Peru. Thence
it spread to Mexico, where the Aztecs dubbed it *xitomatle*.
That was a little too much for marauding but appreciative
conquistadors, who reduced the name to its present form.
Soon these conquistadors, and their neighbors across the
Italian and French borders, were munching tomatoes at all
hours of the day and night. In Italy they became mixed up
with sauces and pizzas; in France, like so many other things
in that wonderful land, with sauces and sex. The French re-

named tomatoes *pommes d'amour,* and whispered that they possessed aphrodisiacal qualities.

The Puritans, after Cromwell's uprising, took no chances with this dangerous edible. They officially decreed that, aphrodisiac or not, tomatoes were *verboten,* and to be avoided as assiduously as toadstools and wolfsbane.

It remained for a publicity-minded benefactor named Robert Gibbon Johnson, of Salem, New Jersey, to put an end to this nonsense in the year 1820. He announced boldly that he would eat one dozen large tomatoes on the steps of the Salem courthouse.

A big crowd assembled, thoughtfully bringing two stomach specialists along with them, but Mr. Johnson calmly ate the twelve tomatoes, patted his midriff, and casually walked the five miles back to his farm. It was one of the stomach specialists who fainted.

* * *

From that day, tomatoes have ranked as our No. 1 home garden favorite, and indeed, what more satisfying sight can there be than a luscious tomato working in her garden? Tomatoes are ambrosial, whether in the guise of aspic, catsup, juice, chili sauce, salad, or cream of tomato soup!

* * *

But cream of tomato is not the only soup Americans have perfected to titillate the palates of gourmets the world over. The Pilgrims borrowed the idea of clam and fish chowder from the Indians. The Cajuns in Louisiana dreamed up creole gumbo. Philadelphians produced pepper pot, and Kentuckians the savory burgoo.

There are "mock turtle" and "mock kangaroo" soups, too, though if the animals named could read, they might be astonished to see what concoctions are merchandised with their names attached.

These are tasteful, but strictly non-turtle and non-kangaroo products devised by ingenious soup inventors and souperdouper selling organizations.

* * *

Plain soup, in fact, is far too healthful for the hoity-toity set. They now insist upon mixing it with gin, vodka, bourbon, and even rum, and labeling the results "bull shots," "bourbon beer," "monks' solace," and heaven knows what else.

In other words, they're now serving soup to nuts.

THE BULLS AND THE BEARS

Wall Street veterans are wont to talk about the crash of 1929 as though it happened just yesterday, but in 1929 all these commonplaces of 1965 were as yet unheard of (points out Joe Alex Morris in *What a Year*): jets, moon shots, the "sound barrier," Polaroid cameras, split-level houses, guided missiles, radar, bulldozers, electric typewriters, color TV, foam rubber, drive-in movie houses, bobby soxers, automatic transmissions for the family car, electric razors, the four-minute mile, and bubble gum—not to mention the United Nations—and the atom bomb!

* * *

Officials of the New York Stock Exchange treasure a request received by mail from a supplicant in Alabama who alleged that he was coming north to sell some hogs and would like "to get a couple of seats for the Stock Exchange which ain't behind no post or around in some corner where we can't see what's going on. Our Uncle Julius says you fellows put on the best show in New York."

Back in 1875, incidentally, a seat on the New York Stock Exchange was valued at $4750. In 1929, an all-time high was reached when a seat sold for $625,000. In the war year of 1942 the value plummeted to $17,000. Present value is in the $200,-000 range. There are 1366 seats on the Exchange today.

* * *

John Wheeler tells about a daring speculator named Charles Flint who operated in Wall Street at the turn of the century. Once he found himself in serious financial straits, and knowing J. P. Morgan, the elder, slightly, he approached him for a loan.

Mr. Morgan consented to take a stroll with him to the Battery. He talked polite nothings, however, the entire time. Finally, after about an hour, Flint blurted, "But, Mr. Morgan, how about that million dollars I want to borrow?"

Morgan held out his hand to say goodbye and answered, "Oh, you won't have any trouble getting it now that we have been seen together."

* * *

Hetty Green, famed "witch of Wall Street," was one of the richest women in the world when she died—also one of the stingiest and most detested. Arthur Lewis tells the whole story superbly in his book, *The Day They Shook the Plum Tree.*

Hetty Green dressed in rags, slept in cold-water flats, ate leftover scraps, and begged for free office space—so she could go on adding to the millions she already had stashed away. Worse still, she denied her son medical aid—so he was doomed to go through life a cripple.

The son, Colonel E. H. Green, when his mother died, proceeded to squander millions on patent medicines and such indulgences as an oceangoing yacht, which he ignored when he found that it made him seasick, and which gave him his first pleasure when it turned turtle and sank. He—and his only sister—derived as little real happiness from their great fortune as had their mother Hetty. Figure the moral for yourselves.

* * *

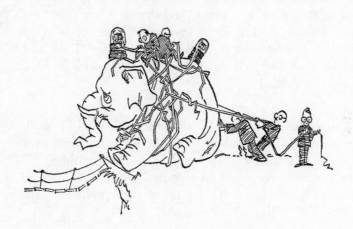

"A Wall Street security analyst," the late Herbert Bayard Swope liked to point out, "is as cautious as an Indian elephant. When one of these sagacious mastadons comes to a bridge, he tests it first with his trunk. If it holds firm, he next plants his front feet on it. If it still stands, he sits on it. After that, he sends another elephant over first!"

* * *

At the annual meeting of a company that was going from bad to worse, the president was interrupted in the middle of his address by his secretary who whispered hoarsely, "The treasurer wants to give his financial report. He's on long distance."

* * *

A partner of a Wall Street brokerage house summoned a pert, capable girl from the outer offices and offered her a big raise and advancement to a different job. "Thank you, sir," she replied demurely, "but if it's all the same to you, I think I'll keep my present pay and hang on to taking care of the stamp box and the petty cash."

* * *

John Straley tells of the stockbroker who was trying on a suit and told the tailor, "I think you might take these pants in about an inch." The tailor squelched him with, "In this business, mister, it's like in yours. You should never argue with the tape." Straley, meanwhile, is toying with the notion of opening a brokerage office in a dirigible moored above Broad and Wall Streets. That way he'll always be able to sell stock for his clients above the market.

* * *

A new customer asked for the head of a Wall Street brokerage house, and once admitted to the inner sanctum, explained succinctly, "I have a really tough investment problem." "We're here precisely for cases like yours," the broker assured him cheerily. "Just what is the nature of your problem?" The customer said, "I haven't any money."

* * *

Dick Bobbitt tells about a wealthy financier who became the virtual slave of a reigning musical comedy queen. After squiring her aggressively for months, he decided to propose matrimony, but cautiously hired a private eye to shadow her for a spell to make sure she wasn't two-timing him. A fortnight later, he received this report: "Miss So-and-So enjoys a spotless reputation, and until this year her behavior has been exemplary. In recent months, however, she has wandered sadly from the paths of virtue, and is now being seen constantly with a banker who is said to be the biggest crook in Wall Street."

* * *

A hard-driving young securities salesman phoned a prospect who chanced to be a certified accountant, and gave him a terrific pitch about a new business equipment stock which he claimed "was certain to double or even triple in less than a year." "I'm glad you think so well of this company," said the accountant warmly. "I happen to be its financial vice president." "Well, I'll be darned!" exclaimed the salesman. "Tell me confidentially, sir, *is the company any good?*"

* * *

Popular story among well-heeled suburbanites: A teacher, lecturing on Puritan fables and customs, asked her class, "What sort of people were punished in the stocks?" To which a bright lad in the front row responded, "The small, unsophisticated investors."

* * *

J. K. Galbraith, witty Professor of Economics at Harvard, explains in his book, *The Affluent Society:* "The nature of a vested interest has an engaging flexibility. In ordinary intercourse it is an improper advantage enjoyed by a political minority to which the speaker does not himself belong. When the speaker enjoys it, it ceases to be a vested interest and becomes a hard-won reward. When a vested interest is enjoyed not by a minority but by a majority, it is a human right."

* * *

A fat dowager aboard a crowded Fifth Avenue bus trod upon the foot of an irritable merchant who was trying to read the stock tables in the evening paper. "Madam," he said coldly, "I will ask you to kindly get off my foot." "Put your foot where it belongs," she replied sharply. "Madam," he murmured reverently, "don't tempt me!"

* * *

Arthur Goodman claims there's a new electronic machine in a big Wall Street brokerage office that is being used to good effect for extracurricular purposes by the staff during the coffee break. One girl inserted a note saying that from the way her boy friend had acted the night before, she figured she was engaged. "What should I do?" she asked the wonderful machine. It answered, "GET IT IN WRITING." Then a customer's man asked about an opportunity just given him to get in on a deal on the ground floor. Advised the machine, "WATCH OUT FOR THE BASEMENT."

* * *

Financial experts will like the story of the securities analyst who came home early one day and found his wife being embraced by a strange gentleman. "What's the meaning of this?" he bellowed. "Keep your shirt on," counseled his wife. "I've gone public."

20. A Turn for the Verse

What sentiment, what emotion a clever versifier can cram into four short lines! Following are a few quotable examples.

Ruminates Rod Terrill:

> The good old days, the good old days,
> We all so fondly speak of,
> Which, if they ever should come back,
> No one could stand a week of.

Character sketch by Frank Connors:

> He wrecked his car, he lost his job
> And yet throughout his life,
> He took his troubles like a man:
> He blamed them on his wife.

Disgusted with a stretch of wretched weather, an English poet (who wouldn't sign his name) dashed off this rhymed lament:

> Oh, what a blamed uncertain thing
> This pesky weather is:
> It blew and snew and then it thew
> And now by jing it friz!

Sayeth Paul Flowers, the Memphis sage:

> All right, go lie upon the beach,
> To bake beyond the water's reach;
> But if you're blistered when you quit,
> Remember that you basked for it.

By Sheldon White:

> I've written lots of letters
> Filled with libelous intent,
> And don't regret a single one—
> Except the few I sent.

Colonel Corncrib's ode to a bore:

> If you can remember so many bad jokes,
> With all of the details that mold them,
> Why can't you recall, with comparable skill,
> All the countless occasions you've told them?

By Herb Ellafson:

> 'Twas in a restaurant they met
> Brave Romeo and Juliet.
> He had no cash to pay his debt
> So Romeo'd what Juli'et.

Frank Boyden, famous headmaster of Deerfield Academy, has a little poem always on tap for lazy students:

> You can't go far just by wishing
> Nor by sitting around to wait:
> The good Lord provides the fishing—
> But you have to dig the bait.

Barbara Jones suggests a new version of an old Mother Goose rhyme:

> There was an old woman
> Who lived in a shoe
> She had so many children
> Her government relief check came to $4892.

Reports Day C. Yeager:

> I took up golf to soothe my nerves,
> But one thing causes mutters:
> If the foursome playing ahead of me
> Instead of putting, putters.

Rueful meditation from D. E. Twiggs:

> Doc said he'd have me on my feet
> The last time I was ill,
> And that he did . . . I sold my car
> So I could pay his bill.

Laments Walter Jacobs:

> A lady drove her little car
> In manner swift and deft,
> But every time she signaled right
> The little car turned left.

Terse verse from Francis Duffy:

> He let his head get swollen up,
> And sniffed at those who hired him.
> He thought himself a great big gun—
> And that is why they fired him.

Ogden Nash, of course, is one of the great masters of the art of the four-liner. These two are included in his sparkling collection, *From Everyone but Thee and Me*:

1.

The truth I do not stretch or shove
When I state the dog is full of love.
I've also proved, by actual test,
A wet dog is the lovingest.

2.

The clam, esteemed by gourmets highly,
Is said to live the life of Riley;
When you are lolling on a piazza
It's what you are happy as a.

The prolific Richard Armour is another of my favorites.
Consider:

1.

You cannot buy, you cannot lease
As durable and crisp a crease
As that your trousers soon acquire
When hung on hangers made of wire.

2.

How cunningly the ice holds back
And lingers underneath
And lets you raise and tilt the glass,
Then smacks you in the teeth!

The late Sam Hoffenstein once sent these lines to a lady
love who was beginning to bore him:

When you're away, I'm restless, lonely,
Wretched, bored, dejected; only
Here's the rub, my darling dear,
I feel the same when you are near.

A knowing light versifier once whipped up this gentle lament:

> When late I attempted your pity to move,
> What made you so deaf to my prayers?
> Perhaps it was right to dissemble your love
> But—why did you kick me downstairs?

Now who would you name as the author of those lines? Ogden Nash? Dorothy Parker? Richard Armour? Phyllis McGinley?

The poet's name was Isaac Bickerstaffe, born in 1735, and dead and gone almost a century and a half ago.

Rhyme marches on!

21. *Wide, Wide World*

THERE'LL ALWAYS BE AN ENGLAND

Hear ye, hear ye, those who chafe under the restrictions of the income tax, to this protest from a recognized authority: "The income tax, we have been told repeatedly, was a temporary measure, and would soon be reduced, if not relinquished altogether. These sanguine expectations have now been proved in vain, and indeed, the income tax is pressing on us more heavily, in peace time, than it did during the war. The very minister, in fact, who told us it would cease, now proposes its augmentation. What practical man now expects to see its end? Who is credulous enough to hope for a year in which he will be granted a reduction?"

The paper in which these words appeared was the London

Economist. The minister referred to was William Gladstone. The date was February 23, 1861!

*   *   *

Peter Fryer, in his book, *Mrs. Grundy: Studies in English Prudery,* tells how one Victorian journal lashed out at the waltz as "an expression of those base, primitive instincts which it is the aim of civilization to suppress. It is an engine of Hell to do the Devil's work!" Another London newspaper, in an article by a pig-raiser on pork and bacon, substituted "sow bacon" for "sowbelly." A third chastely referred to a dancer's navel as her "waist dimple."

Fryer notes that the undergarments issued to the Women's Auxiliary Air Force in World War II were so ludicrously "modest" and hideous that the girls dejectedly dubbed them "passion killers."

*   *   *

The stately and ultradignified Queen Victoria was riding in the royal coach through the streets of London when a loyal subject suddenly burst past the cordon of police and hollered, "Keep up the good work, Vic, old girl!" The miscreant was hustled off, and the Queen was heard to grumble, "That should never have been allowed to happen—but it was gratifying, quite gratifying!"

*   *   *

England's great Prime Minister, Benjamin Disraeli, once discovered a deaf Member of Parliament listening to a dreary debate with the aid of an ear trumpet. Snorted Disraeli, "What a wanton waste of the mercies of God's providence!"

*   *   *

In a debate in England's House of Lords, a tiresome member had been speaking for an hour. When he drew himself up to his full height (5 feet 2) and declaimed, "And now the time has come to ask myself . . ." a voice from the opposite side of the hall interrupted him with, "Well, you're going to get a damn silly answer!"

* * *

A British lady, married to a dashing cavalier ten years younger than herself, was summoned to America and forced to leave her roving-eyed husband alone for the first time since their marriage. Just before she left, she introduced the new butler to her husband.

"This is Rumbold," she said. "Not only will he look after you while I'm away but he'll do the cooking as well."

Some nights later the cavalier invited an old university chum to dinner. The food was ghastly. "What's gone wrong around here, old chap?" inquired the chum testily. "You never used to be satisfied with food like this."

"I know, I know," sighed the husband. "But what kind of cooking can you expect from Scotland Yard?"

* * *

An American in London slipped and fell on Fleet Street one day and was sufficiently bruised to believe a visit to a doctor would be the better part of valor. He accordingly stopped a bearded passerby and asked for the address of the nearest physician.

"Turn up Hind Court and look for Gough Square," advised the passerby. "There's a doctor living on the left hand side, I believe. You'll see the name on a plate outside."

The tourist followed instructions faithfully. He had no trouble finding the house. And there was the plate as promised. It read: HOME OF DR. SAMUEL JOHNSON, BORN, 1709. DIED, 1784.

* * *

Robert Littell, in his book *It Takes All Kinds,* tells of frisky Oxford undergraduates who practice for future Alpine and Himalayan mountain-climbing feats by inching their way up the walls and monuments of the various edifices on the Oxford campus. The fact that this sport is strictly forbidden adds an extra attraction to the activity.

One corpulent don who had been a famous mountain climber in his younger days recently gave a group of these Oxonian scalawags a surprise. Spotting them carefully ascending the outside of the most hallowed building in Oxford, he hurried around to the other side and, puffing heavily, managed to reach the summit first. When the temporarily triumphant undergrads got there themselves, the next voice they heard was the don's. "Gentlemen," he asked calmly, "may I have your names, please?"

* * *

Palm Beach gentry recall with pleasure a crusty, formidable English earl who made his first visit to our shores shortly after the end of World War II.

Austerity was the watchword in Britain that year, and the earl, although one of the wealthiest peers of the realm, with four castles and a hundred servants, felt a bit guilty about evading London's wintry blasts. "I've got it," he suddenly told his wife, Celia. "We'll go without my personal valet, Masters."

Masters had not been ten feet from the earl's side since nursery days, and the news that he now proposed to spend an entire winter without his valet caused a sensation in every club on Pall Mall.

The earl got through the first two days aboard the *Queen Elizabeth* beautifully, faltering only when he had to put on his dinner coat and black tie. A crisis was avoided when the captain of the ship came down from the bridge and helped him personally. But on the third morning, His Lordship looked a fright when he came on deck. There were tufts of hair in odd places on his face, and blood flowed from jagged cuts beneath his chin. "Bertie," gasped his wife Celia. "What have they done to you?"

"It's my beastly razor," explained His Lordship. Lady Celia rushed with him to their suite and found the razor clotted with rust, hair, and gore. "Silly boy," she chided. "You forgot to change the blade."

The earl regarded her in a state of stupefaction. "The *what?*" he inquired.

* * *

The earl referred to in the previous anecdote prided himself on his hunting prowess. "In my day," he informed a beautiful dinner companion at a Palm Beach affair, "I have shot every known variety of wild game but a bongo."

"No bongo," sympathized the beautiful dinner companion (who had never even heard of such a beast). "Why not?"

"It was my stupid beaters," explained His Lordship petulantly. "They couldn't coax one up to the verandah!"

* * *

The first Rolls-Royce automobile was built in an English shed in 1905, and since that day the radiator design has never changed. The No. 2 model, in fact, remained in continuous production for nineteen years.

When Sir Frederick Henry Royce died in 1933, the designers decided on a radical step. The previously red "RR" monogram was changed to *black!* Conservative Britons expressed their disapproval in no uncertain terms.

As for the design of the emblem itself, it has changed only once—and that was when Queen Elizabeth ordered a special ornament from the royal silversmith depicting St. George and the Dragon. Directly after it was finished, the mold was destroyed.

*   *   *

A leading book publisher, famous for his taste in books, wines, and vari-colored shirts, purchased a Rolls-Royce recently with the profits earned from two new books of poetry.

A week after the Rolls had been delivered, the publisher called the Rolls dealer to complain that wheezing noises were emanating from the front end.

"There is only one possible explanation," said the Rolls man huffily. "Your chauffeur has asthma."

*   *   *

Max Bygraves, British comedian, confesses in his autobiography, "When I was a small lad my dad gave me a penny every morning as he patted me on the head. By the time I was fourteen, I had several pounds—and a flat head."

*   *   *

Every session of Britain's House of Commons is called to order by the Speaker, who marches into the halls with the flowing train of his black gown held up by a page, looking for all the world like a character in Gilbert and Sullivan. On the way to the House, he strides through the visitors' hall, a herald preceding him to call out, "Hats Off, Strangers!" Tourists who have gathered from all parts of the world to watch the colorful and traditional ceremony obediently doff their headgear as the procession goes by.

One day a great personal friend of the Speaker, named Neal McLean, was in the gathering in the visitors' hall. The Speaker spotted him as he walked through and impulsively cried out, "Neal! Neal!" Every tourist present promptly dropped to his knees!

*   *   *

Joe McCarthy met an Englishman who had just returned from the Far North and was full of tales of the troubles he had encountered driving a dogsled team over the frozen wasteland. "I kept urging them on with 'Tally-ho,' 'Tally-ho,'" he mourned, "but the confounded dogs wouldn't budge. They just panted a bit and laughed in my face."

"You should have said 'Mush,'" advised McCarthy.

"All right," conceded the Englishman. "The dogs just panted and laughed in my mush."

*　*　*

Martin Gabel, who loves England and the English people, brings back this story of a weekend he spent at a fine old estate in Surrey, complete with stables, prize cattle, peacocks, and extensive gardens. For his first breakfast there, the butler inquired, "Tea, coffee, or milk, sir?" Gabel chose tea. "Very good, sir," said the butler. "And will you take Ceylon, China, or Assam?" "Ceylon," elected Gabel. "And do you use milk, cream, or lemon?" continued the butler. "Milk," said Gabel with finality —but the butler's quiz was not yet concluded. "Very good, sir," said the butler again. "Jersey, Guernsey, or Holstein?"

*　*　*

A distinguished English actor had condescended to play a part in a Hollywood movie—at about six times the salary he commanded at home—but this didn't stop him from criticizing everything and everybody within range. One evening he was invited to dine with the publisher of one of the biggest and best West Coast newspapers. As coffee was being served, the publisher excused himself, explaining, "Every evening we have a staff meeting to discuss policy, and check on the editorials and front-page stories that are going to run in the next day's paper." "Good heavens," exclaimed the English actor. "You don't mean to tell me that you get out that paper of yours *deliberately?*"

*　*　*

It is very difficult to police some of the giant housing projects that now abound in cities around the world. One low-cost development outside of London had so many robberies that the tenants formed their own protective committee, and erected this sign: "Notice to Thieves: You are too late. Early bird miscreants have already purloined from these premises all radio and TV sets in working order, cameras, furs, and jewelry. THERE IS NOTHING OF VALUE LEFT TO TAKE."

Three days later somebody stole the sign.

*   *   *

Bids were solicited for a long-projected tunnel between France and England. Several firms submitted approximately the same estimates: in the neighborhood of twenty million pounds. One little outfit, however—Goldfarb and Company—declared it could do the job for fifty thousand pounds net. Highly amused, the head commissioner sent for Mr. Goldfarb and said, "Your estimate stopped us cold, I admit. How do you figure you can do this enormous job for fifty thousand pounds?" "Nothing to it," shrugged Mr. Goldfarb. "My brother will take a shovel and begin digging from the French side. I'll take a shovel and begin digging from the English side. When we meet—there you are."

"Do you realize," demurred the commissioner, "that the most minute error in calculation will mean that you'll miss each other completely under the middle of the English Channel?" "So what?" said Mr. Goldfarb, unperturbed. "If that happens, you'll simply have two tunnels!"

*   *   *

Sir Winston Churchill, to quote Bob Considine, was more than Britain's "Man of the Century." He was "one with the ages, a titan without boundary, borne to his timeless niche on the wings of a funeral unmatched in a land famed for plumed pomp and circumstance."

Sir Winston's old friend, Somerset Maugham, summed up the unbelievable mark on history made by Churchill in ninety years of tumultuous life when he reflected, "Not one of us would be here today had it not been for him." Churchill himself was perhaps prouder of his eloquence, wit, and genius as a journalist and historian than he was of his achievements in

diplomacy. "Winston," protested one of his parliamentary opponents, "spent the best part of his life preparing impromptu speeches." His valet noted that the preparations often were made in the bathtub. He thought he heard Sir Winston calling him one morning from that sanctuary, but was reminded sharply, "I wasn't talking to you. I was addressing the House of Commons."

One day Churchill remarked ruefully, "There's nothing very good to say about history after 1900. If I were dictator of the world, I probably should kill all the scientists. I should make it a criminal offense for anyone to go around bothering molecules. And the little atom would be left in peace forever." But Lady Churchill demurred, "Why then, Winston, are you always telling the British scientists to get on with their work?" "Because," he explained patiently, "in the first place, I am *not* the dictator of the world. In the second place, I am most unlikely to be elected one on such a platform. So—we just have to keep our end up."

"And," concludes Emmet Hughes, "he did—his life through. He could cock a skeptic's eye at the whole age that hailed him as a hero. And no small man can see so far."

LA BELLE FRANCE

Art Buchwald tells a story that underlines the skullduggery of fake art dealers in Paris, with rich but unwary Americans their chief victims. One such American fell for the old gag of the masterpiece so valuable that the government wouldn't allow its shipment out of the country. "It's a Titian," whispered the dealer, "a Titian every museum director would give his eyeteeth to possess. There's only one way I can sneak it to America for you. Let my assistant Garachi paint over the Titian. Then, when you get home, have the Garachi wiped off, and *voilà*, you have your priceless Titian."

The delighted American wrote out his check for two hundred thousand dollars, went on to the Riviera, and issued the necessary instructions about the painting to his secretary in New York.

Three weeks later he received this cable from New York: "Have received Garachi and cleaned it. Found Titian. Cleaned Titian. Found Garachi. How far should I go?"

*   *   *

"*Mal de mer*," explained Maurice Chevalier to a young lady about to embark upon her first sea trip to the land of De Gaulle, "is merely a Frenchman's way of saying 'You can't take it with you.'"

*   *   *

An American tourist, arrived at Paris's Orly Airport for his first visit abroad, stopped at the restaurant near the customs counter for a bite of breakfast. What an opportunity to try out the French he had studied so laboriously from a set of phonograph records! He hailed a waiter and nervously ordered "*Oeufs! Oeufs!*" (Eggs! Eggs!) The waiter regarded him in disbelief, so again the American cried "*Oeufs! Oeufs!*"

This time the waiter permitted himself the suspicion of a

smile and, in perfect English, said to the tourist, "If you'll stop barking at me, sir, I'll be happy to take your order."

* * *

Red Smith was extolling the virtues of a Paris suburb called Noisy-le-Roi when a not-too-couth associate interrupted him by echoing, "Noisy Leroy?" and adding, "Throw the bum out!"

* * *

A French playwright visited our shores this season with his new and beautiful wife in tow. Unbelievably jealous, he had her shadowed constantly by private detectives until American friends told him, "We don't do things that way over here. Your behavior is an insult to all womanhood. Call off those gumshoes immediately." Reluctantly the French playwright followed their directive. The very next day his bride slapped him across the face, crying, "You do not love me any more!"

* * *

Charles Pintchman claims that cinema star Henry Fonda had a difficult time in a Paris restaurant recently resisting a waiter who insisted that he drink a full glass of absinthe before tackling his dinner. "Why are you so determined on this point?" Mr. Fonda demanded. "Because," said the waiter, "you are my favorite screen personality, and I want you to stay healthy. And I happen to know that absinthe makes the heart grow, Fonda."

* * *

Herb Caen tells of the American exporter who was at the airport, bound for Paris, when he remembered he had failed to equip himself with some negotiable French currency. He phoned his brand-new secretary, "Get me fifty dollars' worth of francs and hightail it out here." She arrived breathlessly twenty minutes later—with two hundred hot dogs.

THE CARING FOR THE GREEN

If you're ever lucky enough to visit Dublin by air, I hope you'll get the same greeting there that awaited my wife, my two boys, and myself: a covey of bright-eyed journalists who made up clever remarks for me in the next day's journals, and a beaker of Irish coffee—which contains more Irish whiskey than coffee, and is a concoction fit for the gods.

The ride into the city of Dublin from the airport is an exhilarating one, too. "Look at the signs on the shops," I exclaimed happily. "Clancy, Gilhooley, Gallagher, O'Toole . . . !" My wife, infinitely calmer and less emotional than I am, doused my childish delight with, "What were you expecting: Nussbaum and Manischewitz?"

Our driver pointed out a railroad crossing where a guard had left the gate half open the day before, causing a traffic tieup clear down to O'Connell Street. A policeman finally cornered the guard and demanded, "What's the idea of leaving this gate half open?" The guard explained, "I'm half expecting a train from Galway."

Our driver also waxed enthusiastic about the literary revival in Ireland. "Those of us who don't read books," he boasted, "are writing them. And those who do neither are writing letters to the newspapers demanding that any book that really says something be suppressed immediately!"

Arriving at Dublin's famous Shelbourne Hotel, our driver pointed a man in the lobby who once was silly enough to confess to an editor, "My name is Patrick Dolan, but I'm not Irish." "When you get to heaven," advised the editor, "just tell 'em your name—and never say another word!"

And how the Irish love to tell stories about themselves! Before I had been in Dublin four days I had chuckled over scores of them. Following are some I liked best (and had time to jot down).

* * *

The archbishop had preached a rousing sermon on the beauties of married life. Two buxom ladies from Bray left the church feeling uplifted and contented. "'Twas a fine sermon His Reverence gave us this morning," observed one. "That it was," agreed the other, "and I wish I knew as little about the matter as he does."

* * *

Honor Tracy tells of a phone call that woke up a minister in the middle of the night. "Hi, Finnegan," there asked a blurred voice he recognized as a parishioner. "Please send around three quarts of Scotch immediately." "This is not Finnegan," said the minister severely. "This is your rector." "Well, for Pete's sake," came the voice in astonishment. "What the heck are you doing in Finnegan's joint?"

* * *

A pugnacious son of Erin, exactly five feet tall and three sheets to the wind, staggered into a bar and loudly declared, "I'm the wild bull of Killarney and I can lick any bum in this joint." The bartender leaned casually across the bar, hit him lightly in the stomach, and sent him sprawling to the floor. It took the Killarneyite a few seconds to regain his composure,

and then he told the bartender reproachfully, "Never hit a wild
bull in the stomach, man. It's the silliest thing you can do!"

* * *

Patrick Clancy was a fighting man from the word go, but unfortunately he was lost in a gale in Galway Bay last winter. A
neighbor stopped by to offer the widow Clancy a bit of conso-
lation.

"Poor Pat," sighed the neighbor, "no doubt he's hitting the
harp with the angels by now."

"Not him," replied Mrs. Clancy. "If I know my Pat, it's more
likely he's hitting the angels with the harp!"

* * *

To prove to you what a smart girl O'Shea picked for his
bride, there's the day they went to be married but didn't have
a cent to pay the clergyman. "Sorry," said the latter, "but strictly
cash in advance is my motto."

"Might you," suggested O'Shea's girl, "be after givin' me
leave to go git the money?" Permission granted, she sped off
and soon returned with the cash. After the ceremony, she
asked, "No matter what you do now, yer riverence, this marriage is official, isn't it?" "It certainly is," the clergyman assured
her.

"Then bless yer heart," said O'Shea's girl. "Here's the ticket
fer yer hat. I picked it up in the vestry and pawned it."

* * *

In the heart of Dublin, reports the *Irish Digest,* there dwells
a soul so pious that he insists on wearing stained glass in his
spectacles during Lent.

* * *

Irish wit Brendan Behan recalled that after his book *Borstal
Boy* became an international best seller, a boyhood crony accosted him in a Dublin pub. "'Tis well you're looking these
days, Brendan," he wheezed. "Could you be giving me the
loan of five quid?" "Why should I," countered Behan coldly.
"Ah, sure, Brendan," said the beggar with tears in his eyes,

"don't I remember you when the rags were floggin' your back?"

"Sorry, Mick," nodded Behan, turning away. "You're out of luck. You don't remember it half as well as I do!"

* * *

The guard at the entrance to a flossy estate barred the way to Shaughnessy, an old drinking acquaintance, who unexpectedly appeared leading by a halter an enormous elephant. "Come now, Shaughnessy," protested the guard. "You know we don't allow no elephants in here."

Back came Shaughnessy the very next day, leading the same elephant. He had, however, pasted a slice of bread on the elephant's trunk and another slice of bread on its tail.

"Didn't I tell you yesterday," roared the guard, "that we don't allow no elephants in this place?"

"So what?" demanded Shaughnessy. "This ain't an elephant, me lad. This is a *sandwich!*"

* * *

A Hibernian laborer, warned not to smoke near explosives, lit his pipe, nevertheless, one day on the job and promptly was blown sky-high.

A foreman dashed to the spot and demanded, "Where's Cassidy?" "He left," explained a fellow toiler. "When?" demanded the foreman. "Boss," declared the toiler solemnly, "if Cassidy comes back as fast as he went, he should have been here yesterday."

* * *

Now that those confounded experts are down to identifying people by numbers instead of names, Elliot Sharp tells about a convivial soul at the Hemisphere Club who introduced two men, explaining, "Number 435-11-9974, it's high time you met your fellow member, Number 632-7-091." The men shook hands warmly, and one said, "Mr. 632-7-091, where do you hail from originally?" "Dublin, Ireland," responded the other proudly. "Funny," mused the first man. "Your name doesn't sound Irish."

*   *   *

Two bricklayers, writes Jerry Shane, were working on a building. A sidewalk superintendent paused to ask precisely what they were building. The more stolid bricklayer replied, "I don't know and I don't care. All I do is slap this crummy mortar on these crummy bricks and pile them up in a crummy line." But the second and more imaginative bricklayer enthused, "I'm helping to build a great cathedral with a beautiful spire that will point straight up to heaven."

So the second man was fired because they were building a garage.

ISRAEL

A story currently popular in Tel Aviv concerns the newly enlisted spy in the Israeli Secret Service who is sent to America on a top-secret mission concerned with finding more water to irrigate the Negev Desert. "When you deplane at Kennedy Airport," he is instructed, "proceed to 171 Riverton Street, ring the bell of Rosenbluth's apartment, and say, 'The sky is blue and the grass is green.' He'll tell you what to do from there on in."

The agent proceeds without incident to 171 Riverton Street, but is perplexed when he discovers that there are two Rosenbluths living there. He take a chance and rings the bell of the Rosenbluth on the first floor. When it is opened, he quickly whispers, "The sky is blue and the grass is green." The man inside tells him, "It isn't I you want, my friend. Rosenbluth, the secret agent, is the one on the *fourth* floor!"

*   *   *

Ephraim Kishon, who writes a popular daily column for a Tel Aviv newspaper, describes Israel as "sprawled on the shore of the Mediterranean in such a way that half an hour's drive from any point in the country will take you either to the seashore or into captivity at the hands of the Arab Legion."

Once Kishon complained in court about being smacked by

a taxicab, but the magistrate quickly put him in his place. "See how Israel has progressed," boasted His Honor. "When the pioneers first came here, some of them had to wait eighteen or twenty years before there *were* any taxicabs to knock them down!"

* * *

An Israeli diplomat tells about a duck that was preparing to paddle across the Suez Canal one day when a scorpion appeared with a bag of grain and said, "All this is yours if you will let me ride across on your back." "My mother always warned me to beware of the treachery of scorpions," demurred the duck. "How do I know you won't sting me in midstream?" "Silly duck," scoffed the scorpion, "in that case wouldn't we both drown?" So the duck said, "Hop aboard," but sure enough, halfway across the Canal the scorpion stung it. As they both went under for the third time the duck gasped, "What made you do it?" The scorpion gasped back, "What else could you expect? This is the Middle East!"

* * *

Messrs. Lapidus and Moskowitz, two wealthy and highly respected merchants from New York, were making their first visit to Israel, and in the course of same, dropped into a Tel Aviv night club where a new comedian had scored a sensational success. His entire monologue was delivered in Hebrew. Lapidus listened to it in silence without cracking one smile, but Moskowitz roared with laughter at each sally.

When the comedian had quit the stage, Lapidus said, "You certainly enjoyed that fellow's routine. I never knew you understood Hebrew." "I don't understand one word of it," answered Moskowitz. "If that's true," countered Lapidus, frowning, "how come you laughed so much at what he was saying?"

"Aha!" beamed Moskowitz. "*I trusted him!*"

* * *

An American tourist in Tel Aviv stopped an Israeli young lady and complimented her on her fine-looking, buxom baby.

"What's his name?" he asked. "Nasser Goldfarb," she replied. "Nasser?" echoed the astonished tourist. "How could you name your son after the enemy of your people, Mrs. Goldfarb?"

She corrected him, "Miss Goldfarb, please."

* * *

A bit of excitement was added to the daily routine at a fashionable Israeli seaside hotel recently. A beautifully proportioned debutante from the U.S.A. went up to the roof on the first day of her visit to Israel to acquire a suntan in the shortest possible time. She kept her bathing suit on for a while, but then, discovering there was not another soul in sight, slipped it off and stretched out, face downward, to absorb the sun's rays, with only a small towel stretched across her back.

Suddenly there was a commotion. A flustered little assistant manager of the hotel dashed into view and gasped apologetically, "Miss, we do not mind your sunning on the roof, but we must beg you to keep on your bathing suit."

A bit miffed, the debutante demanded, "What difference does it make? No one can see me up here, and besides, I've covered my back with a towel."

"I see that," conceded the assistant manager, "but unfortunately, Miss, you are lying on the dining room skylight."

* * *

Latest story from Tel Aviv concerns Israeli private Avrim who tried to wheedle a three-day pass from his captain. "Don't be silly," the captain told him. "To get a three-day pass in this man's Army, you've got to earn it with some spectacular exploit."

A few days later Avrim astounded everybody by capturing

a brand-new Arab tank. Of course, he was rewarded with a three-day pass. Less than a month later, he captured another Arab tank and snagged a second pass. When he bagged a *third* Arab tank he became a national hero, and was promoted to captain himself.

Some time later, Private Moshe, who happened to be Avrim's first cousin, suggested, "Hey, Captain Avrim, how about one of those three-day passes for your favorite cousin?" "Earn one like I did," snapped Captain Avrim. "I couldn't," mourned Moshe. "I haven't your courage, or initiative, or flair for the spectacular."

Captain Avrim locked the door of his office, pulled down the shade, then whispered to his cousin, "Listen, Moshe. It's not as hard as you think. Take one of our own tanks out of the compound some night and drive out into the desert. Pretty soon you'll meet up with some Arab tank driver who's also looking for a three-day pass. . . ."

PEACEFUL COEXISTENCE

Official Washington is likening Red Chinese tactics to those of Hitler when he was in the ascendancy. They call it the "old salami game." "They shave off a slice of salami at a time but never enough to fight over. Finally the victim is left with nothing but the string of the salami—and that's not enough to fight over either."

* * *

At the opening of a three-day conclave in Smolensk, avers Myron Cohen, Soviet Premier Kosygin thundered, "Today, under our wonderful Communist system, every citizen of the Soviet Union is entitled to an electric icebox and a color television set. Is there any comrade in this hall who hasn't got an electric icebox and a color television set?" "Me," declared a little man in the fourteenth row. "Ah ha," nodded Kosygin, "and what is your name?" "Plotzikov," was the answer. "See that Comrade Plotzikov gets what is coming to him," ordered Kosygin immediately.

Toward the close of the third day of the rally, another citizen demanded the floor. "I suppose," sneered Kosygin, "you want to know what's happened to Plotzikov's icebox and TV set?" "Not at all," countered the citizen. "I want to know what's happened to Plotzikov."

* * *

Movie producer Billy Wilder has two gimmicks up his sleeve that he hasn't yet been able to jimmy into a picture. Both involve operatives from behind the Iron Curtain.

In one, the Commies kidnap a great film star in West Berlin and brainwash her. They are completely frustrated, however, because they discover she has no brains to wash.

In the other, a top commissar takes it on the lam and seeks sanctuary in Paris. In revenge, the boys at the Kremlin liquidate his wife and six children. The commissar thereupon hotfoots it right back to Moscow. He's no traitor at all; he just wanted to get rid of his family.

* * *

Comrade Kazotsky dropped in at the polls on election day in Pinsk and was handed a sealed envelope to drop into the ballot box. An official jumped six feet when Kazotsky started to open it. "What's the big idea?" screamed the official. "I want to see who I'm voting for," explained Kazotsky. "You must be out of your mind," decided the official. "Don't you realize that this is a secret ballot?"

* * *

A bold wag in Moscow dared tell about a big bruiser who attended his first track meet and discovered that one of the featured events was the hammer throw. He climbed down from the stadium, doffed his coat, seized a hammer, and threw it farther than a hammer ever had been thrown before.

When the track officials rushed up to congratulate him, the big man said modestly, "You haven't seen anything yet. Let me show you how far I throw the sickle!"

* * *

Caskie Stinnett reports that a passel of French delegates to a Moscow trade fair, understandably alert to the possibilities of their hotel room being bugged, cut through a maze of multi-colored wires they discovered cleverly hidden under the carpet. The floor was thick, but not so thick that it deadened the sound of the chandelier crashing in the room beneath them.

* * *

"Do you know what those Red Chinese are up to now?" grumbled an indignant businessman. "They're making the world's most beautiful girl. They're using Elizabeth Taylor's eyes, Brigitte Bardot's mouth, Ginger Rogers' legs, and Verna Lisi's back." "Boy, oh boy," moaned a man at the next table, "what I could do with what they're throwing away!"

* * *

Russia's increasingly uncensored humor magazine, *Krokodil*, recently ran a cartoon showing William Tell preparing to shoot his arrow. But on his boy's head was a sign readers seemed to recognize. It read, "NO APPLES."

*　*　*

Peter Lind Hayes spotted the most poignant classified ad of the year on the inside page of an East Berlin newspaper. It reads—if you can believe Peter—"WILL EXCHANGE: One fourteen-room, fully air-conditioned East Berlin villa for a hole in the wall."

*　*　*

Two confused Polish Communists were trying to make some kind of sense out of the current chaotic international situation. "Thank the Lord," concluded one, "that between Poland and China there's still one nice buffer state—Russia!"

*　*　*

Two space ships—one from Russia, one from the U.S.A.— predicts Seymour Rankin, will land smack on the moon before 1967, whereupon we may expect this anguished message from lunar males: "Dogs and monkeys we okay for a starter, but from here out, for the sake of universal harmony, boys, send us a couple of dames!"

*　*　*

Wiley Buchanan recalls an old fable that Spanish statesman Salvador de Madaragia told every time he heard Soviet propagandists proposing world disarmament without full inspection. The fable concerned a disarmament conference attended by all the animals. Each animal enthusiastically endorsed the abolition of a weapon he didn't happen to possess. The elephant proposed the abolition of talons. The eagle was equally enthusiastic over the notion of abolishing tusks. The lion wanted horns outlawed; the tiger poisoned quills. And so it went until the bear demanded the floor. "Let's abolish EVERY-THING," declared the bear heartily—"that is, everything except the great universal embrace!"

*　*　*

A preoccupied society matron was giving a dinner-dance for two hundred guests at her Washington residence. One guest named Smith was introduced to her exactly six times. When she asked his name a seventh time, he lost his temper completely and shouted, "Smith, you witch." "Ah," she beamed, "from the Soviet legation, I presume!"

* * *

Sad story from Moscow: An impetuous student in early 1963 drew a ten-year sentence in jail for hollering, "Khrushchev is a bum." Granted an amnesty in late 1964, he decided to get back into favor with the powers that be, and ran into Red Square shouting "Hooray for Khrushchev." Now he's back in the clink for *twenty* years!

WELL PLAID

An American in Aberdeen called up the police station and reported, "In front of the MacTavish National Bank there are two Scotsmen who are violently insane." "What makes you think that?" asked the lieutenant. "They must be," explained the American. "One is throwing his money away on the street and the other is picking it up and handing it back to him."

* * *

The driver of a taxicab suddenly lost control of his vehicle, and it started careening wildly through the dense traffic near London's Trafalgar Square. The passenger, to make matters worse, hailed from Edinburgh. "Can't you stop this cab?" he cried to the driver. "No," admitted the driver, "it's out of control." "There's one thing then that you *can* do," rasped the Edinburgher. "Turn off the meter!"

* * *

MacPherson was driving his girl past a shopping center one hot summer night when they passed a popcorn stand. "Yummy," said the girl. "That popcorn sure smells good."

"Wait a minute," said MacPherson generously, "and I'll drive up closer so you can get a better whiff of it."

* * *

A spoiled young Edinburgh society lass had not been entertained one evening by a new beau in the style she hoped to become accustomed to. As she bade him goodnight, she added in acid tones, "Take care on the way home, Jock—I wouldn't like to hear that you'd been robbed of all that money you saved tonight."

*   *   *

Quizzing a prospective son-in-law, a retired Scotsman demanded, "Are you quite sure you can support a family? Think carefully, young man. There are seven of us."

*   *   *

A traveling Scotsman was given expense money to put over a big deal. His reckless and most unusual spending aroused the suspicions of the bartender on his block. "Don't worry," the Scotsman told him sharply, "I'll know when I get to my own money!"

*   *   *

Workers in the box office of the Majestic Theatre never will forget the night Callahan stood patiently in line for an hour to purchase seats for a melodrama called *The Great Miracle*. Directly ahead of him was a dour Scot, who eventually reached the ticket window.

"Our best orchestra seats," the treasurer told the Scot, "are six-sixty. In the balcony they run as low as two-twenty." "I'll take two of the six-sixty seats," decided the Scot, producing a twenty-dollar bill, "and you may keep the change for being so courteous."

Callahan abruptly stepped out of line and headed for the sidewalk. The man in the box office yelled, "Hey! Don't you want to see *The Great Miracle?*"

"Not me," answered Callahan. "I've *seen* it!"

*   *   *

The fire-spitting three-headed Loch Ness monster, Scottish hotelkeepers' pride and joy, made one of his spectacular appearances one July day and sent vacationers and tourists fleeing, panic-stricken. All but one indomitable American lady, that is. She put down her knitting and patted the three-headed monster gently on the back. "*My* dear boy," she beamed, "have I got a girl for you!"

TRAVEL IN THE JET AGE

By Air . . .

Airline pilots at Kennedy Airport are talking about the ravishing redhead who boarded a jet, stretched out at full length, and explained to passengers around her, "I've got a big day ahead of me in L.A. tomorrow. I have to get some sleep."

The jet roared off into the gloaming, and as the redhead turned and wriggled in her sleep, her skirt crept up and up.

Suddenly the young gentleman in the seat opposite jumped up and reached for the blanket in the overhead rack. Carefully, almost reverently, he draped it over the recumbent figure of the beautiful girl. She awoke with a start. "Beg pardon, Miss," he told her, "but I've got important work also in L.A. tomorrow, and *I've got to get some sleep, too!*"

* * *

For her hundredth birthday, an old lady in the Blue Ridge country was offered a ride to New York in a jet airliner. "You won't get me in one of those fool contraptions," she answered firmly. "I'm gonna sit right here and watch my color TV, like the good Lord intended I should!"

* * *

A lady who weighs something over three hundred pounds had an interesting experience while flying by jet from Denver to New York recently. Shortly after the takeoff a stewardess tapped her on the shoulder and invited her to move from the tourist section to a seat in the first-class compartment. "I'm flattered," said the lady, "but wonder why you've singled me out for this V.I.P. treatment." "Madam," explained the steward-ess candidly, "we have a weight problem."

*   *   *

A jet was about to take off for Seattle from Kennedy Airport when a man rushed up to the gate attendant and demanded, "Will there be time for me to get on that jet and kiss my wife goodbye?" The attendant answered gravely, "That depends, sir, on how long you've been married."

*   *   *

Aboard a jet, one passenger explained to his seatmate that his home was in upstate New York. "How far are you from Manhattan?" asked the seatmate. "I reckon about 250 miles," said the passenger. "Two hundred and fifty miles!" echoed the seatmate. "In Los Angeles where I live, up*town* is farther away than that!"

*   *   *

As a London to Calcutta jet soared through the sky, a rest-less kid kept tugging at the steward's coat to inquire every twenty minutes or so, "What are we flying over now?" After a dozen attempts to give a reasonably accurate reply, the steward finally gave the kid a flight schedule and told him, "If you look at your watch, then study this schedule, you should be able to figure out where we are by yourself."

This kept the young traveler quiet for some time, but sud-denly he was back at the galley, demanding, "Where are we now?" "I told you," said the steward testily, "to look at your watch." "Somebody has stolen my watch," whined the boy. "Stolen, eh?" said the steward. "Then we're over Albania."

*   *   *

At the Honolulu airport, a tourist deplaned and Tony Ran-dall overheard him asking a bystander, "How do you natives pronounce it? Hawaii or Havaii?"

"Havaii," said the native.

"Thank you," said the tourist.

"You're velcome," said the native.

* * *

Stewardesses were being hired to staff a new transpacific airline and the question was asked, "What would you do if the plane had to be ditched, and you found yourself the only girl on a remote tropical isle, garrisoned by ten thousand soldiers and only one officer?"

An English applicant admitted, "I should probably faint."

An American applicant said, "I should expect the lone officer to keep his troops in order."

A French applicant said, "What is ze problem?"

By Sea . . .

Captain MacLean, handsome skipper of the luxury liner *Queen Elizabeth*, had a bit of a problem with a particularly ebullient Texan on a recent westward crossing. It seems the Texan had become so attached to the ship that he insisted upon buying it. Captain MacLean finally dissuaded him with, "I'm afraid it's impossible, sir. You see she's part of a set."

* * *

The *Queen Elizabeth* was about to pull up her gangplank and sail off one morning when a shiny Rolls-Royce glided up to the dock and discharged a heavily furred London matron, followed by fourteen suitcases. Breathlessly, she explained why she was so late: "I told that fool chauffeur to take me to the pier —and he took me to the Pierre!"

* * *

A rich Iowa farmer was such a hi-fi enthusiast that he insisted on taking some elaborate hi-fi equipment with him on a European tour. His favorite platter recorded a variety of railroad sounds—whistles, chuffs, and clangs. He had just played it full blast in his stateroom in midocean when a female voice in the next cabin was heard. "You idiot," screamed the lady in said cabin. "My first sea trip to Europe—and you have to pick out a stateroom next to a railroad yard!"

* * *

A young doctor applied for a job of ship's surgeon for a 'round-the-world cruise. "What would you do," he was asked, "if the captain fainted on the bridge?" "I'd bring him to," answered the applicant. "And if he was still wobbly?" "I'd bring him two more."

* * *

Once upon a time there was a steamship captain who had handled freighters for years and took it as a mortal insult when he was transferred to a spanking new deluxe passenger liner. In fact, he often declared forcefully that any landlubber passenger who dared to get seasick should be tossed overboard forthwith.

One day in a howling gale a deck steward made his way along a line of deck chairs warning the few passengers in sight that the skipper was in a foul mood and might put his idea into execution.

"Throw seasick passengers overboard?" croaked one unfortunate voyager already green around the gills. "Here's a ten-dollar bill for you. Make sure I don't miss my turn!"

To Europe . . .

Back from his first tour of Europe, a disillusioned college student reports that he couldn't get hamburgers in Hamburg, English muffins in England, London broil in London, French toast in France, or even eggs Florentine in Florence. The wines —and the girls—he admitted, however, were wonderful.

*　*　*

The police officer who headed the night shift in a station house on the outskirts of Paris answered the phone, and heard an agitated citizen quaver, "There's a duel to the death scheduled for 6 A.M. in the Bois tomorrow and it's up to you police to put a stop to it." "We know, we know," the officer assured him. "Your adversary has already called us."

*　*　*

In a very, very swank restaurant in Paris, just off the Champs-Elysées, an American tourist was ignored for an unconscionable time by his waiter. Finally he managed to capture the errant waiter's attention and blustered, "My wife and I have been waiting for you for fully half an hour. I want a bottle of your best champagne." "Certainly, monsieur," said the waiter soothingly. "What year?" The tourist cried, "Right NOW!"

*　*　*

Arlene Francis decided to study French cooking recently, and enrolled with a very famous, very expensive Parisian chef.

"Does he let you eat what you cook?" asked her friend, Joan Axelrod.

"Let us?" laughed Arlene. "He *makes* us."

*　*　*

Judge Manders returned from his first trip to the Continent bubbling with enthusiasm. "What a wonderful city Paris is," he reported. "If only I could have gone there twenty years ago!" "You mean when Paris was really Paris?" joshed a friend. "No," said the Judge. "I mean when Manders was really Manders."

* * *

Aboard a luxury liner bound from New York to Le Havre, one elderly first-class passenger was boasting to a chance acquaintance of comparable vintage of a wonderful new watering spot he had discovered in Austria. "I don't know what chemical qualities the water there contains," he declared, "but I do know it's guaranteed to take twenty years off of anybody's life." When the acquaintance registered acute skepticism, the elderly gentleman produced his clinching argument. "You'll believe me," he crowed, "when I tell you of my own experience there. I arrived with a beautiful female friend who was eighteen years old—and in three days she disappeared!"

* * *

George Mikes, a Hungarian by birth and an Englishman by adoption, has written an amusing survey called "How to Be an Alien in Britain, France, Italy, Germany, Switzerland, Israel, and Japan." "In Britain," he notes, "a criminal may improve and become a decent member of society. A foreigner cannot. Once a foreigner, always a foreigner. He may become British; he never can become English."

"In Italy," observes Mikes, "hotel bills are scrupulously honest. If here and there in some of the smaller places, they happen to add the date to the bill, it is an error, committed in perfectly good faith. The only case which puzzled me occurred in Naples. I wondered whether they were justified in adding 230 lire for heating to my bill in the midst of a July heat wave."

* * *

A world traveler has brought back from Frankfurt a paperback English-German phrase book which offers neophytes bound for West Germany the Teutonic equivalents for such everyday English phrases as: 1. "Stand back, the train ran off the metals." 2. "Bring me the curling tongs for my mustache." 3. "Give me a dozen very high, detached collars." 4. "Do you prefer a valve or a crystal set?" Here is a book, obviously, that no tourist bound for Germany can afford to be without!

* * *

Suggestion in a Vienna newspaper for crossing a busy street: "In Italy, traffic will stop promptly if you cross the street with a shapely blonde; in England, if you have a dog on a leash; in America, if you are accompanied by at least three children; in Germany, if you are wearing the uniform of a general."

* * *

Author Aubrey Menen, whose mother was Irish and whose father was Indian, declares that the land in which he ardently desires to spend the rest of his days is Italy, and here is his reason why: "In the first half of my life, I learned to know three people well: the English, the Indians, and the Americans. They were diverse in their ways, but they had one thing in common: all three felt deep within them that they had fewer moral failings than the rest of mankind. They felt that they only had to set the world a moral example, and the world would follow them.

"I suppose the world might have, if they actually had set the example. But they never did. Now I've decided to live among the Italians, who have given up such illusions."

* * *

It's Louis Sobol's story about the American motorist in Rome who stopped a native and asked anxiously, "Do you have any black cats two feet long?" "A few, *signóre*," answered the native. "Any black cats four feet long?" "It is possible," conceded the native. "Well, have you any *six* feet long?" "But no, *signóre*, that is ridiculous," said the native. "It's like I told you, you dope," interrupted the motorist's wife from the back seat. "You've run over a priest!"

* * *

Mary Ann Mobley bought a pair of expensive imported Italian shoes in a Fifth Avenue bootery recently. She knows they're the genuine article, too. They keep pinching her.

* * *

Afdera Fonda tells about a fountain in a town in northern Italy where any wish you make, the legend has it, will ultimately be granted.

One day a tourist and his wife were gazing raptly at the fountain, making their wishes, when the wife suddenly lost her balance and fell in with a mighty splash.

"Golly," exclaimed the husband. "I never realized these things really work!"

* * *

Touring through the south of Italy, an American couple drove through one village square where a brass band of twelve musicians was blaring away, under the violent leadership of a perspiring, uniformed maestro, before a deserted house whose every door and window was tightly shuttered.

The driver stopped and asked an onlooker, "Who are they serenading?" "The mayor," was the answer. "Well, why isn't he at the window acknowledging the compliment?" persisted the driver.

"That's the mayor leading the band," explained the onlooker. "What do you expect him to do? Be in two places at the same time?"

* * *

Two ladies from Montreal toured Italy by motor last summer and inevitably pulled up before the famous Leaning Tower of Pisa. While they were parking their car, a uniformed attendant appeared, handed them a pink ticket, and collected 100 lire therefor. When the ladies returned to their hotel, they asked the concierge, "Who gets the money collected for parking near the Tower?"

The concierge examined their pink ticket, smiled, and explained: "There's no parking charge in Pisa, ladies. What you did here was to insure your car against damage in the event that the Leaning Tower fell on it."

* * *

Outside the Excelsior Hotel in Rome, an American tourist heard a fellow chanting, "Bananas! Bananas! Three for a shilling!" The tourist elbowed his way through the midday traffic and tapped the caller on the shoulder. "Son," he advised, "these Eye-tall-ians don't understand English—and furthermore, they trade in lira, not shillings."

A happy smile spread over the banana vendor's face. "You're just the fellow I've been waiting for," he beamed. "Which way is the railroad station?"

To Africa . . .

A Peace Corps worker from the Deep South, assigned to a turbulent new African state, reported to his superiors in Washington via transatlantic phone, "What we're trying urgently to plant here is peace and harmony." A month later a freighter arrived loaded down with split peas and hominy grits.

*   *   *

A tourist came back from Africa with a trunkful of shrunken heads he hoped to sell, but experienced some difficulty in locating a purchaser. Somebody suggested he try a big sporting goods store. He called up, and after a few moments was connected with a man with a very deep voice. "I want to talk to somebody about selling a collection of shrunken heads," explained the tourist. "You're speaking to the right party," the deep voice assured him. "I'm the head buyer."

*   *   *

Miss Goldfarb, avid young do-gooder, joined the Peace Corps and was assigned a post in darkest Africa. Some months later, her mother answered the doorbell in her Chicago apartment. There stood her daughter, arm-in-arm with a huge man dressed in a lion skin, daubs of paint on his face, great gold earrings, an ebony splint in his nose, and a hideous mask in his disengaged hand. Mrs. Goldfarb gasped and cried out in pain, "No, no, NO, Reba! I told you to marry a RICH doctor!"

*   *   *

An African chieftain's daughter was offered as a bride to the son of a neighboring potentate in exchange for two cows and four sheep. It was agreed that the big swap was to be effected on the shore of the swift-flowing stream that separated the tribes. Pop and his daughter showed up at the appointed time on one side of the stream only to discover that the bridegroom and his livestock were waiting on the other side.

"Stupid fool," grunted the father of the bride. "He doesn't seem to know which side his bride is bartered on."

* * *

An intrepid explorer hired African natives to row him up a river where no white man ever had been seen. It traversed an impenetrable jungle and was laced with treacherous rapids.

For seven days the expedition doggedly progressed into the wilderness. Suddenly the explorer heard a beating of drums—ominous, insistent. Drums maintaining the same rhythm answered from farther up the river.

The explorer pulled out his pistol. "If these warriors attack," he promised, "I'll sell my life dearly."

"Keep your shirt on, mister," advised his boss guide. "Drums only say white sucker on way. Everybody raise prices."

* * *

Sick cannibal joke: Explorer in pot, about to be cooked. Chief asks victim if he has any last words to say. Explorer gasps, "Yes. I'm smoking more and enjoying it less."

* * *

It often happens, laments Olin Miller, that those who try to run the lives of others do more harm than good. Miller cites as an example the missionary who convinced a cannibal it was a sin for him to have five wives. So the cannibal ate four of them.

* * *

Changing world department: Well-informed cannibal chiefs are warning their subjects not to eat any more Americans. "Their fat," explained one fastidious fancier of human flesh, "is contaminated with chlorinated hydrocarbons, and is likely to produce ulcers, liver pains, and acute indigestion!"

Doesn't *anybody* love us any more?

To the Far East . . .

An American tourist gazed in awe at India's famous Taj Mahal. "And to think," he told his wife, "they were able to do it before anybody even had heard of such a thing as foreign aid!"

* * *

A fakir in Delhi cried out, "I've discovered two sacks of brand new nails." "Hurrah," cheered an even bigger fakir nearby. "Let's have a pillow fight."

* * *

Herb Stein tells about a tourist in Bangkok who was approached by a native and asked, "Hey, you like meet beautiful half-caste girl?" "No," said the tourist. "You like see nudist film?" "No." "You want to visit opium parlor?" "No." "What do you like then?" "Could you direct me to the public library?" "Hey, tourist! What's matter? You some kind of nut?"

* * *

Henry Morgan is credited with the story of a yachtsman whose boat foundered in the South Pacific. A giant wave finally swept him ashore on an uncharted island. Warily he crept into the underbrush, and suddenly spotted a wisp of smoke ascending from the foliage in front of him. Was this a nest of cannibals? He maneuvered within a few feet of the smoke-makers and it was then he heard a human voice. It was a woman's—and what she was exclaiming was, "You idiot! Why did you throw away your high trump on that trick? I ought to throw these cards right into your stupid mug!"

"Thank heaven, I'm safe," breathed the relieved yachtsman. "They're civilized!"

*   *   *

There's a very fat lady in Hong Kong who is threatening suit against the owner of a weighing machine there. She stepped on his scale one morning and reached for the card that was supposed to register her net tonnage. The card dropped out all right, but what it said was, "Come back in fifteen minutes—alone."

*   *   *

Danny Kaye, touring the world in behalf of the UN International Children's Emergency Fund, encountered one mean old curmudgeon who derided the whole idea. "The diseases, famines, and floods of the Far East," he insisted, "were always nature's way of counteracting overpopulation. Now you do-gooders are upsetting all the scales and what's the result? Seven hundred million Red Chinese! I don't mean to sound heartless, but . . ."

"Your logic is infallible," interrupted Kaye testily. "Why not put it to the test the next time your own child gets sick?"

*   *   *

Juliet Lowell reports receipt of the following note by a Japanese magistrate:

"Honorable Sir: I am writing school essay about American habits. Kindly enlighten me: how soon after marriage does great festival of divorce?"

*   *   *

To accommodate American tourists in Japan, the telephone company there, some years ago, slapped this notice in many public booths:

(A) Please ready with necessary yen coin, take off the transmitter, put in coin, and lastly send round the dial.

(B) When not connected, put on the transmitter if it was, and the coin will come on the return hole.

(C) For the suburbs communication, please notify it.

(P.S. Japan, infinitely more advanced today, and more conversant with American ways and speech, now has phone booths and equipment of the highest order—and the service is above reproach.)

* * *

A Japanese merchant has also made available for American visitors handy copies of local highway codes and regulations, thoughtfully translated by himself into English.

A typical paragraph: "On encountering pedestrians: when a passenger on the hoof hoves into sight, tootle the horn, trumpet to him melodiously at first. If he still obstacles your passage, tootle him with increasing vigor and express by work of mouth the warning: 'HI! HI.'"

* * *

A pompous history professor from the U.S. was invited to address a group of university students while he was visiting Tokyo. The Japanese dean acted as interpreter, writing the gist of the professor's remarks in Japanese symbols on the blackboard. Soon, however, the Japanese dean put down his chalk and stopped writing. Later the American professor asked him why. "Here in Japan," explained the dean with a respectful bow, "we only write when the speaker says something."

All-American . . .

A wily guide at Niagara Falls earns a big laugh—and extra tips—from every women's group he pilots by this sure-fire device: he herds them close to the brink of the cataract and declaims, "Now ladies, if I can possibly persuade you all to be absolutely silent for two minutes at the same time, you will hear the deafening roar of the cascading waters of Niagara!"

*   *   *

"I'll never forget the morning we first gazed on Niagara Falls," confided Mrs. O'Connor. "My husband's face dropped about a mile." "You mean," asked her friend incredulously, "that Niagara didn't come up to your husband's expectations?" "Not at all," Mrs. O'Connor assured her. "He fell over the rim."

*   *   *

A young mother was riding through Pennsylvania in a day coach with her baby boy cradled in her arms when a man across the aisle leaned over to say, "I must tell you that that child of yours is just about the homeliest I've ever seen." The outraged mother complained immediately to the conductor, who did his best to soothe her. "We aim to please on this railroad," he concluded, "so I want you to ignore this man, and move to a seat in the Pullman car ahead with our compliments. . . . And, by the way, here's a banana for your monkey."

*   *   *

In Albuquerque they talk about a resident who drove all day in 105-degree temperature with every window of his car closed tight, then collapsed of prostration when he got home. "Why didn't you open the windows?" wailed his wife. "What?" he protested weakly, "and let everybody know we haven't got an air-conditioned car?"

*   *   *

A tourist in New Mexico bought a beaded trinket from an Indian for three dollars, upon the assurance that it represented authentic tribal craftsmanship. "My squaw learn art from her great-grandmother," said the Indian.

An hour later the tourist was back, hopping mad. "You faker," he cried to the Indian. "There's a fellow down at the railroad station selling these same gadgets for a dollar. Shows you never can trust an Indian!"

"No," contradicted the unperturbed Indian. "Shows you never can trust white man. Feller who sold me these promised nobody else in town gettum."

*　*　*

New Mexico historians point out with pride that it was an Indian chief from that state who first thought of installing electricity in the tribal washroom. Thus he became the first Indian ever to wire a head for a reservation.

*　*　*

A certain distinguished gentleman from Arizona recently told an enthralled audience what happened when an apprehensive tenderfoot asked an old rancher, "What should I do if a rattlesnake bites me in the arm?" "Get a friend to open the punctures the rattler made and suck the poison out for you," advised the rancher. "And if I get bitten in the leg?" "Follow the identical procedure," nodded the rancher. "But suppose I'm unlucky enough to sit down on one of those darn rattlesnakes?"

"Ah, my boy," said the rancher solemnly, "that's the time you'll find out who your real friends are!"

*　*　*

Epitaph in the cemetery at Tombstone, Arizona: "Here lies Jack Williams. He done his damndest."

*　*　*

A Billings, Montana man told me of a vacation trip he took with his wife through Yellowstone National Park. En route, they met a quiet, amiable couple from New York, and made up a very compatible foursome. Back in Billings, my friend collected dozens of photographs posed by all in front of geysers, bears, waterfalls, and whatnot, and mailed them to the New York couple.

Two weeks later a slick lawyer appeared and announced, "Thank you for sending those pictures. Now I'll need you two as witnesses. I'm representing your gentleman friend's wife in a divorce suit."

"She didn't like the pictures I sent her?" faltered the Billings camera shark.

"She thought they were extremely interesting," nodded the lawyer. "You see, she wasn't the woman who was posing in them."

* * *

Harry Golden tells about a West Coast lady named Sadie whose twelve-year-old son snagged a job during his summer vacation that paid twenty dollars a week. "And Mama," he promised, "it all goes straight to you." When he handed her his first pay envelope, the contents added up to only $19.90. "Ah ha," said Sadie. "Taking out girls already!"

* * *

Notes Neil Morgan in his new book, *Westward Tilt*: Americans today are moving to California in greater numbers than the annual entire immigration to the U.S. The five boroughs of New York City would have to be emptied of every man, woman, and child to match the population increase of the past decade in our eleven Western states." He laments, however, that "people move to a place because it's different. But the minute they get there, they start remaking it into a place that isn't different at all."

* * *

A demon cartographer named Basil Konstantinos has determined that there is only one New York in the United States, and that, of course, is the one that includes Manhattan, Brooklyn, and the Bronx. On the other hand, besides Boston, Massachusetts, there are Bostons in Arkansas, Georgia, Indiana, Kentucky, Missouri, New York, Pennsylvania, Texas, and Virginia (nor should we overlook Bean City, Florida). There are five Philadelphias besides the one in Pennsylvania, no less than twenty-five Washingtons in addition to the nation's capital, twenty-two Princetons, twenty-two Springfields, twenty-one Lincolns, and twenty-one Newports.

No wonder those hard-working lads in the Post Office Department occasionally get confused!

❃   ❃   ❃

James Thurber told about two Alaskans who spent a summer vacation in the northernmost tip of Maine and had the time of their lives. As they were leaving, one of them told his hosts effusively, "Thank you! Thank you! Now I know what they mean by Southern hospitality!"

❃   ❃   ❃

In the gold-rush days at the turn of the century in Alaska, recalls Boyce House, one of the most colorful figures in the territory was Wilson Mizner. To his dying day, Mizner boasted about the time it was so cold he broke three teeth on a frozen doughnut—also the night he pilfered the only typewriter in town and sold it to the butcher, who thought it was a cash register.

"Tragedy struck," reported Mizner, "on a colder day yet. The thermometer got stuck at sixty-nine below zero. The president of the bank stooped over to tie his shoelace and froze in that position. We had to bury the poor fellow in a drum!"

❃   ❃   ❃

The peripatetic John Straley has been investigating the transit situation up in Nome, Alaska: "I wouldn't say in so many words that the transit system remains comparatively primitive in these parts—but yesterday was the first time I ever saw a crosstown bus that barked at me!"

* * *

The Eskimo had a reasonable explanation for leaving his 260-pound wife. He told a sympathetic judge in Sitka, "She wouldn't stop blubbering."

* * *

In Sitka they tell of a lucky Eskimo who won a trip to Seattle in a newspaper numbers contest. He came home with a long lead pipe that he set up in the center of his igloo, with one end protruding through the roof. When his wife asked the purpose of this installation, the Eskimo replied proudly, "New trick I picked up in Seattle. When you want more heat, you just bang on this pipe."

* * *

Anxious to be admitted to the most exclusive club in northern Alaska, a tenderfoot asked what he'd have to do to qualify. "Three things," he was told. "You've got to drink a quart of straight whiskey at one sitting, you've got to hug and kiss an Eskimo girl for three hours without being caught by her parents, and you've got to shoot a full-sized polar bear."

The tenderfoot promptly downed a quart of liquor, and reeled out into the stinging cold with a wild look in his eye. An hour later he was back, his clothing in tatters, and vivid scratches on his countenance. "O.K., O.K.," he reported. "Two out of three tasks accomplished. Now where's that Eskimo girl I'm supposed to shoot?"

* * *

A pair of bemused newlyweds were strolling on the white sands of Paradise Beach in the Bahamas. The groom looked out over the azure sea and declaimed, "Roll on, thou deep and dark blue ocean, roll on." His star-struck bride gazed out at the water for a moment, then gushed, "Oh, Sheldon, you wonderful man! It's doing it!"

※   ※   ※

Two cafe society phonies were discussing ways and means of promoting a loan for a Caribbean fortnight. "I'd call my broker," confessed one, "but his phone has been disconnected."

※   ※   ※

An American tourist fell in love with Montego Bay in Jamaica and decided to build a villa of his own there—offering overtime pay if it could be finished quickly. The contractor got it finished in record time—but the American found one thing missing when he moved in: there was no railing to the stairway. An army of native carpenters rushed out to the house immediately and built a railing in three hours flat. Two hours later the railing collapsed. The outraged owner called the contractor to raise more Cain. "Don't get so excited," soothed the contractor. "Remember: Nothing lasts forever."

※   ※   ※

Last word in optimism: the bullfighter, scheduled to face in the ring the fiercest bull in Mexico City, who put mustard on his sword!

※   ※   ※

Proud but easygoing Brazilians, says John Dos Passos, like to tell this story on themselves. When the Lord Jehovah had finished making Brazil he couldn't help boasting a little to one of his archangels. He had planted the greatest forests, laid out the biggest rivers, built the most magnificent mountains, bays, and beaches—then added untold treasures of gold, iron, and diamonds. "Is it fair, Lord," asked the archangel, "to give so many benefits to just one country?"

"You wait," chuckled the Lord Jehovah, "till you see the people I'm going to put there!"

22. *You Can Say That Again!*

QUOTATIONS

Some people collect stamps and others collect autographs. I collect quotes. I have a little black book that I carry around the country on lecture tours, and every time I read or hear a new or old quote that fascinates me, I make a note.

Here are some of my favorites:

Carl Sandburg: "A baby is God's opinion that the world should go on."

Arnold Glasgow: "A good leader takes a little more than his share of the blame; a little less than his share of the credit."

Ralph Peterson: "Experience is what enables you to make the same mistake again without getting caught."

George Burns: "Laughter feels good all over, but it only shows in one place."

Robert Balzer: "Life is what happens to you while you're making other plans."

William Allen White: "I am not afraid of tomorrow, for I have seen yesterday."

George Bernard Shaw: "Do not do unto others as you would that they should do unto you. Their tastes might not be the same."

Ralph Waldo Emerson: "The louder he talked of his honor, the faster we counted our spoons."

Harold Rome: "The trouble with being punctual is that nobody's there to appreciate it."

Frank Taylor: "A literary party is four authors and their wives who live in the same suburb and loathe each other."

George Santayana: "It is prudent to thank an author for his book before reading it, so as to avoid the necessity of lying about it afterwards."

From a book review by Dorothy Parker: "This is not a novel to be tossed aside lightly. It should be thrown with great force."

Wilson Mizner: "There is something about a closet that makes a skeleton terribly restless."

Franklin P. Adams: "Nothing is more responsible for the good old days than a bad memory."

Christopher Morley: "A man who insists on having his initials embroidered on his pajamas must be uncertain of himself. Surely you ought to know who you are by bedtime."

Somerset Maugham: "Only a mediocre person is always at his best."

Explorer Sir Vivian Fuchs: "If you actually look like your passport photo, you aren't well enough to travel."

George Ade: "A good listener is not only popular everywhere, but after a while he knows something."

Mark Twain: "Few of us can stand prosperity. Another man's, I mean."

Neil Morgan: "Behind every successful man is a surprised woman."

Will Rogers: "The best way to make a fire with two sticks is to make sure one of them is a match."

Abe Martin: "Never slap a man in the face—specially when he's chewing tobacco."

Tony Randall: "Those stretch pants so many young ladies are sporting these days come in three sizes: small, medium, and don't bend over."

Philip Wylie: "In the old days, men rode chargers. Now they marry them."

John Crosby: "A girl's biggest asset is a man's imagination."

Will Rogers: "A husband who is boss in his own house is probably a liar about other things, too."

O. O. McIntyre: "There are no illegitimate children. There are only illegitimate parents."

John Mason Brown: "Reasoning with a child is fine, if you can reach the child's reason without destroying your own."

Rod Cavanaugh: "My neighbor is mighty slow returning tools and commodities he borrows from me, but when it comes to bringing back my small children from his own little boys' birthday parties, golly, is he on time!"

Kim Hubbard: "Most parents don't worry about a daughter till she fails to show up for breakfast and then it's too late."

Doris Lilly: "To make a long story short, there's nothing like having the boss walk in."

Calvin Coolidge: "If you really want a job done, give it to a busy, important man. He'll have his secretary do it."

William Lyon Phelps: "The man who invented pills was a very bright fellow—but the man who put the sugar coating on them was a genius!"

Albert Lasker: "A salesman should never be ashamed of his calling. He should be ashamed of his *not* calling."

William Wrigley, Jr.: "When two men in a business always agree, one of them is unnecessary."

Tony Lema: "A hole in one, scored by pure accident can keep a complete duffer playing golf for the rest of his life."

Jack Benny: "Give me my golf clubs, the fresh air, and a beautiful girl for a partner, and you can keep my golf clubs and the fresh air."

Irving Lazar: "After eating a meal in a first-class restaurant nowadays, you need an after-dinner mint—such as the one in Denver."

Old Yankee pitching ace Lefty Gomez: "Remember this: a pitcher's success depends upon clean living—and a fast, friendly outfield."

Sinclair Lewis: "Don't fret about finding your station in life. Someone's sure to tell you where to get off."

Sigmund Spaeth: "Have you noticed how a concert audience will applaud a familiar encore after a few bars are played? They are applauding neither the performer nor the music. They are applauding themselves because they recognized it."

Sam Levenson: "My mother got up every morning at 5:00 A.M. no matter what time it was."

Chief Sitting Bull (as quoted by Dorothy Fields in *Annie Get Your Gun*): "I got three rules of life: no red meat; no get feet wet; no put money in show business."

David Burns: "In the old days, when a vaudeville comic allowed a pie to be thrown in his face, he wondered how many laughs he'd get. Now he wonders how many calories."

W. C. Fields (with a sensible amendment to an old proverb): "If at first you don't succeed, try, try, a couple of times more. Then quit. There's no sense making a fool of yourself."

Tony Randall: "Every time I find a girl who can cook like my mother—she looks like my father."

Arthur Godfrey: "Common sense gets a lot of credit that belongs to cold feet."

Groucho Marx (buying a frankfurter-on-the-roll): "Give me the bottom one: I'm always for the underdog."

Jackie Gleason: "The second day of a diet is always easier than the first. By the second day you're off it."

Dave Gardner: "Had it not been for Thomas A. Edison, people today would be watching television by candlelight."

Ringo Beatle: "Take a perfectly beautiful day, add six hours of rain and fog—and you have instant London."

Fable over the fireplace of a small hotel near Liverpool: "Fear knocked at the door. Faith went out to it and there was no one there."

Hindu observation: "Parting begins with the first meeting."

Lin Yutang: "When small men begin to cast big shadows, it means that the sun is about to set."

Persian proverb: "Give a horse to him who tells the truth. He'll need it to escape on."

Japanese proverb: "The cat is a saint when there are no mice about."

Vincent Hughes: "Politics is a profession where the paths of glory lead but to the gravy."

Mackenzie King: "The politician's promises of yesterday are the taxes of today."

Karl von Clausewitz: "A conqueror is always a lover of peace. He would like to make his entry into a coveted state unopposed."

Walt Whitman: "Bad officials are elected by good citizens who do not vote."

Adlai Stevenson: "There is nothing more horrifying than stupidity in action."

Ralph Erman: "These days the UN Building seems to be a site for sore allies."

Harry S. Truman: "The President of the United States hears a hundred voices telling him that he is the greatest man in the world. He must listen carefully to hear the one voice that tells him he's not."

Abel Green: "Eighty is a wonderful age—especially if you're ninety."

William Faulkner: "I decline to accept the end of man. I believe that man will not merely endure; he will prevail. He is immortal, not because he alone among creatures has an inexhaustible voice, but because he has a soul, a spirit capable of compassion and sacrifice and endurance."

23. *Roundup*

GRAB BAG

Does the number thirteen terrify you? If it does, points out Wes Lawrence, you are tempting fate every time you finger a U.S. one-dollar bill. The incomplete pyramid on its back has thirteen steps. Above the pyramid are the words "Annuit Cœptis" with thirteen letters. The American bald eagle holds in one talon an olive branch with thirteen leaves, in the other talon a bundle of thirteen arrows. These, of course, are reproductions of the two sides of the Great Seal of the United States, which had thirteen original states.

* * *

"In every organization," observes Dr. Charles Lapp, "there are three kinds of people: rowboat people, sailboat people, and steamboat people. Rowboat people need to be pushed or shoved along. Sailboat people move when a favorable wind is blowing. Steamboat people move continuously, through calm or storm. They are the ones who are masters of themselves, their surroundings, and their fate."

* * *

Jerome Beatty, Jr., has been investigating the new science of "thermodamnics," which concerns itself with the persistent cussedness of inanimate objects. It is hoped that thermodamnics eventually will reveal the secrets of why buttered bread always falls to the floor with the buttered side down, why squirting grapefruit juice always lands squarely on the spoon-wielder's eye, why, when you're dressing in the greatest hurry, a shoelace always breaks, and why, when you're lighting your pipe with your last match, the wind invariably starts to blow.

* * *

Disillusioning bulletin from a highbrow quarterly: bulls are color-blind and don't "see red" at all. . . . Nero couldn't have fiddled while Rome burned because the violin was not invented until the Middle Ages. . . . And it couldn't have been an apple with which Eve tempted Adam, because apples don't grow in that part of the world. An apricot maybe? Or a fig?

* * *

We owe to John Fuller the incidental intelligence that (1) a Boston newspaper headlined a labor disturbance in Belgium "REVOLT IN BRUSSELS SPROUTS," (2) the call letters of a radio station in Arkansas, a region famous for its duck hunting, are KWAK, and (3) a scrupulously honest British writer has dedicated his first novel to "My friend Elspeth Grant, who wrote it for me."

* * *

Will Jones encountered a nudist with a beard down to his waist exiting from a nudist colony near Minneapolis. "Aren't

those whiskers rather strange adornment for a nudist?" asked
Jones. Explained the nudist, "*Somebody* has to go for coffee."

The man with the beard served another purpose at the
camp, it developed. The leader admitted, "We were getting
mighty tired of looking at the same faces all the time."

A police investigation at the camp some time later bogged
down completely. The local D.A. alibied, "There wasn't a soul
in the place I could pin anything on."

Gravestone Humor . . .

In New Mexico: "Here lies Les Moore, killed by four slugs
from a .44. No Les, No Moore."

In Paris: Wife: I Am Waiting for You. A.D. 1920. *Husband:*
Here I Am. A.D. 1952.

In Waukegan: Criminal Lawyer: The Defense Rests.

In Colorado: He Called Coyote Pete a Liar!

In Vermont:

> Under this grass and under these trees
> Lies the body of Jonathan Pease.
> But he's not here: only his pod;
> He has shelled out his soul, and gone to his God!

º º º

Donald Ogden Stewart suggests this epitaph for the inevita-
ble day when one becomes necessary: "Here lies Donald Ogden Stewart. IF NOT . . ." And Groucho Marx asks only this
of posterity: "Bury me next to a straight man."

º º º

Here's a pocket-size test by Jerry Beatty to see how well informed you may be:

1. What's the full Horace Greeley quote that begins, "Go
West, young man"?

2. Was the Potomac the river Washington tossed the dollar
across?

3. Did Hamlet say "Alas, poor Yorick: I knew him well"?

4. Was Frankenstein the name of Mary Shelley's monster?

(Answers.) 1. "Go West, young man and grow up with the country." 2. No, it was the Rappahannock. 3. No. His precise words were: "Alas, poor Yorick. I knew him, Horatio: a fellow of infinite jest, of most excellent fancy." 4. No. Frankenstein was the *inventor* of the monster who ultimately ruined his life.

✿ ✿ ✿

Variations on a theme:

One priest to another: "Read any Good Books lately?"
One bird to another: "Bred any good rooks lately?"
F.B.I. man to D.A.: "Booked any good Reds lately?"
One woman hater to another: "Fled any good looks lately?"
One jail warden to another: "Fed any good crooks lately?"

✿ ✿ ✿

A statistician, understandably breathless, reported recently that only one woman in 1150 now wears black lace panties. To which Olin Miller added this footnote, "What interesting jobs some people can latch on to these days!"

✿ ✿ ✿

Are you working too hard these days and worrying too much? You *might* bear in mind the soothing philosophy of the late Grantland Rice, who always advised his friends: "Take it easy —and don't forget to stop and smell the flowers on the way."

* * *

An ingenious hostess in Westport kept her guests reasonably contented during a sudden Sunday thunderstorm by demanding they attempt these four tasks:

1. Describe the taste of chocolate.

2. Assume that I am color-blind. Describe the color blue to me.

3. Keep your hands folded and describe how you tie your shoelaces.

4. Keep your hands folded and describe a spiral staircase.

* * *

Millionaire inventor Philip K. Saunders has written the story of his unusual life in *Dr. Panto Fogo,* a nickname he acquired one day when his trousers caught fire while he was taking a nap aboard a slow train in Brazil. A few of Mr. Saunders' passing comments bear repetition: (1) Laziness is the mother of nine inventions out of ten; (2) French food is not really good food. It is mediocre food cunningly cooked and disguised with sauces; (3) Africans never talk about sex because there are no sex taboos of any kind and therefore nothing about sex calls for any comment except the expressions of approval.

* * *

A new book called *The Girls' Book of Physical Fitness* conveys the information that just by lying awake but absolutely still you can use up seventy-five calories an hour! Raising your voice in song (whether in the shower or out) consumes 125 calories an hour and playing soft music on the piano burns up fifty. You can triple that hourly consumption at the ivories by shifting your repertoire to uninhibited rock 'n' roll. You can also get a good kick in the sit-spot from an irate neighbor while or immediately after this calorie-consuming activity is pursued.

* * *

Some towns you will agree just *ought* to be, have been invented by Kate Steichen and friends: Noah's, Ark., Near, Miss.,

Hoot, Mon., Either, Ore., Ballpoint, Penn., Fiveand, Tenn., Metre, Cal., Faux, Pa., Nohitsnorunsno, Ariz.

※ ※ ※

A learned gentleman named Les Goldman is convinced that people should choose professions that match their names. He has spent long hours, therefore, persuading one Walter Wall to lay carpets; Warren Peace to enter the diplomatic corps; Hugo Furst to become a paratrooper; Colette O'Day to assume the role of curfew officer; and Dinah Sklubb to go out and sell credit cards.

※ ※ ※

Once upon a time, legend has it, there were two tiny grains of sand in the Paleozoic ooze. One of the grains was possessed of curiosity, and the result is mankind. The other had no curiosity at all—and the result, today, is the oyster.

※ ※ ※

Editor Tom Dreier tells about a Missouri school superintendent who chose this method to present "a picture of the world his students could understand."

If, said the superintendent, the almost-three-billion persons in the world were compressed into a single town of 1000 people, the following contrasts could be seen:

60 persons would represent the U.S.A., 940 all the others.

60 Americans would receive one-half the income, 940 the other half.

303 would be white, 697 non-white.

The 60 Americans would have a life expectancy of over 70, the others of under 40.

The 60 Americans would consume 15 per cent of the town's food supply, and the lowest income group of the Americans would be better off than the average of the 940.

The 60 Americans would have 12 times as much electricity, 22 times as much coal, 21 times as much oil, 50 times as much steel, and 50 times as much equipment as all 940 remaining members of the town.

Still feeling sorry for yourselves?

FABLES

A great Turkish sultan lay dying one summer's day. His latest favorite, a beautiful lass of nineteen, sat weeping by his bedside.

Suddenly the stricken potentate rallied momentarily and ordered the girl to put on her finest raiment, and adorn herself with her costliest jewels.

"How could I do this when you are so ill?" asked the girl.

"Do as I say," commanded the sultan—then whispered to his chief advisers, "It occurred to me that when the Angel of Death comes for my soul, his eyes may light on this beautiful girl, and perchance he'll decide to take her instead of me!"

* * *

There is a fable about a very wise old man who was visited by a delegation of malcontents determined to tell him their troubles.

Suggested the wise man, "Write down your greatest trouble on a piece of paper." He then threw all the papers into a pot and said, "Now each of you draw a paper and by all the laws of probability you all will have brand-new troubles to fret over."

The malcontents followed his suggestion. Then they read the new troubles they had been saddled with. The result: Every single one of them clamored immediately to have his own trouble back!

* * *

Spoke an Arabic sage of a century gone by:

He who knows not, and knows not he knows not—he is a fool. Shun him.

He who knows not, and knows he knows not—he is simple. Teach him.

He who knows, and knows not he knows—he is asleep. Wake him.

But he who knows, and knows he knows—he is wise. Follow him.

* * *

A vain young creature in Wilkes-Barre, Pennsylvania, craved a pearl necklace. One dark night a genie appeared before her and said, "Make one wish. It will come true by morning."

The young creature murmured ecstatically, "Give me what I need for my neck." When she awoke she found next to her pillow a box containing six cakes of soap.

* * *

Once upon a time there was a snail, relates Simons Roof, who set out on a chill winter morning to climb the trunk of a bleak cherry tree. As he painfully inched his way upward, a beetle poked his head out of a hole and advised him, "You're wasting your time, friend. There aren't any cherries up there." But the snail didn't stop moving for a second. "There will be when I get there," he pointed out.

* * *

A young man saw some beautiful objects in a show window, carved from solid gold, and though the street was crowded with people, smashed the window and ran off with several of the costliest trinkets. Of course, he was immediately apprehended.

"How did you expect to get away with such an act in full view of hundreds of people?" asked the magistrate.

"Alas," murmured the culprit. "When I performed the act, I could see only the gold, and none of the people."

* * *

In Java they tell of a young blade who spied a beautiful maiden on the high road and followed her deliberately for a mile. Finally, she wheeled and demanded, "Why do you dog my footsteps?"

"Because," he declared fervently, "you are the loveliest thing I ever have seen and I have fallen madly in love with you at sight. Be mine!"

"But you have merely to look behind you," said the girl, "to see my young sister, who is ten times more beautiful than I am."

The gallant cavalier wheeled about and his gaze fell on as ugly a wench as ever drew breath in Java. "What mockery is this?" he demanded of the beautiful girl. "You lied to me!"

"So did you," she replied. "If you were so madly in love with me, why did you turn around?"

* * *

An extravagant king of Saxony once borrowed every cent that his court jester had put away for a rainy day. "Now," sighed the jester, "I understand the meaning of that old adage: 'A fool and his money are soon parted!'"

* * *

Olin Clark tells about the little boy who, despite all warnings and fables, continued crying "Fire." He turned out to be a wolf.

* * *

Chinese fable: A poor but honest laundryman maintained his modest establishment next door to a great big prosperous restaurant. Each day the laundryman would sit outside his shop, as near to the restaurant as he dared, and sniff the wonderful aromas from within.

One day the laundryman received a bill from his wealthy neighbor for "continuous smell of my food." He took his usual seat that afternoon with his tin money box in hand. After rattling it vigorously for a while, he cried to his creditor, "I hereby pay for the smell of your food with the *sound of my money!*"

❖ ❖ ❖

Once upon a time there were two brothers—farmers both—named Elmer and Rockwell. Elmer was a hard worker who spent fourteen hours a day improving his land and healthy livestock. Rockwell was a bum, who let his fences fall down. His livestock roamed away and his barn burned down.

One day a man with a pocket full of gold came from Washington to buy land. He admired Elmer's beautiful farm, but he bought Rockwell's dilapidated layout because the government was seeking worthless land for a rocket-launching site.

Rockwell took the cash and bought a villa at Monte Carlo, where he dines with royalty, and has a high old time luxuriating in the sun. Elmer still slaves fourteen hours a day on his magnificent farm. He writes to Rockwell faithfully, but Rockwell is too lazy to answer. End of fable.

GHOSTS?

A brilliant and distinguished television producer I know (aren't they all?) has some rich, pedigreed relatives stashed away in a castle in the lake district of England, and this year he flew over by jet to get his first look at the ancestral seat.

It seemed a pretty gloomy place to him at first glance, and the tasteless dinner served to him by a toothless old hag depressed him further. Around the dining hall were faded portraits of what he presumed to be his ancestors—a forbidding lot—though one frame was conspicuously empty. "I must ask about that when I know these people better," he resolved, then, pleading a sick headache, he retreated to his bed-chamber.

There he found a pleasant surprise awaiting him. A young girl, rather oddly dressed but surpassingly beautiful, was bending over his suitcase.

"You don't have to unpack for me," he assured her. "I'm used to doing it myself."

By way of reply, the beautiful young girl did an unusual thing. First she favored him with a sweet, sorrowful smile, then she disappeared into thin air.

The producer rushed breathlessly back to the dining room and cried, "A beautiful girl has just vanished before my eyes."

"Damnation," grumbled his host, with no surprise whatever. "She's come back again, has she? That was your great-great-great-grandmother. She was murdered in that room by her husband—for good and sufficient reasons—in 1837."

The producer's glance wandered involuntarily to the frame that had been empty. There was the portrait of the girl from his room staring gravely at him!

* * *

Jerome Beatty tells about a friendly, publicity-loving ghost who whooshed into a photographer's studio and allowed as how he'd like to have a full-sized picture of himself. The obliging photographer set up his camera and lights, snapped the shutter once, and waved goodbye as the ghost dissolved into space. Alas! The photographer got no picture because the negative, it developed, was underexposed. To put it in a nutshell, the spirit was willing, but the flash was weak.

* * *

Four ghosts were engaged in a hotly contested bridge game when a fifth ghost opened the door to enter, loosing a gust of wind that blew all the cards off the table. "Confound it, Archie," grumbled one of the card-playing ghosts. "Don't you know what a keyhole is for?"

* * *

Ghosts seem to be especially prevalent in Scotland, but the doughty residents take them in stride. For example, an innkeeper in the Trossachs acknowledged cheerfully at breakfast that the family's pet ghost had paid him a bedside visit on the stroke of midnight. "But he didn't stay very long," he added. "He vanished the moment I asked him for a small contribution to the community fund."

* * *

On a country highway, in the pale light of a waning moon, a forlorn pedestrian vainly thumbed a lift into town from the sparse number of automobiles that hurtled by. Finally, at the crest of a rise, one vehicle came to a halt, and the grateful pedestrian climbed in. The vehicle resumed its creaky advance.

A distant clock was just tolling midnight, when the pedestrian noticed that there was no driver at the wheel. Horrified, he jumped out. A shadowy graveyard loomed beyond him. He broke into a run.

Just then he noticed a figure climbing into the abandoned car. "Don't get in," he shouted. "There's something terribly wrong with that machine."

"You're telling me," was the reply. "I've been pushing the darn thing uphill for half a mile."

MARTIANS?

Those Martians are back in town again! The attention of two of them was attracted to a snazzy white motor scooter at a Third Avenue curb. "Isn't she a honey?" enthused one. "I think I'll take her back to Mars with us." "Careful, boy," warned the other. "She may be under age."

* * *

Two visitors from outer space ambled down Fourth Avenue, each one stretching his four legs and waving his six arms in the air. A tailor, standing in the doorway of his shop, saw them coming and cried out to his partner, "Quick, Mawruss, take down that 'Alterations Free' sign!"

* * *

A newly arrived spaceman arrived from Mars a week after his teammate, whom he found gazing intently at a mail-box and a fire alarm box. "The dumpy green fellow with the big mouth doesn't say a word," observed the teammate, "but I warn you not to fool around with the tall red character. He'll scream his head off!"

* * *

Bob Sylvester keeps bumping into Martians in out-of-the-way nooks and crannies. This time they were inspecting gas pumps at a roadside filling station. "What's the matter with those clunks?" worried one of the Martians. "All they do is stand around with their fingers in their ears."

* * *

One of those space travelers with a triangular head, square eyes, and ears made of piano wire landed on Delancey Street, and scared a pushcart peddler into fainting on the spot. The traveler thought the least he could do was tend the cart till the peddler recovered.

A youngster, passing by with his mother, gulped hard, and said, "Mom, isn't that the craziest-looking vegetable peddler you ever did see?"

The mother admitted grimly, "He may *look* crazy, but you'll notice he's getting sixty-one cents a pound for his potatoes!"

* * *

A Martian spaceman brought his contraption down in Las Vegas at the instant a slot machine player hit the jackpot. As the shower of silver dollars poured noisily out, the Martian patted the machine and remarked, "Buddy, you'd better do something for that cold."

*　*　*

At bustling Austin College in Sherman, Texas, I was solemnly informed by a fun-loving senior that Mars is inhabited by a strange-looking race called the Furries, and that the leader of said Furries is distinguished by a giant headpiece that looks like an enlarged hypodermic needle. Is it necessary to add that he is known as the Furry with the syringe on top?

SIGNS OF THE TIMES

Many signs along the nation's highways and byways prove conclusively that the imagination—and sense of humor—of enterprising operators continues to flourish. Even dignified Wall Street institutions are hanging out new-fangled signs these days to prove that the procession is not leaving them behind. One large bank has posted this warning at its entrance: "Careful, girls! Those attractive fellows in our windows are tellers!" A more conservative institution down the block suggests, "Kindly make your deposits quietly. You might wake one of the vice presidents."

*　*　*

A New Orleans dairy advertises, "Our cows are NOT contented. They're always striving to do better.". . . A Dallas restaurant, obviously patronized by oil magnates and booksellers, offers "All you can eat for $100." . . . In the window of a small Italian restaurant: "We offer you a pizza and quiet." . . . At a roadside beanery: "Try our enthusiastic stew. We put everything we had in it!". . . Up in Alaska: "Orange juice, 35 cents; Texas size, 20 cents.". . . Boasts a supermarket in

Paramus: "Here you will discover the finest liquors and the best fruits. It's where the beer and the cantaloupe play.". . . . Admonition of a health food shoppe: "Don't walk on the grass. It may be your supper.". . . . And above the door of a popular downtown eatery is this wonderfully provocative sign: "O'LEARY AND McGRATH. AUTHENTIC CHINESE COOKING."

What the Traffic Will Bear . . .

Warning on the main street of Beverly Hills: "Beware of children going to or from school—especially if they are driving cars."

On the back of a truck: "Watch my rear—not hers."

Outside of a garage: "Invite us to your next blowout."

In Houston, Texas: "Last Cadillac dealer for three blocks."

On the back of a honeymoon couple's car: "Amateur night."

In a Toledo auto repair shop window: "Save the next dents for us."

On a diaper service truck: "Rock a dry baby."

And on the outskirts of a northwestern college town this billboard has been erected by a concerned safety council:

> If heavy necking is your sport,
> Trade in your auto for a davenport!

*   *   *

Mike Connolly spotted this sign on a shuttered magic shop in Hollywood: "Vanished till next season." In the window of a Boston shop specializing in fireplace equipment: "Everything your little hearth desires." In a camera store in Paterson, New Jersey: "Visit our bargain basement on the second floor." On the sidewall of an otherwise prosaic sandblaster's headquarters: "Call us if you have any dirty stories." In a Niagara Falls gifte shoppe: "If you don't need it, we have it."

*   *   *

There's a warning sign posted seven feet high over the door to a famous basketball coach's office in Lexington, Kentucky. It reads, "If you don't have to stoop to enter here, keep out." . . . An ingenious distributor of fishermen's supplies in Colorado has a window full of new rods "guaranteed to get a pike's pique.". . . A Dayton tycoon has this reminder on his desk: "Things to do today: 1. Get organized. 2. Talk to wife. 3. Get reorganized." . . . And Bob O'Brien spotted this intriguing sign at New York's Hayden Planetarium: "This way to the Solar System and the ladies' and gentlemen's rest rooms."

*   *   *

On a church bulletin board: "This church is prayer-conditioned." . . . In an Arizona public garden: "Please do not write on the cactus." . . . A Boston necktie emporium beseeches, "Come in and tie one on." . . . A Rochester plumber suggests, "Do it yourself—then call us before it's too late." . . . A Shreveport realtor advises, "Get lots while you're young." . . . Outside a veterinarian's office: "Hospital zone: No barking." . . . In a fish store: "If our flounders were any fresher, they'd be insulting." . . . In a college book store: "Help fight TV: Buy a book!" . . . December sign in a toy department: "Five Santa Clauses. No waiting."

*   *   *

A scout reports that an automatic laundromat in Corona has two signs tacked alongside the door. The top sign proclaims, "Through this portal pass the finest folk in Corona." The lower sign adds, "Anyone caught putting slugs in the machine will be arrested forthwith."

*　*　*

Government operatives inform us that:

1. After a violent sandstorm had disrupted service in Saudi Arabia, this sign appeared in telephone booths: "Until further notice please limit calls to four wives."

2. In Moscow there's an imposing complex housing the "Commission on Electrification of all Russia." At the entrance there's a card suggesting, "Please knock. The electric bell is out of order."

3. A young porter at the Pentagon is obviously headed for bigger and better things. His wire basket is labeled, "For Top Confidential Trash."

4. A doctor recently was dispatched to an Army induction center to give antivirus injections. Above the entrance to his cubicle in the dispensary he tacked this notice: "To save time, draftees will please back in."

5. This summer the doughty head of a Cape Cod resort center's weather bureau posted this notice: "On account of the Fourth of July, there will be no weather today."

ELEVEN STORIES TALL

The late Irish author, James Stephens, who wrote *The Crock of Gold*, and insisted that he believed in elfs and leprechauns, often pointed out, "what a dull world this would be if every imaginative maker of legends was stigmatized as a liar!"

Trader Horn, for example, was a man after Stephens' heart. The Trader, or Zambesi Jack, as he liked to call himself, popped up in New York in the thirties with a bagful of preposterous reminiscences and an equally unbelievable capacity for liquor in any form.

Zambesi had a pet tiger, to hear him tell it, who insisted upon sleeping across the foot of his bed. One night he kicked the tiger in a moment of absent-mindedness. "Do you know that one kick broke my poor tiger's spirit?" he mourned. "Shows how careful you have to be of the other fellow's feelings."

* * *

One night the house of a neighbor of Lowell Thomas up in Pawling, New York, burned to the ground. With his own eyes, says Lowell solemnly, he saw the family dash to the lawn, followed by their faithful dog. Then the old dog dashed back into the flames to pull out a child they had overlooked. Then in he dashed again to rescue another missing child. It was a dashing affair.

Although everybody in the family was now positively accounted for, Fido fought his way back into the inferno a third time. He emerged just before the house collapsed, exhausted but triumphant. He was carrying in his mouth the insurance policy wrapped in a wet towel.

* * *

In Colorado, legend-loving Stan Peckham reports a Lothario, surprised by his girl's shotgun-toting pa, who made off so fast he overtook two jackrabbits and a gazelle.

He kicked the latter high into the air, muttering, "Get off the road and let somebody run who knows how."

* * *

In Princeton, Florida, according to W. E. Gaby, when pesky mosquitoes get so thick around him he scarcely can see, he just runs two or three times as fast as he can around a telephone pole and then jumps nimbly to one side, leaving the mosquitoes whirling around the pole till they die of dizziness.

* * *

As Mark Twain saw it, mankind can be divided into liars, damn liars, and statisticians. Probably it was in the role of statistician that he told of a night in Hannibal when Old Man Hankinson got locked in the washroom on the fourth floor of his house and hollered for help. There wasn't a ladder in town long enough to reach him.

"I admit I was the hero of the occasion," wrote Twain. "I snatched up a rope and flung the end of it up to Old Man Hankinson, yelling, 'Tie it around your waist!'

"He did as I told him—and I slowly pulled him down to safety."

* * *

Impressive indeed, I think, is this tall tale concocted by Sam Ridings, a grizzled cowboy of Chisholm Trail fame: A tenderfoot from the East, unaware of the abrupt changes of climate out West, once made for himself four harness tugs out of green buffalo hide. The first time he used them a sudden downpour filled his wagon so full of water he had to climb down and trudge beside his team. When he reached town, he turned around and discovered that his wagon was nowhere to be seen. The rawhide had stretched in the rain, and the wagon was a full mile behind on the tugs.

The tenderfoot started back to retrieve his wagon, but just then the sun reappeared and dried the rawhide, which contracted so quickly that the wagon ran right over its owner and killed him.

＊ ＊ ＊

An unholy spell of weather hit Great Falls, Montana too, where the temperature got down to 38 below zero, and a man who left a friendly poker game because he was scared of his wife, froze to death at the first street corner.

"It wasn't so bad, really," explained one of the survivors of the poker game. "We hung a lantern on Old Charlie's ear and used him for a lamppost all winter."

＊ ＊ ＊

Lightning shattered a tree under which Squire Erskine's hired hand had unwisely sought shelter. Squire Erskine found him there unharmed, however, but severely shaken when the downpour abated. "How close do you figure that lightning came to you?" asked the squire. "I dunno exactly," admitted the hired hand, "but my pipe wasn't lit before it struck!"

＊ ＊ ＊

Clem Albright wins a medal for a prize whopper about hunting dogs. "My retriever stopped dead in his tracks one morning and pointed. I didn't see a sign of quail—just an old man napping in the shade. I woke the fellow and asked, 'Notice any quail around here?' 'Not a one,' answered the old man, 'but I've just been dreaming about a couple.'"

＊ ＊ ＊

"Are the bears around here dangerous? Golly, yes," guide Ben Moody tells properly impressed tourists in the Banff, Alberta area. "One of them caught me drowsing in that open field yonder and chased me clear to that oak tree standing alone in the distance. My only chance was to leap up and catch the lowest limb which is a full twenty feet from the ground."

"Did you make it?" some tourist always asks.

"If you must have the truth," confides Moody, "I missed it clean going up—but I caught it on the way back down."

* * *

Vance Randolph tells about an Ozark mountaineer named Lissenbee who "was always blabbing things all over town. He didn't tell no lies; he just told the truth, and that's what made it so bad."

One day a talking turtle stopped him on the road and snapped, "Lissenbee, you talk too darn much." The startled Lissenbee made for the nearest tavern to holler, "I just seen a turtle what talks." Everybody in the tavern hooted in disbelief, but followed Lissenbee nonetheless to the place where the turtle still rested in the shade.

The pesky turtle, however, never said a word, and the crowd melted away in disgust. Lissenbee, brokenhearted, bowed his head in his hands, and muttered, "My reputation is ruined."

The turtle nodded, and said, "It's like I told you, Lissenbee. You talk too darn much."

WORDS TO SIGN OFF WITH

Minutes, the house organ of the Nationwide Insurance Company, has discovered a new language: "Realestatese," which embodies the art of making the description of a house bear as little resemblance as possible to the real appearance of same.

A few prime examples:

Newly decorated: The owner has repainted the front door.

Needs slight additional decorating: The buyer had better not make any weekend plans for the next three years.

Charming cul-de-sac: Deadend street behind a busy supermarket parking lot and a boys' schoolyard.

Magnificent view: The nearest bus stop is at least five miles away.

Prestige community: Two of the neighbors have maids.
Only two left: There were three originally.

*   *   *

What about the incomprehensible gibberish often handed
out by government bigwigs and business tycoons? Is it unintentional or deliberate? Critic Granville Hicks thinks it usually is
deliberate.

"Evasion of clarity," writes Hicks, "is a trait of bureaucrats,
whether they are in government, business, or the professions.
Evasion of clarity is tantamount to the evasion of responsibility, and responsibility is what the average bureaucrat wants as
little as possible of. Evasion becomes a habit, and obscuring,
imprecise words often seem to issue automatically from the lips
of most bureaucrats, even when clarity could do no harm."

*   *   *

In line with the above, George Brathwaits, up to here in
Pentagon longwindedness, thinks this is the way Washington
big brass might have delivered three reasonably famous dec-
larations:

1. It is my command that we relegate the torpedoes to per-
dition. Proceed at maximum celerity at 119 degrees NNE on
our erstwhile established course.

2. Let no homo sapien engage in the firing of his non-nuclear
weapon until the precise moment when the scleras of the
enemy are visible.

3. My expressed desire is to receive not more than one of the
following: (A) Complete freedom, entailing all its pleasures
and responsibilities, or (B) The loss of my life in a manner to
be determined at a later date.

*   *   *

Collecting the quaint expressions of the Pennsylvania Dutch
is a favorite diversion of many Philadelphians. A few that pop
up on most lists are: 1. The sign on a door where the bell was
out of order: "Button don't bell. Bump." 2. The sound tip: "Bet-

ter it is to single live than to the wife the britches give." 3. The housewife's complaint: "The hurrier I go, the behinder I get."

* * *

Famous Critic Brooks Atkinson confesses that when he wants to add some very unusual words to his vocabulary, he consults the works of S. J. Perelman. It was from this prolific source, for instance, that he borrowed, "a firkin of butter and a hectare of gherkins" to describe the fare served at a picnic. Mr. P. shingled his country house, Atkinson discovered, with "second-hand wattles," and he "taps the dottle from his pipe" by "knocking it against the hob." He also frequently "muckles fibre towels" from airplanes that carry him hither and yon.

* * *

Words which are spelled the same way backwards as they are forwards are called palindromes. Examples are: ere, bib, did, bob, eke, ewe, eye, kayak, level, refer, radar, reviver, rotator, deified. Jason Lindsay lists four words which spell *another* word backwards: straw, diaper, deliver, dessert.

* * *

There are just two words in the English language that contain all the vowels (including the optional "y") in their regular order. They are "facetiously" and "abstemiously."

* * *

John Moore, in his new book *Your English Words*, lists some words even John Charles Daly hasn't used on TV. It's a hundred to one you never before encountered these specimens either: 1. quockerwodger; 2. skilligolete; 3. calibogus; 4. jobbernowl; and 5. rumblegumption. Their meanings? 1. A puppet; 2. A soup served sometimes to prisoners or sailors; 3. A mixture of spruce beer and rum; 4. A blockhead; 5. A Scottish word for common sense.

"Increase your word power" with these—if you *can!*

* * *

Come, James! We must clapperclaw that scomm before he wambles from a surfeit of quiddany.

A condensation of Dr. Johnson's famous dictionary has been published for the first time. A few of the unfamiliar words therein are clapperclaw, huzz, fleshmonger, scomm, doubry, quiddany, and wamble. Two to one you don't know the meaning of any of them. I certainly didn't!

*   *   *

At a conclave of half a dozen learned college professors, none could correctly define more than one of these four often-misused words: limpid, livid, stultify, and transpire. Try your own luck—before you go on to read that limpid means clear, transparent, free from obscurity; livid means dark grayish-blue, a bluish appearance due to a bruise; stultify means to make foolish or ridiculous; and transpire means to emit or give off waste matter, or to escape through the pores as moisture or odor. (The use of "transpire" to mean "pass" or "elapse" is distinctly frowned upon by practically all authorities on word usage but Bergen Evans.)

*   *   *

Henry Minott, of United Press International, after years of rigid copy editing, declares these to be the fifteen most commonly misspelled words: uncontrollable, changeable, gauge, naphtha, occurred, discernible, diphtheria, permissible, paraphernalia, likable, judgment, dietitian, embarrass, indispensable, harass.

*　*　*

A student of semantics at Kansas State has summed up the career of a college football coach in eight words: Desired; Wired; Hired; Inspired; Admired; Tired; Mired; Fired.

*　*　*

Cary Grant, a riddle addict of the first water, has found a new way to use the word "fundamental" in a sentence: "I went horseback riding yesterday, and now I have to eat fun da mental." And a precocious fifth-grade student in a Queens public school, asked to fit the word "influential" in a sentence, came up with "I dreamed I was in heaven, and influentials."

*　*　*

The French philosopher Voltaire was told that a certain professor had a five-hundred-word answer for everything. "Heavens!" he exclaimed. "Is he as ignorant as all that?"

*　*　*

Papa Smedkins, under the urgings of his wife, reluctantly postponed his golf game to give his young son a few customary words about the birds and the bees. At the end of his talk, both father and son were obviously impatient. "At least," concluded Papa Smedkins, "I guess you now understand why our cat is about to have kittens." "Thanks to you, pop," said Junior, "I do. She must have gotten stung by a bee."

*　*　*

A very popular middle-aged farmer's wife in a Midwestern town was asked her secret for making and keeping friends. "There's no secret about it," she explained. "I'm just always careful to taste my words real good before I let 'em get past my teeth."

*　*　*

Novelist Barnaby Conrad has compiled a volume of "Famous Last Words." Included is gourmet R. M. Milne's, "My exit is the result of too many entrees." Gambler Wilson Mizner's, "Well, Doc, I guess this is the main event!" And philosopher Hegel's, "Only one man understood me—and he didn't, really!"

Lord Duveen, art collector, died at Claridge's after a lengthy illness during which doctors repeatedly had told him he had only a few days left to live. His last words were, "Well, I fooled 'em for five years!"

* * *

A few other last words to remember are: The smart-alecky motorist's "Well, if he won't turn off his bright lights, I won't turn off mine!"; the chronic alcoholic's "I *thought* that last drink had a peculiar taste"; and the henpecked husband's "Hey, darling, hand me that stack of books to stand on so I can reach this curtain rod."

* * *

And here's a last word from the compiler of *Laugh Day*: There's no getting away from the world of today; you might as well get used to it. If you can adjust yourself to the pace, there's never been so exciting a time to be alive. More momentous things happen in a single year now than our grandparents experienced in a lifetime.

In fact, nobody's ever had it so good before. So laugh more! Make *every* day "Laugh Day"—and see how much happier you'll be!

Index by Categories